Lecture Notes in Computer Science 1283

Edited by G. Goos, J. Hartmanis and J. van Leeuwen

Springer
Berlin
Heidelberg
New York
Barcelona
Budapest
Hong Kong
London
Milan
Paris
Santa Clara
Singapore
Tokyo

Markus Müller-Olm

Modular Compiler Verification

A Refinement-Algebraic Approach Advocating Stepwise Abstraction

Springer

Series Editors

Gerhard Goos, Karlsruhe University, Germany

Juris Hartmanis, Cornell University, NY, USA

Jan van Leeuwen, Utrecht University, The Netherlands

Author

Markus Müller-Olm
Universität Dortmund, Lehrstuhl Informatik V
Baroper Straße 301, D-44221 Dortmund, Germany
E-mail: mmo@ls5.informatik.uni-dortmund.de

Cataloging-in-Publication data applied for

Die Deutsche Bibliothek - CIP-Einheitsaufnahme

Müller-Olm, Markus:
Modular compiler verification : a refinement algebraic approach advocating stepwise abstraction / Markus Müller-Olm. - Berlin ; Heidelberg ; New York ; Barcelona ; Budapest ; Hong Kong ; London ; Milan ; Paris ; Santa Clara ; Singapore ; Tokyo : Springer, 1997
(Lecture notes in computer science ; 1283)
ISBN 3-540-63406-1

CR Subject Classification (1991): D.3.4, D.2.4, D.3.1, J.7, F.3.1, C.3

ISSN 0302-9743
ISBN 3-540-63406-1 Springer-Verlag Berlin Heidelberg New York

Printed in Germany

Typesetting: Camera-ready by author
SPIN 10547711 06/3142 – 5 4 3 2 1 0 Printed on acid-free paper

Foreword

After 40 years of practice and theory in compiler construction and 30 years of experience and teaching in software engineering we still observe that safety-critical high-level language programs are certified only together with the corresponding machine code. The reason is that certification institutions do not trust any compiler. And they are quite right: whereas errors detected in processor hardware are generally perceived as sensations, errors in software, even in system software, are commonplace.

It is high time to reverse this trend. Computer scientists should concentrate their abilities, experiences, and insights on the safe mastery of realistic system software. This particularly concerns realistic compilers for realistic programming languages running on hardware processors, as correct compilers play a central role in the construction of trustworthy application and system programs. Both application programmers and system software engineers need trusted development environments that permit them to concentrate on software specification and high-level implementation instead of wasting their time again and again with compilation problems and machine code inspection.

In order to construct fully correct and realistic compilers useful for safety-critical applications one must master two problems: compiling specification verification and compiler implementation verification. The first problem is to specify and prove semantically correct a mathematical translation function from high-level source programs to realistic target machine code. The second problem is to correctly refine and implement such a function either in a host language for which there is a running and trusted host compiler or in the machine language of a real host processor. Clearly, initially only the second way is trustworthy. M. Müller-Olm lays foundations for both problems.

One of the most characteristic aspects of M. Müller-Olm's way of thinking is his special way of looking at the behavior of hardware processors. He derives successively more elegant views, which allow real processors to be treated as idealized machines with ideal properties. This enables compiling verification techniques to be applied that rely on such machines. Future further propagation of the hierarchy of views promises clearer insights and proofs for the translation of even more ambitious realistic programming languages.

Kiel, May 1997 Hans Langmaack

Preface

Whenever software is developed for safety-critical systems, trusted, verified compilers would be of great value because they would make it possible to reason about software correctness solely on the source language level. Many people, however, are rather skeptical when confronted with the idea of completely verified realistic compilers. They fear that proofs addressing the complexity of compilers generating actual machine code would become long and involved and, therefore, would hardly be convincing. Indeed, the available literature on compiler verification mostly concentrates on particular translation aspects in isolation, illustrated by toy source and target languages. More ambitious efforts usually stop at the level of some abstract machine.

This monograph aims to show that it is possible to reason convincingly about correctness of translations to machine code of actual processors, and, even better, that this can be done in an illuminating and appealing manner. As a case study it provides the verified design of a code generator translating a real-time programming language to the Inmos Transputer. The success of such an effort crucially depends on appropriate structuring and the use of an adequate notation. Moreover, many theoretical topics are involved that are usually studied in isolation. Therefore, part of this monograph is devoted to consistently combining a number of subjects: algebraic reasoning with program-like combinators, data refinement theory, predicate transformer semantics, modeling of timing, and communication behavior. I hope that the resulting formal framework as well as the proof-engineering ideas incorporated in the verified code generator design are of interest even outside the realm of compiler verification.

This monograph is a revised version of my doctoral dissertation, the German equivalent of a Ph.D. thesis, which was submitted to the Technical Faculty of the Christian-Albrechts-University at Kiel and accepted in June 1996. I would like to thank my supervisor Hans Langmaack for support in many ways. I am also indebted to Martin Fränzle, who shared my office in the last few years and who was always willing to discuss technical and non-technical questions. He also gave a number of hints on a draft version that helped to improve the presentation.

The Provably Correct Systems (ProCoS) project provided the environment for writing my dissertation and I thank my colleagues for inspiration, criticism, and discussion, in addition to the aforementioned persons in particular Tony Hoare, He Jifeng, Burghard von Karger, Ernst-Rüdiger Olderog, Anders P. Ravn, and Michael Schenke. I greatly acknowledge the financial support of the European Union which made this project possible by funding it in the ESPRIT programme (BRA 3104 and BRA 7071).

I am also grateful to the referees of my thesis, Hans Langmaack, Juraj Hromkovič, and Bernhard Steffen, for their time and enthusiasm and to the other members of the examination board, Rudolf Berghammer, Helmut Föll, Klaus Potthoff, Roland Schmidt, and Wolfgang Thomas. Last but not least I would like to thank Claudia Herbers for constant encouragement.

I hope that this monograph is a step towards changing people's view of compiler verification: It should be regarded as an aid in correct design rather than as another burden for the compiler builder.

Passau, January 1997 Markus Müller-Olm

Table of Contents

List of Figures

List of Tables

1. Introduction

Much research has been performed in the last decades on verified design of programs. But to establish properties rigorously for high-level programs is worth the effort only if we can ensure that these properties transfer to the machine code that is finally executed. The latter usually is generated from the high-level program by a compiler. As inspection of the generated machine code is tedious and error-prone, it should be avoided by use of trusted compilers. In the area of safety-critical systems, certification could be performed on the source code level if trusted compilers were available, which promises to be less time-consuming and thus less costly as the current practice.

A common approach to increase confidence into a compiler is to compile a collection of test programs, to execute the resulting object code, and to inspect the results. It is questionable whether such a validation procedure can replace target code inspection in safety-critical software development, as test programs usually exhibit rather simple behavior and will not necessarily catch intricate timing and synchronization errors. Hence, development of a reliable compiler for a real-time programming language in our opinion should include formal verification of its vital constituents, in particular of its code generator.

Although the idea of mathematically verified compilers dates back at least to the sixties [54], the complete verification of realistic compilers is still a challenge. Most documented work on compiler verification heads for mathematical understanding of typical or semantically intricate implementation mechanisms. Therefore, generally source and target language are chosen in order to illustrate just the aspects under consideration. In particular, target code for commercially available processors rarely is formally investigated. One can argue that the application to actual machine code is straightforward but burdens the verification with many details of little interest, an attitude which is quite reasonable from a mathematician's point of view.

Besides mathematical insight, however, there is the more practical reason mentioned above for an interest in compiler verification: to justify the correctness of compiler-generated machine code from the correctness of the source code. Such a practical application of compiler verification calls for investigation of realistic processors and actual machine code.

This book provides a case study for the verified design of a code generator translating to an actual processor. The source language is essentially the language of while programs extended by communication statements and upper bound timing, and the target architecture is the Inmos Transputer [46]. The effort put into such a verification is, of course, not so much justified by the particular correctness claim that is proved but by the methodological insights that support and simplify a later undertaking of a similar kind.

The work has been performed in the context of the ProCoS project [13], a basic research action that has been funded by the European Union in the ESPRIT programme from 1989 until 1995 in two phases. ProCoS is an acronym for 'Provably Correct Systems' and the project partners in the second phase have been research groups from the universities in Kiel (Germany, site leader: H. Langmaack), Lyngby (Denmark, site leader: A.P. Ravn), Oldenburg (Germany, site leader: E.-R. Olderog), and Oxford (England, site leader: C.A.R. Hoare). The objective of ProCoS was 'to advance the state of the art of systematic design of complex heterogeneous systems, including both software and hardware; in particular to reduce the risk of error in the specification, design and implementation of embedded safety-critical systems' (cited from ProCoS's technical annex). More specifically, its goal was to develop a tower of notations with a consistent mathematical interpretation that can advantageously be used to document the development process from requirements capture down to implementation by machine code or task-specific hardware [35]. Compiler verification has been an important subtask, for which the Kiel group had the main responsibility.

A difficulty when verifying code for real processors is the large amount of machine-specific details that must be mastered: addressing modes, side effects of instructions, allocation of memory and registers, representation of data, restricted address space, no a-priori separation of program and data store, etc. It is essential to structure the entire proof appropriately such that small parts can independently be approached and checked.

The global structure of compilers is classical; they consist of a scanner, a parser, a well-formedness checker, and a code generator. Like most other work on compiler verification, we concentrate on the correctness proof for code generators, particularly on the semantic correctness of the generated code, because construction of scanners and parsers has been studied in the literature extensively.

Our main emphasis is on structuring code generator verification appropriately when translating to actually available hardware. The chosen structure must support the reader in checking the considerations in detail in order to allow a trustworthy certification of the correctness claim. Therefore, the verification must not consist of a few large monolithic proofs but must be split into (a larger number of) small proofs that can independently be examined. One might object that human control of a verification intended to validate the detailed correctness of a compiler is inherently unreliable due to its size and that the use of mechanical provers is a must. But this is not at all an argument against structuring: experience suggests that a good structure often is the key to the success of a mechanical proof attempt.

But a structured approach to verification should also support the making of the proof. One of the merits of a correctness proof is that assumptions that are left implicit in informal reasoning must be made explicit. Thus after the proof has been completed the side conditions required for execution of the code and the invariants kept by the code are precisely documented. The necessity of explication, however, is one of the sources for the complexity of such a proof. It is not easy to guess a precise formulation of the side conditions and the invariants together with correct code consistently, before starting the proof. Therefore, it is advisable to design the code generation map simultaneously together with the correctness property and the proof, in order to avoid iteration of proof attempts. We are heading for a structure of presentation and preparation that fosters a separation of concerns, such that the writer as well as the reader can concentrate on one particular aspect of the translation at a given time. Ultimate goal of the research reported here is a methodology for the correct construction of code generators.

Of course the construction of a verified code generator does not start from scratch but from a rough intuitive understanding gained from prior compiler building experience and tradition. A useful methodology for the correct construction of code generators must allow to make precise these informal ideas in a stepwise and incremental fashion. Let us sketch the proposal that is exemplified in this book. The core is the stepwise derivation of increasingly ***abstract views*** to the target processor's behavior from a ***base model*** of its execution cycle. Each abstraction step allows to treat one particular aspect of translation or machine program execution in isolation. Then ***compiling-correctness relations*** are defined that specify the intended semantic relationship between source and target code, which is largely simplified by the availability of the abstract views. Afterwards, concrete code patterns are studied by means of theorems about the compiling-correctness relations. From these ***translation theorems*** a code generator can be implemented without further semantic consideration.[1]

It is natural to think of instructions of von Neumann machines as assignments to machine components like accumulators and store. Hence, the effect of machine instructions can conveniently be described by imperative programs. E.g. the effect of the Transputer instruction `ldc(1)`, which loads the constant value 1 to the accumulator called `A`, and moves `A`'s contents to

[1] In order to construct a verified code generator, the implementation must, in principle, be done in machine code (for a trusted processor) because – at least for the first program of this kind – we cannot rely on a trusted compiler. The Verifix project [28] proposes to reduce the amount of manual work necessary for construction of a first, verified implementation in machine code by a bootstrap approach in multiple stages.

accumulator B, as well as B's contents to accumulator C, can be represented by the multiple assignment

$$E(\texttt{ldc}(1)) \quad = \quad \texttt{A},\texttt{B},\texttt{C} := 1,\texttt{A},\texttt{B} \ .$$

Similarly, the effect of $\texttt{stl}(x)$, writing A's contents to variable x, moving B's value to A, C's value to B, and an unspecified value to C, can be described by

$$E(\texttt{stl}(x)) \quad = \quad x,\texttt{A},\texttt{B} := \texttt{A},\texttt{B},\texttt{C} \ ; \texttt{C} :=? \ ,$$

where $\texttt{C} :=?$ abbreviates the nondeterministic choice between all possible assignments to C. If semantics of machine instructions is captured by imperative program fragments, refinement algebra of imperative programs [42] can be used to prove that certain machine instruction sequences refine, i.e. implement, certain source programs. The following calculation, for instance, shows that the code sequence $\langle \texttt{ldc}(1), \texttt{stl}(x)\rangle$, assumed to have the same meaning as the sequential composition of the effects $E(\texttt{ldc}(1))$ and $E(\texttt{stl}(x))$, is correct target code for the assignment $x := 1$:

$$\begin{array}{ll} & E(\texttt{ldc}(1)) \ ; E(\texttt{stl}(x)) \\ = & \text{[Identities above]} \\ & \texttt{A},\texttt{B},\texttt{C} := 1,\texttt{A},\texttt{B} \ ; x,\texttt{A},\texttt{B} := \texttt{A},\texttt{B},\texttt{C} \ ; \texttt{C} :=? \\ = & \text{[(Combine-assign), (Identity-assign)]} \\ & x,\texttt{A},\texttt{B},\texttt{C} := 1,\texttt{A},\texttt{B},\texttt{B} \ ; \texttt{C} :=? \\ = & \text{[(Cancel-assign), (Identity-assign)]} \\ & x := 1 \ ; \texttt{C} :=? \ . \end{array}$$

For the moment the additional effect on the accumulator C is taken to be irrelevant. In this proof we have used the assignment laws

$$\begin{array}{lrcl} \text{(Identity-assign)} & (x := e) & = & (x, y := e, y) \\ \text{(Combine-assign)} & (x := e \ ; x := f) & = & (x := f[e/x]) \\ \text{(Cancel-assign)} & (x, y := e, f \ ; y :=?) & = & (x := e \ ; y :=?) \end{array}$$

where $f[e/x]$ denotes substitution of e for x in expression f (x and y stand for disjoint lists of variable and e and f for lists of expressions of corresponding type).

The above little calculation illustrates a basic idea of our approach, viz. to use an imperative meta-language and refinement laws as proposed by C.A.R. Hoare in [41]. But, of course, the presentation up to now is oversimplified. Firstly, the model of the instruction's effect is too abstract. For example, the Transputer instructions refer to memory locations basically, not to variable identifiers as we assumed in the description of $\texttt{stl}(x)$, and a machine program basically is not a separate entity but the executed instructions are taken from memory, thus running a risk of being overwritten. Secondly, a number of unformalized assumptions have been made in the surrounding text, e.g. that concatenation of machine programs corresponds to sequential composition.

Clearly, an abstract model of the target processor simplifies the compiler verification. But if considerations are based on such a model alone, there is a severe danger of unsoundness because the postulated model might fail to provide a safe abstraction of the processor's actual behavior. To avoid this danger in our case study, we interface directly to the Transputer's documentation and start from a semi-formal model given by Inmos, the manufacturer of the Transputer, in [46]. However, a direct application of this model in a compiler proof results in very long and tedious calculations, which would seriously affect credibility of the proofs. How can we combine simplicity and conciseness of proofs with realistic modeling of the processor?

As mentioned, the idea is to derive a hierarchy of mutually consistent, increasingly abstract views to the Transputer's behavior, starting from bit-code level up to assembly levels with symbolic addressing. Afterwards we can choose for each proof task the model that allows the simplest proof or even mix reasoning at different abstraction levels without risking inconsistencies or unsoundness.

In the tradition of the refinement calculus we use a notation similar to an imperative programming language furnished with a refinement relation [5, 6, 61, 65] as meta-language for describing the various Transputer models and the abstraction maps. The various theorems on abstractions and code sequences are proved by short calculations using algebraic laws about the imperative constructs as proposed in [42, 43]. The imperative notation is interpreted by predicate transformers as in E.W. Dijkstra's wp-calculus. This is classical for internal constructs like assignments [6, 20, 21, 61, 65]. But we extend this to communication and timing by using two distinguished variables *hst* (for modeling the communication history) and *clk* (for modeling the runtime consumption) in a specific way. Non-$\perp$-strict predicate transformers are exploited to assign a reasonable total correctness semantics to non-terminating commands. Following the example of R.J.R. Back and J. von Wright [5], we perform the reasoning in the heterogeneous algebra of monotonic predicate transformers over different state spaces. For performing the abstractions we use a variant of the data refinement theory of R.J.R. Back [5], P.H.B. Gardiner & C.C. Morgan [25], and J.M. Morris [66].

The translation task considered in this book is modest w.r.t. the level of the source language; the complexity mainly stems from the investigation of actual machine code. But there are two aspects of broader interest. On the one hand the source language allows to state upper bound requirements for the execution time of basic blocks, the validity of which must be checked by the compiler. This is complicated by an idealization offered in the source language that is essential for the convenient programming of real-time programs in our opinion, viz. that internal computation is immediate and time proceeds only in communication statements. We can offer this idealization because only the communication behavior of programs is externally observable. The compiler has to distribute the actual execution time of the code implementing internal activity to subsequent communications.

The other interesting translation aspect is that we do not assume that a generally acceptable failure behavior is available. Classically, stopping of programs is assumed to be reasonable in failure situations like stack overflow or arithmetic under- or overflow. This assumption, however, often is wrong in the context of reactive programs: certainly a control program in an aeroplane must not stop under any circumstances. Consequently, machine restrictions must either be reflected on the source language level or checked by the compiler. The former approach allows the program designer to prove that the machine restriction does not affect correctness of the program, which is appropriate e.g. for the restricted arithmetic available on a specific processor. The latter is a reasonable strategy for the storage consumption of programs but excludes e.g. unrestricted use of recursion in the source language.

1.1 Organization of This Book

Almost half of this book is devoted to providing a firm foundation for calculations with the chosen imperative notation. In Chap. 2 we summarize basic results about complete Boolean lattices. The fundamental notion of Galois connections is discussed in Chap. 3. Chapter 4 defines and studies states, valuation functions and predicates. In particular, various 'typed' quantification operators are introduced. In Chap. 5 the basic notations of the imperative meta-language are defined and numerous laws are established. In Chap. 6 we extend this basic language with communication and timing primitives. In particular, we present a trace semantics for communicating processes in the space of predicate transformers which reasonably models non-terminating processes that communicate infinitely often. For this behalf the classic notion of total correctness is extended to communicating processes, which is motivated and studied in an operational framework. Chapter 7 is concerned with data refinement. Essentially, we reformulate the definition of J.M. Morris [66] and P.H.B. Gardiner & C.C. Morgan [25, 63] on the process level. This concludes the first part that provides the notational and mathematical basis for the second part that is concerned more directly with code generator correctness.

In Chap. 8 we formulate the most concrete model of the target processor, viz. the Inmos Transputer. It is obtained by re-stating information from the Transputer instruction set manual [46] as refinement axioms about a certain collection of processes. Chapter 9 defines the source language TPL, a prototypic hard-real time programming language. In Chap. 10 we construct in successive steps more abstract views to the behavior of the Transputer that are exploited when defining in Chap. 11 the semantic compiling-correctness relations that must hold between source and target code. By means of theorems about these relations, concrete correct code patterns are studied in

Chap. 12. How a code generator can be implemented from this collection of translation theorems is illustrated in Chap. 13 by the construction of a functional program. We finish with concluding remarks in Chap. 14. An index at the end of this book is particularly intended to support finding definitions and laws.

1.2 Related Literature on Code Generator Verification

The idea to specify a machine by a high level program is old and present already in the concept of micro-programming [86]. G.M. Brown, A.J. Martin and others [15, 36, 52] use such descriptions as starting point for hardware design and C.A.R. Hoare, H. Jifeng and A. Sampaio [41, 43, 79] propose to utilize them together with a refinement algebra related to the source language [42, 60] for reasoning about code generator correctness. We adopt this proposal but apply it in a different way. From more classical work about compiler correctness [48, 54, 64, 57, 71, 78, 84] we are particularly distinguished by aiming at code for an actually commercially available processor and not for idealized hardware, which puts an emphasis on modularity and on readability of the meta-language used. Another difference to classical methods is that we use refinement as the correctness notion instead of semantic equivalence, which is also borrowed from [43]. This allows a proper treatment of under-specification in the source language's semantics (e.g. of uninitialized variables) and accommodates modularization. Like the work at CLI (Computational Logic Inc.) [7, 59] on the 'verified stack' we put emphasis on consistent interfaces to higher and in particular lower levels of abstraction.

E. Börger, I. Durdanović and D. Rosenzweig [11, 12] are concerned with proving correct compilation of Occam to the Transputer. Their emphasis, however, is more on a mathematical understanding of its specific multitasking and communication mechanisms, while we are more interested in the common phenomena arising when translating to actually available von Neumann processors. The recent impressive work on VLisp by J.D. Guttman, D.P. Oliva, J.D. Ramsdell, V. Swarup and M. Wand [33, 34, 73] is concerned with a verified translator for Scheme, a functional Lisp-like language. The final abstract machine is rather close to actual hardware given the abstractness of the source language Scheme but is still more abstract than code for commercially available processors. They propose to use an operational style of reasoning for the verification at lower levels while we advocate a more abstract denotational style even there. Some of their abstractions rely on the existence of an acceptable failure behavior, which prohibits an immediate application of their work in the area of embedded safety-critical control programs.

2. Complete Boolean Lattices

We assume familiarity with the basic theory of complete Boolean lattices. To make this book reasonably self-contained, however, we repeat the basic definitions and facts in this section. An in-depth exposition of lattice theory is provided by the classic books of G. Birkhoff [9] and G. Grätzer [29]. We also partly follow the introductory sections of [6]. All the results are standard and are therefore reported here without proof.

2.1 Basic Definitions

This section contains the basic definitions and facts of lattice theory. We cite them from the first chapter of [29] mainly.

A *partial order* on a non-empty set A is a binary relation $\leq$ on A that is reflexive, antisymmetric and transitive, i.e. that satisfies the following three axioms.

- *Reflexivity*: for all $a \in A$: $a \leq a$.
- *Antisymmetry*: for all $a, b \in A$: $a \leq b \land b \leq a \Rightarrow a = b$.
- *Transitivity*: for all $a, b, c \in A$: $a \leq b \land b \leq c \Rightarrow a \leq c$.

If $\leq$ is a partial order on a set A then we call the pair $(A, \leq)$ a ***partially ordered set***. If $\leq$ is clear from context, we often call A a partially ordered set omitting an explicit reference to $\leq$.

Assume $(A, \leq)$ is a partially ordered set and let $B \subseteq A$ and $a \in A$. Then a is called an ***upper bound*** of B if $b \leq a$ for all $b \in B$. An upper bound a of B is called the ***least upper bound*** or ***join*** of B if it is smaller than any other upper bound. By antisymmetry of $\leq$, the least upper bound is unique if it exists. We denote the least upper bound of B (if it exists) by $\bigvee B$. Dually, a is called a ***lower bound*** of B if $a \leq b$ for all $b \in B$, and called the ***greatest lower bound*** or ***meet*** of B if it is a lower bound greater than any other lower bound. Like the least upper bound the greatest lower bound of B is unique if it exists and is then denoted by $\bigwedge B$. B is called a ***chain*** if it is non-empty and all its elements are comparable w.r.t. $\leq$, i.e. if for all $b, c \in B$, $b \leq c$ or $c \leq b$.

A partially ordered set $(L, \leq)$ is called a ***lattice*** if for any two elements $a, b \in L$ the least upper bound $\bigvee\{a, b\}$ as well as the greatest lower bound

$\bigwedge\{a,b\}$ exist. It is well-known (and easy to see by induction) that an equivalent requirement is that $\bigvee H$ and $\bigwedge H$ exist for any finite and non-empty subset H of L.

On a lattice $(L, \leq)$ we can define the two binary operations $\wedge$ and $\vee$, also called *meet* and *join*, by the identities

$$a \wedge b = \bigwedge\{a,b\} \quad \text{and} \quad a \vee b = \bigvee\{a,b\} .$$

They satisfy for any $a, b, c \in L$ the following laws.

- *Idempotency*: $a \wedge a = a$ and $a \vee a = a$.
- *Commutativity*: $a \wedge b = b \wedge a$ and $a \vee b = b \vee a$.
- *Associativity*: $(a \wedge b) \wedge c = a \wedge (b \wedge c)$ and $(a \vee b) \vee c = a \vee (b \vee c)$.
- *Absorption identities*: $a \wedge (a \vee b) = a$ and $a \vee (a \wedge b) = a$.

It is well-known (e.g. [29, p. 5, Theorem 1]) that a lattice can be characterized as a non-empty set L equipped with two operations $\wedge$ and $\vee$ satisfying the above four laws.[1] The ordering relation $\leq$ can be regained from meet or join by one of the two equivalences

$$a \leq b \quad \text{iff} \quad a = a \wedge b \quad \text{iff} \quad b = a \vee b .$$

Whenever talking about lattices we assume that we have both views available, viz. as an ordering structure and as an algebraic structure.

A lattice $(L, \leq)$ is called *distributive* if for all $a, b, c \in L$ the two laws

$$a \wedge (b \vee c) = (a \wedge b) \vee (a \wedge c) \quad \text{and} \quad a \vee (b \wedge c) = (a \vee b) \wedge (a \vee c)$$

hold. Each of these laws is a consequence of the other. It suffices, therefore, to require only one of them.

A *bounded lattice* is a lattice $(L, \leq)$ that has a smallest element denoted by $\bot$ (or $\bot_L$ if L is to be emphasized) and a largest element $\top$ (or $\top_L$). In a bounded lattice an element $a \in L$ is called a *complement* of an element $b \in L$ if $a \wedge b = \bot$ and $a \vee b = \top$. In a distributive bounded lattice complements are unique if they exist ([29, p. 47, Lemma 1]).

A *Boolean lattice* is a distributive bounded lattice in which every element has a (unique) complement. We denote the complement of a by $\overline{a}$. In a Boolean lattice the well-known *de Morgan identities* hold ([29, p. 48, Lemma 3]), i.e, for all $a, b \in L$:

$$\overline{a \wedge b} = \overline{a} \vee \overline{b} \quad \text{and} \quad \overline{a \vee b} = \overline{a} \wedge \overline{b} .$$

On Boolean lattices we use the common 'propositional' operators that can be introduced as abbreviations. In particular we write $a \Rightarrow b$ for $\overline{a} \vee b$.

A lattice $(L, \leq)$ is called *complete* if $\bigvee H$ and $\bigwedge H$ exist for any subset H of L. It suffices to require only half of this, e.g. existence of $\bigvee H$ for any $H \subseteq L$, as the second requirement then already is implied. A complete lattice

[1] It suffices to require commutativity, associativity and the absorption identities because the idempotency laws follow already from the absorption identities.

$(L, \leq)$ is always bounded and the smallest element $\bot$ equals $\bigvee \emptyset$ as well as $\bigwedge L$. Dually, the greatest element $\top$ of a complete lattice equals $\bigwedge \emptyset$ and $\bigvee L$.

Example 2.1.1. A canonic example of a complete Boolean lattice is the set $\mathsf{Bool} = \{\mathsf{ff}, \mathsf{tt}\}$, where ff and tt stand for the truth values 'false' and 'true', ordered by the *implication order*,

$$a \leq b \quad \text{iff} \quad a = \mathsf{ff} \text{ or } b = \mathsf{tt} \ ,$$

that is illustrated by the Hasse-diagram. Meet and join correspond to the logical connectives 'and' and 'or' and complementation is negation. □

Example 2.1.2. Another well-known example is the power set $\mathbb{P}(A)$ of a set A ordered by the inclusion relation $\subseteq$. Meet and join are set intersection and set union and the complement $\overline{B}$ of $B \in \mathbb{P}(A)$ is the set-theoretic relative complement $A \setminus B$. □

A non-empty subset K of a lattice $(L, \leq)$ is called a ***sub-lattice*** if $a \wedge b, a \vee b \in K$ for any $a, b \in K$. As expected, a sub-lattice K together with the restriction of $\leq$ to K is a lattice. A non-empty subset K of a complete lattice $(L, \leq)$ is called a ***complete sub-lattice*** if $\bigwedge H, \bigvee H \in K$ for any $H \subseteq K$. A complete sub-lattice K of $(L, \leq)$ together with the restriction of $\leq$ to K is a complete lattice. A standard remark at this point is that a sub-lattice K of a complete lattice $(L, \leq)$ that is complete is not necessarily a complete sub-lattice of $(L, \leq)$. The requirement that arbitrary meets and joins taken in K coincide with the meets and joins taken in L is stronger than the requirement that this only holds for finite ones and that infinite ones exist in K.

2.2 Functions

We denote the set of (total) functions from A to B by $(A \to B)$. The ***identity*** on a set A mapping each $a \in A$ to itself is denoted by Id_A (or Id if A is clear from context). The ***composition*** of two functions $f \in (A \to B)$ and $g \in (B \to C)$ is denoted by $g \circ f$ and is the function from A to C defined by $(g \circ f)(a) = g(f(a))$. Composition of functions is associative and has Id_A as right and Id_B as left unit. We are particularly interested in functions from arbitrary sets to partial orders or lattices, and mappings between lattices.

2.2.1 Functions from a Set to an Ordered Set or Lattice

Suppose A is a set and $(L, \leq)$ is a partially ordered set. The partial order $\leq$ on L can be lifted to a relation $\sqsubseteq$ on $(A \to L)$, the set of total functions from A to L, by the definition

$$g \sqsubseteq g' \quad \text{iff} \quad \forall a \in A : g(a) \leq g'(a) \ .$$

The relation $\sqsubseteq$ is an order on $(A \to L)$ called the *pointwise extension* of $\leq$ to functions. Suppose $H \subseteq (A \to L)$ and $g \in (A \to L)$. It is well-known that

(a) g is an upper bound of H (w.r.t. $\sqsubseteq$) iff $g(a)$ is an upper bound of $\{f(a) \mid f \in H\}$ (w.r.t. $\leq$) for all $a \in A$, and
(b) g is the least upper bound of H (w.r.t. $\sqsubseteq$) iff $g(a)$ is the least upper bound of the set $\{f(a) \mid f \in H\}$ (w.r.t. $\leq$) for all $a \in A$.

By duality, analogous results hold for lower bounds.

If $(L, \leq)$ is a lattice, $((A \to L), \sqsubseteq)$ is a lattice too and meet and join operations on $(A \to L)$ are the pointwise extensions of the meet and join operations on L, i.e., for all $g, g' \in (A \to L)$, $a \in A$

$$(g \sqcap g')(a) \;=\; g(a) \wedge g'(a) \quad \text{and} \quad (g \sqcup g')(a) \;=\; g(a) \vee g'(a) \;.$$

If L is distributive (bounded, Boolean, complete), $(A \to L)$ is distributive (bounded, Boolean, complete) as well. If L is Boolean (and consequently also $(A \to L)$) then the complement $\overline{g}$ of $g \in (A \to L)$ is the pointwise complement, i.e., for all $a \in A$

$$\overline{g}(a) \;=\; \overline{g(a)} \;.$$

Usually we do not notationally distinguish between $\leq$ and $\sqsubseteq$ writing $\leq$ for both the order on L as well as its pointwise extension to $(A \to L)$.

2.2.2 Functions Between Lattices

We now consider functions between lattices; so suppose $(L, \leq)$ and $(L', \leq')$ are lattices. By the results of the previous section $(L \to L')$ ordered by the pointwise extension of $\leq'$ is a lattice (distributive if L is distributive etc.). A function $g \in (L \to L')$ is called

- *monotonic* iff $a \leq b$ implies $g(a) \leq' g(b)$ for all $a, b \in L$,
- *antitonic* iff $a \leq b$ implies $g(b) \leq' g(a)$ for all $a, b \in L$,
- $\bot$*-strict* iff $g(\bot_L) = \bot_{L'}$,
- $\top$*-strict* iff $g(\top_L) = \top_{L'}$.

The set of monotonic functions from L to L' is denoted by $[L \to L']$. The following facts are well-known.

- $[L \to L']$ is a sub-lattice of $(L \to L')$, the lattice of all (total) functions from L to L'.
- If L' (and so also $(L \to L')$) is distributive (bounded, complete) then $[L \to L']$ is distributive (resp. bounded, complete) as well. Arbitrary least upper and greatest lower bounds of subsets $H \subseteq [L \to L']$ exist in $[L \to L']$ iff they exist in $(L \to L')$ and the results whether taken in $[L \to L']$ or $(L \to L')$ coincide.

Note that $[L \to L']$ never is a Boolean lattice (except if L' contains just one element) as the complement of the function $g \in [L \to L']$,

$$g(x) = \begin{cases} \top & \text{if } x \neq \bot \\ \bot & \text{if } x = \bot \end{cases}$$

is not monotonic.

A monotonic function $g \in [L \to L']$ between complete lattices L, L' always is ***super-distributive*** w.r.t. arbitrary joins and ***sub-distributive*** w.r.t. arbitrary meets. This means that for arbitrary $H \subseteq L$ the following two inequalities hold:

$$g(\bigvee H) \;\geq\; \bigvee\{g(h) \mid h \in H\} \quad \text{and} \quad g(\bigwedge H) \;\leq\; \bigwedge\{g(h) \mid h \in H\} .$$

We have required L, L' to be complete lattices in order to guarantee existence of the joins and meets. The two inequalities above also hold for arbitrary monotonic functions between partially ordered sets if the occurring meets and joins exist.

The reverse inequalities have special names. A function g between complete lattices L, L' is said to be

- *universally disjunctive* iff it distributes over arbitrary joins, i.e., if an only if $g(\bigvee H) = \bigvee\{g(h) \mid h \in H\}$ for all $H \subseteq L$,
- *universally conjunctive* iff it distributes over meets, i.e., if and only if $g(\bigwedge H) = \bigwedge\{g(h) \mid h \in H\}$ for all $H \subseteq L$,
- *positively disjunctive* iff it distributes over non-empty joins, i.e., if and only if $g(\bigvee H) = \bigvee\{g(h) \mid h \in H\}$ for all *non-empty* $H \subseteq L$,
- *positively conjunctive* iff it distributes over non-empty meets, i.e., if and only if $g(\bigwedge H) = \bigwedge\{g(h) \mid h \in H\}$ for all *non-empty* $H \subseteq L$, and called
- *continuous* iff it distributes over joins of chains, i.e., if and only if $g(\bigvee H) = \bigvee\{g(h) \mid h \in H\}$ for all chains $H \subseteq L$. The latter property sometimes is called $\vee$-continuity and the dual property $\wedge$-continuity is also considered.

Any function that has one of these properties is monotonic. A function g is universally disjunctive iff it is positively disjunctive and $\bot$-strict; it is universally conjunctive iff it is positively conjunctive and $\top$-strict.

We note some distribution properties of the lattice operators $\wedge$ and $\vee$. Suppose $(L, \leq)$ is a lattice. Then, for any $a \in L$, the function that maps x to $a \wedge x$ is positively conjunctive and the function that maps x to $a \vee x$ is positively disjunctive:

- $a \wedge (\bigwedge H) \;=\; \bigwedge\{a \wedge h \mid h \in H\}$ for all non-empty $H \subseteq L$, and
- $a \vee (\bigvee H) \;=\; \bigvee\{a \vee h \mid h \in H\}$ for all non-empty $H \subseteq L$.

Moreover, in any complete sub-lattice of a complete Boolean lattice $\lambda x \,.\, a \wedge x$ is universally disjunctive and $\lambda x \,.\, a \vee x$ is universally conjunctive (see [29, p. 91, Corollary 11]). These rules sometimes are called the Join Distributive Identity (JDI) and the Meet Distributive Identity (MDI):

$$\text{(JDI)} \qquad a \wedge (\bigvee H) = \bigvee \{a \wedge h \mid h \in H\} \quad \text{for any } H \subseteq L, \text{ and}$$

$$\text{(MDI)} \qquad a \vee (\bigwedge H) = \bigwedge \{a \vee h \mid h \in H\} \quad \text{for any } H \subseteq L.$$

2.3 Fixpoints

Let $g \in (L \to L)$ be a function on an ordered set $(L, \leq)$ and $a \in L$. Then a is called a *fixpoint* of g if $g(a) = a$. If a in addition is smaller than any other fixpoint of g, it is called the *least fixpoint*. By antisymmetry of $\leq$, the least fixpoint is unique if it exists. We denote the least fixpoint of g by μg.

The following so-called Knaster-Tarski fixpoint theorem ensures the existence of least fixpoints for monotonic functions on complete lattices. It is often used in computer science to define the meaning of recursive definitions.

Theorem 2.3.1 (Knaster-Tarski fixpoint theorem). *Let L be a complete lattice and $g \in [L \to L]$. Then g has a least fixpoint and μg is the greatest lower bound of the set of all 'pre-fixpoints' of g:*

$$\mu g = \bigwedge \{x \mid g(x) \leq x\} .$$

The (not very difficult) proof can be found in [83]. An interesting discussion about the attribution of a number of fixpoint theorems that are used to define semantics of recursion to Knaster, Tarski and others is in [49]. By the Knaster-Tarski fixpoint theorem, μg is a lower bound of the set of pre-fixpoints. Thus we have the following corollary.

Corollary 2.3.2. *Suppose L is a complete lattice, $g \in [L \to L]$ and $x \in L$. If x is a pre-fixpoint of g, i.e. if $g(x) \leq x$, then $\mu g \leq x$.*

So, in order to prove that an element $x \in L$ is greater than the least fixpoint of a monotonic function g on L, it suffices to show that x is contracted by g, i.e. that $g(x) \leq x$. In the fixpoint theory on complete partial orders (cpos) this property is called 'Park's lemma'.

Consider now the following situation illustrated by the below diagram: L and L' are complete lattices, $f \in [L \to L]$, $g \in [L' \to L']$ and $h \in (L \to L')$.

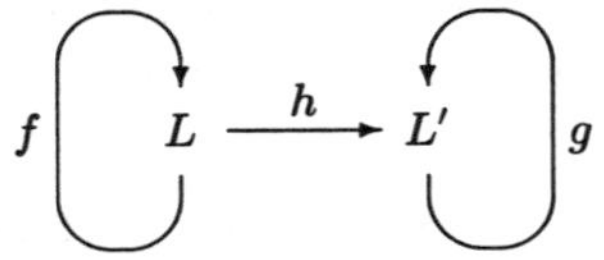

Theorem 2.3.3 (Transfer lemma, μ-fusion rule).
If h is $\perp$-strict and continuous and $h \circ f = g \circ h$ then $h(\mu f) = \mu g$.

This theorem appears under the name 'transfer lemma' e.g. in [2] and is called μ-fusion rule in [53]. For universally disjunctive h there is an elegant proof using the fact that h has an upper adjoint (see, e.g., [26, Lemma 2.3]).

3. Galois Connections

Galois connections provide a means for relating different abstraction levels in presence of incomplete information. For example, in the context of abstract interpretation they have been used for describing the relationship between programming language models of different accuracy (see [18] for an overview on abstract interpretation frameworks and for an extensive bibliography). Their use as a vehicle for describing correctness of implementations is indicated in [55]. The mathematical study of Galois connections goes back to the forties [8, 74, 81].

3.1 Definition and Basic Facts

The notion of a Galois connection can be defined between ordered or even pre-ordered sets and is defined in the literature with monotonic or antitonic functions (sometimes called covariant or contra-variant Galois connections). In category-theoretic terminology Galois connections are adjoint situations between partially ordered sets. H. Herrlich and M. Hušek [37] argue, however, that a generalization to adjoint situations between arbitrary categories is inappropriate as most of the interesting results about Galois connections are no longer valid. We are only interested in (covariant) Galois connections between complete lattices that are defined as follows.

Definition 3.1.1 (Galois connection). *Suppose* $(L, \leq)$ *and* $(L', \leq')$ *are complete lattices and* $F \in [L \to L']$ *and* $G \in [L' \to L]$ *are monotonic functions. Then the pair* (F, G) *is called a* Galois connection between L and L' *if for all* $x \in L$, $y \in L'$

$$F(x) \leq' y \quad \text{iff} \quad x \leq G(y) .$$

F *is called a* lower adjoint *of* G *and* G *is called an* upper adjoint *of* F.

As indicated, Galois connections can be used to relate models of the same system on different abstraction levels. Interpret the orders for a moment as 'refinement', i.e. $a \leq b$ expresses that b is better than a in serving every purpose a does (but possibly more), and assume that L and L' are lattices of descriptions for systems on different abstraction levels. We describe the correspondence between L and L' by a Galois connection (F, G) such that $G(c)$ is the best we can guarantee in the more abstract model L about a system whose behavior is described by c in the more concrete model L'. Consider now a system for which a concrete description $c \in L'$ is known. In order to prove that it implements a specification $a \in L$ formulated in the more abstract model, we can choose whether to reason in L or in L': either we demonstrate $F(a) \leq c$; this amounts to a proof in the concrete model L'; or we check $a \leq G(c)$ – a proof in the abstract model – which is equivalent to $F(a) \leq c$ by the defining condition for Galois connections. We can so to speak choose whether to 'concretize' a or to 'abstract' c if the intended relationship between L and L' is described by a Galois connection. Together with their pleasant structural properties this is one of the main reasons why Galois connections become increasingly popular for formally stating implementation choices.

But we should be careful: that (F, G) is a Galois connection does not immediately guarantee that the described relationship between L and L' is reasonable. In fact there is always the trivial Galois connection defined by

$$F(x) \stackrel{\text{def}}{=} \bot_{L'} \quad \text{and} \quad G(y) \stackrel{\text{def}}{=} \top_L \ ,$$

with respect to which every $y \in L'$ is an implementation of every $x \in L$! The question whether a specific Galois connection describes a reasonable correspondence is subject to a separate (informal or formal) consideration.

When Galois connections are used in this way for relating different abstraction levels, G is called an ***abstraction*** because it maps a description c given in the more concrete model L' to the corresponding (best) description $G(c)$ in the more abstract model L. In this context F is called a *concretization.*

The following results about Galois connections are well-known. We cite them from [37] and [55] where they are either proved or a pointer to a proof in the literature is given. The first is an equivalent characterization of Galois connections.

Theorem 3.1.2 (Alternative characterization). *Let $(L, \leq)$ and $(L', \leq')$ be complete lattices and $F \in [L \to L']$ and $G \in [L' \to L]$ monotonic functions. Then (F, G) is a Galois connection if and only if the following two inequalities hold:*

$$F \circ G \leq' \mathsf{Id}_{L'} \quad \textit{and} \quad \mathsf{Id}_L \leq G \circ F \ .$$

The condition $F \circ G \leq' \mathsf{Id}_{L'}$ captures nicely that abstraction in general is bought by a loss of information: if we have concrete information $c \in L'$ about a system, abstract this information (via G) and then concretize the result (via F), we get less information about the system than we had in the beginning. The gain we usually hope to obtain from abstraction is an advance in tractability. On the other hand concretization might gain additional information due to knowledge about the implementation technology that is coded in the concrete model L.

Theorem 3.1.3 (Existence and uniqueness of adjoints). *Let $(L, \leq)$ and $(L', \leq')$ be complete lattices, $F \in [L \to L']$ and $G \in [L' \to L]$.*

(a) *F has an upper adjoint iff F is universally disjunctive. This means that there is an H such that (F, H) is a Galois connection iff F preserves arbitrary joins. Dually, G has a lower adjoint iff it is universally conjunctive.*
(b) *Suppose (F, G) is a Galois connection. Then F and G determine each other uniquely, i.e., G is the only function $\tilde{G} \in [L' \to L]$ such that $(F, \tilde{G})$ is a Galois connection and F is the only function $\tilde{F} \in [L \to L']$ such that $(\tilde{F}, G)$ is a Galois connection. This justifies to speak of F as* the lower adjoint *of G and of G as* the upper adjoint *of F. Sometimes the notation $G^\flat$ for the lower adjoint of G and $F^\sharp$ for the upper adjoint of F is used.*

The following little lemma shows that both $.^\sharp$ and $.^\flat$ are antitonic.

Lemma 3.1.4 (Comparison of Galois connections). *Let (F, G) and (F', G') be Galois connections between L and L'. Then $F \leq F'$ iff $G \geq G'$.*

Proof. If $F \leq F'$ then

$$\begin{array}{ccccccc} G' & \leq & G \circ F \circ G' & \leq & G \circ F' \circ G' & \leq & G\,. \\ & \uparrow & & \uparrow & & \uparrow & \\ & [\mathsf{Id} \leq G \circ F] & & [F \leq F'] & & [F' \circ G' \leq \mathsf{Id}] & \end{array}$$

The other implication follows by a similar calculation. □

3.2 Distributive Galois Connections

When reasoning about machine language semantics, we apply Galois connections as a vehicle for deriving less detailed descriptions out of more detailed ones. We start from a description on a detailed level. Partial knowledge about the machine behavior is captured by axioms that are formulated as refinement inequalities. The formula

$$M' \;\geq'\; \mathit{Step}' \,;\, M' \,, \tag{3.1}$$

for instance, expresses that the machine described by M' behaves cyclically performing in each cycle the behavior described by Step'. We specify the intended relationship between the detailed concrete model and the less detailed more abstract one by a Galois connection (F, G) and *define* the abstraction M of M' by the identity $M = G(M')$ and the abstraction of Step' by $\mathit{Step} = G(\mathit{Step}')$. Although this is a precise definition of M and Step, it is given only with reference to the detailed concrete model. Therefore, we derive from the axioms about M' and Step' similar inequations about M

that do not refer to the low level objects M' and *Step'*. Distributive Galois connections are of particular importance in this context.

Definition 3.2.1 (Distributive Galois connections). *Let* $(L, \leq)$ *and* $(L', \leq')$ *be complete lattices. Assume that on* L *as well as* L' *a binary monotonic operator* ; *is defined. Let* (F, G) *be a Galois connection between* L *and* L'. *Then* (F, G) *is called a* ;-distributive Galois connection *if*

(a) F *is sub-distributive w.r.t.* ;, *i.e. for all* x, x': $F(x\ ;\ x') \ \leq\ F(x)\ ;\ F(x')$, *and*

(b) G *is super-distributive w.r.t* ;, *i.e. for all* y, y': $G(y\ ;\ y') \ \geq\ G(y)\ ;\ G(y')$.

If the operators ; *are clear from the context, we simply speak of a* distributive Galois connection.

Distributive Galois connections allow to perform abstraction piecewise: if in the above little example the Galois connection (F, G) is distributive, we get from (3.1):

$$M \ =\ G(M') \ \geq\ G(\mathit{Step}'\ ;\ M') \ \geq\ G(\mathit{Step}')\ ;\ G(M') \ =\ \mathit{Step}\ ;\ M\ .$$

This little calculation proves $M \geq \mathit{Step}\ ;\ M$, an inequality formulated solely in the abstract model. This example is only intended to motivate the notion of distributive Galois connections and cannot show the increase of tractability by abstraction. Clearly, the inequality about M has the same complexity as (3.1). Extensive examples of the simplifying effect of abstraction can be found in Chap. 10.

It suffices to require one of the conditions (a) and (b) in the definition of distributive Galois connections.

Lemma 3.2.2 (Distributive Galois connections). *Let* (F, G) *be a Galois connection between the complete lattices* L *and* L' *and assume that in both lattices a binary monotonic operator* ; *is defined. Then* F *is sub-distributive w.r.t.* ; *if and only if* G *is super-distributive w.r.t.* ;.

Proof. We prove only one of the claimed implications (viz. "only if"). The other implication follows by dualization.

Suppose $F(x\ ;\ x') \leq F(x)\ ;\ F(x')$ holds for all $x, x' \in L$. Then for any $y, y' \in L'$:

$$\begin{array}{ll} & F(G(y)\ ;\ G(y')) \\ \leq & \quad [\text{Sub-distributivity of } F] \\ & F(G(y))\ ;\ F(G(y')) \\ \leq & \quad [F \circ G \leq \mathsf{Id} \text{ because } (F, G) \text{ is Galois connection}] \\ & y\ ;\ y'\ . \end{array}$$

An application of the defining equivalence for Galois connections yields, as required, $G(y)\ ;\ G(y') \ \leq\ G(y\ ;\ y')$. □

3.3 Galois Connections Between Power Sets

We now investigate methods for constructing Galois connections. First of all, we consider Galois connections between the power sets of two sets A and B. There is a one-to-one correspondence between relations $R \subseteq A \times B$ and Galois connections (F, G) between $(\mathbb{P}(A), \subseteq)$ and $(\mathbb{P}(B), \subseteq)$. Each such relation R induces a Galois connection (F_R, G_R) and each Galois connection (F, G) (between power sets ordered by inclusion) is induced by a relation. The constructions from relations to Galois connections and reverse are given in the following two theorems.

Theorem 3.3.1 (Relations induce Galois connections). *Suppose given two sets A and B and a relation $R \subseteq A \times B$. Define $F_R \in [\mathbb{P}(A) \to \mathbb{P}(B)]$ and $G_R \in [\mathbb{P}(B) \to \mathbb{P}(A)]$ by*

$$F_R(x) \stackrel{\text{def}}{=} \{b \mid \exists a : (a,b) \in R \wedge a \in x\} \quad \textit{and}$$
$$G_R(y) \stackrel{\text{def}}{=} \{a \mid \forall b : (a,b) \in R \Rightarrow b \in y\}$$

for $x \subseteq A, y \subseteq B$. Then (F_R, G_R) is a Galois connection.

Proof. Monotonicity of F_R and G_R is clear. The defining condition for Galois connections is established by a series of equivalence transformations:

Suppose $x \subseteq A$ and $y \subseteq B$.

$F_R(x) \subseteq y$

iff [Definition of F_R]

$(\forall b : (\exists a : (a,b) \in R \wedge a \in x) \Rightarrow b \in y)$

iff [a does not appear on the right hand side of the implication]

$(\forall a, b : (a,b) \in R \wedge a \in x \Rightarrow b \in y)$

iff [Propositional logic]

$(\forall a, b : a \in x \Rightarrow ((a,b) \in R \Rightarrow b \in y))$

iff [b does not appear on the right hand side of the implication]

$(\forall a : a \in x \Rightarrow (\forall b : (a,b) \in R \Rightarrow b \in y))$

iff [Definition of G_R]

$x \subseteq G_R(y)$. □

Theorem 3.3.2 (Galois connections are induced by relations). *Suppose given sets A, B and a Galois connection (F, G) between $\mathbb{P}(A)$ and $\mathbb{P}(B)$. Define $R \subseteq A \times B$ by*

$$R \stackrel{\text{def}}{=} \{(a,b) \mid b \in F(\{a\})\} .$$

Then $(F, G) = (F_R, G_R)$, where F_R, G_R are defined as in the previous theorem.

Proof. First we show that F coincides with F_R on singletons:
Suppose $a \in A$. Then

$$\begin{array}{ll} & F_R(\{a\}) \\ = & \quad [\text{Definition of } F_R] \\ & \{b \mid \exists c : (c,b) \in R \wedge c \in \{a\}\} \\ = & \quad [\text{Definition of } R] \\ & \{b \mid \exists c : b \in F(\{c\}) \wedge c \in \{a\}\} \\ = & \quad [\text{One point rule}] \\ & F(\{a\}) . \end{array}$$

By Theorem 3.1.3, F as well as F_R are universally disjunctive (both have an upper adjoint, viz. G and G_R). As each set can be constructed as the union of the contained singletons, we can now easily show that F equals F_R:
Suppose $x \subseteq A$. Then

$$\begin{array}{ll} & F_R(x) \\ = & F_R(\bigcup\{\{a\} \mid a \in x\}) \\ = & \quad [F_R \text{ is universally disjunctive}] \\ & \bigcup\{F_R(\{a\}) \mid a \in x\} \\ = & \quad [\text{Above calculation}] \\ & \bigcup\{F(\{a\}) \mid a \in x\} \\ = & \quad [F \text{ is universally disjunctive}] \\ & F(\bigcup\{\{a\} \mid a \in x\}) \\ = & F(x) . \end{array}$$

Thus $F = F_R$. $G = G_R$ follows from the uniqueness of the upper adjoint. □

G. Birkhoff studies in [8] a connection between the power sets $\mathbb{P}(A)$ and $\mathbb{P}(B)$ induced by a relation R between A and B, which he calls ***polarities*** (according to H. Herrlich and M. Hušek [37]). This study motivated O. Ore [74] to introduce and study the notion of (contra-variant) Galois connections of which polarities are a special instance. The above definition of F_R and G_R is a co-variant analogue to polarities. It is interesting that the relationship between R and G_R corresponds to the relationship between relational models and weakest precondition models of program semantics.

3.4 Composing Galois Connections

We now consider the situation illustrated by the following diagram.

$$L \underset{G}{\overset{F}{\rightleftarrows}} L' \underset{G'}{\overset{F'}{\rightleftarrows}} L''$$

Theorem 3.4.1 (Functional composition). *Suppose L, L', L'' are complete lattices, (F, G) is a Galois connection between L and L' and (F', G') a Galois connection between L' and L''. Then $(F' \circ F, G \circ G')$ is a Galois connection between L and L''. If both (F, G) and (F', G') are distributive then $(F' \circ F, G \circ G')$ is distributive as well.*

Proof. Straightforward. □

Galois connections can also be constructed from families of Galois connections by taking their join and meet.

Theorem 3.4.2 (Join and meet of Galois connections). *Suppose $(F_i, G_i)_{i \in I}$ is a family of Galois connections between L and L'. Define $F \in (L \to L')$ and $G \in (L' \to L)$ by*

$$F(x) \stackrel{\text{def}}{=} \bigvee\{F_i(x) \mid i \in I\} \quad \textit{and} \quad G(y) \stackrel{\text{def}}{=} \bigwedge\{G_i(y) \mid i \in I\}$$

for $x \in L, y \in L'$. Then (F, G) is again a Galois connection between L and L'. If for each $i \in I$ the Galois connection (F_i, G_i) is distributive then (F, G) is distributive as well.

Proof. We first check the defining condition for Galois conditions.
Let $x \in L$ and $y \in L'$. Then

$$
\begin{array}{ll}
& F(x) \leq y \\
\text{iff} & [\text{Definition of } F] \\
& \bigvee\{F_i(x) \mid i \in I\} \leq y \\
\text{iff} & [\text{Definition of least upper bound}] \\
& \forall i \in I : F_i(x) \leq y \\
\text{iff} & [(F_i, G_i) \text{ is Galois connection}] \\
& \forall i \in I : x \leq G_i(y) \\
\text{iff} & [\text{Definition of greatest lower bound}] \\
& x \leq \bigwedge\{G_i(y) \mid i \in I\} \\
\text{iff} & [\text{Definition of } G] \\
& x \leq G(y) \;.
\end{array}
$$

Now assume that (F_i, G_i) is a distributive Galois connection for any $i \in I$. Then for any $x, x' \in L$:

$$F(x \,;\, x')$$

$$
\begin{aligned}
= \quad & [\text{Definition of } F] \\
& \bigvee\{F_i(x \,;\, x') \mid i \in I\} \\
\leq \quad & [\text{Distributivity of } (F_i, G_i), \text{ monotonicity of } \bigvee] \\
& \bigvee\{F_i(x) \,;\, F_i(x') \mid i \in I\} \\
\leq \quad & [\text{See below}] \\
& \bigvee\{F_i(x) \mid i \in I\} \,;\, \bigvee\{F_i(x') \mid i \in I\} \\
= \quad & [\text{Definition of } F] \\
& F(x) \,;\, F(x') \; .
\end{aligned}
$$

The justification for the third step is as follows. By monotonicity of ; we have for any $i \in I$

$$F_i(x) \,;\, F_i(x') \;\leq\; \bigvee\{F_i(x) \mid i \in I\} \,;\, \bigvee\{F_i(x') \mid i \in I\} \; .$$

Therefore, $\bigvee\{F_i(x) \mid i \in I\} \,;\, \bigvee\{F_i(x') \mid i \in I\}$ is an upper bound of $\{F_i(x) \,;\, F_i(x') \mid i \in I\}$ and thus greater than the least upper bound. □

4. States, Valuation Functions and Predicates

C.A.R. Hoare considers in [41] translation of a small imperative programming language and proposes to employ refinement algebra [42] for reasoning about correctness. He assumes that the source language is equipped with a refinement relation and that a number of intuitively plausible laws, i.e. semantics preserving or refining program transformation rules, hold. Semantics of the target language is defined by a program in the source language. Thus the correctness relation to be guaranteed between the source program and the generated target program is given essentially by the refinement relationship. The aforementioned refinement laws can, therefore, be exploited for proving correctness of a code generator specification. So the source language is also used as the meta- (or reasoning-) language for the proof.

It sometimes has been overemphasized that source language and reasoning language are identical in this approach. In our opinion, the main insight of [41] is that – when proving code generators correct – a reasoning language should be used that allows concise definitions of source and target language's semantics as well as effective and readable calculations. More specifically, the paper shows that an imperative programming notation together with refinement laws is a very promising candidate for dealing with translation of imperative programming languages to conventional (von-Neumann) processors. Separating source language and reasoning language has a number of pragmatic advantages.

- The reasoning language can be reused for different source and target languages.
- The reasoning language can be designed to facilitate calculations. Sometimes different design decisions are adequate for a reasoning language and a translatable programming language. An example is the treatment of 'undefined expressions' like 1/0. In a programming language one might prefer a special kind of behavior if such an expression is met during execution, e.g. irregular termination with an error message. Such a special treatment of 'undefined' expressions, however, complicates the algebraic rules concerned with expressions. Thus in a reasoning language it is more appropriate to assume that all operators are total (by extending the operators in the 'undefined' cases in an arbitrary but fixed way) as this leads to considerably smoother and easier applicable laws.

- A related point is that it is conceptually simpler to include concepts that assist calculations but cannot be implemented, like 'miracles', into a pure reasoning language.

In the next chapters we introduce the imperative notation that we use as our reasoning language.

A very simple example of a calculation with imperative programs is the equality

$$x := x + 1 \, ; x := x + 1 \quad = \quad x := x + 2 \, .$$

How can we justify such calculations in a mathematically respectable way?

One possible solution, which might be called the *formal approach*, is to follow the example of mathematical logic. First the formal language would be defined in which the reasoning is performed. Parameterized by a signature syntactic categories would be identified:

- variables, e.g. x,
- expressions, e.g. $x + 1$,
- statements, e.g. $x := x + 1$ and $x := x + 1 \, ; x := x + 1$, and
- formulas, e.g. $P = Q$ and $P \leq Q$ for any two statements P, Q.

Afterwards the interpretation of this formal language would be defined (parameterized by an algebra interpreting the symbols from the signature). It would assign, for instance,

- a function from states to values (a *valuation function*) to each expression,
- a predicate transformer to each statement, and
- a truth value to each formula.

Based on the formal language's interpretation we would define the notion of validity of a formula and afterwards establish the soundness of a number of proof rules. In this framework refinement laws correspond to axiom schemata and calculational 'algebraic' proofs are derivations in the formal system. This 'formal approach' is fully respectable and provides the most solid theoretical foundation. It is particularly well-suited if the algebraic reasoning as such is to be investigated. Our main interest, however, is in performing algebraic proofs and not so much in investigating their theoretical foundation. The definition and investigation of a formal system leads to a rather large definitional overhead and seems to distract from our main topic. In particular, all familiar standard reasoning methods of mathematics, which have been well-studied in mathematical logic and to which we are accustomed by years of mathematical training, must be reestablished in the formal system. So the question arises whether we can justify algebraic calculations with imperative programs by 'standard mathematical conventions'.

The basic idea, which is not at all original, is to interpret the assignment sign :=, the sequential composition sign ; etc. as infix operators on suitable domains. A straightforward application of this idea, however, is hindered by some problems connected to the use of variables.

One of them is that in an imperative program a variable does not always denote the same value. Denotational semanticists would say that imperative programs are not 'referentially transparent'. We conclude from this observation that the variables of the mathematical meta-language cannot be used directly as the variables of the imperative notation. Therefore, we make the variables of the programming notation an object of our mathematical investigation and assume given a set X of them. The variables of the mathematical meta-language are called *meta-variables* in order to distinguish them from the members of X that are simply called *variables*.

Another problem is that the right hand side of an assignment, e.g. $x + 1$ in the assignment $x := x + 1$, is to denote a valuation function, whereas in usual mathematical practice it denotes an (integer) value.[1] A related problem, which is also well-known in denotational semantics, is that in an assignment $x := x + 1$ the two references to x on the left and the right hand side denote different kinds of values. In denotational semantics one therefore sometimes distinguishes left hand side value and right hand side value of a variable. We define $:=$ as an operator that has a variable and a valuation function as arguments and gives a predicate transformer as result.

We solve these problems as follows. First we define how constants, variables, operators and relations are lifted to valuations functions. E.g. for a variable $x \in X$ we define x^* to be the valuation function that maps each state σ to $\sigma(x)$. We then agree to omit the lifting stars whenever they are inferable from context. By this convention $x := x + 1$ is considered a notational abbreviation for $x := (x^* +^* 1^*)$. Conventions of this kind that help to keep the notation simple are very common in mathematics: after an embedding has been well-understood the embedding mapping is notationally suppressed. We admit that we are a little dissatisfied about the fact that this approach means that the elegance of the notation to a certain extent is bought by a somehow questionable abbreviation convention. On the other hand, this seems to be the simplest and clearest way to justify algebraic calculations with an imperative programming notation in a framework employing standard mathematical conventions.

The above remarks do not question the soundness of algebraic calculations with imperative programs without an appeal to the above abbreviation convention. Such calculations can be justified by the 'formal approach' just as strict as standard mathematical practice is justified by mathematical logic. The point is that they follow conventions that to a certain extent are incompatible to the conventions used in standard mathematical practice. To work with lifting operators that are notationally suppressed is a trial to preserve

[1] Of course mathematical logic interprets a term by a valuation function in order to explain the use of the (meta-) variables. But operators are interpreted as functions between the atomic data types in the first place and then lifted by pointwise extension to valuation functions. The assignment operator $:=$, however, must be interpreted as a function on pairs of variables and valuation functions that is not a pointwise extension.

the advantages of refinement calculations while staying within the conventions of standard mathematics.

In summary, we opt for a 'semantic approach' for a justification of refinement calculations, where :=, ;, etc. are interpreted as operators on semantic entities like valuation functions, predicates and predicate transformers. The convention to omit lifting stars whenever this does not lead to ambiguities lets our calculations look like calculations with imperative programs.

Let us add the following remark. Since we are using a 'semantic approach', we cannot look at the 'expression' e on the right hand side of an assignment $x := e$ as a syntactic object; the second operator of := is a valuation function and not an expression. Therefore, when formulating, for instance, the well-known law

$$x := e\ ;\ x := f \quad = \quad x := f[e/x]$$

for combining successive assignments, we cannot interpret $f[e/x]$ as a syntactic substitution: e, f are meta-variables for valuation functions not for expressions. (In order to 'see' the expressions defining e and f we must step back into the justification of mathematical notation, i.e. to the syntactic view of mathematical reasoning provided by mathematical logic. But this is just what is to be avoided in a 'semantic approach'.) Therefore, we interpret $.[./.]$ as an operator on valuation functions and variables, the semantic counterpart to a syntactic substitution. This operator satisfies a number of laws that allow essentially the same calculations that are possible if it were interpreted as a syntactic operation. In particular it distributes over all pointwise extensions of functions on elementary data types. Similarly, we have not available a notion of a free variable in an expression in side conditions of refinement laws but must replace it by a semantic notion of independence.

The remainder of the chapter is devoted to the definition of states, valuation function and predicates and the main operations on them, and an investigation of their properties.

4.1 Variables

Assume given a non-empty set X, the member of which are called *variables*. We use a type-writer font for denoting concrete members of X in order to distinguish them from the meta-variables of the mathematical language (so, for example, `A` is a member of X). For any subset V of X we denote by $V^\bullet$ the set of lists of *distinct* variables in V. We use the letters x, y, z as meta-variables ranging over X and the letters u, v, w as meta-variables ranging over $X^\bullet$. We typically use U, V, W for denoting subsets of X.

We sometimes use a set-like notation for the members of $X^\bullet$. In particular we write $x \in u$ to express that the variable x appears in the list u and $x \notin u$ to express the opposite. We write $u \setminus v$ for the list that results from removing all variables appearing in v from u and $u \cap v$ for the list that results from removing all the variables from u that do not appear in v. We write $\{\!|u|\!\}$ for the set consisting of just the variables in u.

For any $x \in X$ we assume given a non-empty set Val_x, called *x's domain*, and denote for any list $u = (x_1, \ldots, x_n)$ the set of value lists of corresponding type by Val_u:

$$\mathsf{Val}_u \stackrel{\text{def}}{=} \{(a_1, \ldots, a_n) \mid a_1 \in \mathsf{Val}_{x_1}, \ldots, a_n \in \mathsf{Val}_{x_n}\} .$$

We call Val_u the *domain of u*. Note that Val_u is non-empty for any u by our assumption that Val_x is non-empty for any x. In particular $\mathsf{Val}_\varepsilon = \{\varepsilon\}$.

4.2 States

Following R.J.R. Back [5] we work with state sets over different sets of variables. For the rest of this chapter we assume that $V \subseteq X$ is the *alphabet* of variables on which the states, valuation functions and predicates (notions yet to be formally specified) are defined.

A *V-state* is a mapping σ assigning to each $x \in V$ an element $\sigma(x) \in \mathsf{Val}_x$. The set of V-states is denoted by State_V, so

$$\mathsf{State}_V \stackrel{\text{def}}{=} \{\sigma \mid \sigma \in (V \to \bigcup_{x \in V} \mathsf{Val}_x) \wedge (\forall x \in V : \sigma(x) \in \mathsf{Val}_x)\} .$$

We use σ to range over State_V.

4.2.1 Variation

Suppose given a state $\sigma \in \mathsf{State}_V$, a variable $x \in V$ and a value $a \in \mathsf{Val}_x$. The *variation of σ in x by a*, denoted by $\sigma[x \mapsto a]$, is the V-state defined by

$$(\sigma[x \mapsto a])(y) \;=\; \begin{cases} \sigma(y) & y \neq x \\ a & y = x \end{cases} \qquad \text{for all } y \in V .$$

For a list of distinct variables $u = (x_1, \ldots, x_n) \in V^\bullet$ and a list $a = (a_1, \ldots, a_n)$ of values of corresponding type $\sigma[u \mapsto a]$ is an abbreviation for $\sigma[x_1 \mapsto a_1] \cdots [x_n \mapsto a_n]$. The following lemma presents some laws about variations.

Lemma 4.2.1 (Some variation laws). *Suppose $x, y \in V$, $a \in \mathsf{Val}_x$, $b \in \mathsf{Val}_y$ and $\sigma \in \mathsf{State}_V$. Then*

$$\sigma[x \mapsto \sigma(x)] \;=\; \sigma . \qquad \textit{(V-void)}$$

$$\sigma[x \mapsto b][x \mapsto a] \;=\; \sigma[x \mapsto a] . \qquad \textit{(V-cancel)}$$

$$\sigma[x \mapsto a][y \mapsto b] \;=\; \sigma[y \mapsto b][x \mapsto a] , \;\; \textit{if } x \neq y . \qquad \textit{(V-commute)}$$

Proof. Straightforward. □

4.3 Valuation Functions

Suppose given a non-empty set A. An (A, V)*-valuation function* (or *valuation function on V with range A*) is any (total) function from State_V to A. The set of (A, V)-valuation functions is denoted by Valfct_V^A:

$$\mathsf{Valfct}_V^A \;=\; (\mathsf{State}_V \rightarrow A) \;.$$

We use φ to range over valuation functions and e, f, g to range over lists of valuation functions.

A V*-predicate* is a valuation function on V with range Bool. We denote the set of V-predicates by Pred_V:

$$\mathsf{Pred}_V \;=\; (\mathsf{State}_V \rightarrow \mathsf{Bool}) \;.$$

We use ϕ to range over Pred_V. **true** is the constant predicate that yields tt for any state and **false** is the constant predicate that always yield ff.

Suppose $u = (x_1, \ldots, x_n) \in V^\bullet$ is a list of distinct variables and $e = (\varphi_1, \ldots, \varphi_n)$ is a list of valuation functions on V. We say that u and e have the *same type* if the lists u and e have the same length (i.e. $n = m$) and φ_i is a (Val_{x_i}, V)-valuation function (for $i = 1, \ldots, n$). By Valfct_V^u we denote the set of lists of valuation functions over V that have the same type as u:

$$\mathsf{Valfct}_V^u \;\stackrel{\text{def}}{=}\; \{(\varphi_1, \ldots, \varphi_n) \mid \varphi_1 \in \mathsf{Valfct}_V^{\mathsf{Val}_{x_1}}, \ldots, \varphi_n \in \mathsf{Valfct}_V^{\mathsf{Val}_{x_n}}\} \;.$$

Usually we assume that each of the pairs u and e, v and f, w and g have the same type.

4.3.1 Projection and Lifting

Each variable $x \in V$ induces a (Val_x, V)-valuation function $x^* \in \mathsf{Valfct}_V^x$, called a *projection*, that is defined by

$$x^*(\sigma) \;=\; \sigma(x) \;.$$

Suppose $A, A_1, \ldots, A_n$ are non-empty sets. Each element $a \in A$ induces the constant (A, V)-valuation function a^* defined by

$$a^*(\sigma) \;=\; a \;.$$

Similarly, each (total) function $F \in (A_1 \times \cdots \times A_n \rightarrow A)$ induces a function $F^* \in (\mathsf{Valfct}_V^{A_1} \times \cdots \times \mathsf{Valfct}_V^{A_n} \rightarrow \mathsf{Valfct}_V^A)$ by pointwise extension, viz.

$$F^*(\varphi_1, \ldots, \varphi_n)(\sigma) \;=\; F(\varphi_1(\sigma), \ldots, \varphi_n(\sigma)) \;,$$

and each relation $R \subseteq A_1 \times \cdots \times A_n$ induces a function $R^* \in (\mathsf{Valfct}_V^{A_1} \times \cdots \times \mathsf{Valfct}_V^{A_n} \rightarrow \mathsf{Pred}_V)$, defined by

$$R^*(\varphi_1, \ldots, \varphi_n)(\sigma) \;=\; \begin{cases} \mathsf{tt} & \text{if } (\varphi_1(\sigma), \ldots, \varphi_n(\sigma)) \in R \\ \mathsf{ff} & \text{if } (\varphi_1(\sigma), \ldots, \varphi_n(\sigma)) \notin R \;. \end{cases}$$

As announced earlier, we omit in most cases the stars lifting variables, values, functions and relations to valuation functions. Usually it is clear from context whether the lift is meant or not. In order to calm the wary reader, however, we discuss possible sources of ambiguity and either justify that they are without harm or agree on a convention that excludes misunderstanding.

Consider, first of all, a meta-expression constructed from constants of basic sets and functions between them. Suppose that this meta-expression is used in a context that requires a valuation function. Then it is not a-priori clear whether the lift is to be taken at the outermost level once or for all the constants and functions individually. An example is the meta-expression $1+2$ in a context that requires an integer valuation function. The expression could be read either as $(1+2)^*$ or as $1^* +^* 2^*$. Fortunately both of these expressions denote the same valuation function, viz. the function that maps each state σ to 3. More generally, we have the following (almost trivial) result that defuses this ambiguity.

Lemma 4.3.1 (Lifting is distributive). *Suppose* $F \in (A_1, \ldots, A_n \to A)$, $a_1 \in A_1, \ldots, a_n \in A_n$. *Then*

$$(F(a_1, \ldots, a_n))^* \;=\; F^*({a_1}^*, \ldots, {a_n}^*) \;.$$

Proof. Let σ be a state. Then

$$\begin{array}{ll} & F^*({a_1}^*, \ldots, {a_n}^*)(\sigma) \\ = & \quad [\text{Definition of } F^*] \\ & F({a_1}^*(\sigma), \ldots, {a_n}^*(\sigma)) \\ = & \quad [\text{Definition of } {a_i}^*] \\ & F(a_1, \ldots, a_n) \\ = & \quad [\text{Definition of lift of values}] \\ & (F(a_1, \ldots, a_n))^*(\sigma) \;. \end{array}$$

□

The second source of ambiguity is more severe. It results from overloading of symbols in mathematical notation. Assume that $\diamond$ is a symbol that denotes both a function from $A_1 \times \cdots \times A_n$ to A as well as a function from $\mathsf{Valfct}_V^{A_1} \times \cdots \times \mathsf{Valfct}_V^{A_n}$ to Valfct_V^{A}. Then, clearly, it could make a difference whether we read a meta-expression $\diamond(a_1, \ldots, a_n)$ as $(\diamond(a_1, \ldots, a_n))^*$ or as $\diamond({a_1}^*, \ldots, {a_n}^*)$. (As we have just seen the third possible reading $\diamond^*({a_1}^*, \ldots, {a_n}^*)$ coincides with the first one.) In the first case we apply $\diamond$'s interpretation as a function from $A_1 \times \cdots \times A_n$ to A, in the second case its interpretation as a function from $\mathsf{Valfct}_V^{A_1} \times \cdots \times \mathsf{Valfct}_V^{A_n}$ to Valfct_V^{A}. We are going to defuse this problem by carefully avoiding overloading of such kind.

A similar problem results from the overloading of the equality sign. Suppose φ, φ' are (A, V)-valuation functions. Then $\varphi = \varphi'$ can denote either the predicate $\varphi =^* \varphi'$ that maps a state σ to the value tt iff φ and φ' coincide in σ. Or it can mean the meta-language proposition claiming that φ and φ'

are equal, i.e. that they coincide on any state σ. This is not a real ambiguity since propositions and predicates have a different status in mathematical symbolism. Nevertheless it can sometimes be confusing. We use the sign $\equiv$ for denoting the meta-level equality of valuation function (and predicates) whenever misunderstanding seems possible. The problem is further defused by the observation that

$$\varphi \equiv \varphi' \quad \text{iff} \quad (\varphi = \varphi') \equiv \mathsf{true} \ ,$$

which means that the distinction breaks down if predicates written at places where meta-language propositions are required are interpreted to claim their equality to **true**. This convention is chosen e.g. by E.W. Dijkstra and C.S. Scholten in [22].

Another kind of ambiguity results from the fact that the lifting star does not mention the alphabet of the state set. For example, x^* denotes a (Val_x, V)-valuation function for any state set V containing x. But this overloading is without harm as usually all these functions are identified (see Sect. 4.3.4).

4.3.2 Substitution

For valuation functions (and thus also for predicates) we now define the semantic counterpart to a syntactic substitution.

Suppose $u = (x_1, \dots, x_n) \in V^\bullet$ is a list of distinct variables, $e = (\varphi_1, \dots, \varphi_n) \in \mathsf{Valfct}_V^u$ and $\varphi \in \mathsf{Valfct}_V^A$. Then $\varphi[e/u]$ is the valuation function defined by

$$(\varphi[\varphi_1, \dots, \varphi_n / x_1, \dots, x_n])(\sigma) \;=\; \varphi(\sigma[x_1 \mapsto \varphi_1(\sigma)] \cdots [x_n \mapsto \varphi_n(\sigma)]) \ ,$$

for any $\sigma \in \mathsf{State}_V$. If $f = (\psi_1, \dots, \psi_m)$ is a list of valuation functions then $f[e/u]$ is defined in the obvious way to be $(\psi_1[e/u], \dots, \psi_m[e/u])$.

Substitution enjoys a number of distribution laws over lifts.

Lemma 4.3.2 (Distributivity of substitution). *Suppose $A, A_1, \dots, A_n$ are non-empty sets, $x \in V$, $u = (y_1, \dots, y_m) \in V^\bullet$, $e = (\psi_1, \dots, \psi_m) \in \mathsf{Valfct}_V^u$, $\varphi_i \in \mathsf{Valfct}_V^{A_i}$ (for $i = 1, \dots, n$), $F \in (A_1 \times \cdots \times A_n)$ and $R \subseteq A_1 \times \cdots \times A_n$.*

(a) If $x \notin u$ then $x^*[e/u] \equiv x^*$.
(b) If $x \in u$, viz. $x = y_i$, then $x^*[e/u] \equiv \psi_i$.
(c) $a^*[e/u] = a^*$.
(d) $F^*(\varphi_1, \dots, \varphi_n)[e/u] = F^*(\varphi_1[e/u], \dots, \varphi_n[e/u])$.
(e) $R^*(\varphi_1, \dots, \varphi_n)[e/u] = R^*(\varphi_1[e/u], \dots, \varphi_n[e/u])$.

Proof. The properties are proved by the following straightforward calculations for an arbitrary state $\sigma \in \mathsf{State}_V$.

(a) $$(x^*[e/u])(\sigma) \underset{\substack{\uparrow \\ \text{[Def. subst.]}}}{=} x^*(\sigma[u \mapsto e(\sigma)]) \underset{\substack{\uparrow \\ \text{[Def. } x^*\text{]}}}{=} (\sigma[u \mapsto e(\sigma)])(x) \underset{\substack{\uparrow \\ \text{[Def. variation, } x \notin u\text{]}}}{=} \sigma(x)$$

$$= \quad x^*(\sigma)\ .$$

(b) $$(x^*[e/u])(\sigma) \underset{\substack{\uparrow\\ \text{[Def. subst.]}}}{=} x^*(\sigma[u \mapsto e(\sigma)]) \underset{\substack{\uparrow\\ \text{[Def. } x^*\text{]}}}{=} (\sigma[u \mapsto e(\sigma)])(x) \underset{\substack{\uparrow\\ \text{[Def. variation, } x = y_i\text{]}}}{=} (\psi_i)(\sigma)\ .$$

(c) $$(a^*[e/u])(\sigma) \underset{\substack{\uparrow\\ \text{[Def. subst.]}}}{=} a^*(\sigma[u \mapsto e(\sigma)]) \underset{\substack{\uparrow\\ \text{[Def. } a^*\text{]}}}{=} a \quad = \quad a^*(\sigma)\ .$$

(d)

$$\begin{aligned}
& (F^*(\varphi_1, \ldots, \varphi_n)[e/u])(\sigma) \\
= \quad & \text{[Def. subst.]} \\
& F^*(\varphi_1, \ldots, \varphi_n)(\sigma[u \mapsto e(\sigma)]) \\
= \quad & \text{[Def. } F^*\text{]} \\
& F(\varphi_1(\sigma[u \mapsto e(\sigma)]), \ldots, \varphi_n(\sigma[u \mapsto e(\sigma)])) \\
= \quad & \text{[Def. subst]} \\
& F((\varphi_1[e/u])(\sigma), \ldots, (\varphi_n[e/u])(\sigma)) \\
= \quad & \text{[Def. } F^*\text{]} \\
& F^*(\varphi_1[e/u], \ldots, \varphi_n[e/u])(\sigma)\ .
\end{aligned}$$

The calculation for (e) is analogous. □

These laws allow to perform a substitution syntactically in a (meta-) expression that defines a valuation function solely in terms of projections and lifted constants, functions and relations. For example, if φ_1 is defined by `A+(B+1)` and φ_2 by `C+1`, then $\varphi_1[\varphi_2/\mathtt{A}]$ equals the valuation function defined by $(\mathtt{C}+1)+(\mathtt{B}+1)$. Note that we applied in all three cases the convention to omit all the lifting stars.

From the laws about variation of states we can easily prove the following laws for substitutions.

Lemma 4.3.3 (Basic substitution laws). *Let $x \in V$, $u = (x_1, \ldots, x_n) \in V^\bullet$ such that $x \notin u$, $e, f \in \mathsf{Valfct}_V^u$, $e = (\varphi_1, \ldots, \varphi_n)$, $\varphi \in \mathsf{Valfct}_V^A$, and ρ be a permutation of $\{1, \ldots, n\}$. Then:*

$$\varphi[\varphi_1, \ldots, \varphi_n/x_1, \ldots, x_n] \quad = \quad \varphi[\varphi_{\rho(1)}, \ldots, \varphi_{\rho(n)}/x_{\rho(1)}, \ldots, x_{\rho(n)}]\ . \qquad \textit{(S-reorder)}$$

$$\varphi[e, x^*/u, x] \quad = \quad \varphi[e/u]\ . \qquad \textit{(S-void)}$$

$$\varphi[\varepsilon/\varepsilon] \quad = \quad \varphi\ . \qquad \textit{(S-empty)}$$

$$\varphi[e/u][f/u] \quad = \quad \varphi[e[f/u]/u]\ . \qquad \textit{(S-comb)}$$

Proof. The laws follow from the laws about variations in Lemma 4.2.1.

– (S-reorder) follows by a multiple application of (V-commute).

- (S-void) follows from (V-void) and the fact that $x^*(\sigma) = \sigma(x)$.
- (S-empty) is clear by definition.
- (S-comb) is seen by the following calculation. For simplicity we assume that the length of all of the lists e, f and u equals 1. For an arbitrarily chosen state σ we then have

$$
\begin{array}{ll}
& \mathrm{LHS}(\sigma) \\
= & \quad [\text{Definition of substitution}] \\
& (\varphi[e/u])(\sigma[u \mapsto f(\sigma)]) \\
= & \quad [\text{Definition of substitution}] \\
& \varphi(\sigma[u \mapsto f(\sigma)][u \mapsto e(\sigma[u \mapsto f(\sigma)])]) \\
= & \quad [\text{(V-cancel), definition of substitution}] \\
& \varphi(\sigma[u \mapsto e[f/u](\sigma)]) \\
= & \quad [\text{Definition of substitution}] \\
& \mathrm{RHS}(\sigma)\ .
\end{array}
$$

The calculation for arbitrary lists is analogous. □

4.3.3 Independence

Heading for a semantic foundation of algebraic calculations with an imperative programming like notation, we need a semantic replacement of the syntactic notion of a free variable in a term. It proves convenient to formalize the opposite concept. That a variable x does not appear free in a term means that the denoted value does not depend on that variable. Thus the notion we are looking for is that of independence of a valuation function from a variable. It is convenient to define the notion of independence for lists of variables.

Definition 4.3.4 (Independence). *Suppose* $\varphi \in \mathsf{Valfct}_V^A$ *is a valuation function and* $u \in V^\bullet$. *Then* φ *is called* independent of u, φ idp u *for short, if for all* $\sigma \in \mathsf{State}_V$ *and* $a \in \mathsf{Val}_u$: $\varphi(\sigma) = \varphi(\sigma[u \mapsto a])$.

Independence can be equivalently characterized without explicitly mentioning states using substitution.

Lemma 4.3.5 (Independence and substitution). *Suppose* e *is a list of valuation functions and* $u \in V^\bullet$. *The following conditions are equivalent:*

(a) e *is independent of* u.
(b) $e \equiv e[f/u]$ *for all* $f \in \mathsf{Valfct}_V^u$.
(c) $e[f, g/u, v] \equiv e[g/v]$ *for any list* $v \in V^\bullet$ *disjoint from* u, $f \in \mathsf{Valfct}_V^u$ *and* $g \in \mathsf{Valfct}_V^v$.

Proof. Equivalence of (a), (b) and (c) is shown by a roundabout argument. For simplicity we assume that u is a single variable. The proof for arbitrary lists is analogous.

(a) implies (c):
Suppose (a) holds and g, f and v are given as in (c). Then, for any state σ,

$$\begin{aligned}
& \mathrm{LHS}(\sigma) \\
= \quad & [(\text{S-reorder}), \text{definition of substitution}] \\
& e(\sigma[v \mapsto g(\sigma)][u \mapsto f(\sigma)]) \\
= \quad & [\text{a}] \\
& e(\sigma[v \mapsto g(\sigma)]) \\
= \quad & [\text{Definition of substitution}] \\
& \mathrm{RHS}(\sigma) .
\end{aligned}$$

(c) implies (b):
(b) is seen to be a special case of (c) by choosing $g = v = \varepsilon$ and applying the law (S-empty).

(b) implies (a):
Assume (b), and suppose $\sigma \in \mathsf{State}_V$ and $a \in \mathsf{Val}_u$ are given. Then we can calculate as follows:

$$\begin{aligned}
& e(\sigma[u \mapsto a]) \\
= \quad & [\text{Definition of } a^*] \\
& e(\sigma[u \mapsto a^*(\sigma)]) \\
= \quad & [\text{Definition of substitution}] \\
& (e[a^*/u])(\sigma) \\
= \quad & [\text{b}] \\
& e(\sigma) .
\end{aligned}$$

This shows independence of e from u. □

Lemma 4.3.2 allows to perform substitutions syntactically for valuation functions defined in terms of projections and lifting. Similarly, the following lemma allows to check independence for such valuation functions.

Lemma 4.3.6 ('Distributivity' of independence). *Let $A, A_1, \ldots, A_n$ be non-empty sets. Suppose $x \in V$, $u \in V^\bullet$, $\varphi_i \in \mathsf{Valfct}_V^{A_i}$ (for $i = 1, \ldots, n$), $F \in (A_1 \times \cdots \times A_n \to A)$ and $R \subseteq A_1 \times \cdots \times A_n$.*

(a) x^* is independent of u if $x \notin u$.
(b) a^* is independent of u.
(c) If $\phi_1, \ldots, \phi_n$ are independent of u, then so are $F^*(\phi_1, \ldots, \phi_n)$ and $R^*(\phi_1, \ldots, \phi_n)$.

Proof. For proving (a) to (c) we check condition (b) of Lemma 4.3.5.
Suppose $e \in \mathsf{Valfct}_V^u$.

(a) If $x \notin u$ then $x^*[e/u] \equiv x^*$ according to Lemma 4.3.2, part (a).
(b) $a^*[e/u] \equiv a^*$ according to Lemma 4.3.2, part (d).
(c) $F^*(\varphi_1, \ldots, \varphi_n)[e/u]$ equals $F^*(\varphi_1[e/u], \ldots, \varphi_n[e/u])$ according to item (d) of Lemma 4.3.2. This in turn equals $F^*(\varphi_1, \ldots, \varphi_n)$ if $\varphi_1, \ldots, \varphi_n$ are independent of u.
The proof for R^* is similar. □

With the above lemma it is immediately clear, for instance, that the valuation function ϕ defined by $\mathtt{A} + 1$ (viz. $\mathtt{A}^* +^* 1^*$) is independent of $\mathtt{B}$.

A word of warning: a valuation function can be independent of a variable although defined by a term containing a reference to that variable. An example is the valuation function $\mathtt{A}^* -^* \mathtt{A}^*$ that is independent of $\mathtt{A}$. Thus independence from a variable x is not a fully accurate semantic replacement of the syntactic condition 'x does not appear free'. This is the reason why in item (c) in the above lemma only an implication holds. Fortunately in all applications the looser condition 'independence of x' is sufficient.

4.3.4 Extending and Restricting the Alphabet

Valuation functions on V can easily be interpreted on state sets with additional components by simply ignoring their value. For a formal explanation assume that $u \in X^\bullet$ is a list of new variables (i.e. $V \cap \{\!|u|\!\} = \emptyset$). Then define the *embedding operator* $\iota_u \in (\mathsf{Valfct}_V^A \to \mathsf{Valfct}_{V \cup \{\!|u|\!\}}^A)$ by

$$\iota_u(\varphi)(\sigma) \;=\; \varphi(\sigma|V)$$

for an (A, V)-valuation function φ and a $(V \cup \{\!|u|\!\})$-state σ. It is easy to see that ι_u is a bijection between the valuation functions on V and the valuation functions on $V \cup \{\!|u|\!\}$ that are independent of u. In practical applications we usually do not distinguish between valuation functions on V and valuation functions on larger alphabets that are independent of the additional components. This identification is consistent with the overloading of the lifting stars for different alphabets.

The embedding operator distributes over substitution in the following sense.

Lemma 4.3.7 (Embedding and substitution). *Suppose* $V \cap \{\!|u|\!\} = \emptyset$, $v \in V^\bullet$, $\varphi_1 \in \mathsf{Valfct}_V^A$ *and* $\varphi_2 \in \mathsf{Valfct}_V^v$. *Then*

$$\iota_u(\varphi_1[\varphi_2/v]) \;\equiv\; \iota_u(\varphi_1)[\iota_u(\varphi_2)/v]\;. \qquad \textit{(S-embedding)}$$

Proof. Straightforward. □

4.4 Predicates

The definitions and results concerning valuation functions apply in particular to predicates because predicates are just valuation functions of a special kind. On the predicate sets Pred_V, however, the lift of the (implication) order on Bool (see p. 11) induces additional structure:

$$\phi \le \phi' \quad \text{iff} \quad \forall \sigma \in \mathsf{State}_V : \phi(\sigma) \le \phi(\sigma')$$

for $\phi, \phi' \in \mathsf{Pred}_V$. By the results reported in Sect. 2.2, Pred_V inherits being a complete Boolean lattice from Bool. Note that $\top_{\mathsf{Pred}_V} = \mathsf{true}$ and $\bot_{\mathsf{Pred}_V} = \mathsf{false}$.

The following law connects substitution in predicates and the pointwise extension of equality to valuation functions.

Lemma 4.4.1 (Substitution and equality). *Let $u \in V^\bullet$, $e, f \in \mathsf{Valfct}_V^u$ and $\phi \in \mathsf{Pred}_V$. Then*

$$(e = f) \wedge \phi[e/u] \quad \equiv \quad (e = f) \wedge \phi[f/u] \; . \qquad \textit{(S-equality)}$$

Proof. The claimed equality is seen from the following chain of equivalences that holds for any $\sigma \in \mathsf{State}_V$:

$$\begin{aligned} & \mathrm{LHS}(\sigma) = \mathsf{tt} \\ \text{iff } & e(\sigma) = f(\sigma) \text{ and } \phi(\sigma[u \mapsto e(\sigma)]) = \mathsf{tt} \\ \text{iff } & e(\sigma) = f(\sigma) \text{ and } \phi(\sigma[u \mapsto f(\sigma)]) = \mathsf{tt} \\ \text{iff } & \mathrm{RHS}(\sigma) = \mathsf{tt} \; . \end{aligned}$$

□

It is easy to see that the embedding operator $\iota_u \in (\mathsf{Pred}_V \to \mathsf{Pred}_{V \cup \{\!|u|\!\}})$ is universally conjunctive as well as universally disjunctive and distributes over complementation. Indeed, it is a Boolean lattice isomorphism between Pred_V and the complete Boolean sub-lattice consisting of the predicates in $\mathsf{Pred}_{V \cup \{\!|u|\!\}}$ that are independent of u.

4.4.1 Quantification

Based on the lattice operations meet and join we can define the quantification operations $\forall_x$ and $\exists_x$ as unary operations on Pred_V by

$$\forall_x(\phi) = \bigwedge_{a \in \mathsf{Val}_x} \phi[a^*/x] \quad \text{and} \quad \exists_x(\phi) = \bigvee_{a \in \mathsf{Val}_x} \phi[a^*/x]$$

for $x \in V$, $\phi \in \mathsf{Pred}_V$. Applied to a predicate $\phi \in \mathsf{Pred}_V$ they always yield predicates that are independent of x. We have also the corresponding quantification operations $\mathbf{A}_x, \mathbf{E}_x \in (\mathsf{Pred}_V \to \mathsf{Pred}_{V \setminus \{x\}})$ that besides quantification remove x from the alphabet:

$$\mathbf{A}_x(\phi)(\sigma) = \begin{cases} \mathsf{tt} & \text{if } \phi(\sigma \cup \{(x,a)\}) = \mathsf{tt} \text{ for all } a \in \mathsf{Val}_x \\ \mathsf{ff} & \text{otherwise} \end{cases}$$

and

$$\mathbf{E}_x(\phi)(\sigma) = \begin{cases} \mathsf{tt} & \text{if there is } a \in \mathsf{Val}_x \text{ such that } \phi(\sigma \cup \{(x,a)\}) = \mathsf{tt} \\ \mathsf{ff} & \text{otherwise} \end{cases}$$

for $x \in V$, $\phi \in \mathsf{Pred}_V$, and $\sigma \in \mathsf{Pred}_{V\setminus\{x\}}$. The following diagram illustrates the functionality of the embedding operator and the quantification operators:

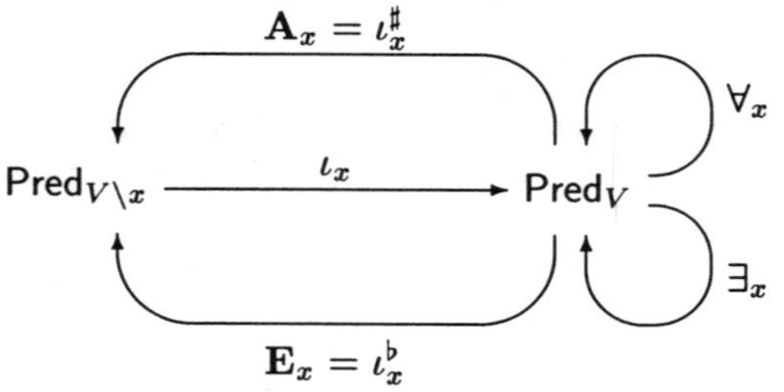

The relationship between the quantification operators and the embedding operator is studied in the following lemma.

Lemma 4.4.2 (Embedding and quantification). *Suppose $x \in V$.*

(a) $\iota_x \circ \mathbf{A}_x = \forall_x \leq \mathsf{Id}$.
(b) $\iota_x \circ \mathbf{E}_x = \exists_x \geq \mathsf{Id}$.
(c) $\mathbf{A}_x \circ \iota_x = \mathsf{Id}$.
(d) $\mathbf{E}_x \circ \iota_x = \mathsf{Id}$.
(e) ι_x *is dual to itself, i.e.* $\iota_x(\overline{\phi}) = \overline{\iota_x(\phi)}$ *for all* $\phi \in \mathsf{Pred}_{V\setminus\{x\}}$.
(f) $\mathbf{A}_x$ *is the dual of* $\mathbf{E}_x$*, i.e.* $\mathbf{A}_x(\overline{\phi}) = \overline{\mathbf{E}_x(\phi)}$ *for all* $\phi \in \mathsf{Pred}_V$.
(g) $\forall_x$ *is the dual of* $\exists_x$*, i.e.* $\forall_x(\overline{\phi}) = \overline{\exists_x(\phi)}$ *for all* $\phi \in \mathsf{Pred}_V$.
(h) $(\iota_x, \mathbf{A}_x)$ *is a Galois connection between* $\mathsf{Pred}_{V\setminus\{x\}}$ *and* Pred_V *and* $(\mathbf{E}_x, \iota_x)$ *is a Galois connection between* Pred_V *and* $\mathsf{Pred}_{V\setminus\{x\}}$.

The order in (a) and (b) is the lift of the order on predicates to predicate transformers.

Proof. The proofs of (a) to (g) are straightforward but tedious. The properties mostly are obvious if one takes into account the intuitive interpretation of the quantification operators and remembers that $\leq$ formalizes implication $\Rightarrow$. The formal proofs can be shortened a little bit by showing the duality results first and exploiting that (a) is dual to (b) and (c) is dual to (d). Property (h) is a direct consequence of properties (a) to (d). □

Instead of defining $\mathbf{A}_x$ and $\mathbf{E}_x$ explicitly, we could have used the fact that they are the upper and lower adjoint of ι_x as their definition. Another possibility is to define them by the equations in (a) and (b) of Lemma 4.4.2.

The next lemma studies commutation properties for successive embeddings and quantifiers to different variables.

Lemma 4.4.3 (Commutation of embeddings and quantifiers). *Let $x, y \in X$ such that $x \neq y$.*

(a) *Successive embeddings commute:* $\iota_x \circ \iota_y = \iota_y \circ \iota_x$.

(b) *Successive quantifiers of same kind commute:* $\mathbf{A}_x \circ \mathbf{A}_y = \mathbf{A}_y \circ \mathbf{A}_x$ *and* $\mathbf{E}_x \circ \mathbf{E}_y = \mathbf{E}_y \circ \mathbf{E}_x$.

(c) *Embeddings commute with quantifiers:* $\iota_x \circ \mathbf{A}_y = \mathbf{A}_y \circ \iota_x$ *and* $\iota_x \circ \mathbf{E}_y = \mathbf{E}_y \circ \iota_x$.

(d) *There is also a weak commutation law for quantifiers of different kind:* $\mathbf{E}_x \circ \mathbf{A}_y \leq \mathbf{A}_y \circ \mathbf{E}_x$.

Strictly speaking, the embeddings and quantifiers occurring on the left and right hand side of above commutation laws have different functionality as illustrated by the following diagram.

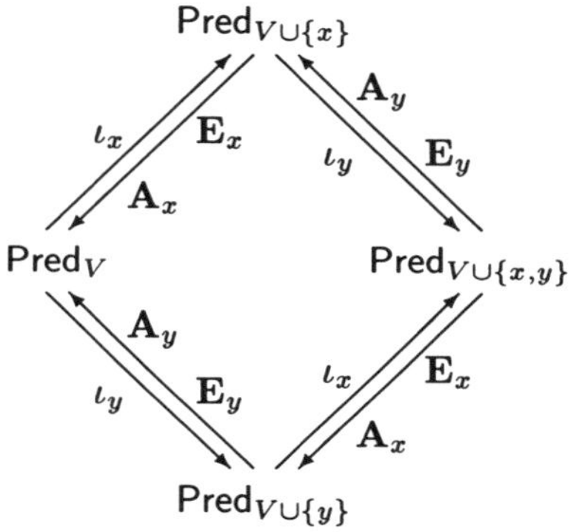

Proof. Like for the previous lemma the proofs are straightforward but tedious. The commutation properties (b) for quantifiers are well-known in logic and essentially hold here for the same reason. Property (d) also formalizes a well-known logical fact but can also be seen by the following little calculation that shows its equivalence to an obvious fact:

$$\mathbf{E}_x \circ \mathbf{A}_y \leq \mathbf{A}_y \circ \mathbf{E}_x$$

iff [$(\mathbf{E}_x, \iota_x)$ is a Galois connection]

$$\mathbf{A}_y \leq \iota_x \circ \mathbf{A}_y \circ \mathbf{E}_x$$

iff [Property (c)]

$$\mathbf{A}_y \leq \mathbf{A}_y \circ \iota_x \circ \mathbf{E}_x$$

iff [$(\mathbf{E}_x, \iota_x)$ is a Galois connection]

$$\mathbf{A}_y \circ \iota_x \leq \mathbf{A}_y \circ \iota_x \ .$$

□

Substitution commutes over quantifiers. The valuation functions in the substitution, however, must be embedded into the larger space.

Lemma 4.4.4 (Substitution and quantifiers). *Suppose* $x \in X \setminus V$, $\phi \in \mathsf{Pred}_{V\cup\{x\}}$, $u \in V^\bullet$, *and* e *is a list of valuation function over* V *such that* u *and* e *have same type. Then*

$$\mathbf{A}_x(\phi)[e/u] \quad = \quad \mathbf{A}_x(\phi[\iota_x(e)/u]) \ . \qquad \textit{(S-forall)}$$

$$\mathbf{E}_x(\phi)[e/u] \quad = \quad \mathbf{E}_x(\phi[\iota_x(e)/u]) \ . \qquad \textit{(S-exists)}$$

The usual care to avoid erroneous capture of variables by the quantifier is not necessary here because we work in a heterogeneous space of predicates. By well-definedness of the substitutions, the valuation functions e are defined on a state space not containing x.

Proof. If you do not consider the properties obvious inspect the following calculation (for $\sigma \in \mathsf{State}_V$) that shows (S-forall):

$$\begin{array}{ll} & (\mathbf{A}_x(\phi)[e/u])(\sigma) \\ = & \text{[Def. Substitution]} \\ & \mathbf{A}_x(\phi)(\sigma[u \mapsto e(\sigma)]) \\ = & \text{[Def. } \mathbf{A}_x\text{]} \\ & \begin{cases} \mathsf{tt} & \text{if } \phi(\sigma[u \mapsto e(\sigma)] \cup \{(x,a)\}) = \mathsf{tt} \text{ f.a. } a \in \mathsf{Val}_x \\ \mathsf{ff} & \text{otherwise} \end{cases} \\ = & \text{[See below]} \\ & \begin{cases} \mathsf{tt} & \text{if } \phi(\sigma \cup \{(x,a)\})[u \mapsto \iota_x(e)(\sigma \cup \{(x,a)\})]) = \mathsf{tt} \text{ f.a. } a \in \mathsf{Val}_x \\ \mathsf{ff} & \text{otherwise} \end{cases} \\ = & \text{[Def. Substitution]} \\ & \begin{cases} \mathsf{tt} & \text{if } \phi[\iota_x(e)/u](\sigma \cup \{(x,a)\}) = \mathsf{tt} \text{ f.a. } a \in \mathsf{Val}_x \\ \mathsf{ff} & \text{otherwise} \end{cases} \\ = & \text{[Def. } \mathbf{A}_x\text{]} \\ & \mathbf{A}_x(\phi[\iota_x(e)/u])(\sigma) \ . \end{array}$$

The equality in the third step exploits that $\sigma[u \mapsto e(\sigma)] \cup \{(x,a)\} = (\sigma \cup \{(x,a)\})[u \mapsto e(\sigma)]$ and $e(\sigma) = \iota_x(e)(\sigma \cup \{(x,a)\})$.

(S-exists) is the dual of (S-forall). □

The quantification operators can easily be generalized to lists $u = (x_1, \ldots, x_n) \in X^\bullet$ of distinct variables by the definitions

$$\mathbf{A}_u \ = \ \mathbf{A}_{x_1} \circ \ldots \circ \mathbf{A}_{x_n} \quad \text{and} \quad \mathbf{E}_u \ = \ \mathbf{E}_{x_1} \circ \ldots \circ \mathbf{E}_{x_n} \ .$$

For the empty list $u = \varepsilon$ the right hand sides are meant to specify Id. $\mathbf{A}_u$ and $\mathbf{E}_u$ are operators from $\mathsf{Pred}_{V \cup \{\!|u|\!\}}$ to Pred_V. The results in Lemma 4.4.2 remain valid and from the results in Lemma 4.4.3 similar commutation properties can easily be established for the generalized operators (see Theorem 5.5.2).

5. The Algebra of Commands

In his famous book 'A Discipline of Programming' [21] E.W. Dijkstra models semantics of guarded commands [20] by their weakest precondition predicate transformer. He states a number of 'healthiness conditions' that are obeyed by any predicate transformer corresponding to an implementable command. More specifically, he requires that the predicate transformers are monotonic, universally conjunctive, $\perp$-strict and $\vee$-continuous. Except of monotonicity all these healthiness conditions have been questioned in the realm of the refinement calculus [3, 6, 25, 38, 60, 61, 65, 70]. The reason is the idea to embed programs into a larger space of specification commands. Although well motivated for implementable programs, the healthiness conditions are inappropriate requirements for specifications and sometimes hinder algebraic manipulations.

Motivated by the observation of J.M. Morris [65] that the monotonic predicate transformers form a lattice and the use of lattice operators by P.H.B. Gardiner and C.C. Morgan in [25] and C.A.R. Hoare et. al. in [42], R.J.R. Back and J. von Wright [5, 6] suggest to treat program and data refinement in a lattice-theoretic framework. We follow their proposal to employ the heterogeneous algebra of monotonic predicate transformers between predicate spaces over different alphabets. A consequence of working in a heterogeneous algebra of commands is that – at least in principle – the concrete commands must be annotated by the state space on which they are working (or even two state spaces, viz. the pre- and the post-state). For example, we have many different versions of the assignment $x :=\ .$, one for each set of variables V that contains x. To be precise we should annotate the assignment by V: $x :=_V\ .$. In practical calculations, however, an annotation is rather inconvenient. Therefore, we assume that $:=$ like ; and the lattice operations is overloaded and let the context resolve the ambiguity.

The main objective of this chapter is to smoothly establish laws [42, 43] that allow algebraic manipulation of predicate transformers written in terms of a concrete imperative programming notation. In this context we call predicate transformers *commands*. We introduce the notation and laws stepwise such that when proving laws we can take advantage of laws already established. More specifically, we are going to introduce the following basic commands:

- the *assignment command* $u := e$ for a list u of distinct variables and a list e of valuation functions,
- the *assertion command* $\{\phi\}$ and the *assumption command* $[\phi]$ for a predicate ϕ,
- the *demonic addition* u^+ and the *angelic addition* $u^\oplus$ of a list of variables u to the state space, and
- the *deletion* u^- of u from the state space.

These commands are supplemented by

- Id, the skip (or 'do nothing') command, and by
- the standard elements $\perp$ and $\top$ of a Boolean lattice. $\perp$ is the worst command, sometimes called 'chaos', that satisfies no non-trivial specification and $\top$ is the best command, sometimes called 'miracle', that satisfies any specification.

From these basic commands compound commands can be constructed by the lattice operations meet and join and by functional composition. As observed already by J.M. Morris [65] it is not necessary to include least fixpoints into the basic language because they can be expressed by a meet according to the Knaster-Tarski fixpoint theorem.

The benefit of reasoning with miraculous processes like $[\phi]$ has been advocated by G. Nelson [70], C.C. Morgan [60] and others. The idea to introduce separate commands for addition to and deletion from the state space instead of a concept of scope is due to R.J.R. Back [5] and used by C.A.R. Hoare, H. Jifeng and A. Sampaio, too, in [43]. The advantage is that the abstraction and concretization which relate the state spaces in a data refinement can be described with the command notation. Therefore, the refinement laws can be used to reason about the data refinement on the command level, i.e. without a direct reference to their interpretation as predicate transformers. A disadvantage is that their definition requires an inhomogeneous algebra and that they cannot properly explain re-declaration of variables.

By the way, all the definitions of ALGOL 60-like blocks that have been proposed in the context of the refinement calculus and of which we are aware [6, 63, 66] do not allow re-declaration of variables or do not properly model that a block that introduces a local variable does not change a global variable with the same name. In a draft of this book we worked with a block operator in a homogeneous space that handled re-declaration correctly. However, its definition was comparatively complicated and data refinement calculations turned out to become inconvenient because only the entire abstraction and concretization of commands could be described on the command level but not the relationship between the state spaces alone.

Based on the basic commands we define and study later in this chapter

- *demonic choice assignments* $u :=?$ and *angelic choice assignments* $u :=!$ for lists u of distinct variables,
- *conditional commands* $P \lhd \phi \rhd Q$, and

– an array-like notation.

Intentionally none of these notations is original. All of them correspond to well-known imperative programming or specification constructs that have been considered in the literature. The reader is invited to check that their formal interpretation as predicate transformers matches his operational intuition. Moreover, he should read the laws with his intuitive understanding in mind. The formal derivation of the laws ensures consistency but most of the laws have a clear and simple intuitive interpretation. One of the most important purposes of the command notation and the laws is to go away from the specific interpretation of commands as predicate transformers and to enable calculations on an intuitive level.

We shall see in Chap. 6 how timing and communication can be treated by using distinguished variables *clk* and *hst* for modeling the runtime and the communication history. We employ there non-$\perp$-strict predicate transformers that allow to speak meaningful not only about terminating but also about non-terminating computations which communicate infinitely often. The operational interpretation of non-$\perp$-strict transformers is partly non-standard. But for non-communicating pieces of commands we use predicate transformers entirely in the classic way. Refinement in the space of predicate transformers can be interpreted as preservation of total correctness properties. The operational interpretation of total correctness in particular for communicating commands is discussed in Chap. 6.

5.1 Definitions

In Chap. 4 we already defined State_V, the set of states, and Pred_V, the set of predicates over an alphabet V. We now define predicate transformers.

Definition 5.1.1 (Predicate transformers). *Let $V, W \subseteq X$. A (V,W)-*predicate transformer *is a mapping from Pred_W to Pred_V. The set of predicate transformers is denoted by PTrans_V^W:*

$$\mathsf{PTrans}_V^W \;=\; (\mathsf{Pred}_W \rightarrow \mathsf{Pred}_V) \; .$$

We range over PTrans_V^W by π.

A (V,W)-predicate transformer models the behavior of a command that starts execution in a V-state and is intended to terminate in a W-state. As it assigns weakest *pre-conditions* to *post-conditions* it maps W-predicates to V-predicates. We say that it *works on a homogeneous state space* if $V = W$. The interpretation of commands by their weakest precondition transformer has been introduced by E.W. Dijkstra in [21].

The implication order $\leq$ on predicates is lifted to predicate transformers:

$$\pi \leq \pi' \quad \text{iff} \quad \forall \phi \in \mathsf{Pred}_W : \pi(\phi) \leq \pi'(\phi)$$

for $\pi, \pi' \in \mathsf{PTrans}_V^W$. By the results reported in Sect. 2.2, PTrans_V^W inherits being a complete Boolean lattice from Pred_V.

PTrans_V^W almost qualifies as a space in which refinement of commands might be approached calculationally. An obstacle, however, is that the composition operator $\circ$ in general is not monotonic in its second argument on PTrans_V^W. As a counter-example consider the constant transformer $\perp, \top \in \mathsf{PTrans}_V^W$,

$$\perp(\phi) = \perp_{\mathsf{Pred}_V} \quad \text{and} \quad \top(\phi) = \top_{\mathsf{Pred}_V} \ ,$$

and the transformer $C \in \mathsf{PTrans}_V^V$ that assigns each predicate its complement. Of course $\perp \leq \top$; but $C \circ \perp = \top$ and $C \circ \top = \perp$ such that $C \circ \perp$ is not smaller than or equal to $C \circ \top$. (We assume here that the predicate space Pred_V is non-trivial in containing at least two elements such that $\perp_{\mathsf{Pred}_V} < \top_{\mathsf{Pred}_V}$; this is the case iff V is non-empty.) In its first argument $\circ$ always is monotonic but $P \circ .$ is monotonic only if P is monotonic. Therefore, it is attractive to restrict attention to the monotonic predicate transformers, that we call *commands*. The set of commands (from V to W) is denoted by Com_V^W:

$$\mathsf{Com}_V^W \ = \ \{P \mid P \in \mathsf{PTrans}_V^W \text{ and } P \text{ is monotonic}\} \ .$$

Note that Com_V^W contains elements that cannot be interpreted as implementable programs, for example $\top$. We use the letters $P, Q, R, \ldots$ for commands. We denote the functional composition of predicate transformers by ; instead of $\circ$ because it models the sequential composition of commands. The order of arguments of ; and $\circ$ is the same, so $P \,;\, Q = P \circ Q$.

By the results reported in Sect. 2.2, Com_V^W is a complete sub-lattice of PTrans_V^W. Moreover, the functional composition of two monotonic predicate transformers is monotonic. Thus ; can be used as an operator on the command space. The order $\leq$ on Com_V^W is interpreted as refinement between commands: a command refines another one if it guarantees all classes of final states for larger classes of initial states. The relationship $P \leq Q$ is verbalized as Q *is better than* P or as P *is worse than* Q. When $P \leq Q$ holds we call Q a *refinement* or *upper estimate* of P and P an *approximation* or *lower estimate* of Q. The greatest lower bound $\bigwedge_{i \in I} P_i$ can operationally be interpreted as a *demonic choice* between the commands P_i and the least upper bounds $\bigvee_{i \in I} P_i$ as an *angelic choice.*

On Com_V^W the sequential composition operator ; is monotonic and the same holds for join and meet. Hence, for any context $C(\,.\,)$ (i.e. any operator) on Com_V^W solely defined using meets, joins and sequential compositions of commands, $P \leq Q$ implies $C(P) \leq C(Q)$. This is a property of tremendous importance for a refinement calculus as it allows to perform local refinements. We apply this property almost always tacitly in calculations and refer otherwise simply to 'monotonicity'.

5.2 Dualization

Dualization of predicate transformers has been investigated in [6]. For a predicate transformer $\pi \in \mathsf{PTrans}_V^W$ the *dual predicate transformer* $\pi^{\circ} \in \mathsf{PTrans}_V^W$ is defined by

$$\pi^{\circ}(\psi) \;=\; \overline{\pi(\overline{\psi})}$$

for $\psi \in \mathsf{Pred}_W$. Dualization is an involution. It is antitonic and distributes over ;. The dual of a join is the meet of the duals and vice versa. These basic properties of dualization are summarized in the following lemma ([6, Lemma 6]).

Lemma 5.2.1 (Properties of dualization). *Let $\pi, \pi_1, \pi_2, \pi_i \in \mathsf{PTrans}_V^W$, where i ranges over an arbitrary index set I. Then*

(a) $(\pi^{\circ})^{\circ} = \pi$.
(b) $\pi_1 \le \pi_2$ *if and only if* $\pi_2{}^{\circ} \le \pi_1{}^{\circ}$.
(c) $(\pi_1 \,;\, \pi_2)^{\circ} = \pi_1{}^{\circ} \,;\, \pi_2{}^{\circ}$.
(d) $(\bigwedge\{\pi_i \mid i \in I\})^{\circ} = \bigvee\{\pi_i{}^{\circ} \mid i \in I\}$.
(e) $(\bigvee\{\pi_i \mid i \in I\})^{\circ} = \bigwedge\{\pi_i{}^{\circ} \mid i \in I\}$.
(f) π *is universally disjunctive if and only if* π° *is universally conjunctive.*
(g) π *is universally conjunctive if and only if* π° *is universally disjunctive.*
(h) π *is monotonic if and only if* π° *is monotonic.*

Property (h) ensures that monotonicity of π implies monotonicity of π^{o}. This enables to use dualization as an operator on Com_V^W. Having similar properties dualization is a partial replacement for complementation that is not available on Com_V^W.

We often exploit that there is a dual law $E^{\circ} \geq F^{\circ}$ for each law $E \leq F$, where E and F are terms standing for commands. The distributive properties of $.^{\circ}$ together with facts about dualization of specific commands normally allow to remove the references to dualization in E° and F°. Thus every law has a corollary, viz. the dual law, that we get almost for free. The remark of G. Grätzer [29, p. 3] about the duality principle of lattice theory applies here as well:

> 'It is hard to imagine that anything as trivial as the Duality Principle could yield anything profound, and it does not; but it can save a lot of work.'

It is easy to see that $\top$ and $\bot$ are duals of each other and that Id is dual to itself.

Lemma 5.2.2 (Duality of $\top$, $\bot$ and Id).

(a) $\top^{\circ} = \bot$ *(b)* $\bot^{\circ} = \top$ *(c)* $\mathsf{Id}^{\circ} = \mathsf{Id}$.

Proof. The proof of (a) and (c) is by little calculations in Boolean algebra; the proof of (b) is by dualizing (a).

Suppose $\psi \in \mathsf{Pred}$. Then we have

$$\text{(a) } \top^{\circ}(\psi) = \overline{\top(\overline{\psi})} = \overline{\top_{\mathsf{Pred}}} = \bot_{\mathsf{Pred}} = \bot(\psi) \,,$$
$$\text{(b) } \bot^{\circ} = (\top^{\circ})^{\circ} = \top \text{ , and}$$
$$\text{(c) } \mathsf{Id}^{\circ}(\psi) = \overline{\mathsf{Id}(\overline{\psi})} = \overline{\overline{\psi}} = \psi = \mathsf{Id}(\psi) \,.$$

□

5.3 Simulations

When considering Galois connections and commands a careful distinction must be drawn between Galois connections between two spaces of commands Com_V^W and $\mathsf{Com}_{V'}^{W'}$, i.e. a pair of monotonic mappings $F \in [\mathsf{Com}_V^W \to \mathsf{Com}_{V'}^{W'}]$ and $G \in [\mathsf{Com}_{V'}^{W'} \to \mathsf{Com}_V^W]$, and pairs of commands (P, Q) that form Galois connections between two predicate spaces Pred_V and Pred_W. In order to reduce the danger of misunderstanding, we call the latter *simulations*, following the terminology used in [43]. As we use the sign ; instead of $\circ$ for denoting the functional composition of commands, simulations can be defined as follows according to the characterization of Galois connections in Theorem 3.1.2.

Definition 5.3.1 (Simulations). *Suppose* $P \in \mathsf{Com}_V^W$, $Q \in \mathsf{Com}_W^V$. *Then the pair* (P, Q) *is called a* simulation *(between* V *and* W*) if*

$$P \,;\, Q \le \mathsf{Id} \quad \textit{and} \quad \mathsf{Id} \le Q \,;\, P \,.$$

This definition does not refer directly to the predicate transformer interpretation of commands. Therefore, we can prove that a pair (P, Q) is a simulation by calculating on the level of commands with the aid of the laws established later in this chapter. We shall see that the following pairs of basic commands are simulations:

- assertions and assumptions $(\{\phi\}, [\phi])$ to the same predicate ϕ,
- deletion and demonic addition (u^-, u^+) of a list u of variables from/to the state space,
- angelic addition and deletion $(u^{\oplus}, u^-)$ of a list u of variables to/from the state space, and
- angelic and demonic choice assignments $(u :=!, u :=?)$.

As simulations are just Galois connections between predicate spaces, we can apply the methods described in Chap. 3 to construct simulations out of simulations. In particular $(P \,;\, P' \,,\; Q' \,;\, Q)$ is a simulation if (P, Q) and (P', Q') are simulations.

Simulations induce Galois connections between command spaces.

Lemma 5.3.2 (Induced Galois connections). *Let* (P, Q) *be a simulation between* V *and* W.

(a) *Define* $F \in [\mathsf{Com}^U_W \to \mathsf{Com}^U_V]$, $G \in [\mathsf{Com}^U_V \to \mathsf{Com}^U_W]$ *by*

$$F(X) = P\,;X \quad \text{and} \quad G(Y) = Q\,;Y\,.$$

Then (F,G) *is a Galois connection between* Com^U_W *and* Com^U_V.

(b) *Similarly, we can define* $F \in [\mathsf{Com}^W_U \to \mathsf{Com}^V_U]$, $G \in [\mathsf{Com}^V_U \to \mathsf{Com}^W_U]$ *by*

$$F(X) = X\,;Q \quad \text{and} \quad G(Y) = Y\,;P\,.$$

Then (F,G) *is a Galois connection between* Com^W_U *and* Com^V_U.

(c) *(a) and (b) can be combined: Define* $F \in [\mathsf{Com}^W_W \to \mathsf{Com}^V_V]$, $G \in [\mathsf{Com}^V_V \to \mathsf{Com}^W_W]$ *by*

$$F(X) = P\,;X\,;Q \quad \text{and} \quad G(Y) = Q\,;Y\,;P\,.$$

Then (F,G) *is a Galois connection between* Com^W_W *and* Com^V_V.

(d) *The Galois connection constructed in (c) is distributive.*

Proof. In each case it is easy to prove from the defining condition for simulations that $F \circ G \le \mathsf{Id}$ and $\mathsf{Id} \le G \circ F$, which suffices by Theorem 3.1.2 to show that (F,G) is a Galois connection. For example (a) is seen from

$$(F \circ G)(X) = F(G(X)) = P\,;Q\,;X \le \mathsf{Id}\,;X = X\,, \text{ and}$$
$$(G \circ F)(Y) = G(F((Y)) = Q\,;P\,;Y \ge \mathsf{Id}\,;Y = Y\,.$$

The proof of (b) and (c) is similar. That the Galois connection constructed in (c) is ;-distributive is seen by the straightforward calculation

$$
\begin{array}{ll}
 & F(X\,;X') \\
= & \quad [\text{Definition of } F] \\
 & P\,;X\,;X'\,;Q \\
= & \quad [\mathsf{Id} \text{ is unit of } ;] \\
 & P\,;X\,;\mathsf{Id}\,;X'\,;Q \\
\le & \quad [\mathsf{Id} \le Q\,;P \text{ because } (P,Q) \text{ is a simulation}] \\
 & P\,;X\,;Q\,;P\,;X'\,;Q \\
= & \quad [\text{Definition of } F] \\
 & F(X)\,;F(X')
\end{array}
$$

for $X, X' \in \mathsf{Com}^W_W$. □

5.4 Basic Homogeneous Commands

In this section we define concrete notations for commands working on a homogeneous state space V and investigate their properties and laws. More specifically, we define multiple assignments $u := e$ (for lists u of variables and evaluation function lists e), assertions $\{\phi\}$ and assumptions $[\phi]$ (for predicates ϕ). R.J.R. Back and J. von Wright show in [6] that any monotonic predicate transformer on a homogeneous state space can be constructed from assignments, assertions and assumptions by sequential composition, meet and join. This is a technical justification for taking these constructs as basis. For the purpose of this book, however, other reasons are even more important. On the one hand it is easy to develop a good intuition about these constructs that is independent of their definition as predicate transformer. This makes them appropriate for specifying source and target language's semantics. On the other hand they enjoy simple and powerful laws, which makes them suitable for algebraic calculations.

All the predicates transformers and predicates considered in this section are of alphabet V. Therefore, we sometimes write Com and Pred for Com_V^V and Pred_V.

5.4.1 Multiple Assignments

The traditional definition of the weakest precondition of an assignment *var* := *exp* is

$$\mathsf{wp}(var := exp)(form) \stackrel{\text{def}}{=} form_{var}^{exp} ,$$

where $form_{var}^{exp}$ denotes the syntactic substitution of the expression *exp* for the variable *var* in the formula *form*. The intuition is that the postcondition *form* holds in the final state of the assignment if and only if it holds in the initial state modified by the value of *exp* in component *var*. The below definition of := as a semantic operator replays this definition semantically. Instead of expressions *exp* it takes valuation functions φ, instead of formulas *form* it transforms (semantic) predicates ϕ, and instead of syntactic substitution it uses the semantic substitution that has been defined in Sect. 4.3.2. Moreover, the weakest precondition interpretation is built into the operator :=, so := is an infix operator that takes a list of variables and a list of valuation functions as arguments and yields a monotonic predicate transformer as result.

Suppose $u \in V^\bullet$ and $e \in \mathsf{Valfct}_V^u$. Then $u := e$ is the predicate transformer defined by

$$(u := e)(\phi) \stackrel{\text{def}}{=} \phi[e/u]$$

for $\phi \in \mathsf{Pred}_V$. It is clear that $u := e \in \mathsf{Com}_V^V$. The dualization and distribution properties are investigated in the next theorem.

Theorem 5.4.1 (Dualization and distribution). *Suppose* $u \in V^\bullet$ *and* $e \in \mathsf{Valfct}_V^u$.

(a) Multiple assignments are dual to themselves: $(u := e)^\circ \;=\; u := e$.
(b) Multiple assignments are $\bot$*- and* $\top$*-strict and universally disjunctive as well as universally conjunctive.*

Proof. The proof of (a) is a little calculation in Boolean algebra. For any $\psi \in \mathsf{Pred}$ we have:

$$(u := e)^{\circ}(\psi) \equiv \overline{(u := e)(\overline{\psi})} \equiv \overline{\overline{\psi}[e/u]} \equiv \overline{\overline{\psi[e/u]}} \equiv \psi[e/u]$$
$$\equiv (u := e)(\psi) .$$

The third step exploits that complementation on Pred is the lift of complementation on Bool and that substitution distributes over lifted operators. Distribution of substitution over the lifted operators disjunction and conjunction as well as the lifted constants $\perp$ and $\top$ establishes (b). □

It is clear from its definition that $u := e$ is just a curried form of the substitution operator on predicates. Therefore, it inherits the basic laws of substitution (Lemma 4.3.3). All of these laws can be written without a reference to predicates. This results in the following familiar laws for assignments.

Theorem 5.4.2 (Basic assignment laws). *Suppose* $u \in V^{\bullet}$, *and* $e \in \mathsf{Valfct}_V^u$, *and let* $x \in V$ *such that* $x \notin u$. *Furthermore, let* $x_1, \ldots, x_n$ *be pairwise distinct variables,* $\varphi_1, \ldots, \varphi_n$ *valuation functions of corresponding type (i.e.* $\varphi_i \in \mathsf{Valfct}_V^{x_i}$ *for* $i = 1, \ldots, n$*), and* ρ *be a permutation of* $\{1, \ldots, n\}$.

(a) *Identical assignments are void:*

$$u := e \quad = \quad u, x := e, x^* . \qquad \textit{(Identity-asg)}$$

(b) *Successive assignments to the same variables can be combined:*

$$u := e\, ; u := f \quad = \quad u := f[e/u] . \qquad \textit{(Comb-asg1)}$$

(c) *An assignment with empty variable and valuation function list is void:*

$$\varepsilon := \varepsilon \quad = \quad \mathsf{Id} . \qquad \textit{(Empty-asg1)}$$

(d) *The specific position of variables and valuation functions in assignments is insignificant. Only the correspondence of variables to valuation function coded in the order is relevant:*

$$x_1, \ldots, x_n := \varphi_1, \ldots, \varphi_n \quad = \quad x_{\rho(1)}, \ldots, x_{\rho(n)} := \varphi_{\rho(1)}, \ldots, \varphi_{\rho(n)} .$$
(Reorder-asg)

Proof. The laws are reformulations of the substitution laws in Lemma 4.3.3. □

By the (Reorder-asg) law a multiple assignment $x_1, \ldots, x_n := \varphi_1, \ldots, \varphi_n$ can be considered an operator on the set of pairs $\{(x_1, \varphi_1), \ldots, (x_n, \varphi_n)\}$, informally speaking. We apply the (Reorder-asg) law (almost) always tacitly to arrange assignments appropriately, i.e. such that they fit to the laws to be applied.

5.4.2 Assertions and Assumptions

Suppose $\phi \in \mathsf{Pred}_V$ is a predicate. The two predicate transformers $\{\phi\}$ and $[\phi]$, called an *assertion* and *assumption* of ϕ are defined by the identities

$$\{\phi\}(\psi) \stackrel{\text{def}}{=} \phi \wedge \psi \quad \text{and} \quad [\phi](\psi) \stackrel{\text{def}}{=} \overline{\phi} \vee \psi$$

for $\psi \in \mathsf{Pred}_V$. It is easy to see that both $\{\phi\}$ and $[\phi]$ are monotonic predicate transformers as $\wedge$ and $\vee$ are monotonic; thus

$$\{\phi\}, [\phi] \in \mathsf{Com}_V^V \quad \text{for } \phi \in \mathsf{Pred}_V \ .$$

The operational intuition is that the assertion $\{\phi\}$ behaves like skip (the identical state transformer) if ϕ holds in the initial state and is otherwise chaotic. So it successfully terminates from an initial state σ in a state satisfying the postcondition ψ iff σ satisfies both ϕ and ψ which motivates its definition. The interpretation of the assumption $[\phi]$ is that it behaves like skip if ϕ holds initially and otherwise succeeds miraculously. So $[\phi]$ establishes from an initial state σ the postcondition ψ if and only if σ satisfies ψ or – by miraculous success – if σ does not satisfy ϕ.

Theorem 5.4.3 (Dualization and distribution). *Suppose* $\phi \in \mathsf{Pred}$.

(a) Assumptions and assertions are dual to each other:

$$\{\phi\}^\circ = [\phi] \quad \textit{and} \quad [\phi]^\circ = \{\phi\} \ .$$

(b) Assertions are $\perp$-strict, positively conjunctive and universally (and thus also positively) disjunctive. In general they are not $\top$-strict and hence not universally conjunctive.

(c) Assumptions are $\top$-strict, universally (and thus also positively) conjunctive and positively disjunctive. In general they are not $\perp$-strict and hence not universally disjunctive.

Proof. (a) The first equality follows from a little calculation in Boolean algebra. Suppose $\psi \in \mathsf{Pred}$. Then:

$$\{\phi\}^\circ(\psi) \quad = \quad \overline{\{\phi\}(\overline{\psi})} \quad = \quad \overline{\phi \wedge \overline{\psi}} \quad = \quad \overline{\phi} \vee \psi \quad = \quad [\phi](\psi) \ .$$

The second equality follows from the first one by dualization:

$$[\phi]^\circ \quad = \quad (\{\phi\}^\circ)^\circ \quad = \quad \{\phi\} \ .$$

(b) $\{\phi\}$ distributes over arbitrary joins by the (JDI) law that is valid in every complete lattice (see p. 14):

$$\begin{aligned}\{\phi\}(\bigvee H) \quad &= \quad \phi \wedge \bigvee H \quad = \quad \bigvee\{\phi \wedge h \mid h \in H\} \\ &= \quad \bigvee\{\{\phi\}(h) \mid h \in H\} \ .\end{aligned}$$

This implies universal and positive disjunctivity and $\perp$-strictness. $\{\phi\}$ is positively conjunctive as the mapping $\phi \wedge .$ is positively conjunctive in every lattice (see p. 13). In general $\{\phi\}$ is not $\top$-strict and, therefore, also not generally conjunctive as

$$\{\bot\}(\top) \;=\; \bot \wedge \top \;=\; \bot \neq \top\,.$$

(c) The distribution properties of assumptions are dual to the properties of assertions and can be justified analogously. □

The next theorem states a number of basic laws for assertions and assumptions.

Theorem 5.4.4 (Basic assertion and assumption laws).
Suppose given $\phi, \phi' \in \mathsf{Pred}$ and $H \subseteq \mathsf{Pred}$.

(a) Asserting false is malicious and asserting true is void; assertions always lie between $\bot$ and Id:

$$\bot \;=\; \{\mathsf{false}\} \;\leq\; \{\phi\} \;\leq\; \{\mathsf{true}\} \;=\; \mathsf{Id}\,. \qquad \textit{(Assert)}$$

Dually, assuming false is miraculous and assuming true is void; assumptions always lie between Id and $\top$:

$$\mathsf{Id} \;=\; [\mathsf{true}] \;\leq\; [\phi] \;\leq\; [\mathsf{false}] \;=\; \top\,. \qquad \textit{(Assume)}$$

(b) The assertion operator is monotonic and the assumption operator antitonic:

$$\{\phi\} \;\leq\; \{\phi'\}\,, \;\; \textit{if}\; \phi \leq \phi'\,. \qquad \textit{(Assert-monotonic)}$$
$$[\phi] \;\leq\; [\phi']\,, \;\; \textit{if}\; \phi' \leq \phi\,. \qquad \textit{(Assume-antitonic)}$$

(c) The assertion operator is universally disjunctive; the assumption operator is universally 'anti-disjunctive':

$$\{\textstyle\bigvee H\} \;=\; \bigvee_{\phi\in H}\{\phi\}\,. \qquad \textit{(Assert-disj)}$$
$$[\textstyle\bigvee H] \;=\; \bigwedge_{\phi\in H}[\phi]\,. \qquad \textit{(Assume-disj)}$$

(d) The assertion operator is positively conjunctive and the assumption operator positively 'anti-conjunctive':

$$\{\textstyle\bigwedge H\} \;=\; \bigwedge_{\phi\in H}\{\phi\}\,, \;\; \textit{if}\; H \neq \emptyset\,. \qquad \textit{(Assert-conj)}$$
$$[\textstyle\bigwedge H] \;=\; \bigvee_{\phi\in H}[\phi]\,, \;\; \textit{if}\; H \neq \emptyset\,. \qquad \textit{(Assume-conj)}$$

(e) Successive assertions can be combined; the same holds for assumptions:

$$\{\phi\}\,;\{\phi'\} \;=\; \{\phi \wedge \phi'\}\,. \qquad \textit{(Comb-assert)}$$
$$[\phi]\,;[\phi'] \;=\; [\phi \wedge \phi']\,. \qquad \textit{(Comb-assume)}$$

Proof. Let us first consider the proof of the results for assertions.

Monotonicity of the assertion operator, i.e. (Assert-monotonic), follows from the monotonicity of $\wedge$.

The disjunctivity of the assertion operator claimed in (c) follows from the 'join distributive identity' (JDI) (p. 14): Suppose $H \subseteq \mathsf{Pred}$ and $\psi \in \mathsf{Pred}$. Then

$$\{\textstyle\bigvee H\}(\psi) \underset{\substack{\uparrow\\ \text{[Def]}}}{=} (\bigvee H) \wedge \psi \underset{\substack{\uparrow\\ \text{[JDI]}}}{=} \bigvee_{\phi\in H} \phi \wedge \psi \underset{\substack{\uparrow\\ \text{[Def]}}}{=} \bigvee_{\phi\in H}\{\phi\}(\psi)$$

$$= (\bigvee_{\phi \in H}\{\phi\})(\psi) .$$
$\uparrow$
[Lifted order]

From this calculation $\{\bigvee H\} = \bigvee_{\phi\in H}\{\phi\}$ follows by extensionality.

The proof of (Assert-conj) is similar but exploits the positive conjunctivity of $. \wedge \phi$ instead of (JDI).

The two equalities stated in the (Assert) law follow from the fact that false is the zero and true the unit of $\wedge$. The inequalities in (a) then follow from (b) because all predicates ϕ lie between false and true.

Law (Comb-assert) in item (e) is proved by the little calculation

$$(\{\phi\} ; \{\phi'\})(\psi) \quad = \quad \phi \wedge (\phi' \wedge \psi) \quad = \quad (\phi \wedge \phi') \wedge \psi \quad = \quad \{\phi \wedge \phi'\}(\psi)$$

for an arbitrarily chosen $\psi \in \mathsf{Pred}$.

These considerations prove the assertion laws. The laws for assumptions follow by dualization. For example, (Assert-disj) is seen from the calculation:

$$[\bigvee H] \quad = \quad \{\bigvee H\}^{\circ} \quad = \quad (\bigvee_{\phi\in H}\{\phi\})^{\circ} \quad = \quad \bigwedge_{\phi\in H}\{\phi\}^{\circ} \quad = \quad \bigwedge_{\phi\in H}[\phi] .$$

□

There are also useful laws to commute subsequent occurrences of basic homogeneous commands of different kind. These laws are collected in the next theorem. There is no generally applicable commutation law for an assertion or assumption followed by an assignment.[1] But we can establish the following rule for transforming such commands: the valuation functions e on the right hand side of the assignment can be replaced by any valuation functions f that coincide with e on all states satisfying the predicate ϕ that is asserted or assumed. The latter condition can formally be expressed as $\phi \leq (e = f)$.

Theorem 5.4.5 (Basic laws for different homogeneous commands). *Suppose $\phi, \phi' \in \mathsf{Pred}_V$, $u \in V^{\bullet}$ and $e, f \in \mathsf{Valfct}_V^u$.*

(a) Assumptions and assertions commute as follows:

$$[\phi] ; \{\phi'\} \quad = \quad \{\phi \Rightarrow \phi'\} ; [\phi] . \qquad \textit{(Assume-assert)}$$
$$\{\phi\} ; [\phi'] \quad = \quad [\phi \Rightarrow \phi'] ; \{\phi\} . \qquad \textit{(Assert-assume)}$$

(b) Assignments commute with assertions and assumptions but the state change must be taken into account in the asserted or assumed predicate:

$$u := e ; \{\phi\} \quad = \quad \{\phi[e/u]\} ; u := e . \qquad \textit{(Assign-assert)}$$
$$u := e ; [\phi] \quad = \quad [\phi[e/u]] ; u := e . \qquad \textit{(Assign-assume)}$$

(c) Asserted or assumed predicates can be exploited for transforming subsequent assignments:

$$\{\phi\} ; u := e \quad = \quad \{\phi\} ; u := f \ , \quad \textit{if} \ \ \phi \leq (e = f) . \qquad \textit{(Exploit-assert)}$$
$$[\phi] ; u := e \quad = \quad [\phi] ; u := f \ , \quad \textit{if} \ \ \phi \leq (e = f) . \qquad \textit{(Exploit-assume)}$$

---

[1] Of course in many cases the laws for the reverse situation that an assignment is followed by an assertion or assumption is applicable from right to left.

Proof. The proofs of (Assume-assert) and (Assign-assert) are small calculations in Boolean algebra.

Suppose $\phi \in \mathsf{Pred}$. Then

$$
\begin{aligned}
([\phi]\,;\{\phi'\})(\psi) &\underset{\substack{\uparrow\\ \text{[Definitions]}}}{=} \overline{\phi} \vee (\phi' \wedge \psi) \underset{\substack{\uparrow\\ \text{[Distributivity]}}}{=} (\overline{\phi} \vee \phi') \wedge (\overline{\phi} \vee \psi) \\
&\underset{\substack{\uparrow\\ \text{[Definition } \Rightarrow]}}{=} (\phi \Rightarrow \phi') \wedge (\overline{\phi} \vee \psi) \underset{\substack{\uparrow\\ \text{[Definitions]}}}{=} (\{\phi \Rightarrow \phi'\}\,;[\phi])(\psi)\ .
\end{aligned}
$$

Moreover,

$$
\begin{aligned}
(u := e\,;\{\phi\})(\psi) &\underset{\substack{\uparrow\\ \text{[Definitions]}}}{=} (\phi \wedge \psi)[e/u] \underset{\substack{\uparrow\\ \text{[Distributivity]}}}{=} \phi[e/u] \wedge \psi[e/u] \\
&\underset{\substack{\uparrow\\ \text{[Definitions]}}}{=} (\{\phi[e/u]\}\,; u := e)(\psi)\ .
\end{aligned}
$$

In order to show (Exploit-assert) we assume that $\psi \in \mathsf{Pred}$ is given such that $\psi \leq (e = f)$. Then

$$
\begin{aligned}
(\{\phi\}\,; u := e)(\psi) &\underset{\substack{\uparrow\\ \text{[Definitions]}}}{=} \phi \wedge \psi[e/u] \underset{\substack{\uparrow\\ [\phi \leq (e=f)]}}{=} \phi \wedge (e = f) \wedge \psi[e/u] \\
&\underset{\substack{\uparrow\\ \text{[S-equality]}}}{=} \phi \wedge (e = f) \wedge \psi[f/u] \underset{\substack{\uparrow\\ [\phi \leq (e=f)]}}{=} \phi \wedge \psi[f/u] \\
&\underset{\substack{\uparrow\\ \text{[Definitions]}}}{=} (\{\phi\}\,; u := f)(\psi)\ .
\end{aligned}
$$

The laws for assumptions are obtained by dualization. □

The next theorem is concerned with a kind of generalized conditional. The idea is to steer the control flow by the value of an A-valuation function φ in the initial state. We assume that for each $a \in A$ we have chosen a command P_a that is to be executed just in case φ's initial value is a. There are two dual intuitions how to describe the resulting command with the operators available up to now, viz. by an angelic choice or by a demonic choice.

In the description with an angelic choice we guard each P_a by the assertion $\{\varphi = a^*\}$. So we get the command

$$\bigvee_{a \in A} \{\varphi = a^*\}\,; P_a\ .$$

The intuition is that the angel is forced to choose in an initial state σ the command $\{\varphi = a^*\}\,; P_a$ where $a = \varphi(\sigma)$ as it must avoid the chaotic behavior that results from a different choice because of the initial (unsatisfied) assertion.

If on the other hand we intend to use a demonic choice instead, we guard each P_a by the assumption $[\varphi = a^*]$, thus obtaining

$$\bigwedge_{a \in A} [\varphi = a^*] \; ; P_a \; .$$

Here the intuition is that the demon performing the choice is forced to decide for the intended path as otherwise an immediate miracle happens (which the demon tries to avoid). The (Span) law below ensures that the two descriptions are equivalent.

Theorem 5.4.6 (Spanning property). *Suppose an A-valuation function $\varphi \in \mathsf{Valfct}_V^A$ and a family of commands $(P_a)_{a \in A}$ indexed by the members of A is given. Then*

$$\bigvee_{a \in A} \{\varphi = a^*\} \; ; P_a \quad = \quad \bigwedge_{a \in A} [\varphi = a^*] \; ; P_a \; . \qquad \textit{(Span)}$$

Proof. Suppose given a predicate ϕ and a state σ. By expanding the definitions it can be shown that both sides applied to ϕ and σ yield tt if and only if $P_a(\phi)(\sigma) = \mathsf{tt}$ for $a = \varphi(\sigma)$.

The calculation that establishes this for the left hand side is as follows:

$\mathrm{LHS}(\phi)(\sigma) = \mathsf{tt}$

iff [Pointwise definition of ordering, definition of the lub]

$(\{\varphi = a^*\} \; ; P_a)(\phi)(\sigma) = \mathsf{tt}$ for some $a \in A$

iff [Definition of assertions and ;]

$((\varphi = a^*) \wedge P_a(\phi))(\sigma) = \mathsf{tt}$ for some $a \in A$

iff [$\wedge$ on predicates is pointwise extension of $\wedge$ on Bool]

$(\varphi = a^*)(\sigma) = \mathsf{tt}$ and $P_a(\phi)(\sigma) = \mathsf{tt}$ for some $a \in A$

iff [Definition of $=$ and a^*]

$\varphi(\sigma) = a$ and $P_a(\phi)(\sigma) = \mathsf{tt}$ for some $a \in A$

iff [One-point rule]

$P_a(\phi)(\sigma) = \mathsf{tt}$ for $a = \varphi(\sigma)$

The calculation for the right hand side is similar. □

An interesting application of the (Span) law is that the conditional `if` ϕ `then` P `else` Q `fi`, which is notated in the infix form $P \lhd \phi \rhd Q$, can equivalently be defined by one of the two identities

$$P \lhd \phi \rhd Q \quad = \quad ([\phi] \; ; P) \wedge ([\overline{\phi}] \; ; Q) \quad \text{and}$$
$$P \lhd \phi \rhd Q \quad = \quad (\{\phi\} \; ; P) \vee (\{\overline{\phi}\} \; ; Q) \; .$$

The right hand sides of these equations follow the structure of the two sides of the (Span) law because ϕ equals $\phi = \mathsf{tt}^*$ and $\overline{\phi}$ equals $\phi = \mathsf{ff}^*$.

5.4.3 Derived Laws for Basic Homogeneous Commands

Up to now we have established laws for assignments, assertions and assumptions by referring to their definition as predicate transformers or by appealing to dualization. Applying only those laws, however, sometimes leads to lengthy calculations. As a step towards shorter calculations we establish some derived laws in the current section. They are called *derived* because their proof refers only to the basic laws and does not appeal to the predicate transformer definition of the constructors.

The (Comb-asg1) law for combining successive assignments has been designed to have a simple formulation such that it is easily remembered and proved. Its disadvantage is that it is applicable to successive assignments $u := e$ and $v := f$ only if the lists of variables u and v are identical. Of course this can always be achieved by prior applications of the laws (Identity-asg) and (Reorder-asg). In practical calculations, however, it is more convenient to have available a more general form of (Comb-asg1) that already embodies the applications of (Identity-asg). Such a law and some other useful derived laws for assignments are collected in the following theorem.

Theorem 5.4.7 (Derived assignment laws). *Suppose* $u, v, w \in V^\bullet$ *and* $e \in \mathsf{Valfct}^u_V$, $f, g \in \mathsf{Valfct}^v_V$ *and* $h \in \mathsf{Valfct}^w_V$.

(a) *This is the promised more general form of (Comb-asg1):*

$$u, v := e, f \,;\, v, w := g, h \quad = \quad u, v, w := e, (g, h)[e, f/u, v] \ ,$$
if u, v, w *are mutually disjoint .* *(Comb-asg)*

(b) *An assignment to a list of variables* v *cancels a preceding assignment to* v *provided the (entire) later assignment does not depend on* v*:*

$$u, v := e, f \,;\, v, w := g, h \quad = \quad u := e \,;\, v, w := g, h \ , \qquad \textit{(Cancel-asg)}$$
if g *and* h *are independent of* v .

(c) *Independent assignments commute:*

$$u := e \,;\, v := f \quad = \quad v := f \,;\, u := e \ , \qquad \textit{(Comm-asg)}$$
if $u \cap v = \varepsilon$, e *is independent of* v, *and* f *is independent of* u .

(d) *There is a generalized form of (Empty-asg1):*

$$u := u^* \quad = \quad \mathsf{Id} \ . \qquad \textit{(Empty-asg)}$$

Proof. The laws correspond to multiple applications of the basic assignment laws.

- An application of the (Comb-asg) law corresponds to a successive application of the laws (Identity-asg) and (Comb-asg1): If u, v, w are mutually disjoint then

$$
\begin{aligned}
& u, v := e, f \ ; v, w := g, h \\
= \quad & [\text{(Identity-asg) two times}] \\
& u, v, w := e, f, w^* \ ; u, v, w := u^*, g, h \\
= \quad & [\text{Comb-asg1}] \\
& u, v, w := (u^*, g, h)[e, f, w^*/u, v, w] \\
= \quad & [\text{Substitute } e \text{ for } u\text{; the substitution of } w^* \text{ for } w \text{ is void}] \\
& u, v, w := e, (g, h)[e, f/u, v] \ .
\end{aligned}
$$

- The (Cancel-asg) law is proved by applying (Comb-asg).
  Suppose g and h are independent of v. The lists u and w are not necessarily disjoint. However, without loss of generality (that is after reordering u and w appropriately) we can choose u', w' and w'' such that $u = u', w'$ and $w = w', w''$ and u' and w'' are disjoint. Let e', e'' and h', h'' be the corresponding partitions of the valuation function lists e and h. Then

$$
\begin{aligned}
& u, v := e, f \ ; v, w := g, h \\
= \quad & [\text{Choice of } u', u'', \ldots \text{, reordering of the first assignment}] \\
& u', v, w' := e', f, e'' \ ; v, w', w'' := g, h', h'' \\
= \quad & [\text{Comb-asg}] \\
& u', v, w', w'' := e', (g, h', h'')[e', f, e''/u', v, w'] \\
= \quad & [g \text{ and } h \text{ are independent of } v] \\
& u', v, w', w'' := e', (g, h', h'')[e', e''/u', w'] \ .
\end{aligned}
$$

  This equals the right assignment as the following calculation shows:

$$
\begin{aligned}
& u := e \ ; v, w := g, h \\
= \quad & [\text{Choice of } u', u'', \ldots \text{, reordering of the second assignment}] \\
& u', w' := e', e'' \ ; w', v, w'' := h', g, h'' \\
= \quad & [\text{Comb-asg}] \\
& u', w', v, w'' := e', (h', g, h'')[e', e''/u', w'] \\
= \quad & [\text{Reordering of the assignment}] \\
& u', v, w', w'' := e', (g, h', h'')[e', e''/u', w'] \ .
\end{aligned}
$$

- The (Comm-asg) law is proved by two applications of (Comb-asg).
  Suppose $u \cap v = \varepsilon$, e is independent of v and f is independent of u.

$$
\begin{aligned}
& u := e \ ; v := f \\
= \quad & [\text{(Comb-asg), } u \cap v = \varepsilon] \\
& u, v := e, f[e/u]
\end{aligned}
$$

$$= \quad [f \text{ idp } u,\ e \text{ idp } v]$$
$$u, v := e[f/v], f$$
$$= \quad [(\text{Comb-asg}),\ u \cap v = \varepsilon]$$
$$v := f\ ;\ u := e\ .$$

– (Empty-asg) follows by a multiple application of (Identity assign) (once for each variable in u) and a final application of (Empty-asg1). □

Quantification of predicates is defined in terms of meet and join. Therefore, the conjunctivity and disjunctivity properties of assertions and assumptions have corollaries for quantification.

Theorem 5.4.8 (Assertions, assumptions and quantification). *Let* $u \in V^\bullet$ *and* $\phi \in \mathsf{Pred}$. *Then*

$$\{\exists_u(\phi)\} \;=\; \bigvee_{a \in \mathsf{Val}_u} \{\phi[a^*/u]\}\ . \qquad (\textit{Assert-}\exists)$$

$$\{\forall_u(\phi)\} \;=\; \bigwedge_{a \in \mathsf{Val}_u} \{\phi[a^*/u]\}\ . \qquad (\textit{Assert-}\forall)$$

Dually, we have

$$[\exists_u(\phi)] \;=\; \bigwedge_{a \in \mathsf{Val}_u} [\phi[a^*/u]]\ . \qquad (\textit{Assume-}\exists)$$

$$[\forall_u(\phi)] \;=\; \bigvee_{a \in \mathsf{Val}_u} [\phi[a^*/u]]\ . \qquad (\textit{Assume-}\forall)$$

Proof. The laws follow from (Assert-disj), (Assert-conj), (Assume disj) and (Assume-conj) since $\exists_u(\phi) = \bigvee_{a \in \mathsf{Val}_u} \phi[a^*/u]$ and $\forall_u(\phi) = \bigwedge_{a \in \mathsf{Val}_u} \phi[a^*/u]$. The proof of (Assert-∀) and (Assume-∀) moreover exploits that Val_u is non-empty. □

The laws for commuting assignments with assertions and assumptions take a simpler form if certain independence conditions hold, and they allow to introduce or remove assertions, assumptions and assignments. Furthermore, it is easy to establish from the commutation laws that assertions and assumptions form a simulation.

Theorem 5.4.9 (Derived laws). *Suppose* $u \in V^\bullet$, $e \in \mathsf{Valfct}_V^u$ *and* $\phi \in \mathsf{Pred}$.

(a) Assignments commute with independent assertions or assumptions:

$$u := e\ ;\{\phi\} \;=\; \{\phi\}\ ;u := e\ ,\ \textit{ if } \phi \text{ idp } u\ . \qquad (\textit{Assign-assert1})$$

$$u := e\ ;[\phi] \;=\; [\phi]\ ;u := e\ ,\ \textit{ if } \phi \text{ idp } u\ . \qquad (\textit{Assign-assume1})$$

(b) The value of u *equals* e *just after an assignment* $u := e$*, provided* e *does not depend on* u*:*

$$u := e \;=\; u := e\ ;\{u^* = e\}\ ,\ \textit{ if } e \text{ idp } u\ . \qquad (\textit{Assign-assert2})$$

$$u := e \;=\; u := e\ ;[u^* = e]\ ,\ \textit{ if } e \text{ idp } u\ . \qquad (\textit{Assign-assume2})$$

(c) Assignments can be introduced by the following laws:

$$\{u^* = e\} \;=\; \{u^* = e\}\,;\, u := e\;. \qquad \textit{(Assign-assert3)}$$

$$[\,u^* = e\,] \;=\; [\,u^* = e\,]\,;\, u := e\;. \qquad \textit{(Assign-assume3)}$$

(d) Assertions and assumptions to the same predicate form a simulation:

$$\{\phi\}\,;\,[\phi] \le \mathsf{Id} \quad \textit{and} \quad \mathsf{Id} \le [\phi]\,;\,\{\phi\}\;. \qquad \textit{(Assert-assume-sim)}$$

Proof. The laws (Assign-assert1) and (Assign-assume1) are corollaries of (Assign-assert) and (Assign-assume) because $\phi[e/u]$ equals ϕ if ϕ is independent of u.

(Assign-assert2) is a corollary of (Assign-assert):
Suppose e idp u. Then

$$u := e\,;\,\{u^* = e\} \underset{\substack{\uparrow\\ \text{[Assign-assert]}}}{=} \{(u^* = e)[e/u]\}\,;\,u := e \underset{\substack{\uparrow\\ [e\ \mathsf{idp}\ u \text{ implies } e[e/u] = e]}}{=} \{e = e\}\,;\,u := e$$

$$\underset{\substack{\uparrow\\ [(e=e)\equiv \mathsf{true}]}}{=} \{\mathsf{true}\}\,;\,u := e \underset{\substack{\uparrow\\ \text{[Assume]}}}{=} u := e\;.$$

(Assign-assert3) is a corollary of (Exploit-assert):

$$\{u^* = e\}\,;\,u := e \underset{\substack{\uparrow\\ \text{[Exploit-assert]}}}{=} \{u^* = e\}\,;\,u := u^* \underset{\substack{\uparrow\\ \text{[Empty-asg]}}}{=} \{u^* = e\}\;.$$

(Assign-assume2) and (Assign-assume3) follow by dualization.
The first inequality of (Assert-assume-sim) is established by

$$\{\phi\}\,;\,[\phi] \underset{\substack{\uparrow\\ \text{[Assert-assume]}}}{=} [\phi \Rightarrow \phi]\,;\,\{\phi\} \underset{\substack{\uparrow\\ [\phi \Rightarrow \phi \equiv \mathsf{true}]}}{=} [\mathsf{true}]\,;\,\{\phi\} \underset{\substack{\uparrow\\ \text{[Assume]}}}{=} \{\phi\} \underset{\substack{\uparrow\\ \text{[Assert]}}}{\le} \mathsf{Id}\;.$$

The second inequality follows by dualization. □

The generalized conditional law (Span) implies the following identity for Id.

Theorem 5.4.10 (A spanned characterization of Id).
Let $\varphi \in \mathsf{Valfct}_V^A$. Then

$$\bigvee_{a\in A} \{\varphi = a^*\} \;=\; \mathsf{Id} \;=\; \bigwedge_{a\in A} [\varphi = a^*]\;. \qquad \textit{(Span1)}$$

Proof. The proof is an application of the (Span) law:

$$\mathsf{Id} \;=\; \textstyle\bigwedge_{a\in A}\mathsf{Id} \underset{\substack{\uparrow\\ \text{[Assume]}}}{\le} \bigwedge_{a\in A}[\varphi = a^*] \underset{\substack{\uparrow\\ \text{[(Span) with } P_a = \mathsf{Id}]}}{=} \bigvee_{a\in A}\{\varphi = a^*\} \underset{\substack{\uparrow\\ \text{[Assert]}}}{\le} \bigvee_{a\in A}\mathsf{Id}$$

$$=\; \mathsf{Id}\;.$$

This shows that all commands appearing in the above calculation equal Id and this in turn proves the result. □

5.5 Basic Heterogeneous Commands

In this section we define three further basic commands, demonic and angelic addition of a list of variables u to the state space denoted by u^+ and $u^\oplus$, and deletion of u from the state space, denoted by u^-. Unlike the homogeneous commands considered in the previous section, they are inhomogeneous in that pre- and post-state have a different alphabet. A typical application of the new commands is for making local a variable used in a command P. $x^+ ; P ; x^-$ behaves akin to an ALGOL 60 block that introduces x as a local variable. Note, however, that this construction cannot model re-declaration of variables. To use separate commands for addition to and deletion from the state space instead of a concept of scope has been proposed by R.J.R. Back [5].

An often used definition for blocks introducing x as a local variable (when syntactic Boolean terms and semantic predicates are identified) is

$$\mathsf{Blk}_x(P)(\phi) \;=\; (\forall x : P(\phi)) \;, \tag{5.1}$$

with the side condition that ϕ does not mention x. This definition is used e.g. by J.M. Morris [66] and by C.C. Morgan and P.H.B. Gardiner [25, 63] when considering data refinement in the refinement calculus.[2] One approach for making the condition 'ϕ does not mention x' precise when working with semantic predicates is to use predicates on different state spaces and interpreting it as 'x is not a component of ϕ's state space', a solution that is chosen or at least indicated in [5, 25]. We adopt this approach that requires to perform the reasoning in a heterogeneous algebra of commands. To be precise, ϕ must be embedded into the larger state space before P can be applied, for, certainly P is intended to work on the larger state space that contains x. The *demonic addition* to and the *deletion* from the state space provide separately the 'state transformations' before and after P such that definition (5.1) corresponds to

$$\mathsf{Blk}_x(P) \;=\; x^+ \,;\, P \,;\, x^- \;.$$

The new operators are just new notations for the universal quantifier $\mathbf{A}_u$ and the embedding operator ι_u. To use a new notation is intended to foster their intuitive interpretation as state transforming commands.

Suppose $u \in X^\bullet$ such that $V \cap \{\!|u|\!\} = \emptyset$. Then

---

[2] Both use a block construct with a built-in initialization condition I that is written as $|[x \mid I \bullet P]|$ by Morgan and Gardiner. They define its meaning by

$$|[x \mid I \bullet P]|(\phi) \;\stackrel{\text{def}}{=}\; (\forall x : I \Rightarrow P(\phi)) \;.$$

The intuition is that I is a condition that is satisfied by the initial value of x in the block. We have specialized their definition to the condition $I = \mathsf{true}$. A block with a non-trivial initialization condition I can be obtained by adding an initial assumption $[I]$ which results in $\mathsf{Blk}_x([I] ; P)$.

$$u^{+} \stackrel{\text{def}}{=} \mathbf{A}_u \quad \text{and} \quad u^{-} \stackrel{\text{def}}{=} \iota_u .$$

At first glance it might be a little confusing that the deletion is the embedding and the addition is the universal quantifier but this results from the reverted order of the interpretation of commands as state transformers and as predicate transformers mapping postconditions to (weakest) preconditions. Why do we call u^{+} a 'demonic' addition? The operational intuition is that a demon performs the choice of u's value. As the demon tries to achieve misbehavior whenever possible a postcondition can be guaranteed only if it holds for all possible values of u. This explains the definition of u^{+} by the universal quantifier. If on the other hand the choice of the initial value is done by an angel that tries to reach success whenever possible it suffices that there is a possible value for u. This motivates the definition of the *angelic addition command*:

$$u^{\oplus} \stackrel{\text{def}}{=} \mathbf{E}_u .$$

Like the basic homogeneous commands, the addition and deletion commands are overloaded notations for commands of different functionality. More specifically, we have for any alphabet V that does not contain any of the variables in u versions of u^{+}, $u^{\oplus}$ and u^{-}:

$$u^{+}, u^{\oplus} \in \mathsf{Com}_V^{V \cup \{\!|u|\!\}} \quad \text{and} \quad u^{-} \in \mathsf{Com}_{V \cup \{\!|u|\!\}}^{V} .$$

Before we investigate the properties of addition and deletion commands let's discuss other methods for providing operators introducing local variables. The side condition 'ϕ does not mention x' of definition (5.1) can be made precise also in a different way; it can be interpreted to require independence of ϕ from x. C.C. Morgan and P.H.B. Gardiner in [63] use definition (5.1) for blocks and add the remark that x should be renamed in $\mathsf{Blk}_x(P)$ to a 'fresh' variable x', i.e. a variable not appearing in ϕ, if it appears in ϕ. At first glance this seems promising for allowing the definition of a sensible block operator in a homogeneous space (which would be advantageous because it would remove the need for overloading the command constructors). Unfortunately, when heading for a *complete* homogeneous space, renaming is no solution. As soon as the set of variables V has been fixed we can construct predicates that depend on all the variables in V. To see why this is the case assume for the moment that all variables in V have the integers as their domain and consider the family $(\{x = 0\})_{x \in V}$ of assertions. Certainly

$$\phi \stackrel{\text{def}}{=} (\bigwedge_{x \in V} \{x = 0\})(\mathsf{true})$$

must be contained in the space of predicates, if we head for a complete space of commands. But ϕ is a predicate depending on all variables in V, for ϕ is true in a state σ if and only if $\sigma(x) = 0$ for all $x \in V$. Thus there are not always 'fresh' variables.

In [6] R.J.R. Back and J. von Wright work in a homogeneous space of predicate transformers and define blocks as follows:

$$\mathsf{Blk}_x(P)(\phi) \stackrel{\text{def}}{=} (\forall x : P(\forall x : \phi)) \ . \tag{5.2}$$

Although this definition seems more reasonable in a homogeneous space than (5.1), it is not fully satisfactory as it does not correctly model re-declaration of variables, which is observed already in [6]. For example with definition (5.2) the block $\mathsf{Blk}_x(\mathsf{Id})$ is not totally correct w.r.t. the precondition $x = 0$ and the same postcondition, in contrast to the intuitive expectation. (On the level of commands the expected identity $\mathsf{Blk}_x(\mathsf{Id}) = \mathsf{Id}$ is not valid.) The problem with definition (5.2) is that it does not capture that the value of x is left unchanged by a block containing x as local variable. A satisfactory definition of blocks in a homogeneous space must restore the old value of x.[3]

Being just new notations for them, addition and deletion commands inherit the dualization and distribution properties from the quantifiers and the embedding operator. For reference purposes we collect them once again in the next theorem.

Theorem 5.5.1 (Dualization and distribution). *Suppose* $u \in X^\bullet$.

(a) Deletion commands are dual to themselves: $(u^-)^o = u^-$.

(b) The demonic and angelic addition commands are duals: $(u^+)^o = u^\oplus$.

(c) The following two pairs are simulations: (u^-, u^+) *and* $(u^\oplus, u^-)$. *More specifically, we have the laws:*

$$u^- \, ; u^+ \leq \mathsf{Id} \quad \text{and} \quad u^+ \, ; u^- = \mathsf{Id} \ . \tag{$--+$-sim}$$

[3] In an earlier version of this book we worked with such a definition instead of using separate addition and deletion commands but we have banished it now because it resulted in rather inconvenient calculations. Our definition was given on the level of commands (that is without a direct reference to predicates) with command notation that was introduced before. The definition had a somewhat operational flavor. The idea was to catch the value of x in the initial state by the construction used in the (Span) law. Afterwards an arbitrary value was assigned to x by a demonic choice assignment (demonic choice assignment had been introduced before blocks) in order to model that x is uninitialized. Then the block's body P was started. After termination of P the old value of x was restored by assigning the initially caught value to x. Thus we had the following definition for blocks:

$$\mathsf{Blk}_x(P) \stackrel{\text{def}}{=} \bigwedge_{a \in \mathsf{Val}_x} [x^* = a^*] \, ; x :=? \, ; P \, ; x := a^* \ .$$

The simpler looking definition $\mathsf{Blk}_x(P) \stackrel{\text{def}}{=} y := x^* \ ; \ x :=? \ ; \ P \ ; \ x := y^*$ could not be used because it requires that y is a 'fresh' variable and, therefore, like (5.1) suffers from the problem that fresh variables do not always exist in a homogeneous complete space. The trick that allowed to work in a homogeneous complete space was the use of the *meta-language variable* a for saving x's value in the pre-state. While this definition provided a *demonic block operator* we had also an *angelic block operator* that played a role similar to angelic addition commands:

$$\mathsf{Blk}^d_x(P) \stackrel{\text{def}}{=} \bigvee_{a \in \mathsf{Val}_x} \{x^* = a^*\} \, ; x :=! \, ; P \, ; x := a^* \ .$$

$$u^- \,;\, u^\oplus \geq \mathsf{Id} \quad \textit{and} \quad u^\oplus \,;\, u^- = \mathsf{Id} \,. \qquad (\oplus\text{-}-\text{-}sim)$$

(d) *Deletion commands* u^- *are universally conjunctive as well as universally disjunctive (and thus also* $\bot$*-strict and* $\top$*-strict.)*

(e) *Demonic addition commands* u^+ *are universally conjunctive (and hence* $\top$*-strict). They are in general not (positively or universally) disjunctive but* $\bot$*-strict.*

(f) *Dually, angelic addition commands* $u^\oplus$ *are universally disjunctive (and thus* $\bot$*-strict). They are in general not (positively or universally) conjunctive but* $\top$*-strict.*

Proof. Properties (a)-(c) transfer from Lemma 4.4.2. (d) is a consequence of the fact that u^- has an upper as well as a lower adjoint. (e) is seen as follows: Universal conjunctivity of u^+ (and thus $\top$-strictness) follows from the fact that it has a lower adjoint (namely u^-). $\bot$-strictness is seen directly from the definition of the universal quantifier. (By the global assumption that all variables have non-empty domains the commonly known logical anomaly that $\mathbf{A}_u(\mathsf{false})$ is true if u's domain is empty does not show through here.) That u^+, i.e. universal quantification, is in general not disjunctive is a well-known logical fact: assuming that Val_u contains at most two distinct elements a, b we have $\mathbf{A}_u(u^* = a^* \vee u^* \neq a^*) \equiv \mathsf{true}$ but $\mathbf{A}_u(u^* = a^*) \vee \mathbf{A}_u(u^* \neq a^*) \equiv \mathsf{false}$. Property (f) is proved either by similar arguments or by dualizing (e). □

In a similar way the commutation properties for quantifiers and embeddings transfer to addition and deletion commands. In Lemma 4.4.3 we investigated those for single variables. In the next lemma we collect their generalization to lists of variables as refinement rules for addition and deletion commands.

Theorem 5.5.2 (Commutation of addition and deletion). *Suppose* $u, v, w \in X^\bullet$, $(x_1, \ldots, x_k) \in V^\bullet$, *and* ρ *is a permutation on* $\{1, \ldots, k\}$.

(a) *The order of the list of variables in addition and deletion commands is insignificant:*[4]

$$x_1, \ldots, x_k{}^\diamondsuit \;=\; x_{\rho(1)}, \ldots, x_{\rho(k)}{}^\diamondsuit \,, \quad \textit{for } \diamondsuit \in \{+, \oplus, -\} \,. \qquad (\diamondsuit\text{-}reorder)$$

(b) *Successive additions or deletions of the same kind can be united:*

$$u^\diamondsuit \,;\, v^\diamondsuit \;=\; u, v^\diamondsuit \,, \quad \textit{for } \diamondsuit \in \{+, \oplus, -\}, \textit{ if } u \cap v = \varepsilon \,. \qquad (\diamondsuit\text{-}union)$$

The side condition '$u \cap v = \varepsilon$*' is required to guarantee well-definedness of the left and right hand side of the rules. Two applications of this law allow to commute successive occurrences of additions or deletions of same kind.*

(c) *Addition or deletion of the empty list of variables is void:*

$$\varepsilon^\diamondsuit \;=\; \mathsf{Id} \,, \quad \textit{for } \diamondsuit \in \{+, \oplus, -\} \,. \qquad (\diamondsuit\text{-}empty)$$

[4] Strictly speaking, ($\diamondsuit$-reorder) stands for three laws that are referenced later more specifically as (+-reorder), ($\oplus$-reorder) and (−-reorder). A similar remark applies to other collective formulation of laws.

(d) *Additions commute with the deletion of other variables:*

$$u^{\triangle} \,;\, v^{-} \;=\; v^{-} \,;\, u^{\triangle} \;, \quad \textit{for } \triangle \in \{+, \oplus\}, \textit{ if } u \cap v = \varepsilon \;.$$

(△-−-comm)

(e) *There is a weak law for commuting successive demonic and angelic addition commands:*

$$u^{+} \,;\, v^{\oplus} \;\geq\; v^{\oplus} \,;\, u^{+} \;, \quad \textit{if } u \cap v = \varepsilon \;. \qquad (+\text{-}\oplus\text{-comm})$$

It has the nice intuitive interpretation that it is better to let the angel choose after the demon because it then might be able to compensate the demon's evil intentions.

(f) *The (△-−-comm) laws together with the simulation laws have corollaries for non-disjoint lists of variables. Suppose (for well-definedness of the occurring commands) that u and v as well as v and w are disjoint.*

$$u, v^{\triangle} \,;\, v, w^{-} \;=\; w^{-} \,;\, u^{\triangle} \;, \quad \textit{for } \triangle \in \{+, \oplus\}, \textit{ if } u \cap w = \varepsilon \;.$$

(△-−-general)

$$u, v^{-} \,;\, v, w^{+} \;\leq\; w^{+} \,;\, u^{-} \;, \quad \textit{if } u \cap w = \varepsilon \;. \qquad (+\text{-}-\text{-general})$$

$$u, v^{-} \,;\, v, w^{\oplus} \;\geq\; w^{\oplus} \,;\, u^{-} \;, \quad \textit{if } u \cap w = \varepsilon \;. \qquad (\oplus\text{-}-\text{-general})$$

Proof. The reorder laws in (a) follow by multiple application of the commutation laws for quantifiers and embeddings in Lemma 4.4.3, (a) & (b). The union laws in (b) and the laws in (c) are obvious from the definition of the quantifiers' generalization to lists (and the associativity of ;). The two commutation laws in (d) and the (+-⊕-comm) law in (e) are the generalization of Lemma 4.4.3, (c) & (d). To illustrate the general argument pattern we show how (e) is proved:

If $u = (x_1, \ldots, x_k)$ and $v = (y_1, \ldots, y_l)$ are disjoint lists then

$$\begin{array}{ll} & x_1, \ldots, x_k{}^{+} \,;\, y_1, \ldots, y_l{}^{\oplus} \\ = & [\text{Definitions}] \\ & \mathbf{A}_{x_1} \circ \ldots \circ \mathbf{A}_{x_k} \circ \mathbf{E}_{y_1} \circ \ldots \circ \mathbf{E}_{y_l} \\ \geq & [\text{Multiple applic. of 4.4.3, (d), } x_k \neq y_i \text{ as } u,\, v \text{ are disjoint}] \\ & \mathbf{A}_{x_1} \circ \ldots \mathbf{A}_{x_{k-1}} \circ \mathbf{E}_{y_1} \circ \ldots \circ \mathbf{E}_{y_l} \circ \mathbf{A}_{x_k} \\ \geq & [\text{Similarly for the other variable } x_i \text{ for } i = 1, \ldots, k-1] \\ & \mathbf{E}_{y_1} \circ \ldots \circ \mathbf{E}_{y_l} \circ \mathbf{A}_{x_1} \circ \ldots \circ \mathbf{A}_{x_k} \\ = & [\text{Definitions}] \\ & y_1, \ldots, y_l{}^{\oplus} \,;\, x_1, \ldots, x_k{}^{+} \;. \end{array}$$

(Strictly speaking, this is an inductive argument; but in this case an explicit induction does not contribute much for increasing confidence. Nevertheless, one should possibly check that the laws are valid for empty lists as well. Fortunately the laws hold trivially if u or v is the empty list since $\varepsilon^{+} = \varepsilon^{\oplus} = \varepsilon^{-} = \mathsf{Id}$.)

The reasoning pattern for the laws in (f) is as follows. First the commands at the left hand side are cut to pieces by the union laws and the fitting simulation property from Theorem 5.5.1 is applied to the middle part. Afterwards the appropriate commutation laws is applied. As an example we explicate the proof for (+−−-general):

If $u \cap w = \varepsilon$ we have

$$
\begin{array}{ll}
 & u, v^- \; ; v, w^+ \\
= & [(\text{−-union}), (\text{+-union})] \\
 & u^- \; ; v^- \; ; v^+ \; ; w^+ \\
\leq & [(\text{−-+-sim}) \text{ tells us that } v^- \; ; v^+ \; \leq \; \mathsf{Id}] \\
 & u^- \; ; w^+ \\
= & [\text{+−−-comm}] \\
 & w^+ \; ; u^- \; .
\end{array}
$$

This completes the proof. □

Addition and deletion commands commute with assertions, assumptions and assignments whenever the occurring variables, predicates, and valuation functions can be understood on both the small and the large state space. Formally this means that the predicates and valuation functions occurring in the homogeneous commands on the larger state space must be embeddings of predicates and valuation functions on the smaller state space. (Recall that this is the case if and only if they are independent of the new variables.) For the variables that occur on the left hand side of an assignment this means distinctness from the variables introduced by the addition command. Apart from these laws we consider initialization and finalization of variables in the next theorem.

Theorem 5.5.3 (Addition, deletion and homogeneous commands). *Let $u \in X^\bullet$ be a list of distinct new variables, i.e. $V \cap \{\!|u|\!\} = \emptyset$. Let further be $\phi \in \mathsf{Pred}_V$, $v \in V^\bullet$, $e \in \mathsf{Valfct}^u_V$, $f \in \mathsf{Valfct}^v_V$, $g \in \mathsf{Valfct}^u_{V \cup \{\!|u|\!\}}$, and $h \in \mathsf{Valfct}^v_{V \cup \{\!|u|\!\}}$.*

(a) Addition commands commute with assertions, assumptions and assignments in the following sense:

$$u^\triangle \; ; \{\iota_u(\phi)\} \;=\; \{\phi\} \; ; u^\triangle \;, \quad \textit{for } \triangle \in \{+, \oplus\} \;. \qquad \textit{(Initial-assert)}$$

$$u^\triangle \; ; [\iota_u(\phi)] \;=\; [\phi] \; ; u^\triangle \;, \quad \textit{for } \triangle \in \{+, \oplus\} \;. \qquad \textit{(Initial-assume)}$$

$$u^\triangle \; ; v := \iota_u(f) \;=\; v := f \; ; u^\triangle \;, \quad \textit{for } \triangle \in \{+, \oplus\}, \textit{ if } u \cap v = \varepsilon \;. \qquad \textit{(Initial-assign)}$$

(b) In the same way deletion commands commute with assertions, assumptions and assignments:

$$u^- \; ; \{\phi\} \;=\; \{\iota_u(\phi)\} \; ; u^- \;. \qquad \textit{(Final-assert)}$$

$$u^- \,;\, [\phi] \;=\; [\iota_u(\phi)] \,;\, u^- \;. \qquad \textit{(Final-assume)}$$
$$u^- \,;\, v := f \;=\; v := \iota_u(f) \,;\, u^- \;,\;\; \textit{if } u \cap v = \varepsilon \;. \qquad \textit{(Final-assign)}$$

(c) *Besides the 'trivial' commutation properties in (a) we have the following more interesting ones for demonic addition commands with assertions and angelic addition commands with assumptions:*

$$u^+ \,;\, \{\phi\} \;=\; \{\mathbf{A}_u(\phi)\} \,;\, u^+ \;. \qquad \textit{(+-assert)}$$
$$u^\oplus \,;\, [\phi] \;=\; [\mathbf{A}_u(\phi)] \,;\, u^\oplus \;. \qquad \textit{(}\oplus\textit{-assume)}$$

(d) *A final assignment to local variables is void:*

$$u := g \,;\, u^- \;=\; u^- \;. \qquad \textit{(Finalization)}$$
$$u, v := g, h \,;\, u^- \;=\; v := h \,;\, u^- \;,\;\; \textit{if } u \cap v = \varepsilon \;. \qquad \textit{(Finalization1)}$$

Disjointness of u and v is assumed in (Finalization1) only for well-definedness purposes.

(e) *An initial assignment to a local variable improves a demonic and diminishes an angelic addition:*

$$u^+ \leq u^+ \,;\, u := g \;\;\textit{and}\;\; u^\oplus \geq u^\oplus \,;\, u := g \;. \qquad \textit{(Initialization)}$$

The intuition is that the influence from the demon's or angel's choice is reduced by the initialization. It is even totally removed if the initialization is proper, *i.e. does not depend on the value chosen by the demon or angel:*

$$u^+ \,;\, u := \iota_u(e) \;=\; u^\oplus \,;\, u := \iota_u(e) \;. \qquad \textit{(Proper-ini)}$$

(f) *An assumption $[\phi]$ following a demonic addition command can control the demon's choice. The intuition is that the demon must choose a value for u that satisfies ϕ because otherwise immediate miraculous success arises (which of course it tries to avoid). The next law is concerned with this situation and shows that an angelic choice is still better provided the demon can choose a value making ϕ true.*

$$u^+ \,;\, [\phi] \;\leq\; [\mathbf{E}_u(\phi)] \,;\, u^\oplus \;. \qquad \textit{(Restrict-demon)}$$

There is also the dual law about restricting the angel's choice by assertions:

$$u^\oplus \,;\, \{\phi\} \;\geq\; \{\mathbf{E}_u(\phi)\} \,;\, u^+ \;. \qquad \textit{(Restrict-angel)}$$

Proof. First of all we prove the (Initial-assert) law for demonic additions by an explicit calculation (for $\psi \in \mathsf{Pred}_{V\cup\{\!|u|\!\}}$):

$$(u^+ \,;\, \{\iota_u(\phi)\})(\psi) \underset{\uparrow\,[\text{Defs}]}{=} u^+(\iota_u(\phi) \wedge \psi) \underset{\uparrow\,[u^+ \text{ conjunctive}]}{=} u^+(\iota_u(\phi)) \wedge u^+(\psi)$$
$$\underset{\uparrow\,[u^+ \,;\, \iota_u = \mathsf{Id}]}{=} \phi \wedge u^+(\psi) \underset{\uparrow\,[\text{Defs}]}{=} (\{\phi\} \,;\, u^+)(\psi) \;.$$

One inequality of (Initial-assume) is proved explicitly as well (for $\psi \in \mathsf{Pred}_{V\cup\{\!|u|\!\}}$):

$$\begin{aligned}
(u^+ ; [\iota_u(\phi)])(\psi) &\underset{\substack{\uparrow\\ \text{[Defs]}}}{=} u^+(\overline{\iota_u(\phi)} \vee \psi) \underset{\substack{\uparrow\\ \text{[Monotonicity]}}}{\geq} u^+(\overline{\iota_u(\phi)}) \vee u^+(\psi) \\
&\underset{\substack{\uparrow\\ [\iota_u \text{ is self-dual}]}}{=} u^+(\iota_u(\overline{\phi})) \vee u^+(\psi) \underset{\substack{\uparrow\\ [u^+ ;\, \iota_u = \mathsf{Id}]}}{=} \overline{\phi} \vee u^+(\psi) \\
&\underset{\substack{\uparrow\\ \text{[Defs]}}}{=} ([\phi] ; u^+)(\psi) .
\end{aligned}$$

The other inequality can be proved more elegantly by exploiting that assertions and assumptions (of the same predicate) form a simulation, using the (Initial-assert) law that has already been established:

$$\begin{aligned}
u^+ ; [\iota_u(\phi)] &\underset{\substack{\uparrow\\ \text{[Simulation]}}}{\leq} [\phi] ; \{\phi\} ; u^+ ; [\iota_u(\phi)] \underset{\substack{\uparrow\\ \text{[Initial-assert]}}}{=} [\phi] ; u^+ ; \{\iota_u(\phi)\} ; [\iota_u(\phi)] \\
&\underset{\substack{\uparrow\\ \text{[Simulation]}}}{\leq} [\phi] ; u^+ .
\end{aligned}$$

(Initial-assert) and (Initial-assume) for angelic addition commands follow by duality.

Exploiting the laws established up to now, (Final-assert) is easily proved by

$$\begin{aligned}
u^- ; \{\phi\} &\underset{\substack{\uparrow\\ [u^+ ;\, u^- = \mathsf{Id}]}}{=} u^- ; \{\phi\} ; u^+ ; u^- \underset{\substack{\uparrow\\ \text{[Initial-assert]}}}{=} u^- ; u^+ ; \{\iota_u(\phi)\} ; u^- \\
&\underset{\substack{\uparrow\\ [u^- ;\, u^+ \leq \mathsf{Id}]}}{\leq} \{\iota_u(\phi)\} ; u^-
\end{aligned}$$

and the analogous calculation with $u^\oplus$ instead of u^+. (Final-assume) follows from (Final-assert) by duality.

(Initial-assign) for demonic addition commands is essentially the distribution law for substitution over universal quantification: for any $\psi \in \mathsf{Pred}_{V \cup \{\!|u|\!\}}$ we have

$$\begin{aligned}
(u^+ ; v := \iota_u(f))(\psi) &\underset{\substack{\uparrow\\ \text{[Defs]}}}{=} \mathbf{A}_u(\psi[\iota_u(f)/v]) \underset{\substack{\uparrow\\ \text{[Lemma 4.4.4]}}}{=} \mathbf{A}_u(\psi)[f/v] \\
&\underset{\substack{\uparrow\\ \text{[Defs]}}}{=} (v := f ; u^+)(\psi) .
\end{aligned}$$

(Initial-assign) for angelic addition commands follows in the same way from the distribution law for the existential quantifier. It is also clear by duality. (Final-assign) can be proved from (Initial-assign) like (Final-assert) was proved from (Initial-assert) (or of course directly).

The law (+-assert) is proved by the following explicit calculation for $\psi \in \mathsf{Pred}_V$:

$$\begin{aligned}(u^+ \,;\, \{\phi\})(\psi) &\underset{\substack{\uparrow\\ [\text{Defs}]}}{=} u^+(\phi \wedge \psi) \underset{\substack{\uparrow\\ [u^+ \text{ is conjunctive}]}}{=} u^+(\phi) \wedge u^+(\psi)\\ &\underset{\substack{\uparrow\\ [\text{Defs}]}}{=} (\{\mathbf{A}_u(\phi)\} \,;\, u^+)(\psi)\ .\end{aligned}$$

($\oplus$-assume) follows by dualization.

Let's now consider the proof of (Finalization1). For any $\psi \in \mathsf{Pred}_V$ we have:

$$\begin{aligned}(u, v := g, h \,;\, u^-)(\psi) &\underset{\substack{\uparrow\\ [\text{Defs}]}}{=} \iota_u(\psi)[g, h/u, v] \underset{\substack{\uparrow\\ [\iota_u(\psi) \text{ idp. } u]}}{=} \iota_u(\psi)[h/v]\\ &\underset{\substack{\uparrow\\ [\text{Defs}]}}{=} (v := h \,;\, u^-)(\psi)\ .\end{aligned}$$

(Finalization) is a corollary of the (Finalization1) law for empty lists v and h because – by (Empty-asg1) – $\varepsilon := \varepsilon = \mathsf{Id}$.

The property claimed for demonic addition commands in the (Initialization) law follows easily from the (Finalization) law by exploiting that (u^-, u^+) is a simulation:

$$u^+ \underset{\substack{\uparrow\\ [u^+ \,;\, u^- = \mathsf{Id}]}}{=} u^+ \,;\, u^- \,;\, u^+ \underset{\substack{\uparrow\\ [\text{Finalization}]}}{=} u^+ \,;\, u := g \,;\, u^- \,;\, u^+ \underset{\substack{\uparrow\\ [u^- \,;\, u^+ \leq \mathsf{Id}]}}{\leq} u^+ \,;\, u := g\ .$$

The inequality claimed for angelic addition commands follows by duality.

By unfolding the definitions one sees that the claim of law (Proper-ini) is that for all $\phi \in \mathsf{Pred}_{V \cup \{\!|u|\!\}}$ the identity $\mathbf{A}_u(\phi[\iota_u(e)/u]) = \mathbf{E}_u(\phi[\iota_u(e)/u])$ holds. The predicate $\phi[\iota_u(e)/u]$ is independent of u. This is easily demonstrated by showing the criterion in Lemma 4.3.5, (b):

$$\phi[\iota_u(e)/u][f/u] \underset{\substack{\uparrow\\ [\text{S-comb}]}}{=} \phi[\iota_u(e)[f/u]/u] \underset{\substack{\uparrow\\ [\iota_u(e) \text{ idp. } u]}}{=} \phi[\iota_u(e)/u]$$

(for $f \in \mathsf{Valfct}^u_{V \cup \{\!|u|\!\}}$). Thus there is $\psi \in \mathsf{Pred}_V$ such that $\iota_u(\psi) = \phi[\iota_u(e)/u]$. Now,

$$\mathbf{A}_u(\phi[\iota_u(e)/u]) \underset{\substack{\uparrow\\ [\text{Choice } \psi]}}{=} \mathbf{A}_u(\iota_u(\psi)) \underset{\substack{\uparrow\\ [\mathbf{A}_u \circ \iota_u = \mathsf{Id}]}}{=} \psi = \mathbf{E}_u(\iota_u(\psi))$$

$$\underset{\substack{\uparrow \\ [\text{Choice } \psi]}}{=} \mathbf{E}_u(\phi[\iota_u(e)/u]) \ ,$$

which shows (Proper-ini).

By unfolding the definitions one sees that (Restrict-demon) holds if and only if for all $\psi \in \mathsf{Pred}_{V \cup \{\!\{u\}\!\}}$ the inequality $\mathbf{A}_u(\overline{\phi} \vee \psi) \leq \overline{\mathbf{E}_u(\phi)} \vee \mathbf{E}_u(\psi)$ is valid. For a given $\psi \in \mathsf{Pred}_{V \cup \{\!\{u\}\!\}}$ one proves this as follows:

$$
\begin{array}{ll}
 & \mathbf{A}_u(\overline{\phi} \vee \psi) \ \leq \ \overline{\mathbf{E}_u(\phi)} \vee \mathbf{E}_u(\psi) \\
\text{iff} & [(x \wedge .\,, \overline{x} \vee .\,) \text{ is Galois connection}] \\
 & \mathbf{E}_u(\phi) \wedge \mathbf{A}_u(\overline{\phi} \vee \psi) \ \leq \ \mathbf{E}_u(\psi) \\
\text{iff} & [(x \wedge .\,, \overline{x} \vee .\,) \text{ is Galois connection}] \\
 & \mathbf{E}_u(\phi) \ \leq \ \mathbf{E}_u(\psi) \vee \overline{\mathbf{A}_u(\overline{\phi} \vee \psi)} \\
\text{iff} & [\mathbf{E}_u \text{ is dual of } \mathbf{A}_u, \text{ de Morgan}] \\
 & \mathbf{E}_u(\phi) \ \leq \ \mathbf{E}_u(\psi) \vee \mathbf{E}_u(\phi \wedge \overline{\psi}) \\
\text{iff} & [\mathbf{E}_u \text{ is universally disjunctive}] \\
 & \mathbf{E}_u(\phi) \ \leq \ \mathbf{E}_u(\psi \vee (\phi \wedge \overline{\psi})) \\
\Leftarrow & [\mathbf{E}_u \text{ is monotonic}] \\
 & \phi \ \leq \ \psi \vee (\phi \wedge \overline{\psi}) \\
\text{iff} & [(x \wedge .\,, \overline{x} \vee .\,) \text{ is Galois connection}] \\
 & \phi \wedge \overline{\psi} \ \leq \ \phi \wedge \overline{\psi} \ .
\end{array}
$$

Note that already after the first step the property to be proved is obvious in the logical interpretation. The law (Restrict-angel) is the dual of (Restrict-demon). □

The reader might wonder whether, in addition to the laws in (b), there are also general commutation properties for other situations in which addition or deletion commands are followed or preceded by an assertion or assumption. In these cases only inequalities are valid in general. They can be obtained from the laws in (a) by strengthening or weakening the assertion or assumption and applying their monotonicity resp. antitonicity. Thus they deserve no explicit formulation. An example is the law

$$u^+ \ ; [\phi] \ \leq \ [\mathbf{A}_u(\phi)] \ ; u^+ \ ,$$

which is obtained by the following calculation:

$$
\begin{array}{ll}
 & u^+ \ ; [\phi] \\
\leq & [(\text{Assume-antitonic}) \colon \phi \geq \mathbf{A}_u(\phi)] \\
 & u^+ \ ; [\mathbf{A}_u(\phi)]
\end{array}
$$

Table 5.1. Distribution properties of basic commands

	$\bot$-strict	$\top$-strict	positive-$\wedge$	universal-$\wedge$	positive-$\vee$	universal-$\vee$
$\{\phi\}$	yes	no	yes	no	yes	yes
$[\phi]$	no	yes	yes	yes	yes	no
$u := e$	yes	yes	yes	yes	yes	yes
u^+	yes	yes	yes	yes	no	no
$u^\oplus$	yes	yes	no	no	yes	yes
u^-	yes	yes	yes	yes	yes	yes

$=$ [Initial-assume]
$[\mathbf{A}_u(\phi)]\ ;\ u^+ .$

5.6 Distribution Properties

In this section we summarize the distribution properties of the basic commands and investigate which distribution properties are preserved by the composition operators. Moreover, we explore the distribution properties of the composition operators itself, i.e. as operators working on the space of commands.

5.6.1 Basic Commands

Table 5.1 summarizes the distribution properties of the basic commands $\{\phi\}$, $[\phi]$, $u := e$, u^+, $u^\oplus$, and u^- (were $\phi \in \mathsf{Pred}_V$, $u \in V^\bullet$ and $e \in \mathsf{Valfct}_V^u$). For each of the commands it tells whether it is $\bot$-strict, $\top$-strict, positively or universally disjunctive and positively or universally conjunctive. An entry 'yes' means that the property always holds, a 'no' means that there are counter-examples.

5.6.2 Preservation of Distribution Properties

Table 5.2 is concerned with the question which distribution properties are preserved by the operators ;, $\wedge$ and $\vee$ on commands. For each property mentioned in the headline of Table 5.2 it is indicated whether the predicate transformers $\pi\ ;\ \pi'$, $\pi \wedge \pi'$ and $\pi \vee \pi'$ have this property if both π and π' enjoy it.

- Sequential composition preserves all the properties. The following calculation that shows preservation of $\bot$-strictness is quite typical.

$$(\pi\ ;\ \pi')(\bot) \quad = \quad \pi(\pi'(\bot)) \quad = \quad \pi(\bot) \quad = \quad \bot\ .$$

Table 5.2. Preservation of distribution properties

	⊥-strict	⊤-strict	positive-∧	universal-∧	positive-∨	universal-∨
;	yes	yes	yes	yes	yes	yes
∧	yes	yes	yes	yes	no	no
∨	yes	yes	no	no	yes	yes

- $\wedge$ preserves $\bot$-strictness as well as $\top$-strictness. E.g. if π and π' are $\top$-strict then

  $$(\pi \wedge \pi')(\top) \;=\; \pi(\top) \wedge \pi'(\top) \;=\; \top \wedge \top \;=\; \top\,.$$

  It preserves all meet properties but no join properties.

  Example 5.6.1. Suppose $x \in V$ is a variable the domain of which contains at least the two distinct elements a and b. Let $\pi = (x := a^*)$ and $\pi' = (x := b^*)$. Then, clearly, π and π' are (universally) disjunctive. However, $\pi \wedge \pi'$ is not disjunctive because $(\pi \wedge \pi')(x^* = a^* \vee x^* = b^*)$ equals

  $$(a^* = a^* \vee a^* = b^*) \wedge (b^* = a^* \vee b^* = b^*)\ ,$$

  which is true, but $(\pi \wedge \pi')(x^* = a^*) \vee (\pi \wedge \pi')(x^* = b^*)$ equals

  $$(a^* = a^* \wedge b^* = a^*) \vee (a^* = b^* \wedge b^* = b^*)\ ,$$

  which is false. □

- The preservation properties of $\vee$ are obtained by dualization.

5.6.3 Distribution Properties of Composition Operators

Table 5.3 examines the distribution properties of the operators ;, $\wedge$ and $\vee$ itself. For a fixed $\pi \in \mathsf{PTrans}$ we investigate the operators $\pi\ ;\ .\,,\ .\ ;\ \pi$ etc.

- Functional composition in its second argument, i.e. $P\ ;\ .$ (as an operator on commands), enjoys a distribution property if and only if P (as an operator on predicates) has the corresponding property. We show the proof for universal disjunctivity; the proof for the other properties is analogous.
  Proof. If π is universally disjunctive (on predicates) then for any family $(\pi_i)_{i\in I}$ (where I is an arbitrary index set) and any predicate ϕ we have

  $$(\pi\ ;\ \vee_i\,\pi_i)(\phi) \underset{\substack{\uparrow\\ [\text{Def}]}}{=} \pi((\vee_i\,\pi_i)(\phi)) \underset{\substack{\uparrow\\ [\text{Pointwise order}]}}{=} \pi(\vee_i\,\pi_i(\phi)) \underset{\substack{\uparrow\\ [\pi\ \text{disj.}]}}{=} \vee_i\ \pi(\pi_i(\phi))$$

  $$\underset{\substack{\uparrow\\ [\text{Def}]}}{=} \vee_i\ (\pi\ ;\ \pi_i)(\phi) \underset{\substack{\uparrow\\ [\text{Pointwise order}]}}{=} (\vee_i\,(\pi\ ;\ \pi_i))(\phi)\ ,$$

which shows that π ; . is universally disjunctive as well. If, on the other hand, π is not disjunctive then there is an index set I and a family $(\phi_i)_{i\in I}$ of predicates such that $\pi(\bigvee_i \phi_i) \neq \bigvee_i \pi(\phi_i)$. Choose for any $i \in I$, π_i to be the constant predicate transformer which maps any predicate to ϕ_i. Then we have for an arbitrary predicate ϕ

$$\begin{aligned}(\pi ; (\bigvee_i \pi_i))(\phi) &\underset{\substack{\uparrow \\ \text{[As above]}}}{=} \pi(\bigvee_i \pi_i(\phi)) \underset{\substack{\uparrow \\ \text{[Choice } \pi_i\text{]}}}{=} \pi(\bigvee_i \phi_i) \underset{\substack{\uparrow \\ \text{[Choice } (\phi_i)_i\text{]}}}{\neq} \bigvee_i \pi(\phi_i) \\ &\underset{\substack{\uparrow \\ \text{[Choice } \pi_i\text{]}}}{=} \bigvee_i \pi(\pi_i(\phi)) \underset{\substack{\uparrow \\ \text{[As above]}}}{=} (\bigvee_i (\pi ; \pi_i))(\phi) ,\end{aligned}$$

which shows that π ; . is not disjunctive. □

- Functional composition in its first argument (i.e. . ; π) distributes over arbitrary pointwise extensions. Hence, it has all distribution properties. Again the proof for universal disjunctivity is typical.
  Proof. For all families $(\pi_i)_{i\in I}$ of predicate transformers and predicates ϕ,

$$\begin{aligned}((\bigvee_i \pi_i) ; \pi)(\phi) &\underset{\substack{\uparrow \\ \text{[Def]}}}{=} (\bigvee_i \pi_i)(\pi(\phi)) \underset{\substack{\uparrow \\ \text{[Pointwise order]}}}{=} \bigvee_i \pi_i(\pi(\phi)) \underset{\substack{\uparrow \\ \text{[Def]}}}{=} \bigvee_i (\pi_i ; \pi)(\phi) \\ &\underset{\substack{\uparrow \\ \text{[Pointwise order]}}}{=} (\bigvee_i (\pi_i ; \pi))(\phi) .\end{aligned}$$

  This shows that . ; π is universally disjunctive. □

- By the (JDI) law (see p. 14) $\pi \wedge$. distributes over arbitrary joins and is thus universally disjunctive, positively disjunctive and $\bot$-strict. It is positively conjunctive (see p. 13) but in general not $\top$-strict as $\bot \wedge \top = \bot \neq \top$. Hence, in general it is also not universally conjunctive. . $\wedge\, \pi$ has the same distribution properties by commutativity of $\wedge$.
- $\vee$ enjoys the dual properties.

R.J.R. Back gives in [4] a table similar to Table 5.1 and Table 5.2.

5.7 Derived Commands

In this section we study some derived commands. The motivation is that the new commands are convenient for specifying semantics of programming languages and machines and for reasoning about the correctness of translation. *Derived* means that the commands are defined on the command level without a direct reference to the predicate transformer interpretation and that all properties are proved by considerations on the command level using the laws

Table 5.3. Distribution properties of predicate transformer operators

	$\bot$-strict	$\top$-strict	positive-$\wedge$	universal-$\wedge$	positive-$\vee$	universal-$\vee$
π ; .	iff π is $\bot$-strict	iff π is $\top$-strict	iff π is positive-$\wedge$	iff π is universal-$\wedge$	iff π is positive-$\vee$	iff π is universal-$\vee$
. ; π	yes	yes	yes	yes	yes	yes
$\pi \wedge .$ $. \wedge \pi$	yes	no	yes	no	yes	yes
$\pi \vee .$ $. \vee \pi$	no	yes	yes	yes	yes	no

that already have been shown. In our opinion this yields clearer and shorter proofs in most cases. It also means that an axiomatization of the command algebra need not contain the derived commands as basic notions but can introduce them as abbreviations without own axioms.

5.7.1 Choice Assignments

The intuitive behavior of an angelic or demonic choice assignment to a list u of variables is that the angel or demon chooses a value to be assigned to u. The behavior is thus very similar to angelic and demonic addition commands. The difference is that choice assignments are homogeneous:

$$u :=?,\ u :=! \ \in \ \mathsf{Com}_V^V \ .$$

Given the strong intuitive similarity of choice assignments and addition commands, it is not astounding that choice assignment can easily be defined in terms of addition and deletion commands. Suppose $u \in V^\bullet$ is a list of distinct variable symbols. *Demonic choice assignments*, written $u :=?$, and their duals *angelic choice assignments*, written $u :=!$ are then defined by

$$u :=? \ \stackrel{\text{def}}{=} \ u^- \,;\, u^+ \quad \text{and} \quad u :=! \ \stackrel{\text{def}}{=} \ u^- \,;\, u^\oplus \ .$$

Our motivation for considering choice assignments is that they provide a convenient and clear way to specify the behavior of machine instructions for which the contents of certain registers is left unspecified by the manufacturer of the processor.

There is an equivalent characterization for choice assignments in terms of assignments and meet and join (i.e. demonic and angelic choice) that more directly captures the intuition about their behavior.

Lemma 5.7.1 (Equivalent characterization). *Let $u \in V^\bullet$. Then*

$$u :=? \ = \ \textstyle\bigwedge_{a \in \mathsf{Val}_u} u := a^* \quad \textit{and} \quad u :=! \ = \ \textstyle\bigvee_{a \in \mathsf{Val}_u} u := a^* \ . \qquad \textit{(Choice)}$$

It is easy to see that the choice assignment commands are just the homogeneous quantifiers $\forall_u$ and $\exists_u$ defined in Sect. 4. Thus the relationship of homogeneous and inhomogeneous quantifiers (Lemma 4.4.2) proves the result. However, to keep the promise given at the beginning of this section, we give also a proof on the command level. It is the rare example of a proof that is more complex than a proof taking the predicate transformer interpretation directly into account.

Proof. We prove the characterization for demonic choice assignments. For angelic choice assignments it follows by duality. First of all,

$$\bigwedge_a u := a^* \underset{\substack{\uparrow \\ [\text{--}\oplus\text{-sim}]}}{\geq} \bigwedge_a u := a^* \,;\, u^- \,;\, u^+ \underset{\substack{\uparrow \\ [\text{Finalization}]}}{=} \bigwedge_a u^- \,;\, u^+ \underset{\substack{\uparrow \\ [\text{Glb singleton}]}}{=} u^- \,;\, u^+ \underset{\substack{\uparrow \\ [\text{Def}]}}{=} u :=? \,.$$

For proving the other inequality we observe first that

$$\bigwedge_a u := a^* \underset{\substack{\uparrow \\ [\text{Assume}]}}{\leq} \bigwedge_a [u^* = a^*] \,;\, u := a^* \underset{\substack{\uparrow \\ [\text{Assign-assume3}]}}{=} \bigwedge_a [u^* = a^*] \underset{\substack{\uparrow \\ [\text{Span1}]}}{=} \mathsf{Id} \,.$$

Moreover,

$$u := a^* \underset{\substack{\uparrow \\ [\text{--+-sim}]}}{\geq} u^- \,;\, u^+ \,;\, u := a^* \underset{\substack{\uparrow \\ [\text{Proper-ini}]}}{=} u^- \,;\, u^\oplus \,;\, u := a^* \underset{\substack{\uparrow \\ [\oplus\text{---sim}]}}{\geq} u := a^* \,,$$

which shows in particular that $u := a^*$ equals $u^- \,;\, u^+ \,;\, u := a^*$ for all a. Thus

$$\bigwedge_a u := a^* \underset{\substack{\uparrow \\ [\text{Above eq.}]}}{=} \bigwedge_a u^- \,;\, u^+ \,;\, u := a^* \underset{\substack{\uparrow \\ [u^-, u^+ \text{ conjunctive}]}}{=} u^- \,;\, u^+ \,;\, \bigwedge_a u := a^* \underset{\substack{\uparrow \\ [\text{Above ineq.}]}}{\leq} u^- \,;\, u^+ \underset{\substack{\uparrow \\ [\text{Def}]}}{=} u :=? \,,$$

which establishes the remaining inequality. □

The dualization and distribution properties of choice assignments follow easily from the corresponding properties of deletion and addition commands.

Theorem 5.7.2 (Dualization and distribution). *Suppose $u \in V^\bullet$.*

(a) Demonic and angelic choice assignments are dual to each other:

$$(u :=?)^\circ = u :=! \quad \textit{and} \quad (u :=!)^\circ = u :=? \,.$$

(b) $(u :=!, u :=?)$ is a simulation, i.e. we have the laws

$$u :=! \,;\, u :=? \leq \mathsf{Id} \quad \textit{and} \quad u :=? \,;\, u :=! \geq \mathsf{Id} \,. \qquad (!\text{-}?\text{-}sim)$$

(c) *Demonic choice assignments are* $\bot$- *and* $\top$-*strict and universally conjunctive.*
(d) *Angelic choice assignments are* $\bot$- *and* $\top$-*strict and universally disjunctive.*

Proof. Result (a) follows from the rule that the dual of a sequential composition is the sequential composition of the duals, the self-duality of u^-, and the fact that u^+ is the dual of $u^\oplus$.

Property (b) follows from Lemma 3.4.1 about the sequential composition of Galois connections since (u^-, u^+) and $(u^\oplus, u^-)$ are simulations.

The distribution properties in (c) and (d) follow from the distribution properties of deletion and addition commands and the fact that ; preserves all those properties (see Table 5.2, p. 68). □

Let us now explore the laws for choice assignments. In order to shorten the presentation we state the laws for demonic choice assignments only. The laws for angelic choice assignments can be obtained by dualization. Whenever we speak about choice assignments without qualifying them as demonic or angelic we refer to demonic ones. First of all we establish some elementary facts.

Theorem 5.7.3 (Set laws). *Let* $u, v \in V^\bullet$, $(x_1, \ldots, x_n) \in V^\bullet$ *and* ρ *be an arbitrary permutation of* $\{1, \ldots, n\}$.

(a) *The order of the variables in a choice assignment is immaterial:*

$$x_1, \ldots, x_n :=? \quad = \quad x_{\rho(1)}, \ldots, x_{\rho(n)} :=? \ . \qquad \textit{(Ch-reorder)}$$

(b) *Successive choice assignments of same kind can be combined:*

$$u :=? \ ; v :=? \quad = \quad u \cup v :=? \ . \qquad \textit{(Ch-union)}$$

(c) *Removing variables from the left hand side improves choice assignments; they can always be compared to* Id*:*

$$u \cup v :=? \quad \leq \quad u :=? \quad \leq \quad \varepsilon :=? \quad = \quad \mathsf{Id} \ . \qquad \textit{(Ch-Id)}$$

Proof. The reorder law follows from the reorder laws for deletions and additions.

For the proof of (Ch-union) assume that w is a list containing the common variables in u and v and that u and v are given as $u = u', w$ and $v = w, v'$ for suitably chosen lists u', v'. (We can assume this situation without loss of generality by the reorder law). Then we have:

$$
\begin{aligned}
& u', w :=? \ ; w, v' :=? \\
= \quad & [\Diamond\text{-union}] \\
& u', w^- \ ; u'^+ \ ; w^+ \ ; w^- \ ; v'^- \ ; w, v'^+ \\
= \quad & [\text{--+-sim}] \\
& u', w^- \ ; u'^+ \ ; v'^- \ ; w, v'^+
\end{aligned}
$$

$$
\begin{aligned}
&= \quad [+\!-\!-\text{-comm}] \\
&\quad u', w^- \;;\; v'^- \;;\; u'^+ \;;\; w, v'^+ \\
&= \quad [\Diamond\text{-union}] \\
&\quad u', w, v'^+ \;;\; u', w, v'^+ \;,
\end{aligned}
$$

which proves (Ch-union). $\varepsilon :=? = \mathsf{Id}$ follows from ($\Diamond$-empty) and $u :=? \leq \mathsf{Id}$ is immediate from (−−+-sim). The remaining first inequality of (Ch-Id) now is shown by:

$$
\underset{\substack{\uparrow \\ [\text{Ch-union}]}}{} u \cup v :=? \;\underset{\substack{\uparrow\\ [\text{Ch-union}]}}{=}\; u :=? \,;\, v :=? \;\underset{\substack{\uparrow\\ [v :=? \,\leq\, \mathsf{Id}]}}{\leq}\; u :=? \;. \qquad \square
$$

(Ch-reorder) shows that the choice assignment operator $\,.\, :=?$ can be considered to work on sets of variables rather than lists, informally speaking. Combining two successive choice assignments corresponds to the union of the sets of variables, hence the name of the law (Ch-union). We apply the reorder law in subsequent calculations tacitly without explicit mention because it is a fairly basic fact.

Theorem 5.7.4 (Commutation with basic commands). *Let* $u, v \in V^\bullet$, $e \in \mathsf{Valfct}^u_{V\setminus\{\!|u|\!\}}$, $f \in \mathsf{Valfct}^v_{V\setminus\{\!|u|\!\}}$, *and* $\phi \in \mathsf{Pred}_{V\setminus\{\!|u|\!\}}$.

(a) Choice assignments to the variables u commute with assertions, assumptions, and assignments to other variables, provided the occurring predicates and valuation functions are independent of u:

$$\{\iota_u(\phi)\} \;;\; u :=? \;=\; u :=? \;;\; \{\iota_u(\phi)\} \;. \qquad \textit{(Ch-assert1)}$$

$$[\iota_u(\phi)] \;;\; u :=? \;=\; u :=? \;;\; [\iota_u(\phi)] \;. \qquad \textit{(Ch-assume1)}$$

$$v := \iota_u(f) \;;\; u :=? \;=\; u :=? \;;\; v := \iota_u(f) \;, \quad \textit{if } u \cap v = \varepsilon \;. \qquad \textit{(Ch-asg)}$$

(b) They commute with deletion commands and demonic addition commands concerning different variables:

$$v^- \;;\; u :=? \;=\; u :=? \;;\; v^- \;, \quad \textit{if } u \cap v = \varepsilon \;. \qquad \textit{(Final-ch)}$$

$$v^+ \;;\; u :=? \;=\; u :=? \;;\; v^+ \;, \quad \textit{if } u \cap v = \varepsilon \;. \qquad \textit{(Initial-ch-=)}$$

Only an inequality holds in general for the commutation with angelic addition commands. It is a further instance of the intuition that is better to let the angel choose after the demon.

$$v^\oplus \;;\; u :=? \;\leq\; u :=? \;;\; v^\oplus \;, \quad \textit{if } u \cap v = \varepsilon \;. \qquad \textit{(Initial-ch-}\neq\textit{)}$$

Proof. (Ch-assert1), (Ch-assume) and (Ch-asg) follow from the corresponding (Initial-...) and (Final-...) laws. The little calculation

$$
\{\iota_u(\phi)\} \;;\; u :=? \;\underset{\substack{\uparrow\\ [\text{Def}]}}{=}\; \{\iota_u(\phi)\} \;;\; u^- \;;\; u^+ \;\underset{\substack{\uparrow\\ [\text{Final-assert}]}}{=}\; u^- \;;\; \{\phi\} \;;\; u^+
$$

$$\underset{\substack{\uparrow\\ \text{[Initial-assert]}}}{=} u^- \,;\, u^+ \,;\, \{\iota_u(\phi)\} \underset{\substack{\uparrow\\ \text{[Def]}}}{=} u :=?\,;\, \{\iota_u(\phi)\}\ ,$$

for instance, proves (Ch-assert1). (Final-ch) follows easily from the commutation laws for additions and deletions:

$$v^- \,;\, u :=? \underset{\substack{\uparrow\\ \text{[Def]}}}{=} v^- \,;\, u^- \,;\, u^+ \underset{\substack{\uparrow\\ \text{[−−−union]}}}{=} u^- \,;\, v^- \,;\, u^+ \underset{\substack{\uparrow\\ \text{[−−+-comm]}}}{=} u^- \,;\, u^+ \,;\, v^-$$

$$\underset{\substack{\uparrow\\ \text{[Def]}}}{=} u :=?\,;\, v^-\ .$$

(Initial-ch-=) and (Initial-ch-≠) follow by similar calculations. The calculation for (Initial-ch-≠) uses (+-⊕-comm) and establishes thus only $\leq$. □

Next we consider initialization and finalization by choice assignments.

Theorem 5.7.5 (Choice assignments and deletions & additions). *Suppose* $u \in V^\bullet$.

(a) Finalization by a choice assignments is void because – intuitively speaking – the chosen value is forgotten immediately:

$$u :=?\,;\, u^- \;=\; u^-\ . \qquad \textit{(Ch-finalization)}$$

(b) Initial choice assignments having the same modality as the addition command are void as well. Intuitively it does not matter whether the demon is allowed to choose a value once or twice:

$$u^+ \,;\, u :=? \;=\; u^+\ . \qquad \textit{(Ch-initialization-=)}$$

(c) Initial choice assignments having a different modality change the modality of the addition:

$$u^\oplus \,;\, u :=? \;=\; u^+\ . \qquad \textit{(Ch-initialization-}\neq\textit{)}$$

The intuition is that the demon's choice overrides the angel's choice.

Proof. The three laws follow easily by unfolding the definition of choice assignments and using the simulation laws for additions and deletions. The proof of (Ch-initialization-≠), for example, reads

$$u^\oplus \,;\, u :=? \underset{\substack{\uparrow\\ \text{[Def]}}}{=} u^\oplus \,;\, u^- \,;\, u^+ \underset{\substack{\uparrow\\ [\oplus\text{-−−sim}]}}{=} u^+\ .$$ □

It is of particular interest to derive laws that concern successive occurrences of choice assignments and assignments to the same variables. We first explore *cancellation laws* that show how choice assignments and normal assignments eliminate each other.

Theorem 5.7.6 (Cancellation laws). *Suppose* $u, v \in V^\bullet$, $e \in \mathsf{Valfct}_V^u$, *and* $f \in \mathsf{Valfct}_V^v$.

(a) Choice assignments cancel preceding (usual) assignments:

$$u, v := e, f \;;\; v :=? \quad = \quad u := e \;;\; v :=? \,. \qquad \textit{(Cancel1)}$$

(b) They are cancelled by successive assignments provided the valuation functions on their left hand side do not depend on the variables assigned to by the choice assignment:

$$u :=? \;;\; u, v := e, f \quad = \quad u, v := e, f \;, \quad \textit{if } e, f \ \mathsf{idp}\ u \,. \qquad \textit{(Cancel2)}$$

Note that $\leq$ *holds without any side condition because of (Ch-Id).*

(c) Choice assignments cancel preceding angelic or demonic choice assignments:

$$u :=! \;;\; u :=? \quad = \quad u :=? \,. \qquad \textit{(Cancel3)}$$

$$u :=? \;;\; u :=? \quad = \quad u :=? \,. \qquad \textit{(Cancel4)}$$

Proof. The laws are established by the following calculations that are straightforward (except possibly the calculation for (Cancel2)).

(Cancel1):

$$u, v := e, f \;;\; v :=? \underset{\text{[Def]}}{\overset{}{\underset{\uparrow}{=}}} u, v := e, f \;;\; v^- \;;\; v^+ \underset{\text{[Finalization1]}}{\underset{\uparrow}{=}} u := e \;;\; v^- \;;\; v^+$$

$$\underset{\text{[Def]}}{\underset{\uparrow}{=}} u := e \;;\; v :=? \,.$$

(Cancel2): '$\leq$' is clear from (Ch-Id); '$\geq$' can be shown as follows:

$$u :=? \;;\; u, v := e, f$$

$=$ [Def., (Comb-asg): f idp u]

$$u^- \;;\; u^+ \;;\; u := e \;;\; v := f$$

$=$ [Proper-ini: e idp u]

$$u^- \;;\; u^\oplus \;;\; u := e \;;\; v := f$$

$\geq$ [$\oplus$-−-sim]

$$u := e \;;\; v := f$$

$=$ [(Comb-asg): f idp u]

$$u, v := e, f \,.$$

(Cancel3):

$$u :=! \;;\; u :=? \underset{\text{[Defs]}}{\underset{\uparrow}{=}} u^- \;;\; u^\oplus \;;\; u^- \;;\; u^+ \underset{[\oplus\text{-−-sim}]}{\underset{\uparrow}{=}} u^- \;;\; u^+ \underset{\text{[Def]}}{\underset{\uparrow}{=}} u :=? \,.$$

(Cancel4):

$$u :=? \,;\, u :=? \underset{\substack{\uparrow \\ \text{[Defs]}}}{=} u^- \,;\, u^+ \,;\, u^- \,;\, u^+ \underset{\substack{\uparrow \\ \text{[−−+-sim]}}}{=} u^- \,;\, u^+ \underset{\substack{\uparrow \\ \text{[Def]}}}{=} u :=? \,. \qquad \square$$

The next theorem is concerned with *conversion laws* that show how choice assignments can be converted to normal assignments and vice versa.

Theorem 5.7.7 (Conversion laws). *Suppose* $u, v \in V^\bullet$, $e \in \mathsf{Valfct}_V^u$, *and* $f \in \mathsf{Valfct}_V^v$.

$$u, v :=? \;\leq\; u := e \,;\, v :=? \;\leq\; u, v := e, f \,. \qquad \textit{(Conv1)}$$

$$u, v :=? \;\leq\; u :=? \,;\, v := f \,. \qquad \textit{(Conv2)}$$

Proof. The second inequality of (Conv1) is proved from (Cancel1) and (Ch-Id):

$$u := e \,;\, v :=? \underset{\substack{\uparrow \\ \text{[Cancel1]}}}{=} u, v := e, f \,;\, v :=? \underset{\substack{\uparrow \\ \text{[Ch-Id]}}}{\leq} u, v := e, f \,.$$

The first inequality of (Conv1) follows from the second one:

$$u, v :=? \underset{\substack{\uparrow \\ \text{[Empty-asg]}}}{=} \varepsilon := \varepsilon \,;\, u, v :=? \underset{\substack{\uparrow \\ \text{[Ch-union]}}}{=} \varepsilon := \varepsilon \,;\, u :=? \,;\, v :=? \underset{\substack{\uparrow \\ \text{[Second inequality]}}}{\leq} u := e \,;\, v :=? \,.$$

The proof of (Conv2) is:

$$u, v :=? \underset{\substack{\uparrow \\ \text{[Ch-union]}}}{=} u :=? \,;\, v :=? \underset{\substack{\uparrow \\ \text{[Conv1]}}}{\leq} u :=? \,;\, v := f \,. \qquad \square$$

Remark 5.7.1. The analogy $u :=? \,;\, v := f \;\leq\; u, v := e, f$ to the second inequality of (Conv1) is wrong in general. A counter-example are the two commands

$$P \;=\; x :=? \,;\, y := x^* \quad \text{and} \quad Q \;=\; x, y := 0, x^* \,.$$

P is totally correct with respect to precondition true and postcondition $x^* = y^*$, however, Q is not; thus Q cannot be better than P. More formally, the argumentation is as follows: P applied to $x^* = y^*$ yields true; but Q applied to $x^* = y^*$ yields $0^* = x^*$ that certainly is not implied by true. $\square$

In the previous theorems we studied the phenomena commutation, cancellation and conversion separately. In practice we often apply the following derived rule that combines all three aspects.

Corollary 5.7.8 (General commutation inequality). *Suppose* $u, v, w \in V^\bullet$ *such that* v *are* w *are disjoint,* $f \in \mathsf{Valfct}_V^v$ *and* $g \in \mathsf{Valfct}_V^w$. *Then*

$$u :=? \,;\, v, w := f, g \;\geq\; v := f \,;\, (u \backslash v) \cup w :=? \,, \qquad \textit{(Ch-comm)}$$

if f *is independent of* u .

Proof. The rule is a consequence of already established laws:

$$\begin{array}{ll} & u :=? \,;\, v, w := f, g \\ \geq & [\text{Conv1}] \\ & u :=? \,;\, v := f \,;\, w :=? \\ = & [(\text{Cancel2}) \text{ exploiting } f \mathsf{\ idp\ } u] \\ & u\backslash v :=? \,;\, v := f \,;\, w :=? \\ = & [(\text{Ch-asg}) \text{ exploiting } f \mathsf{\ idp\ } u] \\ & v := f \,;\, u\backslash v :=? \,;\, w :=? \\ = & [\text{Ch-union}] \\ & v := f \,;\, (u\backslash v) \cup w :=? \,. \end{array}$$

□

An assumption $[\phi]$ just after a demonic choice assignment $u :=?$ can be used as a filter for the chosen value. The intuition is (like in the (Restrict-demon) law in Sect. 5.5) that the demon is forced by the assumption to choose a value that satisfies ϕ because otherwise the assumption enforces miraculous success. This might explain the laws in the below theorem.

Theorem 5.7.9 (Forcing choices). *Suppose* $u \in V^{\bullet}$, $e \in \mathsf{Valfct}_V^u$, *and* $\phi \in \mathsf{Pred}_V$.

(a) *There is a law similar to (Restrict-demon) for choice assignments. It gives a general inequality for commuting choice assignments and assumptions.*

$$u :=? \,;\, [\phi] \;\leq\; [\exists_u(\phi)] \,;\, u :=! \,. \qquad \textit{(Ch-assume2)}$$

Note that the demonic *choice assignment is replaced by an* angelic *choice assignment on the right hand side!*

(b) *Assignments can be sliced into a (demonic) choice assignment and an assumption provided the valuation function on the left hand side does not depend on the variables assigned to:*

$$u := e \;=\; u :=? \,;\, [u^* = e] \,, \quad \textit{if } e \mathsf{\ idp\ } u \,. \qquad \textit{(Assign-by-choice)}$$

(c) *We have the following general commutation law for a choice assignment followed by an assertion:*

$$u :=? \,;\, \{\phi\} \;=\; \{\forall_u(\phi)\} \,;\, u :=? \,. \qquad \textit{(Ch-assert2)}$$

The intuitive explanation is that on the left hand side the demon chooses a value that invalidates ϕ *if such a value exists because this results in immediate chaos.*

Proof. (Ch-assume2) follows essentially from (Restrict-demon):

$$u :=? \,;\, [\phi] \underset{\substack{\uparrow \\ [\text{Def}]}}{=} u^- \,;\, u^+ \,;\, [\phi] \underset{\substack{\uparrow \\ [\text{Restrict-demon}]}}{\leq} u^- \,;\, [\mathbf{E}_u(\phi)] \,;\, u^{\oplus}$$

$$= [\iota_u(\mathbf{E}_u(\phi))] \,;\, u^- \,;\, u^\oplus = [\exists_u(\phi)] \,;\, u :=! \,.$$

$\uparrow$ [Final-assume] $\uparrow$ [Def, Lemma 4.4.2]

(Ch-assert2) follows by a similar calculation from (+-assert). For the proof of (Assign-by-choice) assume e idp u and consider the following calculation:

$$u := e = u :=? \,;\, u := e \le u :=? \,;\, [u^* = e] \,;\, u := e = u :=? \,;\, [u^* = e]$$

$\uparrow$ [(Cancel2), e idp u] $\uparrow$ [Assume] $\uparrow$ [Assign-assume3]

$$\le u := e \,;\, [u^* = e] = u := e \,.$$

$\uparrow$ [Conv1] $\uparrow$ [(Assign-assume2), e idp u]

It demonstrates that all occurring commands are equal which yields (Assign by choice). □

5.7.2 Conditionals

We mentioned in Sect. 5.4.2 that the (Span) law guarantees that the two definitions

$$P \lhd \phi \rhd Q = (\{\phi\} \,;\, P) \vee (\{\overline{\phi}\} \,;\, Q) \quad \text{and}$$
$$P \lhd \phi \rhd Q = ([\phi] \,;\, P) \wedge ([\overline{\phi}] \,;\, Q)$$

for the conditional $P \lhd \phi \rhd Q$ are equivalent. The following lemma is a simple consequence of the first of these identities.

Lemma 5.7.10 (Modularization). *Let $P, Q, R \in \mathsf{Com}_V^W$ and $\phi \in \mathsf{Pred}_V$. The following three propositions are equivalent.*

(a) $P \lhd \phi \rhd Q \le R$.
(b) $\{\phi\} \,;\, P \le R$ *and* $\{\overline{\phi}\} \,;\, Q \le R$.
(c) $P \le [\phi] \,;\, R$ *and* $Q \le [\overline{\phi}] \,;\, R$.

Proof.

(a)

iff [Definition of conditional]

R is greater than the least upper bound of $\{\{\phi\} \,;\, P, \{\overline{\phi}\} \,;\, Q\}$

iff [Definition of lub]

R is an upper bound of $\{\{\phi\} \,;\, P, \{\overline{\phi}\} \,;\, Q\}$

iff [Trivial]

(b)

iff [$(\{\phi\}, [\phi])$ is simulation, Lemma 5.3.2]

(c) □

By duality, there is a similar lemma for the dual proposition $P \lhd \phi \rhd Q \geq R$. Although the modularization lemma is almost trivial, it describes an idea of tremendous practical importance, namely that the refinement proof for a conditional can be split up into two proofs, which can be performed independently. Often this leads to shorter and more readable terms and calculations that are easier to check, a fact that can largely increase confidence into the proof.

We use a related idea for modularizing the semantic description of machine instructions. If their effect is of a different nature for certain classes of initial states, we describe the classes by predicates and capture the behavior for the different classes by separate axioms. Two axioms about conditional jumps, for instance, are concerned with the cases that the jump is taken or not. We exploit that a refinement formula $\{\phi\}\,;P \leq Q$ (or, equivalently, $P \leq [\phi]\,;Q$) speaks about refinement of P by Q for all initial states satisfying ϕ but doesn't claim anything for other initial states. We use such a separation of cases 'at the outermost level' extensively such that conditionals play a minor role in our exposition. This justifies to omit a comprehensive study of them and to note only a few (well-known) laws.

Theorem 5.7.11 (Some conditional laws). *Suppose* $P, Q \in \mathsf{Com}_V^W$, $R \in \mathsf{Com}_W^U$, $\phi \in \mathsf{Pred}_V$, $u \in V^\bullet$, *and* $e \in \mathsf{Valfct}_V^u$.

(a) Sequential composition distributes leftwards over conditionals:

$$(P \lhd \phi \rhd Q)\,; R \;=\; (P\,; R) \lhd \phi \rhd (Q\,; R)\,. \qquad \textit{(;-cond-leftwards)}$$

(b) Assignments distribute rightwards over conditionals but in the guard the assignment must be taken into account:

$$u := e\,; (P \lhd \phi \rhd Q) \;=\; (u := e\,; P) \lhd \phi[e/u] \rhd (u := e\,; Q)\,. \qquad \textit{(Assign-cond)}$$

(c) A conditional with same 'then'- and 'else'-part can be simplified:

$$P \lhd \phi \rhd P \;=\; P\,. \qquad \textit{(Void-cond)}$$

(d) The guard can be exploited to rewrite assignments in the 'then'- or 'else'-part:

$$(u := e\,; P) \lhd \phi \rhd Q \;=\; (u := f\,; P) \lhd \phi \rhd Q\,, \quad \textit{if } \phi \leq (e = f)\,.$$
$$P \lhd \phi \rhd (u := e\,; Q) \;=\; P \lhd \phi \rhd (u := f\,; Q)\,, \quad \textit{if } \overline{\phi} \leq (e = f)\,. \qquad \textit{(Exploit-cond)}$$

Proof. The proofs are by straightforward calculations that exploit the corresponding laws for assertions and the distribution properties of the basic commands and the composition operators. As an example we present the proof of (Void-cond):

$$P \lhd \phi \rhd P \underset{\substack{\uparrow\\ \text{[Def]}}}{=} (\{\phi\}\,; P) \vee (\{\overline{\phi}\}\,; P) \underset{\substack{\uparrow\\ [.\,;P \text{ is disj.}]}}{=} (\{\phi\} \vee \{\overline{\phi}\})\,; P$$

$$= \{\phi \vee \overline{\phi}\} ; P \underset{[\phi \vee \overline{\phi} \equiv \mathsf{true}]}{\overset{\uparrow}{=}} P . \qquad \square$$

$$\underset{[\text{Assertion-disj}]}{\uparrow}$$

5.7.3 Arrays

Almost any practical imperative programming language makes variables available that allow an indexed access to a number of component variables of same type. Traditionally such variables are called *array variables*. In the context of this book – the proof of code generators – such variables are convenient for modeling the memory of the target processor. Therefore, we investigate in this section some additions to our notations related to array variables. We consider only one-dimensional arrays. Like in denotational semantics [80, 82], in the context of 'Hoare-style' program proving of programs with arrays [19], or 'Dijkstra-style' program development [30] it proves convenient to treat array variables not as collections of variables but as variables of a functional type. As an example consider the following PASCAL declaration of an array variable AX.

```
VAR AX : ARRAY [1..10] OF BOOLEAN;
```

AX can be modeled by a variable x of type $\mathsf{Val}_x = (\{1, \ldots, 10\} \rightarrow \mathsf{Bool})$. Selection of the current value of the i'th component variable ($1 \leq i \leq 10$) is modeled by applying x's current value to i. Updates of components can be expressed by updates of x and function variation. For example, the PASCAL assignment

```
AX [1] := AX [2]
```
(5.3)

can be modeled by the command $x := x[1 \mapsto x(2)]$.

These considerations motivate the following terminology. The variable $x \in X$ is called an *array variable* if there are sets I and C such that $\mathsf{Val}_x = (I \rightarrow C)$. I is called the *index set* and C the *component value set.* A pair consisting of an array variable x with index set I and an I-valuation function φ is called a *component variable.* We usually write component variables in the form $x[\varphi]$. For the remainder of this section we assume that x is an array variable with index set I and component value set C.

In order to increase readability of specifications written in the language of commands, it is desirable to write updates of component variables similar to the PASCAL notation (5.3). The basic idea is to agree that $x[\varphi_1] := \varphi_2$ is just another notation for $x := x[\varphi_1 \mapsto \varphi_2]$. However, a certain care is necessary to obtain a sensible convention for multiple assignments. The problem is that multiple occurrences of component variables on the left hand side of an assignment can lead to aliasing. Consider, for instance, the assignment

$$x[\varphi_1], x[\varphi_2] := \psi_1, \psi_2 .$$

The value of φ_1 and φ_2 might coincide for some initial state and then it is not clear whether the final value of the corresponding array component is determined by ψ_1 or ψ_2. (For multiple assignments to normal variables this problem is avoided by requiring that the variables on the left hand side are distinct. If component variables are allowed on the left hand side of assignments, however, disjointness is a state-dependent property and, therefore, cannot be decided statically). We adopt a convention that is borrowed e.g. from [30] to resolve this problem: while the evaluation of the valuation functions is assumed to proceed 'in parallel', i.e. to determine their value in the initial state, the assignment of the resulting values to the component variables is assumed to be sequential from left to right. By this convention the command $x[1], x[1] := 2, 3$ has the same effect as $x[1] := 3$ because the assignment of the value 2 to the first component of x is immediately overwritten by the assignment of the value 3.

In order to describe the convention by which the effect of sequential assignment to component variables is achieved, we must first parameterize the general situation. Suppose $n \geq 1$, $u_0, \ldots, u_n$ are disjoint lists of variables that do not contain x, and $e_0, \ldots, e_n$ are lists of valuation functions such that $e_i \in \mathsf{Valfct}_V^{u_i}$ for $i = 0, \ldots, n$. Furthermore, let $\varphi_1, \ldots, \varphi_n \in \mathsf{Valfct}_V^I$ and $\psi_1, \ldots, \psi_n \in \mathsf{Valfct}_V^C$. We consider

$$u_0, x[\varphi_1], u_1, x[\varphi_2], \ldots, x[\varphi_n], u_n := e_0, \psi_1, e_1, \psi_2, \ldots, \psi_n, e_n \tag{5.4}$$

to be just another notation for

$$u_0, u_1, \ldots, u_n, x := e_0, \ldots, e_n, x[\varphi_1 \mapsto \psi_1] \cdots [\varphi_n \mapsto \psi_n] \ . \tag{5.5}$$

Left to right assignment to the component variables is expressed by the order of the variations on the right hand side of (5.5). As subsequent variations do not commute in general, the order of the component variables on the left hand side of (5.4) is significant. In particular the reorder law for multiple assignments does *not* generalize to assignments with component variables. We refrain from investigating laws for this generalized kind of assignment. Instead we always resolve (5.4) implicitly to (5.5) when applying assignment laws.

We considered only a single one-dimensional array here. The generalization to more than one array or to multi-dimensional arrays is obvious but is not needed in the remainder of this book.

5.8 Discussion

In the introduction to Chap. 4 we stressed that calculations with imperative programs follow conventions that are different from usual mathematical practice in particular w.r.t. the use of variables. Therefore, we have drawn a careful distinction between variables of the mathematical meta-language and variables as object of consideration, between terms of the meta-language and valuation functions, and between propositional terms of the meta-language and predicates. Moreover, we up to now very carefully distinguished predicates defined on different state spaces and made the necessary embeddings explicit.

This is sensible for studying the refinement laws. But when the command language is applied, spelling out all the necessary lifts and embeddings tends to hide the view to the more essential details. Therefore, the distinctions are notationally suppressed in practice, and valuation functions and predicates are denoted by mathematical (value or propositional) terms in which the command language variables are used like meta-variables. We write e.g. $x := x + 1$ for the assignment $x := x^* +^* 1^*$ and $[x = y]$ for the assumption $[x^* =^* y^*]$.

There is more to be said than just that embeddings and liftings are omitted, for, the command language variables and the mathematical terms are used with two different interpretations depending on the context. If a propositional term appears, say, inside an assertion, then it is interpreted as a predicate. But if it is not used at such a place it is understood as a proposition and all the occurring variables are interpreted as meta-variables. The attractiveness of reasoning with the command notation partly stems from the fact that these two interpretations are compatible.

If, in particular, two predicates ϕ and ϕ' are given by the propositional terms p and p', then $\phi \leq \phi'$ holds if and only if the implication $p \Rightarrow p'$ is universally valid in the second interpretation for p and p' as propositions. In practice this shift of interpretation is performed without explicit mention.

Example 5.8.1. Suppose $\mathtt{A}, \mathtt{B}, \mathtt{C} \in V$ are variables with domain IN and let ϕ be the predicate defined by $\mathtt{A} = \mathtt{B} \wedge \mathtt{B} = \mathtt{C}$ and ϕ' the predicate defined by $\mathtt{A} = \mathtt{C}$, i.e.

$$\phi \;=\; (\mathtt{A}^* =^* \mathtt{B}^* \wedge \mathtt{B}^* =^* \mathtt{C}^*) \quad \text{and} \quad \phi' \;=\; (\mathtt{A}^* =^* \mathtt{C}^*) \; .$$

Then $\phi \leq \phi'$ holds if and only if

$$\mathtt{A} = \mathtt{B} \text{ and } \mathtt{B} = \mathtt{C} \quad \text{implies} \quad \mathtt{A} = \mathtt{C} \;\text{ for all } \mathtt{A}, \mathtt{B}, \mathtt{C} \in \mathsf{IN} \; .$$

In practice we show validity of this implication and conclude then directly with the (Assert-monotonic) law that $\{\mathtt{A} = \mathtt{B} \wedge \mathtt{B} = \mathtt{C}\} \leq \{\mathtt{A} = \mathtt{C}\}$. □

The basic operations on predicates have been defined to make their correspondence to usual logical operations straightforward. In particular, both the homogeneous quantifiers $\forall_u, \exists_u$ as well as the inhomogeneous ones $\mathbf{A}_u, \mathbf{E}_u$ correspond to universal and existential quantification. The difference between the homogeneous and inhomogeneous versions, viz. their result space, is blurred because we usually do not distinguish explicitly between a valuation function or predicate and its embedding into a larger state space. The state space on which they are interpreted must be inferred from context. This means that embedding operators have no correspondence (or rather correspond to the identity) as they just indicate interpretation on another state space. But whenever a refinement law containing an embedding operator, say ι_u, is applied it is important to check that the mathematical term at that place can actually be interpreted on the smaller state space. Due to the relationship between embedding and independence, this just means that the denoted valuation function or predicate must be independent of u (on the larger state space).

There is one point that deserves special attention: valuation functions and predicates are total. Hence, we must take care that the mathematical terms written instead of them are defined for all possible values of the command language variables. We ensure this by extending operations that are partial in the common interpretation. For example, we agree that the division operations $\div$ and rem yield zero in all cases that traditionally are undefined (see Chap. 8).

6. Communication and Time

We study the space of commands in order to provide a formal basis for the code generator correctness proof in the second part of this book where we approach translation of a timed programming language to Transputer code. The most important correctness condition of that translation is the preservation or, more precisely, refinement of the communication behavior w.r.t. the values that are communicated, the identity of the channels on which they are communicated, and the time instants at which this happens. But the command notation introduced up-to-now speaks neither about communication nor about timing. How can we do so in the space of commands?

The idea is to use two distinguished variables $clk, hst \in X$ that are furnished with a specific interpretation. The variable clk ranges over real values and records elapse of time; hst, on the other hand, ranges over *timed traces*, i.e. sequences of communication events, a communication event being a triple consisting of the name of the channel on which the communication happens, the value that is communicated, and a real-valued time stamp describing the time instant at which the communication happens.

When applying the command language, we refer to clk and hst only indirectly via the following commands that are introduced later in this chapter:

- *input processes* $in\,?\,x$,
- *output processes* $out\,!\,\varphi$,
- the *stop process* Stop,
- *delays* $\Delta\, d$ of at most d time units, and
- *time bounds* $|\,P\,| \preceq d$ that restrict execution time of P to at most d time units.

The laws that relate these new commands to the old ones like assignments, assertions, etc. are thus investigated only for the case that the old constructs do not refer to clk or hst.

We define delays, time bounds, inputs, outputs and stop in terms of basic commands. This enables to exploit the laws for basic commands when establishing laws which shortens the proofs. The basic commands occurring in the definitions refer to clk and hst, which is the reason why we didn't separate them from the other variables just from start.

In order to motivate how the variable hst is used for describing communication traces let us consider a simplified situation: output to just one integer channel. Moreover, we do not consider timing now. A first idea is to use *hst* as an actual history variable [1] that records the communications that have happened in the past. The command $!\varphi$, which intuitively writes the value of the integer valuation function φ in the initial state onto the single channel, would be defined by

$$!\varphi \stackrel{\text{def}}{=} hst := hst \cdot \varphi \;, \tag{6.1}$$

where $\cdot$ denotes the operator that extends a sequence by one element. Unfortunately, this definition does not properly explain non-terminating programs if loops are defined by least fixpoints w.r.t. the refinement order; it leads to the identity

$$\texttt{while true do } !\varphi \texttt{ od} \;=\; \bot \;,$$

which shows that in this model `while true do` $!\varphi$ `od` carries no information about the outputs that happen intuitively. The reason is that by (6.1) $!\varphi$ is $\bot$-strict. In our actual definition inputs, outputs, and stop are modeled by commands that are not $\bot$-strict such that (infinite) loops do not necessarily become trivial.

A solution that is often advocated in the context of denotational semantics is to use more complex orders for approximation of fixpoints that take into account the approximation of final (possibly infinite) communication sequences by their finite prefixes. Fortunately, this additional complexity can be avoided by exploiting the richness of the space of commands. In a definition like (6.1), the postcondition speaks about the communications that have happened during program execution (for terminating programs). The idea now is to speak about the communications that will happen in the precondition. Thus *hst* is used similar to a prophecy variables in the sense of [1].

The classic definition of total correctness for a non-communicating imperative program π w.r.t. a precondition *pre* and a postcondition *post* (based on a formalized or non-formalized operational intuition about program execution) is composed of two conditions.

(a) Firstly, π must be partially correct w.r.t. *pre* and *post* (which means that each final state s' resulting from a terminating computation of π from a state s that satisfies the precondition *pre* must satisfy the postcondition *post*).
(b) Secondly, π must terminate regularly from any initial state satisfying *pre*.

In formalisms that allow to speak about the pre-state in the postcondition (like in C.B. Jones' version of VDM, the Vienna Development Method [47]) requirement (a) can be expressed by the postcondition alone. In such formalisms partial correctness w.r.t. *pre* and *post* is equivalent to partial correctness w.r.t. the trivial precondition true and the post condition $pre \Rightarrow post$. The second purpose of the precondition, however, is more fundamental and cannot be transferred to the postcondition: it excludes initial states from which unwanted anomalous behavior is possible that can prevent regular termination. Examples are divergence or deadlock. (Another example is irregular termination caused e.g. by an operator application outside its range. We ignore irregular termination in the following exposition but mention that it can be treated like deadlock. In the semantics of TPL (see Chap. 9) 'undefined' operator applications cannot arise as all operators are total.)

We replace the absolute notions of divergence and deadlock by the trace-dependent notions 'divergence after a trace h' and 'deadlock after a trace h'. Total correctness requires in particular that validity of the precondition in a state σ excludes divergence and deadlock after trace $\sigma(hst)$. The weakest precondition transformer $\mathsf{wp}(\pi)$ of a (syntactic) program π thus speaks indirectly about the traces after which deadlock or divergence is possible.

The program that communicates the infinite sequence $\langle 0, 1, 2, \ldots \rangle$, for instance, is modeled by the predicate transformer *Count* that maps any postcondition *post* to the precondition $Count(post) = (hst \neq \langle 0, 1, 2, \ldots \rangle)$. This implies that *Count* cannot deadlock or diverge under traces distinct from $\langle 0, 1, 2, \ldots \rangle$. As of course deadlock can only occur after finite traces this means that *Count* cannot deadlock at all. But it can diverge with $\langle 0, 1, 2, \ldots \rangle$. This is its only possible behavior because termination after some finite trace contradicts $Count(\mathsf{false})$.

We shall see below that preservation of total correctness (that is command refinement) implies inclusion of the set of possible communication traces if there is no internal divergence. We now explain our approach more precisely in a small prototypic framework.

6.1 An Operational Framework

We discuss a language of (syntactic) statements π that write to one single integer channel and use variables from a fixed set $V \subseteq X$ as actual program variables. Assume that $hst \in X \setminus V$ is a variable, called the ***history variable***, that ranges over traces. In this simple case a ***trace*** is just a finite or infinite sequence of integers, so $\mathsf{Val}_{hst} = \mathsf{Int}^* \cup \mathsf{Int}^\omega$. Let $V' = V \cup \{hst\}$.

We distinguish between ***proper states*** $s \in \mathsf{State}_V$ that interpret only the actual program variables and ***(general) states*** $\sigma \in \mathsf{State}_{V'}$ that also interpret the history variable hst. For a proper state s and a trace h we denote by $s \oplus h$ the general state $s \cup \{(hst, h)\}$.

Assume given an abstract machine that executes syntactic statements. Its steps are formalized by a transition relation $\xrightarrow{h}$ on configurations (π, s), where π is a syntactic program, s is a proper state, and h is a finite trace consisting of the communications that are emitted within that step. In particular for an internal step h equals ε. The ***terminal configurations*** in which the abstract machine terminates regularly are of the form $(\mathtt{Skip}, s)$. We assume that from a terminal configuration no further transition is possible.

We can now formally define the notions used in the introductory discussion. Suppose s, s' are proper states, h, h' are traces and $pre, post \in \mathsf{Pred}_{V'}$ are predicates over general states.

- We say that π *can diverge from s under h*, $(s,h) \overset{\pi}{\hookrightarrow}$ for short, if there is an infinite sequence of transitions

  $$(\pi, s) = (\pi_0, s_0) \xrightarrow{h_1} (\pi_1, s_1) \xrightarrow{h_2} \cdots$$

  such that $h_1 \cdot \ldots \cdot h_i$ is a prefix of h for all $i \in \mathbb{N}$. Note that we do not require that h is communicated entirely; it suffices that a prefix is emitted. This way of defining divergence under h fits to the definition of loops by least fixpoints w.r.t. the refinement order as we shall see below.
- We say that π *can deadlock from s under h*, $(s,h) \overset{\pi}{\longrightarrow\!\!\|}$ for short, if there is a finite sequence of transitions

  $$(\pi, s) = (\pi_0, s_0) \xrightarrow{h_1} \cdots \xrightarrow{h_n} (\pi_n, s_n)$$

  $(n \geq 0)$ with $h = h_1 \cdot \ldots \cdot h_n$ and $\pi_n \neq \mathtt{Skip}$ such that there is no further transition, i.e. such that there are no $h_{n+1}, \pi_{n+1}, s_{n+1}$ with $(\pi_n, s_n) \xrightarrow{h_{n+1}} (\pi_{n+1}, s_{n+1})$.
- We say π *can terminate from s under h in s′ without consuming h′*, $(s,h) \overset{\pi}{\rightsquigarrow} (s', h')$ for short, if there is a finite sequence of transitions

  $$(\pi, s) = (\pi_0, s_0) \xrightarrow{h_1} \cdots \xrightarrow{h_n} (\pi_n, s_n) = (\mathtt{Skip}, s')$$

  $(n \geq 0)$ with $h = h_1 \cdot \ldots \cdot h_n \cdot h'$.
- π is called *partially correct w.r.t. pre, post* if for all proper states s, s' and traces h, h':

  $$pre(s \oplus h) = \mathrm{tt} \ \wedge\ (s,h) \overset{\pi}{\rightsquigarrow} (s', h') \quad \text{implies} \quad post(s' \oplus h') = \mathrm{tt}\ .$$

- π is called *totally correct w.r.t. pre, post* if
  - π is partially correct w.r.t. *pre*, *post*, and
  - for all proper states s and traces h with $pre(s \oplus h) = \mathrm{tt}$ neither $(s,h) \overset{\pi}{\hookrightarrow}$ nor $(s,h) \overset{\pi}{\longrightarrow\!\!\|}$ holds.

This definition of total correctness leads to the following characterization of the weakest precondition for achieving a postcondition *post* with a program π:

$$\mathsf{wp}(\pi)(post)(s \oplus h) = \mathrm{tt} \tag{6.2}$$

if and only if

(a) $post(s' \oplus h') = \mathrm{tt}$ for all s', h' with $(s,h) \overset{\pi}{\rightsquigarrow} (s', h')$, and
(b) neither $(s,h) \overset{\pi}{\longrightarrow\!\!\|}$ nor $(s,h) \overset{\pi}{\hookrightarrow}$.

For condition (a) we sometimes say that 'there is no terminating computation of π from (s, h) contradicting *post*'.

We emphasize that we do not propose to use the above notions of partial and total correctness directly for specifying programs. How they speak about communications can sometimes be a little bit confusing and is thus not appropriate for specification purposes. We only intend to use the induced notion of weakest precondition transformers as semantic basis for the interpretation of communicating commands.

The definition of total correctness treats – as a generalization of the classic notion – divergence and deadlock under a trace h as unwanted behavior. But we perform a certain shift in the interpretation. We are interested mainly in the communication behavior of commands that is described by the deadlocking and diverging computations. In particular, the semantics of TPL (see Chap. 9) agrees that a program stops when its main body terminates, such that TPL programs as a whole have no 'terminating' computations at all! So deadlocking and diverging is considered the regular behavior. Therefore, it is important that we can regain the deadlocking and diverging traces from the weakest precondition transformer of a statement π. We have namely

$$\{(s,h) \mid (s,h) \xrightarrow{\pi}\!\!\| \text{ or } (s,h) \overset{\pi}{\hookrightarrow}\} \;=\; \{(s,h) \mid \mathsf{wp}(\pi)(\mathsf{true})(s \oplus h) = \mathsf{ff}\}$$

as can be seen from the above characterization of the weakest precondition and the additional consideration that for trivial reasons no terminating computation can contradict the postcondition true. It is easy to see from this identity that refinement of the weakest precondition implies inclusion of the sets of deadlocking and diverging traces: if $\mathsf{wp}(\pi) \leq \mathsf{wp}(\pi')$, then $\mathsf{wp}(\pi')(\mathsf{true}) = \mathsf{ff}$ implies $\mathsf{wp}(\pi)(\mathsf{true}) = \mathsf{ff}$ such that

$$\{(s,h) \mid (s,h) \xrightarrow{\pi'}\!\!\| \text{ or } (s,h) \overset{\pi'}{\hookrightarrow}\} \subseteq \{(s,h) \mid (s,h) \xrightarrow{\pi}\!\!\| \text{ or } (s,h) \overset{\pi}{\hookrightarrow}\} \; .$$

This shows that command refinement is sensible also with this shifted interpretation. We should, however, remind the reader that $(s, h) \overset{\pi}{\hookrightarrow}$ holds also if π diverges internally after only emitting a proper prefix of h so that inclusion of the 'actual' diverging and deadlocking traces can only be guaranteed if π does not diverge internally. The presence of this 'chaotic closure' is quite common in total correctness frameworks and is well-known for the classic weakest precondition semantics for non-communicating programs.

6.1.1 Communication Commands

From the characterization (6.2) we can derive how to define the communication commands as weakest precondition predicate transformer because their operational meaning is clear. As an example consider again the command $!\varphi$.[1] Operationally its behavior is described by the single rule

[1] Strictly speaking, we should use a syntactic expression instead of a (semantic) valuation function as component of a syntactic output statement. But we are

$$(!\varphi, s) \xrightarrow{\varphi(s)} (\texttt{Skip}, s) \ .$$

There is no state s from which $!\varphi$ diverges or deadlocks under some trace h. So condition (b) in the weakest precondition characterization holds always. Condition (a) is satisfied for trivial reasons if h is empty or does not start with $\varphi(s)$ because in these cases there are no s', h' with $(s,h) \overset{\pi}{\leadsto} (s',h')$. It holds non-trivially if h starts with $\varphi(s)$ and post holds for s together with the tail of h. So we have

$$\mathsf{wp}(!\varphi)(post) \;=\; hst = \varepsilon \;\vee\; hd(hst) \neq \varphi \;\vee\; post[tl(hst)/hst] \ .$$

This predicate transformer can also be defined on the command level by

$$\mathsf{wp}(!\varphi) \;=\; [hst \neq \varepsilon \wedge hd(hst) = \varphi] \ ; \ hst := tl(hst)$$

as is seen by unfolding the definitions.

The weakest precondition transformer of an input command $?x$ (where $x \in V$) is similar. For explaining the principle we use *hst* now for recording the input events. Operationally the behavior of an input command $?x$ is described by the family of rules (one rule for each $a \in \mathsf{Val}_x$)

$$(?x, s) \xrightarrow{a} (\texttt{Skip}, s[x \mapsto a]) \ .$$

Again deadlock and divergence is not possible, so condition (b) holds trivially. Condition (a) is satisfied if and only if h is empty or if *post* holds for the state obtained by modifying the initial state in x and *hst* by $hd(h)$ resp. $tl(h)$. So the weakest precondition transformer induced by the input statement $?x$ is

$$\mathsf{wp}(?x)(post) \;=\; hst = \varepsilon \;\vee\; post[hd(hst), tl(hst)/x, hst] \ ,$$

which can be described on the command level by

$$\mathsf{wp}(?x) \;=\; [hst \neq \varepsilon] \ ; \ x, hst := hd(hst), tl(hst) \ . \tag{6.3}$$

This identity can also be written as

$$\mathsf{wp}(?x) \;=\; x :=? \ ; \ [hst \neq \varepsilon \wedge hd(hst) = x] \ ; \ hst := tl(hst) \ .$$

as one can see either directly or by a short calculation from (6.3).

By similar considerations one can check from straightforward assumptions about the operational semantics of statements that $x := \varphi$ indeed is the weakest precondition transformer of an assignment and that the sequential and conditional composition of predicate transformers model correctly the sequential and conditional composition of statements. This means, for instance, that the identity

$$\mathsf{wp}(\mathsf{Seq}(\pi, \pi')) \;=\; \mathsf{wp}(\pi) \ ; \ \mathsf{wp}(\pi')$$

holds, where $\mathtt{Seq}(\pi, \pi')$ stand for the sequential composition of syntactic statements.

interested here only in the execution at the statement level and not in the evaluation of expressions. It is convenient to assume a valuation function as component because this saves a number of applications of semantic interpretation functions.

6.1.2 Loops

We would like to turn our attention to a more interesting question, viz. the weakest precondition transformer of a while-loop. We write the loop statement as $\phi * \pi$ instead of the familiar but more clumsy `while` ϕ `do` π `od`. The *body* π of the loop is a syntactic statement and the guard ϕ is a semantic predicate.[2] We assume that ϕ is a predicate on proper states, i.e. $\phi \in \mathsf{Pred}_V$. It generalizes the standard practice for non-communicating programs to define the semantics of $\phi * \pi$ as the least fixpoint of the functional $W_{\phi,\pi} \in (\mathsf{Com}_{V'}^{V'} \to \mathsf{Com}_{V'}^{V'})$,

$$W_{\phi,\pi}(Y) \;=\; (\mathsf{wp}(\pi)\;;Y) \lhd \iota_{hst}(\phi) \rhd \mathsf{Id}\;.$$

We show that this indeed gives the weakest precondition transformer of the loop $\phi * \pi$.

Theorem 6.1.1 (Adequacy of loop definition). $\mu W_{\phi,\pi} \;=\; \mathsf{wp}(\phi * \pi)\;.$

Of course the proof relies on some assumptions about the operational semantics of loops. Intuitively, executions of the loop $\phi * \pi$ are induced by (ϕ,π)-paths.

- A *finite* (ϕ,π)*-path from* (s,h) *to* (s',h') is a non-empty sequence of state/trace-pairs $p = \langle(s_1,h_1),\ldots,(s_n,h_n)\rangle$ $(n \geq 1)$ that starts with (s,h) and finishes with (s',h'), i.e. $(s,h) = (s_1,h_1)$ and $(s',h') = (s_n,h_n)$, such that in all but the last situation ϕ holds and neighboured pairs stand in $\overset{\pi}{\leadsto}$-relation:

$$\phi(s_i) = \mathsf{tt} \;\text{ and }\; (s_i,h_i) \overset{\pi}{\leadsto} (s_{i+1},h_{i+1}) \quad \text{for all } 1 \leq i < n\;.$$

- An *infinite* (ϕ,π)*-path from* (s,h) is an infinite sequence of state/trace-pairs $p = \langle(s_1,h_1),(s_2,h_2),\ldots\rangle$ that starts with (s,h), i.e. $(s,h) = (s_1,h_1)$, such that in all situations ϕ holds and neighboured pairs stand in $\overset{\pi}{\leadsto}$-relation:

$$\phi(s_i) = \mathsf{tt} \;\text{ and }\; (s_i,h_i) \overset{\pi}{\leadsto} (s_{i+1},h_{i+1}) \quad \text{for all } i \geq 1\;.$$

Finite and infinite (ϕ,π)-paths model finite or infinite iterations of the loop. Note that (ϕ,π)-paths of length one represent zero iterations. We can now formulate our assumptions about the execution of loops.

(A1) The terminating computations of the loop $\phi * \pi$ are induced by finite (ϕ,π)-paths that lead to a situation in which ϕ does not hold:

$$(s,h) \overset{\phi*\pi}{\leadsto} (s',h') \quad \text{iff} \quad \text{there is a finite } (\phi,\pi)\text{-path from } (s,h) \text{ to } (s',h') \text{ and } \phi(s') = \mathsf{ff}\;.$$

[2] Again it is convenient to assume that the guard is given by a semantic predicate rather than a Boolean expression.

(A2) The deadlocking computations of $\phi * \pi$ arise from deadlocks in an execution of the body π after some iterations:

$$(s,h) \xrightarrow{\phi*\pi}\!\!\| \quad \text{iff} \quad \text{there is a finite } (\phi,\pi)\text{-path from } (s,h) \text{ to a situation } (s',h') \text{ where } \phi(s') = \mathsf{tt} \text{ and } (s',h') \xrightarrow{\pi}\!\!\| \ .$$

(A3) The diverging computations of $\phi * \pi$ result either from infinite iteration or from divergence in the body after finitely many iterations:

$$(s,h) \overset{\phi*\pi}{\hookrightarrow} \quad \text{iff} \quad \text{there is an infinite } (\phi,\pi)\text{-path from } (s,h)\text{, or there is a finite } (\phi,\pi)\text{-path from } (s,h) \text{ to some situation } (s',h') \text{ where } \phi(s') = \mathsf{tt} \text{ and } (s',h') \overset{\pi}{\hookrightarrow} .$$

(A3) relies on the fact that divergence under a trace h does not require that h is emitted entirely because there might be infinite (ϕ,π)-paths from (s,h) that make only internal steps after emitting just a proper prefix of h.

The most interesting part of Theorem 6.1.1 is the fact that the weakest fixpoint of $W_{\phi,\pi}$ is not too weak:

Lemma 6.1.2. $\mu W_{\phi,\pi} \;\geq\; \mathsf{wp}(\phi * \pi)$.

Proof. Writing W for $W_{\phi,\pi}$ we have to show that for all $post, s, h$

$$\mu W(post)(s \oplus h) \;\geq\; \mathsf{wp}(\phi * \pi)(post)(s \oplus h) \ . \tag{6.4}$$

Suppose $post, s, h$ are given. If $\mu W(post)(s \oplus h) = \mathsf{tt}$, inequality (6.4) holds trivially, so assume $\mu W(post)(s \oplus h) = \mathsf{ff}$.

If there is a finite (ϕ,π)-path from (s,h) to some entry (s',h') such that

- $\phi(s') = \mathsf{tt}$ and $(s',h') \xrightarrow{\pi}\!\!\|$ or $(s',h') \overset{\pi}{\hookrightarrow}$, or
- $\phi(s') = \mathsf{ff}$ and $post(s' \oplus h') = \mathsf{ff}$,

then – by the operational assumptions and the definition of wp – $\mathsf{wp}(\phi * \pi)(post)(s \oplus h) = \mathsf{ff}$ and (6.4) holds. So assume that such a finite (ϕ,π)-path does not exists.

We can now inductively construct an infinite (ϕ,π)-path from (s,h) (see below). Its existence shows that $\phi * \pi$ can diverge from (s,h), which implies that $\mathsf{wp}(\phi * \pi)(post)(s \oplus h) = \mathsf{ff}$. This completes the proof.

Let us now construct the infinite (ϕ,π)-path $p = \langle (s_1,h_1),(s_2,h_2),\ldots\rangle$ from (s,h) promised above. It has the additional property that $\mu W(post)(s_i \oplus h_i) = \mathsf{ff}$ for all $i \geq 1$ which we show simultaneously with its construction.

Let $(s_1,h_1) = (s,h)$. That $\mu W(post)(s \oplus h) = \mathsf{ff}$ has been assumed above.

Suppose that the first n entries of the infinite (ϕ,π)-path have already been constructed. We collect them to the finite (ϕ,π)-path $p_n = \langle (s_1,h_1),\ldots,(s_n,h_n)\rangle$. By construction we have

$$\begin{aligned} &\mathsf{ff} \\ = \;&\mu W(post)(s_n \oplus h_n) \end{aligned}$$

$$
\begin{aligned}
&= \quad [\text{Fixpoint property}] \\
&\quad W(\mu W)(post)(s_n \oplus h_n) \\
&= \quad [\text{Spelling out the definition of } W] \\
&\quad \begin{cases} \mathsf{wp}(\pi)(\mu W(post))(s_n \oplus h_n), & \text{if } \phi(s_n) = \mathsf{tt} \\ post(s_n \oplus h_n), & \text{if } \phi(s_n) = \mathsf{ff} \end{cases} .
\end{aligned}
$$

If $\phi(s_n) = \mathsf{ff}$, we have thus $post(s_n \oplus h_n) = \mathsf{ff}$. But this means the existence of the finite (ϕ, π)-path p_n that contradicts the post-condition which is excluded by our above assumption. Therefore, $\phi(s_n) = \mathsf{tt}$ must hold, which implies that $\mathsf{wp}(\pi)(\mu W(post))(s_n \oplus h_n) = \mathsf{ff}$. By the definition of wp this means that we have at least one of the following situations.

(i) π can diverge or deadlock from s_n under h_n: $(s_n, h_n) \overset{\pi}{\hookrightarrow}$ or $(s_n, h_n) \overset{\pi}{\longrightarrow}\!\!\|$.
(ii) There is a terminating computation from s_n under h_n that contradicts $\mu W(post)$, i.e. there are s_{n+1}, h_{n+1} such that $(s_n, h_n) \overset{\pi}{\rightsquigarrow} (s_{n+1}, h_{n+1})$ and $\mu W(post)(s_{n+1} \oplus h_{n+1}) = \mathsf{ff}$.

Validity of (i) implies that there is the finite (ϕ, π)-path p_n after which π can deadlock or diverge. But we assumed that such a path does not exist. Hence, (ii) must hold. (s_{n+1}, h_{n+1}) is the sought entry that extends the already constructed part of the infinite (ϕ, π)-path. □

The remaining inequality follows from the fact that $\mathsf{wp}(\phi * \pi)$ is a fixpoint of $W_{\phi,\pi}$. This is of course expected but let us explicate the argumentation.

Lemma 6.1.3. $\mu W_{\phi,\pi} \leq \mathsf{wp}(\phi * \pi)$.

Proof. We write again W for $W_{\phi,\pi}$. It suffices to show $W(\mathsf{wp}(\phi * \pi)) \leq \mathsf{wp}(\phi * \pi)$ (by Corollary 2.3.2), which means validity of

$$W(\mathsf{wp}(\phi * \pi))(post)(s \oplus h) \leq \mathsf{wp}(\phi * \pi)(post)(s \oplus h) \tag{6.5}$$

for all $post, s, h$. By unfolding the definition of W one sees that

$$
\begin{aligned}
&W(\mathsf{wp}(\phi * \pi))(post)(s \oplus h) \\
&\quad = \begin{cases} \mathsf{wp}(\pi)(\mathsf{wp}(\phi * \pi)(post))(s \oplus h), & \text{if } \phi(s) = \mathsf{tt} \\ post(s \oplus h), & \text{if } \phi(s) = \mathsf{ff} \end{cases} .
\end{aligned} \tag{6.6}
$$

If $\mathsf{wp}(\phi * \pi)(post)(s \oplus h) = \mathsf{tt}$, inequality (6.5) holds trivially, so assume $\mathsf{wp}(\phi * \pi)(post)(s \oplus h) = \mathsf{ff}$. By the definition of wp and the operational assumptions (A1) – (A3) about loop execution, this means that

(i) there is an infinite (ϕ, π)-path from (s, h), or
(ii) there is a finite (ϕ, π)-path from (s, h) to some (s', h')
 (a) after which π deadlocks or diverges, i.e. $\phi(s') = \mathsf{tt}$ and $(s', h') \overset{\pi}{\longrightarrow}\!\!\|$ or $(s', h') \overset{\pi}{\hookrightarrow}$, or
 (b) that contradicts $post$, i.e. $\phi(s') = \mathsf{ff}$ and $post(s' \oplus h') = \mathsf{ff}$.

If there is an infinite (ϕ, π)-path from (s, h), we can write it in the form $p = \langle (s, h), (s_1, h_1), (s_2, h_2), \ldots \rangle$. It is clear that $\langle (s_1, h_1), (s_2, h_2), \ldots \rangle$ is again an infinite (ϕ, π)-path from (s_1, h_1), which implies that $\mathsf{wp}(\phi * \pi)(\mathit{post})(s_1 \oplus h_1) = \mathsf{ff}$. Therefore, $(s, h) \overset{\pi}{\rightsquigarrow} (s_1, h_1)$ (which holds because p is a (ϕ, π)-path) is a computation of π that contradicts the post-condition $\mathsf{wp}(\phi * \pi)(\mathit{post})$, so

$$\mathsf{wp}(\pi)(\mathsf{wp}(\phi * \pi)(\mathit{post}))(s \oplus h) \;=\; \mathsf{ff}\;.$$

Moreover, $\phi(s) = \mathsf{tt}$ because p is a (ϕ, π)-path. This implies that

$$W(\mathsf{wp}(\phi * \pi))(\mathit{post})(s \oplus h) \;=\; \mathsf{wp}(\pi)(\mathsf{wp}(\phi * \pi)(\mathit{post}))(s \oplus h) \;=\; \mathsf{ff}\;.$$

In a similar way one argues if the finite (ϕ, π)-path in (ii) has two or more entries. If on the other hand it consists of just one entry it equals $\langle (s, h) \rangle$ such that $s' = s$ and $h' = h$. Hence, we have to explore the cases:

(a) $\phi(s) = \mathsf{tt}$ and $(s, h) \overset{\pi}{\longrightarrow}\!\!\|$ or $(s, h) \overset{\pi}{\hookrightarrow}$, and
(b) $\phi(s) = \mathsf{ff}$ and $\mathit{post}(s \oplus h) = \mathsf{ff}$.

If condition (a) holds, then certainly $\mathsf{wp}(\pi)(\mathsf{wp}(\phi * \pi)(\mathit{post}))(s \oplus h) = \mathsf{ff}$. By the above identity (6.6) and the conditions on $\phi(s)$ in (a) and (b), we have thus $W(\mathsf{wp}(\phi * \pi))(\mathit{post})(s \oplus h) = \mathsf{ff}$ in both cases. □

Theorem 6.1.1 is now obvious from Lemma 6.1.2 and Lemma 6.1.3. Note that this result does not rely on a finite non-determinism assumption. Infinite non-determinism can lead to non-continuity of $W_{\phi,\pi}$ such that its least fixpoint not necessarily equals the least upper bound of the chain $\{W^i_{\phi,\pi}(\bot) \mid i \in \mathbb{N}\}$ but requires transfinite approximation. Nevertheless, the least fixpoint captures exactly the weakest precondition transformer of the loop $\phi * \pi$.

6.1.3 Remarks

This simple operational framework is not intended to explain angelic notions like assumptions or angelic choice. Although more complex operational frameworks exist for the classic non-communicating case in which such notions can be explained, we want to avoid their additional complexity here. We are interested in a formal operational interpretation only for the demonic concepts and consider the angelic concepts only to be convenient completions of the space of commands that foster abstract reasoning.

We studied here a trace semantics of communication. It is clear that a proper definition of external choice and parallel composition requires additional information as provided e.g. by refusal or readiness sets [14, 40, 72]. We believe that such a semantics can be embedded into a predicate transformer framework in a similar way, e.g. by using an additional special variable *rdy*, and that all the laws for commands that are used in the code generator proof remain valid for such a semantics. This would mean that the code generator proof is 'sealed' against these semantic details.

Embedding the semantics of communication into a predicate transformer framework has the advantage that for the development of internal parts of programs the classic methods for non-communicating imperative programs can directly be applied.

6.2 Definitions

Let us now set the stage for the formal definition of the communication and timing commands. Assume given disjoint sets InChan and $\mathsf{OutChan}$ of input and output channel names and let $\mathsf{Chan} = \mathsf{InChan} \cup \mathsf{OutChan}$. For simplicity we assume that both InChan and $\mathsf{OutChan}$ are disjoint from X, the set of variables. We let *in* range over InChan, *out* over $\mathsf{OutChan}$ and c over Chan. We assume furthermore that each $c \in \mathsf{Chan}$ has associated a non-empty set Val_c, the set of values that can be communicated via channel c.

A *communication event* is a triple (c, a, t) consisting of a channel name c, a value $a \in \mathsf{Val}_c$, and a *time stamp* $t \in \mathrm{IR}$. A communication event (c, a, t) models that the value a is communicated via channel c at time t.[3] The set of communication events is called ComEvt:

$$\mathsf{ComEvt} \stackrel{\text{def}}{=} \{(c, a, t) \mid c \in \mathsf{Chan},\ a \in \mathsf{Val}_c,\ t \in \mathrm{IR}\} .$$

A communication event (c, a, t) is called an *input event* if $c \in \mathsf{InChan}$; it is called an *output event* if $c \in \mathsf{OutChan}$. Note that each communication event is either an input event or an output event but never both because InChan and $\mathsf{OutChan}$ are disjoint.

A *communication trace* or *history* is a finite or infinite sequence of communication events:

$$\mathsf{Hist} \stackrel{\text{def}}{=} \mathsf{ComEvt}^* \cup \mathsf{ComEvt}^\omega .$$

The domain of *hst* is the set of histories, i.e. $\mathsf{Val}_{hst} = \mathsf{Hist}$. As we model time points by real numbers we let $\mathsf{Val}_{clk} = \mathrm{IR}$.

We mentioned earlier that we refer to *hst* and *clk* only indirectly via the new commands introduced in this chapter. To prepare this we agree that Y stands for the set of variables distinct from *clk* and *hst*, and – for any $V \subseteq Y$ – VALFCT_V^A and PRED_V for valuation functions and predicates that are independent of *clk* and *hst* (A being a non-empty set):

$$\begin{aligned} Y &\stackrel{\text{def}}{=} X \setminus \{clk, hst\} \\ \mathsf{VALFCT}_V^A &\stackrel{\text{def}}{=} \{\varphi \in \mathsf{Valfct}_{V\cup\{clk,hst\}}^A \mid \varphi \ \mathsf{idp}\ clk \text{ and } \varphi \ \mathsf{idp}\ hst\} \\ \mathsf{PRED}_V &\stackrel{\text{def}}{=} \{\phi \in \mathsf{Pred}_{V\cup\{clk,hst\}} \mid \phi \ \mathsf{idp}\ clk \text{ and } \phi \ \mathsf{idp}\ hst\} . \end{aligned}$$

[3] We do not fix how the time in the model is related to real-time. This question is of no importance for the current considerations which are largely independent of specific choices.

We call commands for which *clk* and *hst* are interpreted in the special way *processes* and denote the set of processes with proper pre-alphabet V and proper post-alphabet W by Proc_V^W :

$$\mathsf{Proc}_V^W \stackrel{\text{def}}{=} \mathsf{Com}_{V\cup\{hst,clk\}}^{W\cup\{hst,clk\}} .$$

We write Proc_V for Proc_V^V and agree that from now on P, Q, R range over Proc_V^W. Moreover, x, y, z range over Y, u, v, w over $Y^\bullet$, U, V, W over subsets of Y, φ, e and ϕ over valuation functions, lists of valuation functions and predicates that are independent of *clk* and *hst*. As for Valfct, we use VALFCT_V^u as an abbreviation for $\mathsf{VALFCT}_V^{\mathsf{Val}_u}$ and VALFCT_V^c as an abbreviation for $\mathsf{VALFCT}_V^{\mathsf{Val}_c}$.

6.3 Input and Output Processes

For an output channel $out \in \mathsf{OutChan}$ and a valuation function $\varphi \in \mathsf{VALFCT}_V^c$ we define the *output process* $out\,!\,\varphi$ by

$$out\,!\,\varphi \stackrel{\text{def}}{=} [hst \neq \varepsilon \wedge hd(hst) = (out, \varphi, clk)] \;;\; hst := tl(hst) .$$

Similarly, we define for an input channel $in \in \mathsf{InChan}$ and a variable x such that $\mathsf{Val}_x = \mathsf{Val}_{in}$ the *input process* $in\,?\,x$ by

$$in\,?\,x \stackrel{\text{def}}{=} x :=? \;;\; [hst \neq \varepsilon \wedge hd(hst) = (in, x, clk)] \;;\; hst := tl(hst) .$$

These two definitions differ from the simplified ones in Sect. 6.1 only in the addition of channel names and time stamps to the communication events. We do not study laws for communication processes extensively but collect only a few that are needed in the second part of this book.

Theorem 6.3.1 (Laws for input and output processes). *Suppose* $in \in \mathsf{InChan}$, $x, y \in Y$ *such that* $\mathsf{Val}_x = \mathsf{Val}_y = \mathsf{Val}_c$, $out \in \mathsf{OutChan}$, $u \in Y^\bullet$, $\varphi \in \mathsf{VALFCT}_V^{out}$, $\varphi' \in \mathsf{VALFCT}_{V\backslash\{\!|u|\!\}}^{out}$, $e \in \mathsf{VALFCT}_V^u$.

(a) Assignments and outputs commute in the following way:

$$u := e \;;\; out\,!\,\varphi \;=\; out\,!\,\varphi[e/u] \;;\; u := e . \qquad \textit{(Assign-output)}$$

(b) Outputs commute with choice assignments provided the value written by the output process does not depend on the variables appearing in the choice assignment; the same holds for addition commands:

$$u :=? \;;\; out\,!\,\varphi \;=\; out\,!\,\varphi \;;\; u :=? \;, \quad \textit{if } \varphi \;\mathsf{idp}\; u . \qquad \textit{(Ch-ass-output)}$$

$$u^+ \;;\; out\,!\,\iota_u(\varphi') \;=\; out\,!\,\varphi' \;;\; u^+ . \qquad \textit{(Initial-output)}$$

(c) The variable in an input process can be exchanged by the following law:

$$in\,?\,x \;;\; y := x \;=\; in\,?\,y \;;\; x := y . \qquad \textit{(Input-asg)}$$

Proof. The (Assign-output) law in (a) is established by the straightforward calculation:

$$u := e \; ; \; out\,!\,\varphi$$

$=$ [Def. of output process, (Assign-assume)]

$$[hst \neq \varepsilon \wedge hd(hst) = (out, \varphi[e/u], clk)] \; ; \; u := e \; ; \; hst := tl(hst)$$

$=$ [(Comm-asg), def. of output process]

$$out\,!\,\varphi[e/u] \; ; \; u := e \; .$$

The side condition of (Comm-asg) in the second step follows from the antecedent $u \in Y^\bullet$ and $e \in \mathsf{VALFCT}_V^u$, which in particular implies that e is independent of hst.

The proof of (Ch-ass-output) and (Initial-output) is also straightforward. But the proof of (Input-asg) is more interesting. It is based on a similar property of choice assignments:

$$x :=? \; ; \; y := x \;\; = \;\; y :=? \; ; \; x := y \; . \tag{6.7}$$

Without loss of generality we can assume that x and y are distinct (both (6.7) as well as (Input-asg) are trivial otherwise). As (6.7) is symmetric in x and y it suffices to prove one of the inequalities obtained by replacing $=$ by $\leq$ resp. $\geq$:

$$x :=? \; ; \; y := x \underset{\substack{\uparrow \\ \text{[Cancel2]}}}{=} x, y :=? \; ; \; y := x \underset{\substack{\uparrow \\ \text{[Conv2]}}}{\leq} y :=? \; ; \; x := y \; ; \; y := x$$

$$\underset{\substack{\uparrow \\ \text{[Comb-asg]}}}{=} y :=? \; ; \; x, y := y, y \underset{\substack{\uparrow \\ \text{[Identity-asg]}}}{=} y :=? \; ; \; x := y \; .$$

This establishes (6.7). Now the proof of (Input-asg) is simple:

$$in\,?\,x \; ; \; y := x$$

$=$ [Def. input, (Comm-asg): $x, y \in Y$ implies the side condition]

$$x :=? \; ; \; [hst \neq \varepsilon \wedge hd(hst) = (in, x, clk)] \; ; \; y := x \; ; \; hst := tl(hst)$$

$=$ [Assign-assert1]

$$x :=? \; ; \; y := x \; ; \; [hst \neq \varepsilon \wedge hd(hst) = (in, x, clk)] \; ; \; hst := tl(hst)$$

$=$ [Choice assignment property (6.7)]

$$y :=? \; ; \; x := y \; ; \; [hst \neq \varepsilon \wedge hd(hst) = (in, x, clk)] \; ; \; hst := tl(hst)$$

$=$ [Assign-assert]

$$y :=? \; ; \; [hst \neq \varepsilon \wedge hd(hst) = (in, y, clk)] \; ; \; x := y \; ; \; hst := tl(hst)$$

$=$ [(Comm-asg): $x, y \in Y$ implies the side condition; def. of input]

$$in\,?\,y \; ; \; x := y \; .$$

□

6.4 Stop

Let us motivate the definition of the stop process Stop by an operational consideration. According to our intuition the stop process deadlocks immediately, i.e. there is no transition from Stop. Therefore, Stop diverges or terminates under no trace. So condition (a) of characterization (6.2) of the weakest precondition on p. 88 holds trivially. But (b) does not hold for the empty trace because Stop deadlocks immediately. Thus Stop is modeled by the predicate transformer

$$\mathsf{Stop}(post) \;=\; hst \neq \varepsilon \;,$$

which can be expressed on the command level by either of the identities

$$\mathsf{Stop} \overset{\text{def}}{=} \{hst \neq \varepsilon\} \;;\, \top \quad \text{and} \quad \mathsf{Stop} \overset{\text{def}}{=} [hst = \varepsilon] \;;\, \bot \;.$$

Note that Stop is an overloaded notation for processes of arbitrary pre- and post-alphabet V and W. Again we do not extensively study the laws for stop but mention just very few. They are easily established from the laws for the basic constructors.

Theorem 6.4.1 (Stop laws). *Suppose* $P \in \mathsf{Proc}_V^W$ *and* $u \in Y^\bullet$.

(a) Stop is a left zero of sequential composition:

$$\mathsf{Stop} \;;\, P \;=\; \mathsf{Stop} \;. \qquad \textit{(Stop-zero)}$$

(b) Stop absorbs addition commands:

$$u^+ \;;\, \mathsf{Stop} \;=\; \mathsf{Stop} \;. \qquad \textit{(Initial-stop)}$$

Proof. (Stop-zero) follows from the fact that $\top$ is a left zero of ;, i.e. that ; is $\top$-strict in its first argument. (Initial-stop) follows from (Initial-assert) and the fact that u^+ is $\top$-strict. □

6.5 Delays

We allow non-negative real numbers and the special value ∞ (that represents no constraint on the elapsing time) as arguments d for delays $\Delta\, d$. So let

$$\mathsf{Time} \overset{\text{def}}{=} \mathsf{IR}_{\geq 0} \cup \{\infty\} \;. \qquad (6.8)$$

The usual ordering on $\mathsf{IR}_{\geq 0}$ is extended to Time in such a way that $d \leq \infty$ for any $d \in \mathsf{Time}$. Moreover, we extend addition (that is defined on $\mathsf{IR}_{\geq 0}$ as usual) to Time by agreeing that $d_1 + d_2$ equals ∞ iff d_1 or d_2 equals ∞.

Suppose $d \in \mathsf{Time}$. The *delay process* $\Delta\, d$ models a delay of at most d time units. It enhances *clk* demonically by an arbitrary (non-negative) amount not greater than d:[4]

$$\Delta\, d \stackrel{\text{def}}{=} \bigwedge_{0 \le r \le d} clk := clk + r\ .$$

It is understood that r ranges over real values and cannot take the value ∞. Like many of the other process constructors, $\Delta\, d$ is an overloaded notation for arbitrary pre- and post-alphabet. A number of laws for delays are collected in the following theorem. Possibly the most important fact that one should remember about delays is the absence of certain laws: in general they do *not* commute with communication processes.

Theorem 6.5.1 (Δ-laws). *Let* $d, d_1, d_2 \in \mathsf{Time}$, $u \in Y^\bullet$, $e \in \mathsf{VALFCT}_V^u$, $\phi \in \mathsf{PRED}_V$, *and* $P, Q \in \mathsf{Proc}_V^W$.

(a) Delays are $\bot$- and $\top$-strict and universally conjunctive.

(b) The delay operator is antitonic:

$$\Delta\, d_1 \ \le\ \Delta\, d_2\ ,\quad \text{if } d_2 \le d_1\ . \qquad (\Delta\text{-refine})$$

(c) A zero delay is void:

$$\Delta\, 0 \ =\ \mathsf{Id}\ . \qquad (\Delta\text{-void})$$

(d) Successive delays can be summed up:

$$\Delta\, d_1\, ;\, \Delta\, d_2 \ =\ \Delta\, d_1 + d_2\ . \qquad (\Delta\text{-add})$$

(e) Delays commute with all 'internal' processes: assertions, assumptions, assignments, and choice assignments:

$$\{\phi\}\, ;\, \Delta\, d \ =\ \Delta\, d\, ;\, \{\phi\}\ . \qquad (\Delta\text{-assert})$$

$$[\phi]\, ;\, \Delta\, d \ =\ \Delta\, d\, ;\, [\phi]\ . \qquad (\Delta\text{-assume})$$

$$u := e\, ;\, \Delta\, d \ =\ \Delta\, d\, ;\, u := e\ . \qquad (\Delta\text{-assign})$$

$$u :=?\, ;\, \Delta\, d \ =\ \Delta\, d\, ;\, u :=?\ . \qquad (\Delta\text{-choice})$$

(f) Delays commute with addition and deletion commands:

$$u^+\, ;\, \Delta\, d \ =\ \Delta\, d\, ;\, u^+\ . \qquad (\text{Initial-}\Delta)$$

$$\Delta\, d\, ;\, u^- \ =\ u^-\, ;\, \Delta\, d\ . \qquad (\text{Final-}\Delta)$$

---

[4] It is not difficult to generalize to state-dependent delays but we do not need them. The argument of Δ is then a Time-valuation functions φ instead of a Time value d. The definition is

$$\Delta\, \varphi \stackrel{\text{def}}{=} \bigwedge_{r \ge 0} [\phi \le r]\, ;\, clk := clk + r\ .$$

For state-dependent delays the (Δ-assign) law in the below Theorem 6.5.1 takes the form

$$u := e\, ;\, \Delta\, \varphi \ =\ \Delta\, \varphi[e/u]\, ;\, u := e\ .$$

The laws combining delays with choice assignment, addition or deletion commands require that φ is independent from u.

(g) Delays are absorbed by the stop process:

$$\Delta\, d\, ;\, \mathsf{Stop} \;=\; \mathsf{Stop}\ . \qquad (\Delta\text{-}stop)$$

(h) Delays distribute over conditionals:

$$\Delta\, d\, ;\, (P \lhd \phi \rhd Q) \;=\; (\Delta\, d\, ;\, P) \lhd \phi \rhd (\Delta\, d\, ;\, Q)\ . \qquad (\Delta\text{-}cond)$$

The laws in (e) and (f) critically depend upon the fact that the occurring valuation functions and predicates do not depend on *clk* and that the variable list u does not contain *clk*.

Proof. The distribution properties in (a) follow from the $\bot$- and $\top$-strictness of assignments and their universal conjunctivity and the fact that these properties are preserved by meets.

(Δ-refine) follows from the fact that the greatest lower bound of a set is a lower bound for any subset of that set. (Δ-void) follows from the fact that the greatest lower bound of a singleton equals its element together with the law (Identity-asg). For the proof of (Δ-add) note first that

$$
\begin{aligned}
& \Delta\, d_1\ ;\ \Delta\, d_2 \\
=\ & \quad [\text{Defs}] \\
& \bigwedge_{0\le r\le d_1} \mathit{clk} := \mathit{clk} + r\ ;\ \bigwedge_{0\le r'\le d_2} \mathit{clk} := \mathit{clk} + r' \\
=\ & \quad [\text{Assignments are conjunctive}] \\
& \bigwedge_{0\le r\le d_1}\ \bigwedge_{0\le r'\le d_2} \mathit{clk} := \mathit{clk} + r\ ;\ \mathit{clk} := \mathit{clk} + r' \\
=\ & \quad [\text{Comb-asg}] \\
& \bigwedge_{0\le r\le d_1}\ \bigwedge_{0\le r'\le d_2} \mathit{clk} := \mathit{clk} + r + r'\ .
\end{aligned}
$$

We have to show that this equals $\Delta\, d_1 + d_2 \;=\; \bigwedge_{0\le s\le d_1+d_2} \mathit{clk} := \mathit{clk} + s$. It is easy to see that $\Delta\, d_1\ ;\ \Delta\, d_2$ is a lower bound of the set $\{\mathit{clk} := \mathit{clk} + s \mid 0 \le s \le d_1 + d_2\}$. If s with $0 \le s \le d_1 + d_2$ is given we can certainly choose r and r' such that $s = r + r'$, $0 \le r \le d_1$, and $0 \le r' \le d_2$, which implies

$$
\begin{aligned}
& \mathit{clk} := \mathit{clk} + s \\
=\ & \quad [\text{Choice of } r \text{ and } r'] \\
& \mathit{clk} := \mathit{clk} + r + r' \\
\ge\ & \quad [\text{Greatest lower bound property}] \\
& \bigwedge_{0\le r'\le d_2} \mathit{clk} := \mathit{clk} + r + r'
\end{aligned}
$$

$\geq$ [Greatest lower bound property]

$$\bigwedge_{0\leq r\leq d_1} \bigwedge_{0\leq r'\leq d_2} clk := clk + r + r'$$

$=$ [Identity above]

$$\Delta\, d_1 \; ; \Delta\, d_2 \; .$$

Therefore, $\Delta\, d_1 \; ; \Delta\, d_2 \leq \Delta\, d_1 + d_2$. The other inequality is proved by a similar consideration.

The commutation properties in item (e) and (f) are shown by straightforward calculations that exploit the positive conjunctivity of the occurring commands. As an example we present the proof of (Δ-assume):

$$[\phi] \; ; \Delta\, d \underset{\substack{\uparrow \\ \text{[Def]}}}{=} [\phi] \; ; \bigwedge_{0\leq r\leq d} clk := clk + r \underset{\substack{\uparrow \\ \text{[Assertions are positive conj.]}}}{=} \bigwedge_{0\leq r\leq d} [\phi] \; ; clk := clk + r$$

$$\underset{\substack{\uparrow \\ \text{[Assert-assume1]}}}{=} \bigwedge_{0\leq r\leq d} clk := clk + r \; ; [\phi] \underset{\substack{\uparrow \\ [\,\cdot\; ; \pi \text{ is conj}]}}{=} (\bigwedge_{0\leq r\leq d} clk := clk + r) \; ; [\phi]$$

$$\underset{\substack{\uparrow \\ \text{[Def]}}}{=} \Delta\, d \, ; [\phi] \; .$$

The proof of (Δ-stop) and (Δ-cond) is even simpler because the laws that have already been established can be applied. For example,

$$\Delta\, d \, ; \mathsf{Stop} \underset{\substack{\uparrow \\ \text{[Def]}}}{=} \Delta\, d \, ; \{hst \neq \varepsilon\} \; ; \top \underset{\substack{\uparrow \\ [\Delta\text{-assert}]}}{=} \{hst \neq \varepsilon\} \; ; \Delta\, d \; ; \top$$

$$\underset{\substack{\uparrow \\ [\Delta\, d \text{ is } \top\text{-strict}]}}{=} \{hst \neq \varepsilon\} \; ; \top \underset{\substack{\uparrow \\ \text{[Def]}}}{=} \mathsf{Stop}$$

establishes (Δ-stop). We exploit here that (Δ-assert) remains valid if ϕ depends on *hst*. □

6.6 Time Bounds

We now consider the *time bound* operator. Intuitively $|\, P \,| \preceq d$ restricts the execution time of P until termination to at most d time units. Formally we define for $d \in \mathsf{Time}$ and $P \in \mathsf{Proc}_V^W$

$$|\, P \,| \preceq d \stackrel{\text{def}}{=} \bigwedge_{a \in \mathbb{R} \cup \{\infty\}} [clk + d = a] \; ; P \; ; [clk \leq a] \; .$$

$|\, P \,| \preceq d$ is again in Proc_V^W. The meta-variable a catches the initial value of $clk + d$ by the generalized conditional construction that has been discussed in connection with the (Span) law. This value is an upper bound for the final value of *clk*. Any implementation of $|P| \preceq d$ must produce its result in up to d time units as it cannot implement the miracle that arises otherwise.[5]

The final assumption only restricts the value of the *clk* variable for terminating computations of P. Hence, a time bound does not enforce termination. Indeed one of the time bound laws in Theorem 6.6.1 below states that $|\bot| \preceq d = \bot$, which shows this at an extreme example.

Clearly, $|P| \preceq d$ is monotonic in P. Moreover, the (Span) law shows that $|P| \preceq d$ can be equivalently defined by the identity

$$|P| \preceq d \;=\; \bigvee_{a \in \mathbb{R} \cup \{\infty\}} \{clk + d = a\} \,;\, P \,;\, [clk \leq a] \,. \tag{6.9}$$

A number of laws for time bounds are collected in the following theorem.

Theorem 6.6.1 (Laws for time bounds). *Suppose* $P, P_1 \in \mathsf{Proc}_V^W$, $P_2 \in \mathsf{Proc}_W^U$, $d, d_1, d_2 \in \mathsf{Time}$, $\phi \in \mathsf{PRED}_V$, $u \in Y^\bullet$, $e \in \mathsf{VALFCT}_V^u$, $in \in \mathsf{InChan}$, $x \in Y$, *with* $\mathsf{Val}_x = \mathsf{Val}_{in}$, $out \in \mathsf{OutChan}$, *and* $\varphi \in \mathsf{VALFCT}_V^{out}$.

(a) *An infinite upper bound poses no constraint:*

$$|P| \preceq \infty \;=\; P \,. \qquad \textit{(Void-bound)}$$

(b) *Decreasing an upper bound improves a process, i.e. the bound operator is antitonic in its Time argument:*

$$|P| \preceq d_1 \;\geq\; |P| \preceq d_2 \,, \;\; \textit{if } d_1 \leq d_2 \,. \qquad \textit{(Bound-refine)}$$

(c) *Any process is improved by introducing a new time bound:*

$$|P| \preceq d \;\geq\; P \,. \qquad \textit{(Bound-intro)}$$

(d) *Nested bounds can be combined:*

$$||P| \preceq d_1| \preceq d_2 \;=\; |P| \preceq Min(d_1, d_2) \,. \qquad \textit{(Bound-comb)}$$

(e) *Splitting a bound over a sequential composition is an improving transformation:*

$$|P_1| \preceq d_1 \,;\, |P_2| \preceq d_2 \;\geq\; |P_1 \,;\, P_2| \preceq d_1 + d_2 \,. \qquad \textit{(Bound-add)}$$

(f) *Assertions, assumptions, assignments, addition and deletion commands, input and output processes,* $\top$, $\bot$, Id *and* Stop *distribute rightwards over time bounds:*

$$Q \,;\, |P| \preceq d \;=\; |Q \,;\, P| \preceq d \,, \qquad \textit{(Bound-initial)}$$
$$Q \in \{\{\phi\}, [\phi], u := e, u^+, u^\oplus, u^-, in\,?\,x, out\,!\,\varphi, \top, \bot, \mathsf{Id}, \mathsf{Stop}\} \,.$$

---

[5] Like delays, time bounds can easily be generalized to state-dependent time bounds $|p| \preceq \varphi$. Just replace d by φ in the definition. But, again, we do not need this generality. For state-dependent time bounds the (Bound-add) law (see Lemma 6.6.1 below) is more complicated because φ_2's value must not be changed by P_1. Moreover, (Bound-initial) for assignments looks as follows:

$$u := e \,;\, |P| \preceq \varphi \;=\; |u := e \,;\, P| \preceq \varphi[e/u] \,.$$

(g) *Assumptions, assignments, addition and deletion commands, inputs, outputs,* $\top$, Id *and* Stop *distribute leftwards over time bounds:*

$$|P| \preceq d\,;Q \;=\; |P\,;Q| \preceq d\;, \qquad \textit{(Bound-final)}$$
$$\textit{for } Q \in \{[\phi], u := e, u^+, u^\oplus, u^-, in\,?\,x, out\,!\,\varphi, \top, \mathsf{Id}, \mathsf{Stop}\}\;.$$

(h) *Restricting the execution time of an assignment or of skip is redundant as immediate execution is part of their semantics:*

$$|\,u := e\,| \preceq d \;=\; u := e\;. \qquad \textit{(Bound-asg)}$$
$$|\,\mathsf{Id}\,| \preceq d \;=\; \mathsf{Id}\;. \qquad \textit{(Bound-}\mathsf{Id}\textit{)}$$

(i) $\perp$, $\top$ *and* Stop *are fixpoints of time bounds:*

$$|\,Q\,| \preceq d \;=\; Q\;,\;\; \textit{for } Q \in \{\perp, \top, \mathsf{Stop}\}\;. \qquad \textit{(Bound-fixpoint)}$$

(j) *A time bound that bounds just a single delay can be expressed by a single delay alone:*

$$|\,\Delta\, d_1\,| \preceq d_2 \;=\; \Delta\, Min(d_1, d_2)\;. \qquad \textit{(}\Delta\textit{-bound)}$$

(k) *Time bounds distribute over conditionals:*

$$|\,P \lhd \phi \rhd Q\,| \preceq d \;=\; (|\,P\,| \preceq d) \lhd \phi \rhd (|\,Q\,| \preceq d)\;. \qquad \textit{(Bound-cond)}$$

For the validity of (f) and (g) independence of ϕ and e from *clk* and *hst* is not required. In addition (f), (g) and (h) remain valid if u contains *hst*. However, absence of *clk*, which is implied by $u \in Y^\bullet$, is essential.

Once again one should memorize the exceptions to rightward and leftward distribution. The most prominent exceptions are delays, which in general distribute neither rightwards nor leftwards over time bounds. Leftward distribution, moreover, does not hold for assertions and $\perp$.

Proof. The proof is by straightforward considerations and calculations. For some proofs it is advantageous to use the identity (6.9) instead of the definition of time bounds. □

6.7 Discussion

The distinguished use of *clk* and *hst* puts a certain asymmetry into the space of processes. The duals of communications, delays, bounds and stop can be defined easily. But we do not yet have any use for them.

We consider only upper-bounded delays and time bounds here. Their treatment provides the largest challenge in a code generator proof. Lower bounded delays are usually implemented directly by some service available on the target processor like timers or timeout mechanisms.

As mentioned earlier, the trace model of communications is not able to explain external choice and parallel composition properly. We believe that this can be done by using the variable *hst* not only for traces but for failures like in CSP [40], or by adding another special variable *rdy*. But an investigation of this question is outside the scope of this monograph.

The definition of timing implicitly assumes that the user is interested only in the timing of external communications, which can be observed via the trace variable *hst*, but not in the timing of internal steps.

7. Data Refinement

The use of data refinement in program development is an instance of the general strategy of separation of concerns. The idea is to develop programs first on 'abstract' data types, which are chosen to ease the description and algorithmic solution of the problem at hand. The representation of these (abstract) data types by the (more concrete) data types available in the programming language of the implementation is treated afterwards as a separate task. It is this transition from abstract to concrete data types that traditionally is called data refinement. In order to achieve an actual separation of algorithm design and data representation, data refinement should preserve the algorithmic structure of programs.

Classic references for data refinement are C.A.R. Hoare's paper 'Proof of Correctness of Data Representation' [39] and the work done in the context of the Vienna Development Method VDM [10, 47]. Data refinement is approached there in the context of procedural imperative programming. A data type is modeled by a set of distinguished (global) variables, called *data type variables*, that are used only by a distinguished set of procedures, called *operations* of the data type. The above references describe rules for proving that a data type, called the *abstract* data type, can be replaced by another data type with corresponding operations, called the *concrete* data type, without affecting overall correctness of the program. The key ideas are the use of data type invariants and of retrieve mappings.

A *data type invariant* is a condition on the values of the data type variables. It must be established by their initialization and be preserved by each operation of the data type. The purpose of a data type invariant essentially is to allow data types that are not represented as a Cartesian product.

A *retrieve mapping* describes the relationship between the concrete and the abstract data type in a data refinement. It assigns to each concrete state, i.e. to each collection of values for the concrete variables which satisfy the invariant of the concrete data type, the represented abstract state. For demonstrating correctness of a data refinement it must be shown that the retrieval state always satisfies the invariant of the abstract data type and that corresponding operations of the abstract and concrete data type are well-behaved with respect to the retrieve mapping. The latter essentially is a proof that

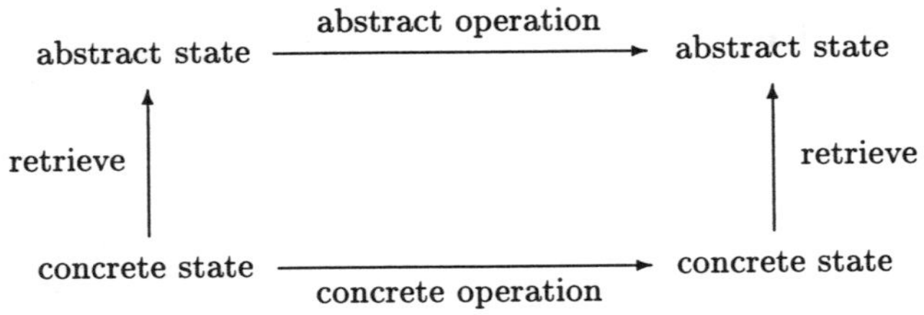

Fig. 7.1. Proof obligation for operations

the diagram in Fig. 7.1 commutes. The exact form of these proof obligations is complicated by partiality and possible non-determinacy of operations.

In the context of weakest precondition semantics and the refinement calculus data refinement has been approached by R.J.R. Back & J. von Wright [3, 4, 5], D. Gries & J. Prins [32], J.M. Morris [66], C.C. Morgan & P.H.B. Gardiner [25, 63] and W. Chen & J.T. Udding [17]. We refer here mainly to the work of Morris and Morgan & Gardiner who formalize data refinement in the same way except of some minor technical variations. They understand data refinement as a relation $\prec_{a,c,CI}$ between commands (= predicate transformers) that is parameterized by

- a list of *abstract variables* a,
- a list of *concrete variables* c, and
- a *coupling (or abstraction) invariant* CI.

CI is a formula that describes the relationship between the abstract and concrete variables. It couples corresponding values of a and c, which explains its name [31]. CI can be an arbitrary formula which means that the method is not restricted to a functional relationship like retrieve mappings. The use of data type invariants and retrieve mappings can be considered as a special instance. The data type invariants are represented by formulas Inv_a (in the variables a) and Inv_c (in the variables c) and the retrieve mapping by a list of expressions e (in the variables c). The coupling invariant is chosen to be

$$CI \stackrel{\text{def}}{=} Inv_a \Rightarrow (Inv_c \wedge a = e) \ .$$

This special case that frequently occurs in practice is called *functional data refinement* [66].

The most important condition for $\prec_{a,c,CI}$ being reasonable is that data refinement implies the algorithmic refinement of the blocks in which the variables a and c are made local. Writing $|[u \mid I \bullet P]|$ for a block with local variables u, initialization condition I and body P this is made precise by the implication

$$\text{if } A \prec_{a,c,CI} C \text{ and } I_c \Rightarrow (\exists a : CI \wedge I_a) \text{ then } |[a \mid I_a \bullet A]| \leq |[c \mid I_c \bullet C]|$$

for any two commands A, C (with appropriate alphabet). This property formalizes the intuitive idea that the change from a to c when developing C

from A does not invalidate observable properties. Morgan and Gardiner call this property the 'soundness of data refinement' and prove it as a theorem for their definition of $\prec_{a,c,CI}$ [63, Theorem 1]. Morris [66] establishes a similar theorem.

The intuitive requirement that the algorithmic structure can be preserved in a data refinement is addressed by showing that data refinement can be performed piecewise. For example the two components of a sequential composition $P ; Q$ can be independently 'data-refined' as the following theorem shows [63, theorem2].

$$\text{If } P \prec_{a,c,CI} P' \text{ and } Q \prec_{a,c,CI} Q' \text{ then } P ; Q \prec_{a,c,CI} P' ; Q' \;. \tag{7.1}$$

At first glance this property seems to be monotonicity of ; w.r.t. $\prec_{a,c,CI}$. However, this interpretation is a bit misleading because $\prec_{a,c,CI}$ is not an ordering relation: in general it is neither reflexive nor antisymmetric nor transitive.

Morris as well as Morgan & Gardiner define the relation $\prec_{a,c,CI}$ between commands as follows:

$$P \prec_{a,c,CI} Q \;\text{ iff }\; \begin{array}{l}\text{for all formulas } \psi \text{ not containing } c \text{ free we have} \\ (\exists a : CI \wedge [\![P]\!]\psi) \Rightarrow [\![Q]\!](\exists a : CI \wedge \psi) \;.\end{array} \tag{7.2}$$

It is understood that P does not use c and Q does not use a. This definition is given in the mixture of syntax and semantics style that unfortunately is so common in the context of predicate transformer semantics. A definition in a strictly semantic space requires the introduction of alphabets in order to enable a precise interpretation of the condition 'ψ is a formula not containing c free' and the implicit assumptions that P does not use c and Q does not use a. Below we give such a definition of data refinement in our framework. Besides of aiming for a precise formulation, we differ from the Morris/Morgan/Gardiner definition only in two respects.

- We express the definition on the level of commands without referring directly to their interpretation as predicate transformers. This allows to calculate with the laws for commands established in Chap. 5 when reasoning about general properties or deriving concrete instances of data refinement.
- We capture data refinement by a Galois connection $(Co_{a,c,CI}, Ab_{a,c,CI})$ in the first place not by a relation $\prec_{a,c,CI}$.

$Co_{a,c,CI}$ as well as $Ab_{a,c,CI}$ can be understood as unary operators on commands. The intuition is as follows: if A is a command that works on a and some global variables g then $Co_{a,c,CI}(A)$ is the worst command that works on c, g instead of a, g corresponding to A. The relationship between a and c in the initial and final state is described by the coupling invariant CI. Similarly, for a command C working on the concrete variables c (and the global variables g), $Ab_{a,c,CI}(C)$ is the best command working on a, g instead of c, g that is data-refined by C. Thus the relation $A \prec_{a,c,CI} C$, A is data-refined by C w.r.t. a, c, CI, can be defined by one of the two conditions

$$Co_{a,c,CI}(A) \leq C \quad \text{or} \quad A \leq Ab_{a,c,CI}(C) \ ,$$

which are equivalent because $(Co_{a,c,CI}, Ab_{a,c,CI})$ is a Galois connection.

Treating data refinement by operators on commands enables to derive data refinements by normal refinement calculations: if we are looking for a data refinement of a command P that is specified by a, c, CI we can simply take $Q = Co_{a,c,CI}(P)$. We sometimes call this *definitional data refinement.* Q is a correct data refinement by definition but it is given only by reference to P. By applying normal refinement laws we can hopefully remove the reference to P and derive more concrete data refinements since every refinement R of Q is a data refinement of P.

In contrast when capturing data refinement only by a relation $\prec_{a,c,CI}$ calculation of data refinements in the above sense is not possible. As noticed earlier, $\prec_{a,c,CI}$ is not an ordering relation, thus we cannot calculate sensibly with $\prec_{a,c,CI}$-chains. Hence, we must either use a calculation on the meta-level, i.e. with meta-level implications, or establish a data refinement for a composed term in one step.[1] Let's look at the 'distributivity of data refinement' in order to illustrate this point. In the Morris/Morgan/Gardiner framework it is expressed by the meta-level implication (7.1); in the Galois connection framework it is just sub-distributivity of $Co_{a,c,CI}$ and super-distributivity of $Ab_{a,c,CI}$:

$$Co_{a,c,CI}(P_1 \ ; P_2) \ \leq \ Co_{a,c,CI}(P_1) \ ; Co_{a,c,CI}(P_2) \quad \text{and}$$
$$Ab_{a,c,CI}(Q_1 \ ; Q_2) \ \geq \ Ab_{a,c,CI}(Q_1) \ ; Ab_{a,c,CI}(Q_2) \ .$$

These laws can be applied in linear refinement calculations.

The idea of treating data refinement as a sub-distributive operator instead of as a relation between commands and the detection of the benefits for a calculational approach is due to C.A.R. Hoare, H. Jifeng and J.W. Sanders [44]. Their work is in a different semantic framework, viz. relational semantics.

Data refinement classically is applied for the representation of abstract data types during program design. The Galois connection $(Co_{a,c,CI}, Ab_{a,c,CI})$, however, can just as well be used for the reverse process, viz. for data abstraction. Similar to data refinement the Galois connection framework here enables *definitional abstraction*: if Q is a command that is to be 'data-abstracted' w.r.t. a, c, CI then we can simply take $P = Ab_{a,c,CI}(Q)$. By definition P and each approximation to P, i.e. each command R with $R \leq P$, is a correct data

[1] Admittedly the latter is often practicable. The rules established in [25, 63, 66] facilitate such one step data refinements. Moreover, it is advisable to consider data refinement of components in isolation first. Their combination corresponds to the application of a meta-level implication. But neither the approach to formulate and exploit rules facilitating one-step data refinements nor the modularity offered by isolated consideration of components is lost in the Galois connection framework. Only their status is reduced from a must to an option.

Strictly speaking, the Galois connection framework also appeals to a one-step data refinement but has a very simple rule, viz. $P \prec_{a,c,CI} Co_{a,c,CI}(P)$. The essential considerations are then performed by refining $Co_{a,c,CI}(P)$.

abstraction of Q. Such approximations can be derived by calculations with $\leq$-chains using the refinement laws and exploiting the super-distributivity of $Ab_{a,c,CI}$. These remarks about definitional concretization and abstraction apply to all concretizations and abstractions described by distributive Galois connections. Data refinement is just an often arising special instance.

We now define the data refinement Galois connection. Suppose $V \subseteq X$ is the set of global variables that are not affected by the data refinement.

Definition 7.1.1 (Data refinement Galois connection). *Suppose given disjoint lists of variables $a \in (X \setminus V)^\bullet$ and $c \in (X \setminus V)^\bullet$ and a predicate $CI \in \mathsf{Pred}_{V \cup \{a\} \cup \{c\}}$.*

(a) The pair $(Co_{a,c,CI}, Ab_{a,c,CI})$ of mappings

$$Co_{a,c,CI} \in [\mathsf{Com}_{V\cup\{a\}}^{V\cup\{a\}} \to \mathsf{Com}_{V\cup\{c\}}^{V\cup\{c\}}]$$
$$Ab_{a,c,CI} \in [\mathsf{Com}_{V\cup\{c\}}^{V\cup\{c\}} \to \mathsf{Com}_{V\cup\{a\}}^{V\cup\{a\}}]$$

defined by

$$Co_{a,c,CI}(P) \overset{\text{def}}{=} a^\oplus \,;\, \{CI\} \,;\, c^- \,;\, P \,;\, c^+ \,;\, [\,CI\,] \,;\, a^-$$
$$Ab_{a,c,CI}(Q) \overset{\text{def}}{=} c^+ \,;\, [\,CI\,] \,;\, a^- \,;\, Q \,;\, a^\oplus \,;\, \{CI\} \,;\, c^-$$

is called the data refinement Galois connection *w.r.t. abstract variables a, concrete variables c and coupling invariant CI.*

(b) P is called data-refined *by Q w.r.t. a, c, CI iff $P \leq Ab_{a,c,CI}(Q)$.*

$Co_{a,c,CI}$ and $Ab_{a,c,CI}$ describe the concretization and abstraction of entire commands. Let us illustrate their definition by the representation of a Boolean variable a by an integer variable c in such a way that odd numbers represent the Boolean value true and even numbers the value false. This data refinement is described by the coupling invariant $CI \equiv (a = odd(c))$. Thus we have

$$Co_{a,c,CI}(P) = a^\oplus \,;\, \{a = odd(c)\} \,;\, c^- \,;\, P \,;\, c^+ \,;\, [a = odd(c)] \,;\, a^-$$
$$Ab_{a,c,CI}(Q) = c^+ \,;\, [a = odd(c)] \,;\, a^- \,;\, Q \,;\, a^\oplus \,;\, \{a = odd(c)\} \,;\, c^- \,.$$

$Ab_{a,c,CI}(Q)$ is the best command working on a that corresponds to a given command Q working on c. Intuitively it behaves as follows: c is initialized with some representation of a's initial value and Q is executed. After termination of Q the Boolean value represented by the final value of c is assigned to a. As $Ab_{a,c,CI}(Q)$ is to be a command working on a instead of c, the change to c caused by Q is hidden by the surrounding c^+ and c^- commands. The demonic addition command c^+ together with the assumption $[a = odd(c)]$ also gives rise to c's proper initialization. Intuitively, Q is a command that does not use a. In the Morris/Morgan/Gardiner formulation this is a (not entirely formalized) syntactic condition. Here it is expressed by the alphabet $V \cup \{c\}$ of Q that is disjoint from a. The commands a^- and $a^\oplus$ embed Q into the state space $V \cup \{a\} \cup \{c\}$. The angelic addition command $a^\oplus$ together with the assertion $\{a = odd(c)\}$ also gives rise to the assignment of a proper final value to a. $Co_{a,c,CI}$ can be interpreted in a similar way.

$(Co_{a,c,CI}, Ab_{a,c,CI})$ is induced by the simulation (A, C) between $V \cup \{c\}$ and $V \cup \{a\}$ defined by

$$A = a^{\oplus} ; \{CI\} ; c^{-} \quad \text{and} \quad C = c^{+} ; [CI] ; a^{-} .$$

Thus by Lemma 5.3.2, (d), $(Co_{a,c,CI}, Ab_{a,c,CI})$ is a distributive Galois connection. A is the (non-deterministic) state transformer that computes corresponding abstract states from concrete states and C is the (non-deterministic) state transformer that computes concrete states from abstract ones. From Lemma 5.3.2 and the definition of Galois connections we obtain also that each of the following conditions expresses that P is data-refined by Q:

- $P \leq Ab_{a,c,CI}(Q)$.
- $Co_{a,c,CI}(P) \leq Q$.
- $A ; P \leq Q ; A$.
- $P ; C \leq C ; Q$.

As mentioned, our definition of data refinement is just a reformulation and formalization of Morris, Morgan and Gardiner's definition. This becomes clear by considering the following chain of equivalences and comparing the result to (7.2):

P is data-refined by Q

iff [Third characterization above, definition of A]

$a^{\oplus} ; \{CI\} ; c^{-} ; P \leq Q ; a^{\oplus} ; \{CI\} ; c^{-}$

iff [Definition of basic commands and the order on commands]

$\mathbf{E}_a(CI \wedge \iota_c(P(\psi))) \leq Q(\mathbf{E}_a(CI \wedge \iota_c(\psi)))$, for all $\psi \in \mathsf{Pred}_{V \cup \{a\}}$.

The soundness result for data refinements can be proved by calculation on the command level.

Theorem 7.1.2 (Soundness of data refinement). *If P is data-refined by Q w.r.t. a, c and CI then*

$$a^{+} ; P ; a^{-} \leq c^{+} ; [\mathbf{E}_a(CI)] ; Q ; c^{-} .$$

Proof. Since P is data-refined by Q we have $P \leq c^{+} ; [CI] ; a^{-} ; Q ; a^{\oplus} ; \{CI\} ; c^{-}$. Thus

$a^{+} ; P ; a^{-}$

$\leq$ [Above inequality]

$a^{+} ; c^{+} ; [CI] ; a^{-} ; Q ; a^{\oplus} ; \{CI\} ; c^{-} ; a^{-}$

$=$ [$\Diamond$-union]

$c^{+} ; a^{+} ; [CI] ; a^{-} ; Q ; a^{\oplus} ; \{CI\} ; a^{-} ; c^{-}$

$$\begin{aligned}
\leq\ & [\text{(Assertion Id) yields } \{CI\} \leq \mathsf{Id}] \\
& c^+ \,;\, a^+ \,;\, [CI] \,;\, a^- \,;\, Q \,;\, a^\oplus \,;\, a^- \,;\, c^- \\
\leq\ & [\text{Restrict-demon}] \\
& c^+ \,;\, [\mathbf{E}_a(CI)] \,;\, a^\oplus \,;\, a^- \,;\, Q \,;\, a^\oplus \,;\, a^- \,;\, c^- \\
=\ & [\oplus\text{-}{-}\text{-sim}] \\
& c^+ \,;\, [\mathbf{E}_a(CI)] \,;\, Q \,;\, c^- \ . \qquad \square
\end{aligned}$$

From the command laws we could derive laws about $Co_{a,c,CI}$ and $Ab_{a,c,CI}$, which could assist concrete data refinements and would correspond to the rules established by Morris and Morgan & Gardiner. But this is beyond the scope of this book.

We often apply ***pure data abstractions***, which are data abstractions with an empty list of abstract variables, i.e. $a = \varepsilon$. In this case the definition of $Ab_{a,c,CI}$ simplifies to

$$Ab_{\varepsilon,c,CI}(Q) \ = \ c^+ \,;\, [CI] \,;\, Q \,;\, \{CI\} \,;\, c^- \ .$$

$Ab_{\varepsilon,c,CI}(Q)$ can be interpreted as a description of Q that abstracts from the variables c but assumes that CI holds initially and is guaranteed upon termination. So CI essentially describes an invariant on c. Pure data abstractions are sensible if the invariant CI embodies all the information about c's use.

In this chapter we captured data refinement by distributive Galois connections. This shows that concretization and abstraction by Galois connections generalizes the classic technique of data refinement. Most but not all abstractions for the Transputer's behavior in Chap. 10 are data abstractions.

8. Transputer Base Model

Traditionally one assumes as basis for code generator verification that source and target language semantics are completely known. But if code for an actual processor is to be generated this is not realistic. The documentation provided by the manufacturer of the processor usually presents a model of the processor's execution cycle rather than a semantics of a machine language. An example is the Transputer's instruction manual [46], which gives in Appendix F such a model in a semi-formal manner. There is not even a notion of an executed machine program but the computation is steered by the contents of the memory cell pointed to by an instruction pointer. Of course, the description of the execution cycle is justified by an implicit idea of machine programs and such an idea is also implicit in the informal notion of instructions; but it is not explicit in the model. The Transputer manual is a quite typical example for the information that is obtained from the manufacturer of a processor (although not for the form in which this information is presented; in this respect the rather precise way of [46] is a positive exception rather than the rule).

A model of the execution cycle allows a more accurate and straightforward specification of the processor's behavior than a semantics of a machine language. For example, it explains immediately the behavior of self-modifying code. Although compilers usually do not exploit self-modifying code, system programs like loaders and operating systems clearly do. For the compiler builder it is surely essential to ensure that the target code does not destroy itself. But whether the taken care is sufficient or not can only be judged if the reference model does not ignore this effect, which is the case or at least likely for the simplistic models that are frequently used in the compiler verification literature. Anyhow, if we base the correctness considerations on an abstract semantics, which assumes machine programs as independent entities, we leave a gap between the assumed semantics and the documentation provided by the manufacturer. In order to avoid this gap for our case study and to interface to the Transputer's documentation, we start from a model of the Transputer's execution cycle that is presented in this chapter. We do not discuss the Transputer architecture in detail here. The reader is referred to the relevant literature in this respect, in particular to [46]

In Sect. 8.1 we define basic constants, data-types and operators. In particular we agree on conventions that make the arithmetic operators total on Transputer words. In Sect. 8.2 we study the relevant components of the Transputer and discuss how they are represented in the language of processes. Section 8.3 discusses the format of Transputer instructions and introduces some related operators. In Sect. 8.4 we reformulate the Transputer model of [46, Appendix F] by a structured set of axioms in the form of refinement formulas for a certain collection of processes that model various parts of Transputer execution. Some remarks in Sect. 8.5 about the presented model conclude this chapter.

8.1 Basic Data-Types and Constants

Like the description in the Transputer instruction set manual [46], our formalization of the Transputer is parameterized with some constants that vary with the word length. It therefore applies like that description to Transputers of different word length by adjustment of these constants. We cite their definition essentially from [46, p. 127]. *bpw* (bytes per word) is the number of bytes in a word. A typical value for *bpw* is four. We assume that *bpw* is a power of two as this simplifies some of the following definitions and is the case for all available Transputers. *wordlength* is the number of bits in a word and is given by

$$wordlength \;=\; bpw * 8 \;.$$

byteselectlength is the smallest number of bits needed to distinguish the bytes in a word. The value of this constant is characterized by being the unique solution of

$$2^{byteselectlength-1} < bpw \leq 2^{byteselectlength} \;.$$

The mask *byteselectmask* is used to extract these bits from a pointer. It is given by

$$byteselectmask \;=\; 2^{byteselectlength} - 1 \;.$$

We use the following basic value sets and operators.

- Word is the set of words, i.e. of bit strings of length *wordlength*. The members of Word are identified with numbers x in the range $\mathsf{MostNeg} \leq x \leq \mathsf{MostPos}$ by two's complement representation, where $\mathsf{MostNeg} \stackrel{\text{def}}{=} -2^{wordlength-1}$ and $\mathsf{MostPos} \stackrel{\text{def}}{=} 2^{wordlength-1} - 1$.
- Byte is the set of bytes, i.e. bit strings of length eight, identified with numbers in the range $0 \leq x < 256$.
- Nibble is the set of nibbles, i.e. bit strings of length four, identified with numbers in the range $0 \leq x < 16$.

- Hexadecimal number representations are written with a leading **$** before the numerals. So **$2A** is the hexadecimal notation for the number 42.
- On word values we use bitnot for denoting bitwise not, bitor for bitwise or and bitand for bitwise and. $\ll$ denotes (arithmetic) shift left and $\gg$ (arithmetic) shift right of their first (Word) argument by the number of bits specified in the second (non-negative integer) argument. $+$ is used for denoting wrapped around addition. In particular, $\mathsf{MostPos} + 1 = \mathsf{MostNeg}$. Similarly, we use the other common arithmetic operators $-$, $*$, $\div$, and rem as total operators on Word values. For the division operators $\div$ and rem we agree that quotient as well as remainder of a division by zero and of the division of $\mathsf{MostNeg}$ by -1 is zero. We use the operator $-$ and $+$ also as unary operator on Word in such a way that $-w$ equals $0 - w$. Note that this in particular implies that $-\mathsf{MostNeg} = \mathsf{MostNeg}$.
  It is usually clear from context whether the arithmetic operators refer to the corresponding operations on Word or on integers. If a misunderstanding seems possible, we index the operations on Word by w (writing e.g. $+_\mathsf{w}$) and the integer operations by i (as in $+_\mathsf{i}$). As usual we write the binary operations on words and integers in infix form.
- For capturing the situations in which the Transputer sets its error flag when performing an arithmetic operation, we use the functions *AddOvFl*, *SubOvFl*, *MulOvFl*, *DivOvFl* $\in (\mathsf{Word} \times \mathsf{Word} \to \mathsf{Bool})$. The first three yield true if and only if the corresponding arithmetic operation on integers yields a value that is not in Word, e.g. we have

$$AddOvFl(v, w) \quad = \quad \begin{cases} \mathsf{tt} & \text{if } v +_\mathsf{i} w \notin \mathsf{Word} \\ \mathsf{ff} & \text{otherwise} \end{cases}$$

  for $v, w \in \mathsf{Word}$. The definition of *DivOvFl* takes in addition into account the 'undefinedness' of a division by zero:

$$DivOvFl(v, w) \quad = \quad \begin{cases} \mathsf{tt} & \text{if } v = \mathsf{MostNeg} \text{ and } w = -1 \text{ or if } w = 0 \\ \mathsf{ff} & \text{otherwise} \end{cases}$$

  for $v, w \in \mathsf{Word}$.
- The length of a sequence s is denoted by $|\, s\,|$ and the concatenation of two sequences s, t by $s \cdot t$.

On the Transputer a word $w \in \mathsf{Word}$ can be used as a pointer that identifies a byte in memory. Considered as a pointer it is divided into two parts. The least significant bits form a *byte selector*, the remaining bits identify the word in memory. The number of bits used for the byte selector depends on the wordlength and is given by *byteselectlength*. A word used as a pointer to a byte is called a *byte address*. A *word address* identifies a word in memory. It is a word w for which all the bits in the byte selector are cleared, i.e. a word satisfying w bitand *byteselectmask* $= 0$. For a byte address w, $BaseAdr(w)$ is the word address of the word to which the byte with address w belongs. It is obtained from w by clearing the byte selector:

$$BaseAdr(w) \stackrel{\text{def}}{=} w \ \mathsf{bitand}\,(\mathsf{bitnot}\ byteselectmask)\ .$$

A word address can be characterized by the condition $w = BaseAdr(w)$. We denote the set of word addresses by WordAdr:

$$\mathsf{WordAdr} \stackrel{\text{def}}{=} \{w \in \mathsf{Word} \mid w = BaseAdr(w)\} .$$

8.2 Modeling the Transputer's Components

The description of Transputer semantics is based on the semi-formal specification given in Appendix F of the Transputer instruction set manual [46]. We model the Transputer by a collection of processes. The various registers and flags of interest are modeled by variables. The links are modeled by channels. In this section we list the interesting machine components and identify their type.

8.2.1 Registers

The Transputer has the three registers Areg, Breg and Creg that are used as a small evaluation stack, an instruction pointer Iptr, an operand register Oreg used to build large operands by prefix instructions and the workspace pointer Wptr. Each of this registers can store a word. Thus they are modeled by variables of type Word:

Word `A`, `B`, `C`, `Ip`, `Oreg`, `Wptr`

The above line indicates that `A`, `B`, ... are distinct variables (i.e. distinct members of Y) with value domain Word, i.e. such that $\mathsf{Val}_\mathrm{A} = \mathsf{Val}_\mathrm{B} = \ldots = \mathsf{Word}$. We have shortened some of the register names but their correspondence to the Transputer's registers should be clear.

Additionally the Transputer has some flags. For our purpose only the error flag is of interest. It is modeled by a Boolean variable.

Bool `Eflg`

This means that `Eflg` $\in Y$ and $\mathsf{Val}_\mathrm{Eflg} = \mathsf{Bool}$.

8.2.2 Memory

Appendix F of [46] uses three addressing modes for referencing the memory (see p. 129):

- as byte values stored at byte addresses,
- as word values stored at word addresses, and
- as word values stored at word offsets from `Wptr`.

In our formalization only one view of the memory is used, viz. as a mapping from word addresses to word values. The conversion to the other addressing modes is made explicit. As word addresses are words we model memory by a variable $\texttt{Mem} \in Y$ of type

$$\mathsf{Memory} \stackrel{\text{def}}{=} (\mathsf{Word} \rightarrow \mathsf{Word}) ,$$

i.e. such that $\mathsf{Val}_{\mathsf{Mem}} = \mathsf{Memory}$. Using this simple model of the memory might be questioned for a number of reasons.

(a) Only words with cleared byte select mask are word addresses.
(b) Certain memory locations at the bottom of the address space are used as auxiliary registers by the Transputer (see [46, Table 10.1 on p. 84]) and must not be used by application programs.
(c) Usually memory is provided only for part of the possible address space.
(d) In realistic Transputer systems the width of the address bus is restricted such that words w, w' that differ only in their upper bits refer to the same memory location.

In order to remedy these problems we assume given a set $\mathsf{Addr} \subseteq \mathsf{WordAdr}$ of *valid word addresses* that tells us which addresses are available to application programs. Each memory access with a pointer w will be guarded by an assertion $\{w \in \mathsf{Addr}\}$. So each access to an address not in Addr is considered catastrophic in the initial processor description. This poses the obligation to prove absence of such possibly bad access. In order to solve the above mentioned problems we assume the following.

(a) Addr contains only word addresses:

$$w \in \mathsf{Addr} \quad \Rightarrow \quad (w \ \mathsf{bitand}\ \mathit{byteselectmask}) = 0 .$$

(b) Addr contains only those locations available to application programs; in particular, for all $w \in \mathsf{Addr}$ memory is provided in the Transputer system, and no pointer to the special locations at the bottom of the address space is contained in Addr.
(c) No two different words $w, w' \in \mathsf{Addr}$ point to the same memory location.

Like [46] we use a mapping $\mathit{Index} \in (\mathsf{WordAdr} \times \mathsf{Word} \rightarrow \mathsf{Word})$. For a word address x and an arbitrary word y, $\mathit{Index}(x, y)$ is the word address y words past the base address x. Since bpw is a power of two, Index can be defined by

$$\mathit{Index}(x, y) \stackrel{\text{def}}{=} x + \mathit{bpw} * y .$$

A word w is a ***valid byte address*** if its base address is valid. So the set Baddr of valid byte addresses is defined by

$$\mathsf{Baddr} \stackrel{\text{def}}{=} \{w \mid \mathit{BaseAdr}(w) \in \mathsf{Addr}\} .$$

Loading of a single byte from memory is described by the mapping $Byte \in (\textsf{Memory} \times \textsf{Word} \rightarrow \textsf{Byte})$. $Byte(\texttt{Mem}, w)$ is the byte residing at the byte address w in the memory $\texttt{Mem}$. It is defined as follows.

$$Byte(\texttt{Mem}, w) \stackrel{\text{def}}{=} b_k \ ,$$

where $k = (w \ \textsf{bitand} \ byteselectmask)$ is the value of w's byte selector and $b_0, \ldots, b_{bpw-1} \in \textsf{Byte}$ are chosen such that

$$\sum_{i=0}^{bpw-1} b_i * 256^i \ = \ \texttt{Mem}(BaseAdr(w)) \ .$$

Note that $b_0, \ldots, b_{bpw-1} \in \textsf{Byte}$ are uniquely determined by uniqueness of 256-adic number representation.

8.2.3 Links

The Transputer has four bi-directional links. They are modeled by four input- and four output-channels of type Word. More specifically, we assume that $\texttt{In}_0, \ldots, \texttt{In}_3 \in \textsf{InChan}$, $\texttt{Out}_0, \ldots, \texttt{Out}_3 \in \textsf{OutChan}$ and $\textsf{Val}_{\texttt{In}_0} = \ldots = \textsf{Val}_{\texttt{Out}_3} = \textsf{Word}$.

8.3 Instructions and Operations

Each Transputer instruction is one byte long and is divided into two 4 bit parts. The four most significant bits are a function code, and the four least significant bits are a data value ([46, p. 7]).

Code	Data
7 4	3 0

Having four bits for coding a function the Transputer has sixteen *direct functions*. We refer to them by their symbolic names `pfix`, `nfix`, `ldc`, `ldl`, `stl`, `ldlp`, `adc`, `eqc`, `j`, `cj`, `ldnl`, `stnl`, `ldnlp`, `call`, `ajw`, `opr`. The set consisting of these names is called *InstrName*. Instructions are modeled as pairs of a direct function name and a nibble:

$$Instr \stackrel{\text{def}}{=} InstrName \times \textsf{Nibble} \ .$$

We use *instr* as a meta-variable ranging over *InstrName*. The set of sequences of instructions is called IS:

$$\textsf{IS} \stackrel{\text{def}}{=} Instr^* \ .$$

We typically range over IS by the letters a, b, c and m and call the members of IS also *machine programs*. The instruction code for a direct function *instr* is defined for example in Appendix D.1 of [46, p. 116] and is denoted *InstrCode*(*instr*), e.g.

$$\mathit{InstrCode}(\texttt{pfix}) = \texttt{\$20} \ .$$

Note that we consider $20 to be the instruction code of `pfix`, not $2, i.e. the instruction code is a full instruction byte with cleared data part. Both of these conventions are used in the Transputer manual at different places. To use a full instruction byte, simplifies some definitions by saving shift operations. By this convention,

$$\mathit{InstrCode}(\mathit{instr}) \ \mathsf{bitand}\ \texttt{\$0F} = 0 \tag{8.1}$$

for all *instr*. An instruction $i = (\mathit{instr}, n)$ is coded by

$$\mathit{Code}(i) \stackrel{\text{def}}{=} \mathit{InstrCode}(\mathit{instr}) \ \mathsf{bitor}\ n \tag{8.2}$$

in the Transputer memory (see the picture above). From (8.1) it is easy to see that the data part n and the instruction code *instr* of an instruction $i = (\mathit{instr}, n)$ can be recovered from $\mathit{Code}(i)$:

$$\mathit{Code}(i) \ \mathsf{bitand}\ \texttt{\$0F} = n \tag{8.3}$$

$$\mathit{Code}(i) \ \mathsf{bitand}\ \texttt{\$F0} = \mathit{InstrCode}(\mathit{instr}) \ . \tag{8.4}$$

The homomorphic extension of *Code* to instruction sequences (machine programs) is also called *Code*, i.e.

$$\mathit{Code}(\varepsilon) \stackrel{\text{def}}{=} \varepsilon \ , \tag{8.5}$$

$$\mathit{Code}([i] \cdot a) \stackrel{\text{def}}{=} [\mathit{Code}(i)] \cdot \mathit{Code}(a) \ . \tag{8.6}$$

The `opr` instruction is special in that it causes the contents of the operand register `Oreg` to be interpreted as the operation code of an *operation*. The set of operation names is denoted *OprName* and *op* is used as (meta-) variable ranging over *OprName*. Operation names are for example `add`, `bcnt`, `rev`, `stopp`, `not`, `mint`, `gt`, `outword`, `in` etc. The opcode of an operation *op* is denoted by *OpCode*(*op*) and is defined for example in Appendix D.2 of [46] where also a complete list of the operations available on the Transputer can be found.

8.4 Capturing the Dynamic Behavior

The Transputer's behavior is formalized as a process *Transputer* that communicates via the four input channels $\texttt{In}_0, \ldots, \texttt{In}_3$ and the four output channels $\texttt{Out}_0, \ldots, \texttt{Out}_3$ of type Word that model the links. As a whole the Transputer is sitting in a package and has thus no variables accessible in its pre- or post-state, so $\mathit{Transputer} \in \mathsf{Proc}_\emptyset$. But its behavior is described referring to internal registers, flags and the memory. These are modeled by variables, the type of which has been described in the previous section. We call the list of these variables Tc (for *Transputer components*):

$$Tc \stackrel{\text{def}}{=} \texttt{A}, \texttt{B}, \texttt{C}, \texttt{Oreg}, \texttt{Wptr}, \texttt{Ip}, \texttt{Eflg}, \texttt{Mem} .$$

The Transputer's behavior is composed of two phases, a *reset* and a *run* phase. The reset phase is entered when the Transputer is started and typically is used to initialize its internal state and external memory interface and to boot a program to be executed. The run phase on the other hand is concerned with the cyclic execution of instructions. Letting *Reset* stand for the process modeling the reset phase and *Run* for the process modeling the run phase, the Transputer's total behavior is described by the axiom:

$$\mathit{Transputer} \;=\; Tc^{+} \;;\; \mathit{Reset} \;;\; \mathit{Run} \;;\; Tc^{-} . \tag{8.7}$$

The alphabet of *Reset* and *Run* is

$$\alpha_0 \stackrel{\text{def}}{=} \{\texttt{A}, \texttt{B}, \texttt{C}, \texttt{Oreg}, \texttt{Wptr}, \texttt{Ip}, \texttt{Eflg}, \texttt{Mem}\} \;=\; \{\!|\, Tc \,|\!\}$$

but the internal state components Tc are hidden in the Transputer axiom (8.7) by the surrounding addition and deletion command. Of course the simple axiom (8.7) is useless without further knowledge about *Reset* and *Run*.

This book is concerned with translation correctness but not with correctness of boot programs or loaders. Since translation correctness can be formulated in terms of *Run*, it suffices for our purpose to capture *Run* formally. As we shall see, a certain precondition for the Transputer's state is required to execute code. The program, for instance, must be loaded to the memory and the instruction pointer must point to its first instruction. The task of a boot or loader program is to establish this precondition from any possible start state of the Transputer. Therefore, verification of a boot program requires to capture properties of *Reset* formally.

Run operates cyclically. Letting *Step* be the process that describes one execution cycle this is captured by the axiom

$$\mathit{Run} \;=\; \mathit{Step} \;;\; \mathit{Run} . \tag{8.8}$$

The run phase like most actual processors does not terminate regularly.[1] We can therefore assume that

$$\mathit{Run} \;;\; X \;=\; \mathit{Run} \;;\; Y \tag{8.9}$$

for all $X, Y \in \mathsf{Proc}^{\alpha}_{\alpha_0}$ (α an arbitrary alphabet).[2] We should mention that these axioms do not exclude irregular termination in the *Step* process. Furthermore, it is important to remember that we can deal with diverging processes. In particular, the below axioms about the communication operations

[1] We do not require that *Run* is the weakest solution of equation (8.8). Although this assumption is quite reasonable, we do without for stylistic reasons. This is possible because we restrict attention to preservation of total correctness. Therefore, non-termination is not implied by axiom (8.8). For the weakest solution the below axiom (8.9) follows from (8.8).

[2] (8.9) is equivalent to the simpler looking axiom $\mathit{Run} \;;\; \bot \;=\; \mathit{Run}$.

(in connection with the other axioms) imply that *Step* is not $\perp$-strict such that $Run = \perp$ is no solution for (8.8).

The *current instruction* is the memory byte pointed to by the instruction pointer. In each instruction cycle the behavior is composed of a fetch phase, which loads the data part of the current instruction to the lower four bits of the operand register and increments the instruction pointer, and the specific effect of the direct function specified in the current instruction's code part. Thus the behavior of *Step* is characterized by the family of axioms (one axiom for each direct function *instr*)

$$[CurFct(instr)] \; ; \; Step \;\geq\; Fetch \; ; \; E_0(instr) \; , \tag{8.10}$$

where

$$CurFct(instr) \stackrel{\text{def}}{\equiv} (Byte(\texttt{Mem}, \texttt{Ip}) \text{ bitand } \texttt{\$F0}) = InstrCode(instr) \; ,$$

$$Fetch \stackrel{\text{def}}{=} \texttt{Oreg}, \texttt{Ip} := \texttt{Oreg} \text{ bitor } (Byte(\texttt{Mem}, \texttt{Ip}) \text{ bitand } \texttt{\$0F}), \texttt{Ip} + 1 \; ,$$

and $E_0(instr)$ models the behavior of the direct function *instr*. The index 0 is used to distinguish this initial description of the direct functions' effect from the more abstract views derived in Chap. 10. The predicate $CurFct(instr)$ is true iff the memory location pointed to by the instruction pointer `Ip` contains the instruction code of the instruction *instr* and *Fetch* describes the behavior of the fetch phase. The alphabet of the processes *Step*, *Fetch* and $E_0(instr)$ is of course again α_0.

The effect of the direct functions is described by Z-like schemata in Appendix F.3 of [46]. (The fetch phase, too, is described by a schema called 'InstrDecode'.) For the load constant function `ldc`, for instance, which loads the contents of the operand register `Oreg` to the evaluation stack, the following schema is provided [46, p. 132].

ldc	#4_	load constant
Areg′ = Oreg^0		
Breg′ = Areg		
Creg′ = Breg		
Oreg′ = 0		
Iptr′ = *NextInst*		

Primed names represent the values of the corresponding register after execution and unprimed names the values before. Oreg^0 stands for the operand register's contents after the fetch phase.

In the current framework the effect of `ldc` is captured by an axiom about $E_0(\texttt{ldc})$. As we are using an imperative programming notation, there is no need to use primed and superscripted variables to distinguish register values at different stages of execution. Rather we differentiate between them implicitly by the places at which they are written in the formulae. In particular, we can describe the register updates simply by an assignment command:

$$E_0(\texttt{ldc}) \geq \Delta 1 \,;\, \texttt{A},\texttt{B},\texttt{C},\texttt{Oreg} := \texttt{Oreg},\texttt{A},\texttt{B},0 \;.$$

In addition to the effect on the registers the above axiom describes by the delay process that `ldc` needs at most one clock cycle for execution. The information about the execution time is taken from [46, Appendix D]. The careful reader might have noticed that incrementation of the instruction pointer is missing in the axiom compared to the Z-like schema. We have decided to move it consistently for all direct functions to the fetch phase as this is slightly more convenient for the following exposition.

Table 8.1. Axioms for various direct functions

$$E_0(\texttt{pfix}) \geq \Delta 1 \,;\, \texttt{Oreg} := \texttt{Oreg} \ll 4 \tag{8.11}$$
$$E_0(\texttt{nfix}) \geq \Delta 1 \,;\, \texttt{Oreg} := (\mathsf{bitnot}\ \texttt{Oreg}) \ll 4 \tag{8.12}$$
$$E_0(\texttt{ldc}) \geq \Delta 1 \,;\, \texttt{A},\texttt{B},\texttt{C},\texttt{Oreg} := \texttt{Oreg},\texttt{A},\texttt{B},0 \tag{8.13}$$
$$E_0(\texttt{ldl}) \geq \Delta 2 \,;\, \{\mathit{Index}(\texttt{Wptr},\texttt{Oreg}) \in \mathsf{Addr}\} \,;\, \texttt{A},\texttt{B},\texttt{C},\texttt{Oreg} := (\texttt{Mem}(\mathit{Index}(\texttt{Wptr},\texttt{Oreg}))),\texttt{A},\texttt{B},0 \tag{8.14}$$
$$E_0(\texttt{stl}) \geq \Delta 1 \,;\, \{\mathit{Index}(\texttt{Wptr},\texttt{Oreg}) \in \mathsf{Addr}\} \,;\, \texttt{Mem}[\mathit{Index}(\texttt{Wptr},\texttt{Oreg})],\texttt{A},\texttt{B},\texttt{Oreg} := \texttt{A},\texttt{B},\texttt{C},0 \,;\, \texttt{C} :=? \tag{8.15}$$
$$E_0(\texttt{ldlp}) \geq \Delta 1 \,;\, \texttt{A},\texttt{B},\texttt{C},\texttt{Oreg} := \mathit{Index}(\texttt{Wptr},\texttt{Oreg}),\texttt{A},\texttt{B},0 \tag{8.16}$$
$$E_0(\texttt{adc}) \geq \Delta 1 \,;\, \texttt{A},\texttt{Eflg},\texttt{Oreg} := \texttt{A}+\texttt{Oreg},\texttt{Eflg} \vee \mathit{AddOvFl}(\texttt{A},\texttt{Oreg}),0 \tag{8.17}$$
$$E_0(\texttt{eqc}) \geq \Delta 2 \,;\, \texttt{A},\texttt{Oreg} := \mathsf{if}\ \texttt{A} = \texttt{Oreg}\ \mathsf{then}\ 1\ \mathsf{else}\ 0\ \mathsf{fi},0 \tag{8.18}$$
$$E_0(\texttt{j}) \geq \Delta 3 \,;\, \texttt{Ip},\texttt{Oreg} := \texttt{Ip}+\texttt{Oreg},0 \,;\, \texttt{A},\texttt{B},\texttt{C} :=? \tag{8.19}$$
$$E_0(\texttt{cj}) \geq \Delta 2 \,;\, \{\texttt{A} \neq 0\} \,;\, \texttt{A},\texttt{B},\texttt{Oreg} := \texttt{B},\texttt{C},0 \,;\, \texttt{C} :=? \tag{8.20}$$
$$E_0(\texttt{cj}) \geq \Delta 4 \,;\, \{\texttt{A} = 0\} \,;\, \texttt{Ip},\texttt{Oreg} := \texttt{Ip}+\texttt{Oreg},0 \tag{8.21}$$
$$E_0(\texttt{opr}) \geq \{\mathit{CurOpr}(op)\} \,;\, E_0(op) \,;\, \texttt{Oreg} := 0 \tag{8.22}$$

In a similar way we obtain the axioms in Table 8.1 for various other instructions. For the conditional jump `cj` we have the two axioms (8.20) and (8.21) that describe the cases whether the jump is taken or not separately. It is a benefit of using refinement instead of equality (or equivalence) that enables such a modular specification. The axiom for the operate instruction `opr` is based on processes $E_0(op)$ that capture the behavior of operations *op*. Furthermore, a predicate *CurOpr* is used, which is true iff the operand register contains the opcode of the operation *op*:

$$\mathit{CurOpr}(op) \stackrel{\text{def}}{\equiv} \texttt{Oreg} = \mathit{OpCode}(op) \;. \tag{8.23}$$

Similar to the direct functions, the Transputer manual describes the effect of operations by Z-like schemata. By rewriting them we obtain the axioms in Table 8.2 for the operations needed in the code generator for TPL.

The specification of input and output operations is partly informal in the Transputer manual. We formalize here our assumptions about the behavior of `in` and `outword` considering only communication via links and

Table 8.2. Axioms for various operations

$$E_0(\texttt{add}) \geq \Delta 1 \; ; \texttt{A},\texttt{B},\texttt{Eflg} := \texttt{B}+\texttt{A},\texttt{C},\texttt{Eflg} \vee \mathit{AddOvFl}(\texttt{B},\texttt{A}) \; ; \texttt{C} :=? \quad (8.24)$$

$$E_0(\texttt{sub}) \geq \Delta 1 \; ; \texttt{A},\texttt{B},\texttt{Eflg} := \texttt{B}-\texttt{A},\texttt{C},\texttt{Eflg} \vee \mathit{SubOvFl}(\texttt{B},\texttt{A}) \; ; \texttt{C} :=? \quad (8.25)$$

$$E_0(\texttt{mul}) \geq \Delta\, bpw + 6 \; ; \; \texttt{A},\texttt{B},\texttt{Eflg} := \texttt{B}*\texttt{A},\texttt{C},\texttt{Eflg} \vee \mathit{MulOvFl}(\texttt{B},\texttt{A}) \; ; \texttt{C} :=? \quad (8.26)$$

$$E_0(\texttt{div}) \geq \Delta\, bpw + 10 \; ; \{\neg \mathit{DivOvFl}(\texttt{B},\texttt{A})\} \; ; \texttt{A},\texttt{B} := \texttt{B} \div \texttt{A},\texttt{C} \; ; \texttt{C} :=? \quad (8.27)$$

$$E_0(\texttt{div}) \geq \Delta\, bpw + 10 \; ; \{\mathit{DivOvFl}(\texttt{B},\texttt{A})\} \; ; \texttt{B},\texttt{Eflg} := \texttt{C},\mathsf{true} \; ; \texttt{A},\texttt{C} :=? \quad (8.28)$$

$$E_0(\texttt{rem}) \geq \Delta\, bpw + 5 \; ; \{\neg \mathit{DivOvFl}(\texttt{B},\texttt{A})\} \; ; \texttt{A},\texttt{B} := \texttt{B}\ \mathsf{rem}\ \texttt{A},\texttt{C} \; ; \texttt{C} :=? \quad (8.29)$$

$$E_0(\texttt{rem}) \geq \Delta\, bpw + 5 \; ; \{\mathit{DivOvFl}(\texttt{B},\texttt{A})\} \; ; \texttt{B},\texttt{Eflg} := \texttt{C},\mathsf{true} \; ; \texttt{A},\texttt{C} :=? \quad (8.30)$$

$$E_0(\texttt{diff}) \geq \Delta 1 \; ; \texttt{A},\texttt{B} := \texttt{B}-\texttt{A},\texttt{C} \; ; \texttt{C} :=? \quad (8.31)$$

$$E_0(\texttt{testerr}) \geq \Delta 3 \; ; \texttt{A},\texttt{B},\texttt{C},\texttt{Eflg} := \mathsf{if}\ \texttt{Eflg}\ \mathsf{then}\ 0\ \mathsf{else}\ 1\ \mathsf{fi},\texttt{A},\texttt{B},\mathsf{false} \quad (8.32)$$

$$E_0(\texttt{stoperr}) \geq \{\texttt{Eflg}\} \; ; \mathsf{Stop} \quad (8.33)$$

$$E_0(\texttt{stoperr}) \geq \Delta 2 \; ; \{\neg \texttt{Eflg}\} \quad (8.34)$$

$$E_0(\texttt{bcnt}) \geq \Delta 2 \; ; \texttt{A} := \texttt{A} * bpw \quad (8.35)$$

$$E_0(\texttt{rev}) \geq \Delta 1 \; ; \texttt{A},\texttt{B} := \texttt{B},\texttt{A} \quad (8.36)$$

$$E_0(\texttt{stopp}) \geq \mathsf{Stop} \quad (8.37)$$

$$E_0(\texttt{not}) \geq \Delta 1 \; ; \texttt{A} := (\mathsf{bitnot}\ \texttt{A}) \quad (8.38)$$

$$E_0(\texttt{mint}) \geq \Delta 1 \; ; \texttt{A},\texttt{B},\texttt{C} := \mathsf{MostNeg},\texttt{A},\texttt{B} \quad (8.39)$$

$$E_0(\texttt{gt}) \geq \Delta 2 \; ; \texttt{A},\texttt{B} := \mathsf{if}\ \texttt{B} > \texttt{A}\ \mathsf{then}\ 1\ \mathsf{else}\ 0\ \mathsf{fi},\texttt{C} \; ; \texttt{C} :=? \quad (8.40)$$

leaving communication on internal channels unspecified. This is enabled by the use of refinement, which once again turns out to be advantageous. Intuitively, the operation `in` reads a message of `A` bytes from the channel pointed to by `B` to the memory at `C` (see [46, p. 138]). The channel control words for the input channels on the links reside in the memory cells $\mathit{Index}(\mathsf{MostNeg}, 4), \ldots, \mathit{Index}(\mathsf{MostNeg}, 7)$ according to a proper interpretation of Table 10.1 in [46, p. 84]. Thus reading a single word from link i (for $0 \leq i \leq 3$) can be achieved with the `in` operation:

$$\begin{aligned} E_0(\texttt{in}) \geq\ & \{\texttt{A} = bpw \wedge \texttt{B} = \mathit{Index}(\mathsf{MostNeg}, i+4) \wedge \texttt{C} \in \mathsf{Addr}\} \; ; \\ & \Delta\, \mathit{indelay}_1 \; ; \\ & \texttt{In}_\mathsf{i}\, ?\, \texttt{A} \; ; \\ & \texttt{Mem}[\texttt{C}] := \texttt{A} \; ; \\ & \texttt{A},\texttt{B},\texttt{C} :=? \; ; \\ & \Delta\, \mathit{indelay}_2 \; . \end{aligned} \quad (8.41)$$

We assume that $\mathit{indelay}_1$ and $\mathit{indelay}_2$ are estimates for the delays before and after the actual communication.[3] Note that in this axiom the value is

[3] Explicit values for these constants can only be determined after a certain reference point for the timing has been fixed in the communication protocol. We do not decide for a specific convention here but assume that for any such choice suitable constants can be provided. Furthermore, we assume that the timing re-

read to register A first because we have not explained inputs to component variables.

The channel control words for the output channels provided by the links are contained in the memory cells $\mathit{Index}(\mathsf{MostNeg}, 0), \ldots, \mathit{Index}(\mathsf{MostNeg}, 3)$ ([46, p. 84]). Therefore, the `outword` operation that outputs the content of register A via the channel pointed to by B satisfies

$$\begin{aligned} E_0(\texttt{outword}) \geq\ & \{\texttt{B} = \mathit{Index}(\mathsf{MostNeg}, i)\}\ ; \\ & \Delta\ \mathit{outdelay}_1\ ; \\ & \texttt{Out}_\mathrm{i}\ !\ \texttt{A}\ ; \\ & \texttt{A} :=?\ ;\ \texttt{Mem}[\mathit{Index}(\texttt{Wptr}, 0)] := \texttt{A}\ ; \\ & \texttt{A}, \texttt{B}, \texttt{C} :=?\ ; \\ & \Delta\ \mathit{outdelay}_2\ , \end{aligned} \tag{8.42}$$

where $\mathit{outdelay}_1$ and $\mathit{outdelay}_2$ are assumed to be appropriate timing constants. Note how we express that the final contents of $\texttt{Mem}[\mathit{Index}(\texttt{Wptr}, 0)]$ is unspecified. This somewhat indirect approach is used because undetermined assignments to component variables have not been investigated.[4]

8.5 Discussion

The axioms about the direct functions and operations are reformulations of the Z-like description given in Appendix F.3 of [46] and the timing is taken from the tables in Appendix D of that document. So we interface directly to the documentation provided by Inmos, the manufacturer of the Transputer. Note that the modularity of the description in [46] is kept or even improved: each direct function and operation is described independently by one or several axioms. This allows to treat abstraction of single functions and operations in isolation, which leads to short independent proofs instead of a monolithic proof for the entire instruction set. In addition it allows formal reasoning without formalizing the complete instruction set. Only the actually needed part has to be considered. To use refinement as basic concept instead of equality or equivalence allows to describe the effect by safe approximations if it is not completely known. For example, (8.19 does not specify the values left in the registers A, B, C after a jump instruction and we specified the operations `in` and `outword` only for external communications.

Although its description is well-structured, the base model is of a rather low level of abstraction. For example, it has no explicit notion of an executed machine program. As a consequence it is able to explain behavior that cannot be interpreted in more abstract models. An example is 'self-modifying' code as mentioned already. The base model describes what happens if a certain byte is

quirements in TPL programs refer to the same convention such that we can leave open this question in this book.

[4] It is straightforward to define them but their laws are rather complicated.

written to memory and then executed. But this generality is closely connected to its largest disadvantage namely that reasoning directly with the base model results in long and complicated proofs. In Chap. 10 we derive stepwise ever more abstract models that facilitate reasoning about 'well-structured' code.

Besides the meta-language used for formalization our model differs from the semi-formal description in Appendix F of [46] in the following respects.

- We make explicit that the memory is accessed in byte-sized quantities in the processes *CurFct* and *Fetch* in contrast to the InstrDecode schema in Appendix F.3.
- We describe the incrementation of the instruction pointer `Ip` in the fetch phase and not in the effect processes for the direct functions.
- We use basically only one view of the memory and describe the different addressing modes based on this single view.
- We describe the effect of instructions on the error flag explicitly. In contrast [46] relies on side-effects of arithmetic operators.
- We need not use an extra name for the value of Oreg after the fetch phase, since we formalize semantics by processes that can access assignable variables. In the Transputer manual the intermediate value of Oreg is called Oreg^0.
- The assignment of arbitrary values to the registers `A`, `B`, `C` by an (unconditional) jump instruction is missing in the specification given in the Transputer manual (due to the convention that registers not mentioned in a schema are left unchanged). That the registers `A`, `B`, `C` might be changed by a jump instruction on an actual Transputer can be inferred from the fact that a jump instruction can cause a process to be de-scheduled.
- We do not model the scheduling and multi-tasking capabilities of the Transputer. After all we are interested in an exemplary study of the general phenomena arising with commercially available von Neumann processors more than in the specifics of the Transputer.

9. A Small Hard Real-Time Programming Language

In this chapter we define a prototypic hard real-time programming language, called TPL, that is the source language in the compiler correctness considerations. Essentially it is the language of while programs extended by communication statements and upperbound timing.

Classically, translation of (imperative) programming languages assumes that stopping (with an error message) is an acceptable behavior for abnormal situations like arithmetic over- or underflow or stack overflow. The availability of such an *acceptable failure behavior* allows to offer in the source language idealizations like infinite number domains or unconstrained recursion that cannot fully be implemented on actual hardware.

For programs running in a safety-critical environment, however, an acceptable failure behavior often does not exist. E.g. an autopilot in an aeroplane must not stop if it detects an arithmetic overflow during a calculation in its control program. Failures of this kind simply must not occur at run-time. In order to allow the program designer to prove their absence, all restrictions of the execution mechanism must be reflected on the source language level. Moreover, the compiler must guarantee that all total correctness properties valid for the source program transfer to the target code.

We, therefore, include into TPL only finite data-types that can fully be represented on the target hardware. More specifically, TPL has the types Bool and Word, where Word is the subset of the integers representable by Transputer machine words. We define all arithmetic, relational and Boolean operators totally such that there are no arithmetic under- and overflows in TPL. This has no disadvantage compared to performing a special kind of failure behavior (like stopping the execution in undefined or under- or overflow situations) in an environment where the failure behavior is not generally acceptable. Anyway the program designer must prove absence of such situations in order to avoid the non-acceptable failure behavior. In all other situations, however, the total operations on words agree with the corresponding operations on integers. Moreover, as argued already in Chap. 4, total operators facilitate algebraic program transformations.

As in the programming language Occam [45] there is no (explicit) recursion in TPL, only iteration by loops. Apart from simplicity the reason is that the compiler, in general, cannot determine the stack size that is necessary for the execution of a recursive program. This is also a difficult task for the program designer, which makes a mixed approach between compiler and program designer unattractive. Excluding recursion and dynamic data-types from the language allows to determine storage consumption of programs statically.

It is fundamental to distinguish between internal and external aspects when considering the correctness of implementations. Important is only the preservation of the externally visible behavior, internal behavior on the other hand can be changed arbitrarily as long as the external behavior is not affected.[1] (This is the reason why code optimizers generally are accepted: their transformations ideally do not change the results of programs.) In TPL internal behavior is described by means of assignable variables and external behavior by means of synchronous channels $\mathtt{In}_0, \ldots, \mathtt{In}_3, \mathtt{Out}_0, \ldots, \mathtt{Out}_3$ that correspond to the Transputer's links. We distinguish the syntactic categories of statements and programs. The meaning of statements comprises both the external communication behavior as well as the internal state-transforming behavior. The latter is needed in order to define the composition operators correctly. The meaning of programs, however, is concerned only with the external communication behavior. Similarly, the code generator correctness condition for statements speaks besides external communication about representation of variables, which is necessary for a compositional code specification, while the correctness condition for programs speaks only about external communication.

The traditional approach to ensure a sufficient performance of the machine code for a real-time application is either by extensive testing or by analysis of the machine code that has been hand-crafted or generated by a compiler. Typically the latter involves counting of processor execution cycles. In TPL we follow a different approach (in the tradition of TimedPL [24, 67], the programming language that has been considered in the ProCoS II project): the program designer is enabled to specify the timing requirements (for basic blocks) in the source program. It is the compiler's task to check whether these requirements are satisfied by the generated code. The upperbound statement constructor provided in TPL allows to constrain the *active time* consumption

---

[1] In practice external behavior is not preserved literally but a pre-defined representation is required at the external interface; synchronous communication, for instance, is physically represented by a protocol running on electrical wires in Transputer architectures or characters are represented by certain pixel patterns on the computer monitor. But in contrast to the representation of the internal components, the external representation is not chosen by the compiler builder but is fixed a-priori. We consider it thus an (often implicit) part of the compiler's specification. For the purpose of this book we work with the simplified picture that external behavior is literally preserved, which is enabled by modeling synchronous communication in the source language (TPL) and in the target processor model (the Transputer model) on the same abstraction level. In our opinion the correctness of the external representation in general and the physical implementation of synchronous communication by the Transputer's link protocol in particular is not a compiler issue.

of the enclosed statement. In connection with synchronous communication, the active time spent by a process can be interpreted as its execution time minus the time it is waiting for a communication partner. Only the active time can be predicted for the code, and this explains why the notion 'active time' has been introduced. However, our considerations are largely independent of the specific details of the definition of active time. They depend only on the use of the same definition in TPL and the Transputer model, which we take for granted.

Besides a construct to control the requirements on the execution time of code, lower-bounded delays are needed in real-time programs. These are typically implemented directly by a service provided by the target processor or the operating system, like a timer. The compiler just transfers this service to the source language level. In our opinion this does not lead to any particular compiler correctness problem. We do not include lower-bounded delays into TPL because they would complicate our semantic framework.

The fact that internal behavior can be changed by the implementation allows to offer in TPL, as in later version of TimedPL, the idealization that all internal activity – like assignments or the selection in a conditional – is immediate and that only the communication statements consume time. We hope that such an assumption simplifies the design of real-time programs. The execution time actually needed for the implementing code for, say, an assignment is shifted by the compiler to the subsequent communication. The difference between the immediate execution 'fiction' and the actual behavior of the code cannot be detected by an external observer as the assignment cannot be monitored directly. (A similar idea has been described recently by R. Gerber and S. Hong [27].)

In TPL external behavior is described by synchronous communication. This is not essential for these considerations but results from the choice of the Transputer as the target architecture. For other architectures other programming language means might be employed for specifying the external behavior. For example, writing to a (memory-mapped) port could be described by an assignment to a variable that is shared with the environment. The distinction between internal and external statements can be preserved by labeling the externally visible variables. The idealization that internal activity executes immediately and the idea to shift the computation time could, therefore, be applied in such a context as well.

We now define the abstract syntax and the static and dynamic semantics of TPL.

9.1 Abstract Syntax

TPL has three syntactic categories: programs <u>Prog</u>, statements <u>Stat</u>, and expressions <u>Expr</u>. These categories are simultaneously defined by the grammar in Table 9.1, where *prog* ranges over <u>Prog</u>, *stat* over <u>Stat</u>, and *expr* over <u>Expr</u>.

The meta-variable *bop* ranges over Bop, the set of binary operators, and *mop* over Mop, the set of monadic operators. These sets are defined by

$$\mathsf{Bop} \stackrel{\text{def}}{=} \{\underline{\textbf{plus}}, \underline{\textbf{minus}}, \underline{\textbf{times}}, \underline{\textbf{div}}, \underline{\textbf{rem}}, \underline{\textbf{eq}}, \underline{\textbf{ne}}, \underline{\textbf{leq}}, \underline{\textbf{geq}}, \underline{\textbf{le}}, \underline{\textbf{ge}}, \underline{\textbf{and}}, \underline{\textbf{or}}\}$$

$$\mathsf{Mop} \stackrel{\text{def}}{=} \{\underline{\textbf{plus}}, \underline{\textbf{minus}}, \underline{\textbf{not}}\} .$$

Because it slightly simplifies the semantics definition, we do not use a new set of identifiers for TPL but utilize the variables from the process space. We assume that only variables with domain Word or Bool appear in TPL programs. For technical reasons we reserve a set Aux of auxiliary variables; we assume in particular that the variables used in the Transputer base model are contained in Aux such that they do not conflict with variables in TPL programs. So x ranges over

$$Z \stackrel{\text{def}}{=} \{x \in Y \mid \mathsf{Val}_x \in \{\mathsf{Word}, \mathsf{Bool}\}\} \setminus \mathsf{Aux}$$

in Table 9.1. Similarly we do not use new sets of channel identifiers but use the channel names from the Transputer base model. So let $\mathsf{InCh} = \{\mathtt{In}_0, \dots, \mathtt{In}_3\}$ ($\subseteq \mathsf{InChan}$) be the set of input channel names and $\mathsf{OutCh} = \{\mathtt{Out}_0, \dots, \mathtt{Out}_3\}$ ($\subseteq \mathsf{OutChan}$) the set of output channel names; we range over InCh by *inch* and over OutCh by *outch*. The letter k ranges over the set $\mathsf{Bool} \cup \mathsf{Word}$ and t over $\mathsf{IR}_{\geq 0}$. As usual a vertical bar | separates the different alternatives in a rule.

Table 9.1. Abstract syntax of TPL

prog	::=	$\underline{\textbf{prog}}\,(stat)$
stat	::=	$\underline{\textbf{skip}} \mid \underline{\textbf{stop}} \mid \underline{\textbf{assign}}\,(x, expr) \mid \underline{\textbf{input}}\,(inch, x) \mid$ $\underline{\textbf{output}}\,(outch, expr) \mid \underline{\textbf{seq}}\,(stat_1, stat_2) \mid \underline{\textbf{if}}\,(expr, stat_1, stat_2) \mid$ $\underline{\textbf{while}}\,(expr, stat) \mid \underline{\textbf{upperbound}}\,(stat, t) \mid \underline{\textbf{block}}\,(x, stat)$
expr	::=	$\underline{\textbf{var}}\,(x) \mid \underline{\textbf{const}}\,(k) \mid \underline{\textbf{bin}}\,(bop, expr_1, expr_2) \mid \underline{\textbf{mon}}\,(mop, expr)$

The intuitive semantics of expressions and statements should be clear from the names of the constructors.

9.2 Static Semantics

The static semantics of TPL requires some conditions that must hold for *valid* TPL programs in addition to their tree construction as described by the context-free grammar of the abstract syntax. Some of these conditions are based on the notion of an expression's type: TPL expressions can be either Boolean or word expressions. The additional requirements are the following.

- There must be no free variables in a program **prog** (*stat*).
- The variable x declared in a block **block** $(x, stat)$ must be new, i.e., it is not allowed that a variable which is already used is re-declared. (The reason is that otherwise semantics is not easily explained with addition and deletion commands.)
- The expressions occurring in the different process constructors must have the correct type. In the **if** and **while** constructor only Boolean expressions and in the **output** constructor only word expressions are allowed. In an assignment the variable's value domain and the expression's type must fit together.
- In the **input** constructor only variables with value domain Word are allowed.
- Expressions must be well-typed. The arithmetic operators **plus**, **minus**, etc., for instance, can only have sub-expressions of type word, not of type Boolean.

These requirements are formally expressed by a family of functions (one function for each syntactic categories of TPL) that are defined inductively over the construction of the abstract trees. The signature of these functions is

$$\begin{aligned} \mathsf{SP} &: \underline{\mathsf{Prog}} \to \{\mathsf{valid}, \mathsf{invalid}\} \\ \mathsf{SS} &: \underline{\mathsf{Stat}} \to (\mathbb{P}^{\mathrm{f}}(Z) \to \{\mathsf{valid}, \mathsf{invalid}\}) \\ \mathsf{SE} &: \underline{\mathsf{Expr}} \to (\mathbb{P}^{\mathrm{f}}(Z) \to \{\mathsf{Bool}, \mathsf{Word}, \mathsf{invalid}\}) \ , \end{aligned}$$

where $\mathbb{P}^{\mathrm{f}}(Z)$ is the set of finite subsets of Z (recall that Z is the set of variables that can appear in TPL programs). The $\mathbb{P}^{\mathrm{f}}(Z)$ argument of SS and SE is interpreted as the set of variables that is permitted in the statement or expression; no other variable is allowed. The interpretation of SP, SS and SE's final result is straightforward. For example, $\mathsf{SE}(expr)(V) = \mathsf{Bool}$ means that the expression $expr \in \underline{\mathsf{Expr}}$ is a well-formed Boolean expression that contains at most the variables from the (finite) set $V \subseteq Z$. Clearly, it would be sufficient to supply instead of the value sets Bool and Word just certain constants **bool** and **word** as results of SE. However, to supply the value sets sometimes is notationally more convenient. The straightforward inductive definition of SP, SS and SE is given in Table 9.2.

Prog, Stat, Expr (without an underbar) stand for the sets of valid programs, statements and expressions; Stat_V and Expr_V are the set of valid statements and expressions that contain at most the variables in V free:

$$\begin{aligned} \mathsf{Prog} &\stackrel{\text{def}}{=} \{prog \in \underline{\mathsf{Prog}} \mid \mathsf{SP}(prog) = \mathsf{valid}\} \\ \mathsf{Stat}_V &\stackrel{\text{def}}{=} \{stat \in \underline{\mathsf{Stat}} \mid \mathsf{SS}(stat)(V) = \mathsf{valid}\} \\ \mathsf{Expr}_V &\stackrel{\text{def}}{=} \{expr \in \underline{\mathsf{Expr}} \mid \mathsf{SE}(expr)(V) \in \{\mathsf{Word}, \mathsf{Bool}\}\} \\ \mathsf{Stat} &\stackrel{\text{def}}{=} \textstyle\bigcup_{V \subseteq Z} \mathsf{Stat}_V \\ \mathsf{Expr} &\stackrel{\text{def}}{=} \textstyle\bigcup_{V \subseteq Z} \mathsf{Expr}_V \ . \end{aligned}$$

Table 9.2. Static semantics of TPL

$$\mathsf{SP}(\,\underline{\mathbf{prog}}\,(stat)) = \mathsf{SS}(stat)(\emptyset)$$

$$\mathsf{SS}(\,\underline{\mathbf{skip}}\,)(V) = \mathsf{valid}$$

$$\mathsf{SS}(\,\underline{\mathbf{stop}}\,)(V) = \mathsf{valid}$$

$$\mathsf{SS}(\,\underline{\mathbf{assign}}\,(x, expr))(V) = \begin{cases} \mathsf{valid} & \text{if } \mathsf{Val}_x = \mathsf{SE}(expr)(V) \text{ and } x \in V \\ \mathsf{invalid} & \text{otherwise} \end{cases}$$

$$\mathsf{SS}(\,\underline{\mathbf{input}}\,(inch, x))(V) = \begin{cases} \mathsf{valid} & \text{if } \mathsf{Val}_x = \mathsf{Word} \text{ and } x \in V \\ \mathsf{invalid} & \text{otherwise} \end{cases}$$

$$\mathsf{SS}(\,\underline{\mathbf{output}}\,(outch, expr))(V) = \begin{cases} \mathsf{valid} & \text{if } \mathsf{SE}(expr)(V) = \mathsf{Word} \\ \mathsf{invalid} & \text{otherwise} \end{cases}$$

$$\mathsf{SS}(\,\underline{\mathbf{seq}}\,(stat_1, stat_2))(V) = \begin{cases} \mathsf{valid} & \text{if } \mathsf{SS}(stat_i)(V) = \mathsf{valid} \text{ for } i = 1,2 \\ \mathsf{invalid} & \text{otherwise} \end{cases}$$

$$\mathsf{SS}(\,\underline{\mathbf{if}}\,(expr, stat_1, stat_2))(V) = \begin{cases} \mathsf{valid} & \text{if } \mathsf{SE}(expr)(V) = \mathsf{Bool} \text{ and} \\ & \mathsf{SS}(stat_i)(V) = \mathsf{valid} \text{ for } i = 1,2 \\ \mathsf{invalid} & \text{otherwise} \end{cases}$$

$$\mathsf{SS}(\,\underline{\mathbf{while}}\,(expr, stat))(V) = \begin{cases} \mathsf{valid} & \text{if } \mathsf{SE}(expr)(V) = \mathsf{Bool} \text{ and} \\ & \mathsf{SS}(stat)(V) = \mathsf{valid} \\ \mathsf{invalid} & \text{otherwise} \end{cases}$$

$$\mathsf{SS}(\,\underline{\mathbf{block}}\,(x, stat))(V) = \begin{cases} \mathsf{valid} & \text{if } \mathsf{SS}(stat)(V \cup \{x\}) = \mathsf{valid} \text{ and} \\ & x \notin V \\ \mathsf{invalid} & \text{otherwise} \end{cases}$$

$$\mathsf{SS}(\,\underline{\mathbf{upperbound}}\,(stat, t))(V) = \mathsf{SS}(stat)(V)$$

$$\mathsf{SE}(\,\underline{\mathbf{var}}\,(x))(V) = \begin{cases} \mathsf{Val}_x & \text{if } x \in V \\ \mathsf{invalid} & \text{otherwise} \end{cases}$$

$$\mathsf{SE}(\,\underline{\mathbf{const}}\,(k))(V) = \begin{cases} \mathsf{Bool} & \text{if } k \in \mathsf{Bool} \\ \mathsf{Word} & \text{if } k \in \mathsf{Word} \end{cases}$$

$$\mathsf{SE}(\,\underline{\mathbf{bin}}\,(bop, expr_1, expr_2))(V) = \begin{cases} \mathsf{Bool} & \text{if } bop \in \{\,\underline{\mathbf{and}}\,,\,\underline{\mathbf{or}}\,\} \text{ and} \\ & \mathsf{SE}(expr_i)(V) = \mathsf{Bool} \text{ for } i = 1,2 \\ \mathsf{Bool} & \text{if } bop \in \{\,\underline{\mathbf{eq}}\,,\,\underline{\mathbf{ne}}\,,\,\underline{\mathbf{leq}}\,,\,\underline{\mathbf{geq}}\,,\,\underline{\mathbf{le}}\,,\,\underline{\mathbf{ge}}\,\} \\ & \text{and } \mathsf{SE}(expr_i)(V) = \mathsf{Word} \\ \mathsf{Word} & \text{if } bop \in \{\,\underline{\mathbf{plus}}\,,\,\underline{\mathbf{minus}}\,,\,\underline{\mathbf{times}}\,, \\ & \underline{\mathbf{div}}\,,\,\underline{\mathbf{rem}}\,\} \text{ and} \\ & \mathsf{SE}(expr_i)(V) = \mathsf{Word} \text{ for } i = 1,2 \\ \mathsf{invalid} & \text{otherwise} \end{cases}$$

$$\mathsf{SE}(\,\underline{\mathbf{mon}}\,(mop, expr))(V) = \begin{cases} \mathsf{Bool} & \text{if } \mathsf{SE}(expr)(V) = \mathsf{Bool} \text{ and} \\ & mop \in \{\,\underline{\mathbf{not}}\,\} \\ \mathsf{Word} & \text{if } \mathsf{SE}(expr)(V) = \mathsf{Word} \text{ and} \\ & mop \in \{\,\underline{\mathbf{plus}}\,,\,\underline{\mathbf{minus}}\,\} \\ \mathsf{invalid} & \text{otherwise} \end{cases}$$

From now on the meta-variables *prog*, *stat* and *expr* range over Prog, Stat and Expr.

9.3 Dynamic Semantics

The dynamic semantics of TPL assigns valuation functions to valid expressions and processes to valid statements and programs. For expressions and statements we define families of meaning functions for each set of variables $V \subseteq X$. The resulting valuation functions and processes have the same alphabet V. The alphabet of the process denoted by a program is empty because only external communications are visible. Thus we have meaning functions

$$\begin{array}{lcl} \mathsf{MP} & : & \mathsf{Prog} \to \mathsf{Proc}_{\emptyset}\ , \\ \mathsf{MS}_V & : & \mathsf{Stat}_V \to \mathsf{Proc}_V\ , \mathit{and} \\ \mathsf{ME}_V & : & \mathsf{Expr}_V \to \mathsf{VALFCT}_V^{\mathsf{Bool}} \cup \mathsf{VALFCT}_V^{\mathsf{Word}} \end{array}$$

that are defined inductively in Table 9.3.

Table 9.3. Dynamic semantics of TPL

$$\begin{array}{rcl} \mathsf{MP}(\underline{\mathbf{prog}}\,(stat)) & = & \mathsf{MS}_{\emptyset}(stat)\ ;\ \mathsf{Stop} \\ \hline \mathsf{MS}_V(\underline{\mathbf{skip}}\,) & = & \mathsf{Id} \\ \mathsf{MS}_V(\underline{\mathbf{stop}}\,) & = & \mathsf{Stop} \\ \mathsf{MS}_V(\underline{\mathbf{assign}}\,(x, expr)) & = & x := \mathsf{ME}_V(expr) \\ \mathsf{MS}_V(\underline{\mathbf{input}}\,(inch, x)) & = & \Delta\infty\ ;\ inch?x \\ \mathsf{MS}_V(\underline{\mathbf{output}}\,(outch, expr)) & = & \Delta\infty\ ;\ outch!\mathsf{ME}_V(expr) \\ \mathsf{MS}_V(\underline{\mathbf{seq}}\,(stat_1, stat_2)) & = & \mathsf{MS}_V(stat_1)\ ;\ \mathsf{MS}_V(stat_2) \\ \mathsf{MS}_V(\underline{\mathbf{if}}\,(expr, stat_1, stat_2)) & = & \mathsf{MS}_V(stat_1) \lhd \mathsf{ME}_V(expr) \rhd \mathsf{MS}_V(stat_2) \\ \mathsf{MS}_V(\underline{\mathbf{while}}\,(expr, stat)) & = & \mu\, W_{\mathsf{ME}_V(\mathsf{expr}),\mathsf{MS}_V(\mathsf{stat})} \\ \mathsf{MS}_V(\underline{\mathbf{block}}\,(x, stat)) & = & x^+\ ;\ \mathsf{MS}_{V\cup\{x\}}(stat)\ ;\ x^- \\ \mathsf{MS}_V(\underline{\mathbf{upperbound}}\,(stat, t)) & = & |\,\mathsf{MS}_V(stat)\,| \preceq t \\ \hline \mathsf{ME}_V(\underline{\mathbf{var}}\,(x)) & = & x^* \\ \mathsf{ME}_V(\underline{\mathbf{const}}\,(k)) & = & k^* \\ \mathsf{ME}_V(\underline{\mathbf{bin}}\,(bop, expr_1, expr_2)) & = & \mathsf{MB}(bop)^*(\mathsf{ME}_V(expr_1), \mathsf{ME}_V(expr_2)) \\ \mathsf{ME}_V(\underline{\mathbf{mon}}\,(mop, expr)) & = & \mathsf{MM}(mop)^*(\mathsf{ME}_V(expr)) \end{array}$$

Having available a suitable notation for processes similar to the program constructs of TPL, the definition is easily given. It is straightforward to see that the side conditions for the process constructors are met and that Boolean and word expressions are interpreted by corresponding valuation functions. The timing conventions deserve special attention. As explained earlier we let time progress only in the communication statements; all other operators are immediate. More specifically, time progresses only before the actual communication takes place. In our language of processes all constructs except of delays are immediate. Therefore, the timing convention is easily expressed by using (indefinite) delays just before the communication processes in the clauses for **input** and **output**.

The functional $W_{\phi,P} \in (\mathsf{Proc}_V \to \mathsf{Proc}_V)$ (for a predicate ϕ and a process P) that is used in the clause for **while** is defined by

$$W_{\phi,P}(X) \;=\; (P\,;X) \lhd \phi \rhd \mathsf{Id}\;.$$

Of course $W_{\phi,P}$ is monotonic because ; and $. \lhd \phi \rhd .$ are monotonic. Therefore, its least fixpoint exists according to the Knaster-Tarski fixpoint theorem. That the definition of loop semantics by the least fixpoint of $W_{\varphi,P}$ is operationally adequate has been shown in Chap. 6.

Note that we agree that programs stop finally if their body terminates.

The stars used in the clauses for ME_V are the operators from Chap. 4 that lift variables and values to valuation functions and operation on values to operations on valuation functions. $\mathsf{MB}(bop)$, the interpretation of the binary operators bop, and $\mathsf{MM}(mop)$, the interpretation of the monadic operators mop, are defined as follows.

- The arithmetic binary operators $bop \in \{$ **plus**, **minus**, **times**, **div**, **rem** $\}$ and the monadic operators $mop \in \{$ **plus**, **minus** $\}$ are interpreted by the corresponding operations of type $(\mathsf{Word} \times \mathsf{Word} \to \mathsf{Word})$ resp. $(\mathsf{Word} \to \mathsf{Word})$ on words that have been defined in Sect. 8.1. In particular the conventions to make them total are described there.
- The relational operators $bop \in \{$ **eq**, **ne**, **leq**, **geq**, **le**, **ge** $\}$ are interpreted by the corresponding comparison operations of signature $(\mathsf{Word} \times \mathsf{Word} \to \mathsf{Bool})$. The comparison operations on words are obtained from the restrictions of the usual ordering relations on integers.
- The Boolean operators **and**, **or** and **not** are interpreted by conjunction, disjunction and complementation on Bool. So $\mathsf{MB}($**and**$), \mathsf{MB}($**or**$) \in (\mathsf{Bool} \times \mathsf{Bool} \to \mathsf{Bool})$ and $\mathsf{MM}(mop) \in (\mathsf{Bool} \to \mathsf{Bool})$.

10. A Hierarchy of Views

In principle it is possible to use the Transputer base model of Chap. 8 directly in a correctness predicate relating machine code with source programs. But this leads to a complicated definition because of the large conceptual distance between the source language semantics and the target machine model. Therefore, a direct employment of the base model in a code generator proof is unattractive; it would make the proof long, tedious, and error-prone. Moreover, with such a model as basis the assumption becomes unrealistic that we have complete knowledge about the correctness predicate to be established by the code generator before starting the proof. Execution of code requires quite a number of side conditions, e.g. that registers contain appropriate values initially as well as finally. Moreover, additional invariants are necessary to facilitate a compositional specification of the code generator. To guess all these conditions correctly right from the beginning is very difficult.

We make a virtue out of necessity and develop the correctness predicate stepwise by means of a hierarchy of increasingly abstract views to the Transputer's behavior. These views are successively concerned with the following topics, which in this way can be treated in isolation:

- symbolic representation of the control point, which results in a treatment of the executed machine program as a separate entity;
- word-size operands for direct functions;
- convenient access to the workspace;
- symbolic variables instead of workspace addresses;
- hiding the registers.

Each abstraction level comprises a collection of processes as illustrated in Fig. 10.1. The base model is at the bottom. On each higher abstraction level we have processes $I_i(a, b)$, which model the total behavior caused by starting the machine program $a \cdot b$ with the first instruction of b, and processes $E_i(\mathit{instr})$ (or $E_i(\mathit{instr}, w)$) and $E_i(\mathit{op})$ that describe the state change induced by the direct function instr and the operation op. From level 2 onwards direct functions are considered together with word operands w. The levels 4 and 5 are parameterized with a dictionary δ, which describes the set of variables introduced on level 4 as well as their representation.

Each abstraction is performed by defining the collection of processes for the more abstract view in terms of the collection for the more concrete one.

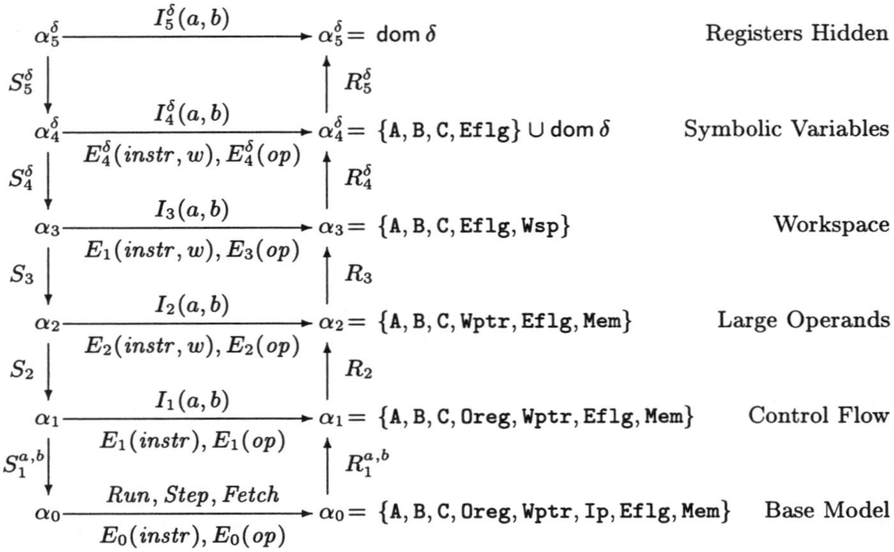

Fig. 10.1. The processes constituting the abstraction levels and their alphabet; association of a process P to the arrow from alphabet α to alphabet β means that $P \in \mathsf{Proc}_\alpha^\beta$; a and b are code sequences, w is a Transputer word, and δ is a dictionary; the occurring processes are defined below

These definitions are induced by the process pairs (S_i, R_i) on the vertical arrows in Fig. 10.1, which form a simulation in each case form.[1] Afterwards we establish sufficiently strong theorems that allow to reason with the abstract family of processes alone, without referring to the concrete family. This is essential for meeting the objective of abstraction, viz. to increase tractability. Table 10.1 shows the drastic effect of abstraction in reducing the complexity of the process terms describing the effect of the instruction `ldl` (load local) on the various abstraction levels. The assertions present at the lower abstraction levels make the inequalities applicable only if the referenced address is valid. From level 3 onwards this is ensured by a global assumption about the storage allocated for the workspace. The models in the hierarchy are consistent by construction, i.e. by definition and calculation.[2]

The abstraction levels are similar to assembler languages. But we concentrate on semantic issues and *derive* the semantic descriptions instead of

[1] The first abstraction that introduces the symbolic representation of the control point is induced by a family of simulations parameterized with a pair of code sequences a, b rather than by a single simulation.

[2] Of course this does not mean that errors cannot happen. But all errors can be traced back to mistakes in calculations and might, therefore, be uncovered by careful inspection or mechanic replay of the proofs.

Table 10.1. Illustration of abstraction levels; for simplicity the timing is ignored; we assume that $1 \leq v \leq l_W$ and that $x \in \mathsf{dom}\,\delta$ is a variable of type word

$E_5^\delta(\mathtt{ldl}, adr_x)$	$\geq$	Id
$E_4^\delta(\mathtt{ldl}, adr_x)$	$\geq$	$\mathtt{A}, \mathtt{B}, \mathtt{C} := x, \mathtt{A}, \mathtt{B}$
$E_3(\mathtt{ldl}, v)$	$\geq$	$\mathtt{A}, \mathtt{B}, \mathtt{C} := \mathtt{Wsp}(v), \mathtt{A}, \mathtt{B}$
$E_2(\mathtt{ldl}, w)$	$\geq$	$\{Index(\mathtt{Wptr}, w) \in \mathsf{Addr}\}$;
		$\mathtt{A}, \mathtt{B}, \mathtt{C} := \mathtt{Mem}(Index(\mathtt{Wptr}, w)), \mathtt{A}, \mathtt{B}$
$E_1(\mathtt{ldl})$	$\geq$	$\{Index(\mathtt{Wptr}, \mathtt{Oreg}) \in \mathsf{Addr}\}$;
		$\mathtt{A}, \mathtt{B}, \mathtt{C}, \mathtt{Oreg} := \mathtt{Mem}(Index(\mathtt{Wptr}, \mathtt{Oreg})), \mathtt{A}, \mathtt{B}, 0$
$E_0(\mathtt{ldl})$	$\geq$	$\{Index(\mathtt{Wptr}, \mathtt{Oreg}) \in \mathsf{Addr}\}$;
		$\mathtt{A}, \mathtt{B}, \mathtt{C}, \mathtt{Oreg} := \mathtt{Mem}(Index(\mathtt{Wptr}, \mathtt{Oreg})), \mathtt{A}, \mathtt{B}, 0$

postulating them. Moreover, the abstraction can be performed in a modular fashion, viz. separately for each instruction. Therefore, we can treat those instructions needed in our application formally even without formalizing the rest of the instruction set. This allows to use the language of an actual processor instead of a toy language in an effort of still modest size.

The choice of the abstraction levels is not accidental. They correspond to increasingly abstract ways of speaking about Transputer code that occasionally are used in [46] without formal introduction. We count it as a merit rather than a weakness that our levels formally reflect concepts used in informal argumentation as this suggests that they are natural and intuitively clear. The advantage of their formalization is that the assumptions on which the informal argumentation relies are made explicit.

Why do we work bottom-up from a model reflecting a low-level of abstraction rather than top-down from an abstract model? The reason is that the task of a compiler constructor usually is to produce code for a given processor for which only a low-level description is available. Trying to hit this description in a top-down development is almost hopeless. A top-down approach would be appropriate if our task would be to *design* a processor.

10.1 Symbolic Representation of Control Point

The base model of the Transputer in Chap. 8 has no formal notion of a machine program but execution is steered from the contents of the memory. However, it is quite natural to think of the executed machine program as a separate entity that consists of a sequence of instructions. The point of execution, which is represented on the machine by the instruction pointer's contents, can be modeled by a distinguished position in that instruction sequence. More elegantly, we can use a pair of instruction sequences (a, b), where a stands for the part of the machine program before the distinguished position and b for the part thereafter; i.e. the complete machine program is $a \cdot b$ and the next instruction to be executed is the first instruction of b. Progress of execution can be expressed by partitioning the sequence $a \cdot b$ in another way. Sometimes we call such a pair (a, b) of code sequences a ***partitioned code sequence***.

The current section is concerned with such a symbolic representation of the control point. We fix a distinguished region of the memory, the ***program storage***, which is used solely to hold the executed machine program. The abstraction's definition below ensures that any attempt to change its contents is considered catastrophic. So on the resulting abstraction level we can no longer reason meaningfully about self-modifying code. The advantage is that we need not prove explicitly that the executed program is not changed as this is reflected already in the derived descriptions.

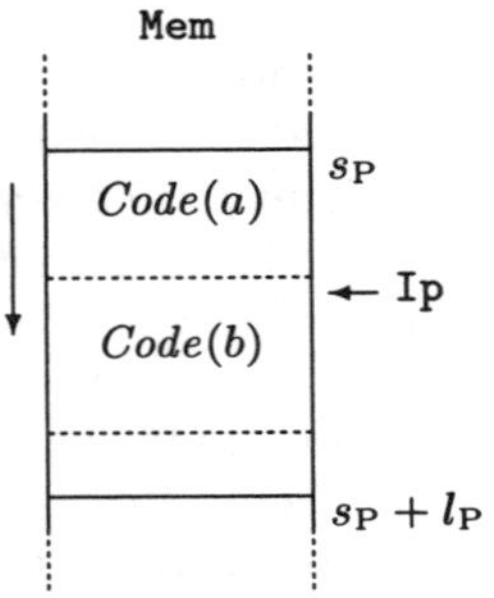

Fig. 10.2. Illustration of $\Lambda(a, b)$

Assume that s_P is the byte address of the program storage's first cell and that l_P is the number of reserved bytes. The predicate $\Lambda(a, b)$, which is illustrated in Fig. 10.2, is used to define the first abstraction. It holds if and only if the machine program $a \cdot b$ is loaded into the program storage and `Ip` points to the first instruction of b.

$$\Lambda(a, b) \stackrel{\text{def}}{\equiv} \mathit{Loaded}(a \cdot b) \wedge \mathit{IpAfter}(a) \ ,$$

where *Loaded* and *IpAfter* are defined by

$$\begin{aligned} \mathit{Loaded}(c) &\stackrel{\text{def}}{\equiv} |\, c \,| \leq l_P \wedge \\ &\qquad [\mathit{Byte}(\mathtt{Mem}, s_P), \ldots, \mathit{Byte}(\mathtt{Mem}, s_P + |\, c \,| - 1)] = \mathit{Code}(c) \\ \mathit{IpAfter}(c) &\stackrel{\text{def}}{\equiv} \mathtt{Ip} = (s_P + |\, c \,|) \end{aligned}$$

for arbitrary $c \in \mathsf{IS}$. *Loaded*(c) holds whenever the program storage contains the code sequence c, which in particular requires that c is not longer than l_P. *IpAfter*(c) is true whenever the instruction pointer `Ip` points to the first location behind the instruction sequence c in the program storage. An abstract view to the behavior of the Transputer's run phase executing the code $a \cdot b$ starting with the first instruction of b is provided by

$$I_1(a,b) \stackrel{\text{def}}{=} \texttt{Ip}^+ \; ; \; [\Lambda(a,b)] \; ; \; Run \; ; \; \{\Lambda(a,b)\} \; ; \; \texttt{Ip}^- \; .$$

The addition and the deletion command hide *Run*'s effect on the instruction pointer Ip, which is no longer of interest because we represent the point of control symbolically from now on. Thus the alphabet of the new view is

$$\alpha_1 \stackrel{\text{def}}{=} \{\texttt{A}, \texttt{B}, \texttt{C}, \texttt{Oreg}, \texttt{Wptr}, \texttt{Eflg}, \texttt{Mem}\} = \alpha_0 \setminus \{\texttt{Ip}\} \; .$$

The assumption $[\Lambda(a,b)]$ ensures that the machine program is loaded and the instruction pointer is initialized appropriately. There is no intuitive reason for the assertion $\{\Lambda(a,b)\}$ but there is a formal one: it shows that the abstraction is induced by the simulation $(R_1^{a,b}, S_1^{a,b})$, where

$$R_1^{a,b} \stackrel{\text{def}}{=} \{\Lambda(a,b)\} \; ; \; \texttt{Ip}^- \quad \text{and} \quad S_1^{a,b} \stackrel{\text{def}}{=} \texttt{Ip}^+ \; ; \; [\Lambda(a,b)] \; .$$

The assertion does not harm because the run phase does not terminate. Using axiom (8.9) we can easily prove that removal of the assertion does not change the definition. Strictly speaking, we have defined a family of processes $(I_1(a,b))_{a,b \in \mathsf{IS}}$ (and a family of simulations), viz. one process for each pair of instruction sequences (a,b), each of which has alphabet α_1.

We also define abstractions of the effect processes $E_0(instr)$ and $E_0(op)$. These ensure by a final assertion and by taking the greatest lower bound over all possible instruction sequences a, b that neither the loaded program (whatever it might be) nor the position of execution is changed or, more precisely, that changes lead to chaotic behavior (remember that in the base model the instruction pointer is incremented by the *Fetch* process and not by the individual effect processes):

$$E_1(instr) \stackrel{\text{def}}{=} \bigwedge\nolimits_{a,b} \texttt{Ip}^+ \; ; \; [\Lambda(a,b)] \; ; \; E_0(instr) \; ; \; \{\Lambda(a,b)\} \; ; \; \texttt{Ip}^- \; .$$
$$E_1(op) \stackrel{\text{def}}{=} \bigwedge\nolimits_{a,b} \texttt{Ip}^+ \; ; \; [\Lambda(a,b)] \; ; \; E_0(op) \; ; \; \{\Lambda(a,b)\} \; ; \; \texttt{Ip}^- \; .$$

Again this definition is induced by the family of simulations $(R_1^{a,b}, S_1^{a,b})_{a,b \in \mathsf{IS}}$.

Note that the abstraction is implicitly parameterized by the program storage's start address s_{P} and length l_{P}. All subsequent considerations apply to all possible choices of these implicit parameters. Implicit parameterization is convenient for entities that remain constant over a large portion of a mathematical investigation because it helps to keep the notation simple. A possible danger is that global assumptions on implicit parameters are overlooked when interpreting finally established theorems in isolation. To avoid this we apply global parameterization only in a few cases.

Since $\bigwedge$ is the greatest lower bound operator, we have for arbitrary a, b

$$E_1(instr) \leq \texttt{Ip}^+ \; ; \; [\Lambda(a,b)] \; ; \; E_0(instr) \; ; \; \{\Lambda(a,b)\} \; ; \; \texttt{Ip}^- \; .$$

Indeed, the greatest lower bound has been used in the definition of E_1 for achieving just this property. The deeper motivation for the definition of E_1 is that a machine program which is loaded and started with some instruction *instr* with (four-bit) operand n behaves as follows: n is bitwise or-ed with the value in the operand register (this loads n to the least significant four bits in `Oreg` since any previous instruction leaves these bits cleared), and then the (abstracted) effect of *instr* is executed. Afterwards it behaves as if the same program is executed starting at the subsequent instruction. We write $instr(n)$ for the code sequence consisting of the single direct function *instr* with four-bit operand n, i.e. $0 \le n < 16$.

Theorem 10.1.1 (General instruction theorem).

$$I_1(a, instr(n) \cdot b) \ \ge\ \texttt{Oreg} := \texttt{Oreg}\ \mathsf{bitor}\ n\ ;\ E_1(instr)\ ;\ I_1(a \cdot instr(n), b)\ .$$

Before we present the proof we investigate Λ. The proved properties are not at all surprising but reflect formally our expectations.

Changing the value of `Ip` changes the point of control.

Lemma 10.1.2 (Λ and `Ip`). *Suppose $a \cdot b = c \cdot d$. Then*

$$(\Lambda(a,b))[\texttt{Ip} + |\,d\,| - |\,b\,|/\texttt{Ip}] \ =\ \Lambda(c,d)\ .$$

Proof.

$$\begin{array}{ll} & (\Lambda(a,b))[\texttt{Ip} + |\,d\,| - |\,b\,|/\texttt{Ip}] \\ \equiv & [\text{Distributivity of substitution, } \mathit{Loaded}(a) \text{ is independent of } \texttt{Ip}] \\ & \mathit{Loaded}(a \cdot b)\ \wedge\ (\texttt{Ip} + |\,d\,| - |\,b\,|) = (s_P + |\,a\,|) \\ \equiv & [a \cdot b = c \cdot d, \text{ arithmetic}] \\ & \mathit{Loaded}(c \cdot d)\ \wedge\ \texttt{Ip} = s_P + |\,a\,| + |\,b\,| - |\,d\,| \\ \equiv & [a \cdot b = c \cdot d \text{ implies } |\,c\,| = |\,a\,| + |\,b\,| - |\,d\,|] \\ & \mathit{Loaded}(c \cdot d)\ \wedge\ \texttt{Ip} = s_P + |\,c\,| \\ \equiv & [\text{Definition of } \mathit{IpAfter} \text{ and } \Lambda(a,b)] \\ & \Lambda(c,d)\ . \end{array}$$

□

Validity of $\Lambda(a, instr(n) \cdot b)$ implies that the data part of the byte pointed to by the instruction pointer contains n and the code part contains the function code of *instr*. The latter means that the predicate $\mathit{CurFct}(instr)$ holds.

Lemma 10.1.3 (Λ and instruction loading).
(a) $\Lambda(a, instr(n) \cdot b) \ \le\ (\mathit{Byte}(\texttt{Mem}, \texttt{Ip})\ \mathsf{bitand}\ \$0F) = n\ .$
(b) $\Lambda(a, instr(n) \cdot b) \ \le\ \mathit{CurFct}(instr)\ .$

Proof. Assume that $\Lambda(a, instr(n) \cdot b)$ holds. Then $\texttt{Ip} = s_P + |\,a\,|$ and $\mathit{Loaded}(a \cdot instr(n) \cdot b)$, which implies that

$$\mathit{Byte}(\texttt{Mem}, \texttt{Ip}) \underset{\substack{\uparrow \\ [\mathit{IpAfter}(a)]}}{=} \mathit{Byte}(\texttt{Mem}, s_P + |\,a\,|) \underset{\substack{\uparrow \\ [\mathit{Loaded}(a \cdot instr(n) \cdot b)]}}{=} \mathit{Code}(instr, n)\ .$$

Hence, $\mathit{Byte}(\texttt{Mem}, \texttt{Ip})\ \mathsf{bitand}\ \$0F \ =\ \mathit{Code}(instr, n)\ \mathsf{bitand}\ \$0F \ =\ n$ according to equation (8.3), which shows (a).

Similarly, identity (8.4) implies that

$$\begin{aligned} \mathit{Byte}(\texttt{Mem}, \texttt{Ip}) \texttt{ bitand } \$\texttt{F0} &= \mathit{Code}(\mathit{instr}, n) \texttt{ bitand } \$\texttt{F0} \\ &= \mathit{InstrCode}(\mathit{instr}) \ , \end{aligned}$$

which shows validity of $\mathit{CurFct}(\mathit{instr})$ and thus (b). □

The fetch phase moves the control point by one instruction and bitwise disjuncts the operand register with the data part of the current instruction.

Lemma 10.1.4 (Λ and *Fetch*).

$$\begin{aligned} &[\Lambda(a, \mathit{instr}(n) \cdot b)] \ ; \mathit{Fetch} \ = \\ &\qquad \texttt{Oreg}, \texttt{Ip} := \texttt{Oreg bitor } n, \texttt{Ip} + 1 \ ; [\Lambda(a \cdot \mathit{instr}(n), b)] \ . \end{aligned}$$

Proof. We start calculating on the right hand side:

$$\begin{aligned} & \texttt{Oreg}, \texttt{Ip} := \texttt{Oreg bitor } n, \texttt{Ip} + 1 \ ; [\Lambda(a \cdot \mathit{instr}(n), b)] \\ = \quad & [\text{(Assign-assert)}, \Lambda(a \cdot \mathit{instr}(n), b) \text{ is independent of } \texttt{Oreg}] \\ & [(\Lambda(a \cdot \mathit{instr}(n), b))[\texttt{Ip} + 1/\texttt{Ip}]] \ ; \texttt{Oreg}, \texttt{Ip} := \texttt{Oreg bitor } n, \texttt{Ip} + 1 \\ = \quad & [\text{Lemma 10.1.2 with } a \leftarrow a \cdot \mathit{instr}(n),\ c \leftarrow a,\ d \leftarrow \mathit{instr}(n) \cdot b] \\ & [\Lambda(a, \mathit{instr}(n) \cdot b)] \ ; \texttt{Oreg}, \texttt{Ip} := \texttt{Oreg bitor } n, \texttt{Ip} + 1 \\ = \quad & [\text{(Exploit assume) using Lemma 10.1.3, (a)}] \\ & [\Lambda(a, \mathit{instr}(n) \cdot b)] \ ; \mathit{Fetch} \ . \end{aligned}$$

□

The following lemma is concerned with the situation just after the fetch phase.

Lemma 10.1.5 (I_1 after *Fetch*).

$$\begin{aligned} & I_1(a, \mathit{instr}(n) \cdot b) \ \geq \\ & \qquad \texttt{Oreg} := \texttt{Oreg bitor } n \ ; S_1^{a \cdot \mathit{instr}(n), b} \ ; E_0(\mathit{instr}) \ ; \mathit{Run} \ ; S_1^{a, \mathit{instr}(n) \cdot b} \ . \end{aligned}$$

Proof.

$$\begin{aligned} & I_1(a, \mathit{instr}(n) \cdot b) \\ \geq \quad & [\text{Definition of } I_1, \text{ axiom (8.8)}] \\ & S_1^{a, \mathit{instr}(n) \cdot b} \ ; \mathit{Step} \ ; \mathit{Run} \ ; R_1^{a, \mathit{instr}(n) \cdot b} \\ = \quad & [\text{Lemma 10.1.3, (b) and (Comb-assume)}] \\ & S_1^{a, \mathit{instr}(n) \cdot b} \ ; [\mathit{CurFct}(\mathit{instr})] \ ; \mathit{Step} \ ; \mathit{Run} \ ; R_1^{a, \mathit{instr}(n) \cdot b} \\ \geq \quad & [\text{Axiom (8.10)}] \\ & S_1^{a, \mathit{instr}(n) \cdot b} \ ; \mathit{Fetch} \ ; E_0(\mathit{instr}) \ ; \mathit{Run} \ ; R_1^{a, \mathit{instr}(n) \cdot b} \\ = \quad & [\text{Definition } S_1, \text{ Lemma 10.1.4}] \\ & \texttt{Ip}^+ \ ; \texttt{Oreg}, \texttt{Ip} := \texttt{Oreg bitor } n, \texttt{Ip} + 1 \ ; [\Lambda(a \cdot \mathit{instr}(n), b)] \ ; \end{aligned}$$

$$E_0(instr) \; ; \; Run \; ; \; R_1^{a, instr(n) \cdot b}$$
$$\geq \quad [\text{Comb-asg}]$$
$$\mathtt{Ip}^+ \; ; \; \mathtt{Ip} := \mathtt{Ip} + 1 \; ; \; \mathtt{Oreg} := \mathtt{Oreg} \; \mathsf{bitor} \; n \; ; \; [\Lambda(a \cdot instr(n), b)] \; ;$$
$$E_0(instr) \; ; \; Run \; ; \; R_1^{a, instr(n) \cdot b}$$
$$\geq \quad [\text{(Initialization), (Initial-assign), definition } S_1]$$
$$\mathtt{Oreg} := \mathtt{Oreg} \; \mathsf{bitor} \; n \; ; \; S_1^{a \cdot instr(n), b} \; ; \; E_0(instr) \; ; \; Run \; ; \; R_1^{a, instr(n) \cdot b} . \quad \square$$

After these preparations we can easily prove Theorem 10.1.1.

Proof.

$$I_1(a, instr(n) \cdot b)$$
$$\geq \quad [\text{Lemma 10.1.5}]$$
$$\mathtt{Oreg} := \mathtt{Oreg} \; \mathsf{bitor} \; n \; ; \; S_1^{a \cdot instr(n), b} \; ; \; E_0(instr) \; ; \; Run \; ; \; R_1^{a, instr(n) \cdot b}$$
$$= \quad [\text{Axiom (8.9)}]$$
$$\mathtt{Oreg} := \mathtt{Oreg} \; \mathsf{bitor} \; n \; ; \; S_1^{a \cdot instr(n), b} \; ; \; E_0(instr) \; ; \; Run \; ; \; R_1^{a \cdot instr(n), b}$$
$$\geq \quad [(S_1^{a \cdot instr(n), b}, R_1^{a \cdot instr(n), b}) \text{ is a simulation}]$$
$$\mathtt{Oreg} := \mathtt{Oreg} \; \mathsf{bitor} \; n \; ; \; S_1^{a \cdot instr(n), b} \; ; \; E_0(instr) \; ; \; R_1^{a \cdot instr(n), b} \; ;$$
$$S_1^{a \cdot instr(n), b} \; ; \; Run \; ; \; R_1^{a \cdot instr(n), b}$$
$$= \quad [\text{Definitions}]$$
$$\mathtt{Oreg} := \mathtt{Oreg} \; \mathsf{bitor} \; n \; ; \; E_1(instr) \; ; \; I_1(a \cdot instr(n), b) \; . \quad \square$$

While Theorem 10.1.1 somehow transfers axiom (8.8) to I_1, the next lemma is concerned with the second axiom (8.9) about the run phase.

Lemma 10.1.6 (Non-termination).

$$I_1(a, b) \; ; \; X \; = \; I_1(a, b) \; ; \; Y \; \textit{for all } X, Y \in \mathsf{Proc}_{\alpha_1}^{\alpha} \; .$$

A corresponding property holds for all views I_i derived later in this chapter but will not be stated explicitly.

Proof.

$$I_1(a, b) \; ; \; X$$
$$= \quad [\text{Def}]$$
$$S_1^{a,b} \; ; \; Run \; ; \; R_1^{a,b} \; ; \; X$$
$$= \quad [\text{Axiom (8.9) with } R_1^{a,b} \; ; \; X \text{ for } X \text{ and } R_1^{a,b} \; ; \; Y \text{ for } Y]$$
$$S_1^{a,b} \; ; \; Run \; ; \; R_1^{a,b} \; ; \; Y$$
$$= \quad [\text{Def}]$$
$$I_1(a, b) \; ; \; Y \; . \quad \square$$

Approximations for $E_1(instr)$ can be calculated separately for each direct function *instr*. Together with Theorem 10.1.1 these approximations yield concrete descriptions for the effect of entire code sequences. In order to prove that P is an approximation of $E_1(instr)$, i.e. that $E_1(instr) \geq P$, it suffices to show that

$$\mathtt{Ip}^+ \; ; [\Lambda(a,b)] \; ; E_0(instr) \; ; \{\Lambda(a,b)\} \; ; \mathtt{Ip}^- \;\geq\; P \tag{10.1}$$

for all code sequences a, b, because $E_1(instr)$ is just the greatest lower bound of all these processes. For the load constant instruction, for instance, we obtain the following approximation.

Theorem 10.1.7 (Approximation for ldc).

$$E_1(\mathtt{ldc}) \;\geq\; \Delta 1 \; ; \mathtt{A,B,C,Oreg} := \mathtt{Oreg,A,B},0 \; .$$

Proof. For any $a, b \in \mathsf{IS}$ we have

$$\begin{aligned}
& \mathtt{Ip}^+ \; ; [\Lambda(a,b)] \; ; E_0(\mathtt{ldc}) \; ; \{\Lambda(a,b)\} \; ; \mathtt{Ip}^- \\
\geq \quad & [\text{Axiom (8.13)}] \\
& \mathtt{Ip}^+ \; ; [\Lambda(a,b)] \; ; \Delta 1 \; ; \mathtt{A,B,C,Oreg} := \mathtt{Oreg,A,B},0 \; ; \{\Lambda(a,b)\} \; ; \mathtt{Ip}^- \\
= \quad & [(\Delta\text{-assert}) \text{ and } (\text{Initial-}\Delta)] \\
& \Delta 1 \; ; \mathtt{Ip}^+ \; ; [\Lambda(a,b)] \; ; \mathtt{A,B,C,Oreg} := \mathtt{Oreg,A,B},0 \; ; \{\Lambda(a,b)\} \; ; \mathtt{Ip}^- \\
= \quad & [(\text{Assign-assert1}) \text{ and } (\text{Initial-assign})] \\
& \Delta 1 \; ; \mathtt{A,B,C,Oreg} := \mathtt{Oreg,A,B},0 \; ; \mathtt{Ip}^+ \; ; [\Lambda(a,b)] \; ; \{\Lambda(a,b)\} \; ; \mathtt{Ip}^- \\
\geq \quad & [(\text{Assert-assume-sim}), (\text{--+-sim})] \\
& \Delta 1 \; ; \mathtt{A,B,C,Oreg} := \mathtt{Oreg,A,B},0 \; .
\end{aligned}$$

□

A closer look at the proof indicates that all approximations for E_0 that neither assign to `Mem` nor refer to `Ip` transfer to E_1 thus easily. Note, however, that their alphabet is changed. All approximations collected in Table 10.2 except of the one for $E_1(\mathtt{stl})$ can be obtained in this way. With respect to modularity it is important to notice that each can be proved separately by a little calculation.

The approximation for $E_0(\mathtt{stl})$ in the axiom (8.15), however, assigns to `Mem`. Intuitively, an approximation for $E_1(\mathtt{stl})$ must ensure that the program storage is not corrupted. In order to express this obligation, we use a predicate *AdmAdr* that is true for a word w iff w belongs to the user accessible addresses Addr but does not point into the program storage. A word satisfying these two conditions is called an *admissible address*:

$$\begin{aligned} AdmAdr(w) \;\stackrel{\text{def}}{\equiv}\; & w \in \mathsf{Addr} \;\wedge \\ & (\forall v : s_P \leq v < s_P + l_P : BaseAdr(v) \neq w) \; . \end{aligned} \tag{10.12}$$

By expanding the definitions one shows easily that for all words v, w and machine programs c,

Table 10.2. Approximations for instructions I

$E_1(\texttt{pfix}) \geq \Delta 1 ; \texttt{Oreg} := \texttt{Oreg} \ll 4$		(10.2)
$E_1(\texttt{nfix}) \geq \Delta 1 ; \texttt{Oreg} := (\mathsf{bitnot}\ \texttt{Oreg}) \ll 4$		(10.3)
$E_1(\texttt{ldc}) \geq \Delta 1 ; \texttt{A}, \texttt{B}, \texttt{C}, \texttt{Oreg} := \texttt{Oreg}, \texttt{A}, \texttt{B}, 0$		(10.4)
$E_1(\texttt{ldl}) \geq \Delta 2 ; \{Index(\texttt{Wptr}, \texttt{Oreg}) \in \mathsf{Addr}\} ;$ $\texttt{A}, \texttt{B}, \texttt{C}, \texttt{Oreg} := (\texttt{Mem}(Index(\texttt{Wptr}, \texttt{Oreg}))), \texttt{A}, \texttt{B}, 0$		(10.5)
$E_1(\texttt{stl}) \geq \Delta 1 ; \{AdmAdr(Index(\texttt{Wptr}, \texttt{Oreg}))\} ;$ $\texttt{Mem}[Index(\texttt{Wptr}, \texttt{Oreg})], \texttt{A}, \texttt{B}, \texttt{Oreg} := \texttt{A}, \texttt{B}, \texttt{C}, 0 ; \texttt{C} :=?$		(10.6)
$E_1(\texttt{ldlp}) \geq \Delta 1 ; \texttt{A}, \texttt{B}, \texttt{C}, \texttt{Oreg} := (Index(\texttt{Wptr}, \texttt{Oreg})), \texttt{A}, \texttt{B}, 0$		(10.7)
$E_1(\texttt{adc}) \geq \Delta 1 ; \texttt{A}, \texttt{Eflg}, \texttt{Oreg} := \texttt{A} + \texttt{Oreg}, \texttt{Eflg} \vee AddOvFl(\texttt{A}, \texttt{Oreg}), 0$		(10.8)
$E_1(\texttt{eqc}) \geq \Delta 2 ; \texttt{A}, \texttt{Oreg} := \mathsf{if}\ \texttt{A} = \texttt{Oreg}\ \mathsf{then}\ 1\ \mathsf{else}\ 0\ \mathsf{fi}, 0$		(10.9)
$E_1(\texttt{cj}) \geq \Delta 2 ; \{\texttt{A} \neq 0\} ; \texttt{A}, \texttt{B}, \texttt{Oreg} := \texttt{B}, \texttt{C}, 0 ; \texttt{C} :=?$		(10.10)
$E_1(\texttt{opr}) \geq \{CurOpr(op)\} ; E_1(op) ; \texttt{Oreg} := 0$		(10.11)

$$AdmAdr(w) \wedge Loaded(c) \leq Loaded(c)[\texttt{Mem}[w \mapsto v]/\texttt{Mem}] , \tag{10.13}$$

i.e. memory updates at admissible addresses do not affect loaded machine programs. Exploiting this property we can prove an approximation for $E_1(\texttt{stl})$. It shows that `stl` behaves as expected if it writes to an admissible address but guarantees nothing otherwise.

Theorem 10.1.8 (Approximation for `stl`).

$$E_1(\texttt{stl}) \geq \Delta 1 ; \{AdmAdr(Index(\texttt{Wptr}, \texttt{Oreg}))\} ;$$
$$\texttt{Mem}[Index(\texttt{Wptr}, \texttt{Oreg})], \texttt{A}, \texttt{B}, \texttt{Oreg} := \texttt{A}, \texttt{B}, \texttt{C}, 0 ; \texttt{C} :=? .$$

Proof. We show the criterion (10.1). Let P be the process

$$\{Index(\texttt{Wptr}, \texttt{Oreg}) \in \mathsf{Addr}\} ;$$
$$\texttt{Mem}[Index(\texttt{Wptr}, \texttt{Oreg})], \texttt{A}, \texttt{B}, \texttt{Oreg} := \texttt{A}, \texttt{B}, \texttt{C}, 0 ;$$
$$\texttt{C} :=? .$$

Then we have

$$\texttt{Ip}^+ ; [\Lambda(a,b)] ; E_0(\texttt{stl}) ; \{\Lambda(a,b)\} ; \texttt{Ip}^-$$
$\geq$ [Axiom (8.15)]
$$\texttt{Ip}^+ ; [\Lambda(a,b)] ; \Delta 1 ; P ; \{\Lambda(a,b)\} ; \texttt{Ip}^-$$
$=$ [Δ-laws]
$$\Delta 1 ; \texttt{Ip}^+ ; [\Lambda(a,b)] ; P ; \{\Lambda(a,b)\} ; \texttt{Ip}^-$$
$=$ [Assertion laws using that $\Lambda(a,b)$ is independent of $\texttt{A}, \texttt{B}, \texttt{C}, \texttt{Oreg}$]
$$\Delta 1 ; \texttt{Ip}^+ ; [\Lambda(a,b)] ; \{(\Lambda(a,b))[\texttt{Mem}[Index(\texttt{Wptr}, \texttt{Oreg}) \mapsto \texttt{A}]/\texttt{Mem}]\} ;$$
$$P ; \texttt{Ip}^-$$

$\geq$ [(Assert-monotonic), property (10.14) below]
$\Delta 1$; $\mathtt{Ip}^+$; $[\Lambda(a,b)]$; $\{\Lambda(a,b) \wedge \mathit{AdmAdr}(\mathit{Index}(\mathtt{Wptr},\mathtt{Oreg}))\}$;
P ; $\mathtt{Ip}^-$

$\geq$ [(Comb-assert), assertions and assumption form simulation]
$\Delta 1$; $\mathtt{Ip}^+$; $\{\mathit{AdmAdr}(\mathit{Index}(\mathtt{Wptr},\mathtt{Oreg}))\}$; P ; $\mathtt{Ip}^-$

$=$ [Definition of P, (Initial-assert), (Initial-assign), (Initial-ch-=)]
$\Delta 1$; $\{\mathit{AdmAdr}(\mathit{Index}(\mathtt{Wptr},\mathtt{Oreg}))\}$;
$\{\mathit{Index}(\mathtt{Wptr},\mathtt{Oreg}) \in \mathsf{Addr}\}$;
$\mathtt{Mem}[\mathit{Index}(\mathtt{Wptr},\mathtt{Oreg})], \mathtt{A}, \mathtt{B}, \mathtt{Oreg} := \mathtt{A}, \mathtt{B}, \mathtt{C}, 0$; $\mathtt{C} :=?$;
$\mathtt{Ip}^+$; $\mathtt{Ip}^-$

$=$ [(−−+-sim), (Comb-assert)]
$\Delta 1$; $\{\mathit{AdmAdr}(\mathit{Index}(\mathtt{Wptr},\mathtt{Oreg})) \wedge \mathit{Index}(\mathtt{Wptr},\mathtt{Oreg}) \in \mathsf{Addr}\}$;
$\mathtt{Mem}[\mathit{Index}(\mathtt{Wptr},\mathtt{Oreg})], \mathtt{A}, \mathtt{B}, \mathtt{Oreg} := \mathtt{A}, \mathtt{B}, \mathtt{C}, 0$; $\mathtt{C} :=?$

$=$ [$\mathit{AdmAdr}(w)$ implies $w \in \mathsf{Addr}$ for any w]
$\Delta 1$; $\{\mathit{AdmAdr}(\mathit{Index}(\mathtt{Wptr},\mathtt{Oreg}))\}$;
$\mathtt{Mem}[\mathit{Index}(\mathtt{Wptr},\mathtt{Oreg})], \mathtt{A}, \mathtt{B}, \mathtt{Oreg} := \mathtt{A}, \mathtt{B}, \mathtt{C}, 0$; $\mathtt{C} :=?$.

The key property used in this calculation is that for arbitrary words v, w

$$\Lambda(a,b) \wedge \mathit{AdmAdr}(w) \leq (\Lambda(a,b))[\mathtt{Mem}[w \mapsto v]/\mathtt{Mem}] . \qquad (10.14)$$

This inequality formally expresses that updates at admissible addresses affect neither loaded programs nor the instruction pointer. It follows from (10.13) and the fact that *IpAfter* is independent of Mem. □

The approximations in Table 10.3 for various operations can be proved by calculations, the complexity of which is comparable to the proof of Theorem 10.1.7. Furthermore, we have the following approximations for $E_1(\mathtt{in})$ and $E_1(\mathtt{outword})$.

Theorem 10.1.9 (Operations in and outword). *Suppose* $i \in \{0, \ldots, 3\}$.

$$\begin{aligned} E_1(\mathtt{in}) \geq\ & \{\mathtt{A} = \mathit{bpw} \wedge \mathtt{B} = \mathit{Index}(\mathsf{MostNeg}, i+4) \wedge \mathit{AdmAdr}(\mathtt{C})\} ; \\ & \Delta\, \mathit{indelay}_1 ; \\ & \mathtt{In}_i\, ?\, \mathtt{A} ; \\ & \mathtt{Mem}[\mathtt{C}] := \mathtt{A} ; \\ & \mathtt{A}, \mathtt{B}, \mathtt{C} :=? ; \\ & \Delta\, \mathit{indelay}_2 \end{aligned}$$

$$\begin{aligned} E_1(\mathtt{outword}) \geq\ & \{\mathtt{B} = \mathit{Index}(\mathsf{MostNeg}, i) \wedge \mathit{AdmAdr}(\mathit{Index}(\mathtt{Wptr}, 0))\} ; \\ & \Delta\, \mathit{outdelay}_1 ; \\ & \mathtt{Out}_i\, !\, \mathtt{A} ; \\ & \mathtt{A} :=? ; \mathtt{Mem}[\mathit{Index}(\mathtt{Wptr}, 0)] := \mathtt{A} ; \\ & \mathtt{A}, \mathtt{B}, \mathtt{C} :=? ; \\ & \Delta\, \mathit{outdelay}_2 \end{aligned}$$

Table 10.3. Approximations for operations I

$E_1(\mathtt{add})$	$\geq$	$\Delta 1 ; \mathtt{A}, \mathtt{B}, \mathtt{Eflg} := \mathtt{B} + \mathtt{A}, \mathtt{C}, \mathtt{Eflg} \vee \mathit{AddOvFl}(\mathtt{B}, \mathtt{A}) ; \mathtt{C} :=?$	(10.15)
$E_1(\mathtt{sub})$	$\geq$	$\Delta 1 ; \mathtt{A}, \mathtt{B}, \mathtt{Eflg} := \mathtt{B} - \mathtt{A}, \mathtt{C}, \mathtt{Eflg} \vee \mathit{SubOvFl}(\mathtt{B}, \mathtt{A}) ; \mathtt{C} :=?$	(10.16)
$E_1(\mathtt{mul})$	$\geq$	$\Delta\, \mathit{bpw} + 6 ;$ $\mathtt{A}, \mathtt{B}, \mathtt{Eflg} := \mathtt{B} * \mathtt{A}, \mathtt{C}, \mathtt{Eflg} \vee \mathit{MulOvFl}(\mathtt{B}, \mathtt{A}) ; \mathtt{C} :=?$	(10.17)
$E_1(\mathtt{div})$	$\geq$	$\Delta\, \mathit{bpw} + 10 ; \{\neg \mathit{DivOvFl}(\mathtt{B}, \mathtt{A})\} ; \mathtt{A}, \mathtt{B} := \mathtt{B} \div \mathtt{A}, \mathtt{C} ; \mathtt{C} :=?$	(10.18)
$E_1(\mathtt{div})$	$\geq$	$\Delta\, \mathit{bpw} + 10 ; \{\mathit{DivOvFl}(\mathtt{B}, \mathtt{A})\} ; \mathtt{B}, \mathtt{Eflg} := \mathtt{C}, \mathsf{true} ; \mathtt{A}, \mathtt{C} :=?$	(10.19)
$E_1(\mathtt{rem})$	$\geq$	$\Delta\, \mathit{bpw} + 5 ; \{\neg \mathit{DivOvFl}(\mathtt{B}, \mathtt{A})\} ; \mathtt{A}, \mathtt{B} := \mathtt{B}\ \mathsf{rem}\ \mathtt{A}, \mathtt{C} ; \mathtt{C} :=?$	(10.20)
$E_1(\mathtt{rem})$	$\geq$	$\Delta\, \mathit{bpw} + 5 ; \{\mathit{DivOvFl}(\mathtt{B}, \mathtt{A})\} ; \mathtt{B}, \mathtt{Eflg} := \mathtt{C}, \mathsf{true} ; \mathtt{A}, \mathtt{C} :=?$	(10.21)
$E_1(\mathtt{diff})$	$\geq$	$\Delta 1 ; \mathtt{A}, \mathtt{B} := \mathtt{B} - \mathtt{A}, \mathtt{C} ; \mathtt{C} :=?$	(10.22)
$E_1(\mathtt{testerr})$	$\geq$	$\Delta 3 ; \mathtt{A}, \mathtt{B}, \mathtt{C}, \mathtt{Eflg} := \mathsf{if}\ \mathtt{Eflg}\ \mathsf{then}\ 0\ \mathsf{else}\ 1\ \mathsf{fi}, \mathtt{A}, \mathtt{B}, \mathsf{false}$	(10.23)
$E_1(\mathtt{stoperr})$	$\geq$	$\{\mathtt{Eflg}\} ; \mathsf{Stop}$	(10.24)
$E_1(\mathtt{stoperr})$	$\geq$	$\Delta 2 ; \{\neg \mathtt{Eflg}\}$	(10.25)
$E_1(\mathtt{bcnt})$	$\geq$	$\Delta 2 ; \mathtt{A} := \mathtt{A} * \mathit{bpw}$	(10.26)
$E_1(\mathtt{rev})$	$\geq$	$\Delta 1 ; \mathtt{A}, \mathtt{B} := \mathtt{B}, \mathtt{A}$	(10.27)
$E_1(\mathtt{stopp})$	$\geq$	Stop	(10.28)
$E_1(\mathtt{not})$	$\geq$	$\Delta 1 ; \mathtt{A} := (\mathsf{bitnot}\ \mathtt{A})$	(10.29)
$E_1(\mathtt{mint})$	$\geq$	$\Delta 1 ; \mathtt{A}, \mathtt{B}, \mathtt{C} := \mathsf{MostNeg}, \mathtt{A}, \mathtt{B}$	(10.30)
$E_1(\mathtt{gt})$	$\geq$	$\Delta 2 ; \mathtt{A}, \mathtt{B} := \mathsf{if}\ \mathtt{B} > \mathtt{A}\ \mathsf{then}\ 1\ \mathsf{else}\ 0\ \mathsf{fi}, \mathtt{C} ; \mathtt{C} :=?$	(10.31)

Proof. Similar to the proof of Theorem 10.1.8. □

The reader might wonder whether Theorem 10.1.1 is true also for jump instructions, since a jump does not pass control to the next instruction unless it is the trivial jump $\mathtt{j}(0)$. The answer is that the theorem is still true (after all it's a theorem!); but it is not useful because we cannot prove an approximation for $E_1(\mathtt{j})$ that is significantly better than $\perp$. Therefore, we need a special theorem for jumps and, for similar reasons, for conditional jumps that are taken. A conditional jump that is not taken, however, can be handled with the general mechanism for instructions, i.e. with Theorem 10.1.1 and inequation (10.10).

Theorem 10.1.10 (Jumps).

(a) Suppose $c \cdot d = a \cdot \mathtt{j}(n) \cdot b$ *and* l bitor $n = |\,b\,| - |\,d\,|$. *Then*

$$\mathtt{Oreg} := l ; I_1(a, \mathtt{j}(n) \cdot b) \;\geq\; \Delta 3 ; \mathtt{Oreg} := 0 ; \mathtt{A}, \mathtt{B}, \mathtt{C} :=? ; I_1(c, d) \; .$$

(b) Suppose $c \cdot d = a \cdot \mathtt{cj}(n) \cdot b$ *and* l bitor $n = |\,b\,| - |\,d\,|$. *Then*

$$\mathtt{Oreg} := l ; I_1(a, \mathtt{cj}(n) \cdot b) \;\geq\; \Delta 4 ; \{\mathtt{A} = 0\} ; \mathtt{Oreg} := 0 ; I_1(c, d) \; .$$

Proof. Proposition (a) is proved by the calculation

$$\mathtt{Oreg} := l ; I_1(a, \mathtt{j}(n) \cdot b)$$

$\geq$ [Lemma 10.1.5]

$\mathtt{Oreg} := l\ ;\ \mathtt{Oreg} := \mathtt{Oreg}\ \mathsf{bitor}\ n\ ;\ \mathtt{Ip}^+\ ;\ [\Lambda(a \cdot \mathtt{j}(n), b)]\ ;$
$E_0(\mathtt{j})\ ;\ \mathit{Run}\ ;\ \mathtt{Ip}^-$

$\geq$ [(Comb-asg), (8.19)]

$\mathtt{Oreg} := l\ \mathsf{bitor}\ n\ ;\ \mathtt{Ip}^+\ ;\ [\Lambda(a \cdot \mathtt{j}(n), b)]\ ;$
$\Delta 3\ ;\ \mathtt{Ip}, \mathtt{Oreg} := \mathtt{Ip} + \mathtt{Oreg}, 0\ ;\ \mathtt{A}, \mathtt{B}, \mathtt{C} :=?\ ;\ \mathit{Run}\ ;\ \mathtt{Ip}^-$

$=$ [Δ-laws, $l\ \mathsf{bitor}\ n = |\,b\,| - |\,d\,|$]

$\Delta 3\ ;\ \mathtt{Oreg} := |\,b\,| - |\,d\,|\ ;\ \mathtt{Ip}^+\ ;\ [\Lambda(a \cdot \mathtt{j}(n), b)]\ ;$
$\mathtt{Ip}, \mathtt{Oreg} := \mathtt{Ip} + \mathtt{Oreg}, 0\ ;\ \mathtt{A}, \mathtt{B}, \mathtt{C} :=?\ ;\ \mathit{Run}\ ;\ \mathtt{Ip}^-$

$=$ [(Initial-assign), (Assign-assert1), (Comb-asg)]

$\Delta 3\ ;\ \mathtt{Ip}^+\ ;\ [\Lambda(a \cdot \mathtt{j}(n), b)]\ ;$
$\mathtt{Ip}, \mathtt{Oreg} := \mathtt{Ip} + (|\,b\,| - |\,d\,|), 0\ ;\ \mathtt{A}, \mathtt{B}, \mathtt{C} :=?\ ;\ \mathit{Run}\ ;\ \mathtt{Ip}^-$

$=$ [Lemma 10.1.2]

$\Delta 3\ ;\ \mathtt{Ip}^+\ ;\ [(\Lambda(c, d))[\mathtt{Ip} + |\,b\,| - |\,d\,| / \mathtt{Ip}]\ ;$
$\mathtt{Ip}, \mathtt{Oreg} := \mathtt{Ip} + (|\,b\,| - |\,d\,|), 0\ ;\ \mathtt{A}, \mathtt{B}, \mathtt{C} :=?\ ;\ \mathit{Run}\ ;\ \mathtt{Ip}^-$

$=$ [(Assign-assert), $\Lambda(c, d)$ is independent of $\mathtt{Oreg}$, (Ch-assume1)]

$\Delta 3\ ;\ \mathtt{Ip}^+\ ;$
$\mathtt{Ip}, \mathtt{Oreg} := \mathtt{Ip} + (|\,b\,| - |\,d\,|), 0\ ;\ \mathtt{A}, \mathtt{B}, \mathtt{C} :=?\ ;\ [\Lambda(c, d)]\ ;\ \mathit{Run}\ ;\ \mathtt{Ip}^-$

$\geq$ [–-+-sim]

$\Delta 3\ ;\ \mathtt{Ip}^+\ ;\ \mathtt{Ip}, \mathtt{Oreg} := \mathtt{Ip} + (|\,b\,| - |\,d\,|), 0\ ;\ \mathtt{A}, \mathtt{B}, \mathtt{C} :=?\ ;\ \mathtt{Ip}^-\ ;$
$\mathtt{Ip}^+\ ;\ [\Lambda(c, d)]\ ;\ \mathit{Run}\ ;\ \mathtt{Ip}^-$

$=$ [(Final-ch), (Finalization1), (Final-assign)]

$\Delta 3\ ;\ \mathtt{Ip}^+\ ;\ \mathtt{Ip}^-\ ;\ \mathtt{Oreg} := 0\ ;\ \mathtt{A}, \mathtt{B}, \mathtt{C} :=?\ ;$
$\mathtt{Ip}^+\ ;\ [\Lambda(c, d)]\ ;\ \mathit{Run}\ ;\ \mathtt{Ip}^-$

$=$ [–-+-sim]

$\Delta 3\ ;\ \mathtt{Oreg} := 0\ ;\ \mathtt{A}, \mathtt{B}, \mathtt{C} :=?\ ;\ \mathtt{Ip}^+\ ;\ [\Lambda(c, d)]\ ;\ \mathit{Run}\ ;\ \mathtt{Ip}^-$

$=$ [Definition I_1]

$\Delta 3\ ;\ \mathtt{Oreg} := 0\ ;\ \mathtt{A}, \mathtt{B}, \mathtt{C} :=?\ ;\ I_1(c, d)\ .$

The proof of (b) is similar. □

10.2 Large Operands

The purpose of the Transputer's operand register is to provide word-size operands for the direct functions. The idea is that the operand register is filled with the operand in portions of four bits by a sequence of `pfix` and `nfix` instructions preceding the instruction for the actual function, the operand part of which provides only the least significant four bits. This special purpose and use of the operand register, however, is not directly reflected in the behavioral description of the Transputer we have available up-to-now, where `Oreg` is treated like the other registers. This section is concerned with an abstraction that allows to interpret the code sequence consisting of leading `pfix` and `nfix` instructions together with a trailing non-`pfix` and non-`nfix` instruction as a multi-byte instruction with a word operand. In the resulting view we no longer need to reason explicitly about the operand register. The mechanism by which large operands are built is proved correct once and for all when deriving the abstraction.

The prefixing mechanism works only from states with a cleared operand register. Each instruction except of `pfix` and `nfix` clears the operand register finally in order to prepare execution of a subsequent prefixed instruction. The abstraction thus ensures in particular that the invariant $\mathtt{Oreg} = 0$ is kept.

First of all, we cite from [46, Chap. 4] the definition of $\mathit{prefix} \in (\mathit{Instr} \times \mathsf{Word} \to \mathsf{IS})$, the function that describes the standard scheme for generation of `pfix`/`nfix` sequences. Intuitively, $\mathit{prefix}(\mathit{instr}, w)$ is a sequence of instructions that applies the direct function instr to the word operand w. prefix is defined by

$$\mathit{prefix}(\mathit{instr}, w) = \begin{cases} \mathit{instr}(w) & 0 \le w < 16 \\ \mathit{prefix}(\mathtt{pfix}, w \gg 4) \cdot \mathit{instr}(w \ \mathsf{bitand}\ \mathsf{\$0F}) & w \ge 16 \\ \mathit{prefix}(\mathtt{nfix}, (\mathsf{bitnot}\ w) \gg 4) \cdot \mathit{instr}(w \ \mathsf{bitand}\ \mathsf{\$0F}) & w < 0 \ . \end{cases}$$

The function $\mathit{ldt} \in (\mathsf{Word} \to \mathsf{IN})$ yields the number of `pfix` and `nfix` instructions needed for loading a word operand w. Since `pfix` as well as `nfix` uses one clock cycle for execution, $\mathit{ldt}(w)$ is also the number of additional clock cycles needed for loading w. This is the reason for calling it ldt as an abbreviation for *loading time*. ldt's definition follows the scheme of prefix's definition:

$$\mathit{ldt}(w) = \begin{cases} 0 & 0 \le w < 16 \\ \mathit{ldt}(w \gg 4) + 1 & w \ge 16 \\ \mathit{ldt}((\mathsf{bitnot}\ w) \gg 4) + 1 & w < 0 \ . \end{cases}$$

10.2.1 Some Properties of *prefix*

We prepare the second abstraction by investigating *prefix*. First of all, a simple syntactic property is established.

Lemma 10.2.1 (Form of prefix sequences). *Suppose instr and w are given. Then there is a code sequence m such that*

$$\mathit{prefix}(\mathit{instr}, w) = m \cdot \mathit{instr}(w \ \mathsf{bitand}\ \mathsf{\$0F}) \ .$$

Proof. $0 \le w < 16$ implies $w = w \ \mathsf{bitand}\ \mathsf{\$0F}$. Everything else is obvious from the definition of *prefix*. □

The prefixing sequence loads w except of its four least significant bits, provided it is started with a cleared operand register.

Lemma 10.2.2 (*prefix* **and I**). *Suppose instr and w are given and the code sequence m and the four-bit value n are chosen such that prefix(instr, w) = m · instr(n). Then*

$$\texttt{Oreg} := 0 \,;\, I_1(a, m \cdot \mathit{instr}(n) \cdot b) \;\geq\; \Delta\, \mathit{ldt}(w) \,;\, \texttt{Oreg} := (w \gg 4) \ll 4 \,;\, I_1(a \cdot m, \mathit{instr}(n) \cdot b)\ .$$

Proof. The proof is by Noetherian induction on w using the Noetherian order on Word defined by

$$w \sqsubset w' \quad \text{iff} \quad w' < 0 \leq w \text{ or } 0 \leq w < w'\ ,$$

where $<$ is the usual ordering on the integers and $\leq$ means $<$ or equal. Suppose w is given and assume that the proposition is valid for all $w' \sqsubset w$.

$0 \leq w < 16$:
In this case $m = \varepsilon$, $(w \gg 4) \ll 4 = 0$ and $\mathit{ldt}(w) = 0$. Therefore, the proposition is trivial as $\Delta 0 = \mathsf{Id}$ is the unit of sequential composition.

$w \geq 16$:
In this case $m = \mathit{prefix}(\texttt{pfix}, v) = m' \cdot \texttt{pfix}(v \text{ bitand } \texttt{\$0F})$ for suitably chosen m' and $v = w \gg 4$. Note first that $v \sqsubset w$. Therefore,

LHS

$\geq$ [Induction assumption]

$\Delta\, \mathit{ldt}(v) \,;\, \texttt{Oreg} := (v \gg 4) \ll 4 \,;$
$I_1(a \cdot m', \texttt{pfix}(v \text{ bitand } \texttt{\$0F}) \cdot \mathit{instr}(w \text{ bitand } \texttt{\$0F}) \cdot b)$

$\geq$ [Theorem 10.1.1, (10.2)]

$\Delta\, \mathit{ldt}(v) \,;\, \texttt{Oreg} := (v \gg 4) \ll 4 \,;$
$\texttt{Oreg} := \texttt{Oreg} \text{ bitor } (v \text{ bitand } \texttt{\$0F}) \,;$
$\Delta 1 \,;\, \texttt{Oreg} := \texttt{Oreg} \ll 4 \,;\, I_1(a \cdot m, \mathit{instr}(w \text{ bitand } \texttt{\$0F}) \cdot b)$

$\geq$ [(Δ-assign), (Δ-add), (Comb-asg)]

$\Delta\, \mathit{ldt}(v) + 1 \,;\, \texttt{Oreg} := (((v \gg 4) \ll 4) \text{ bitor } (v \text{ bitand } \texttt{\$0F})) \ll 4 \,;$
$I_1(a \cdot m, \mathit{instr}(w \text{ bitand } \texttt{\$0F}) \cdot b)$

$=$ [Binary arithmetic]

$\Delta\, \mathit{ldt}(v) + 1 \,;\, \texttt{Oreg} := v \ll 4 \,;\, I_1(a \cdot m, \mathit{instr}(w \text{ bitand } \texttt{\$0F}) \cdot b)$

$=$ [Definition *ldt*, choice of v]

RHS .

$w < 0$:
In this case $m = \mathit{prefix}(\texttt{nfix}, v) = m' \cdot \texttt{nfix}(v \text{ bitand } \texttt{\$0F})$ for suitably chosen m' and $v = (\text{bitnot } w) \gg 4$. Note that $v \sqsubset w$. Therefore,

LHS

$\geq$ [Induction assumption]

$\Delta\, ldt(v)$; $\mathtt{Oreg} := (v \gg 4) \ll 4$;

$I_1(a \cdot m', \mathtt{nfix}(v \text{ bitand } \$0F) \cdot instr(w \text{ bitand } \$0F) \cdot b)$

$\geq$ [Theorem 10.1.1, (10.3)]

$\Delta\, ldt(v)$; $\mathtt{Oreg} := (v \gg 4) \ll 4$;

$\mathtt{Oreg} := \mathtt{Oreg} \text{ bitor } (v \text{ bitand } \$0F)$;

$\Delta\, 1$; $\mathtt{Oreg} := (\text{bitnot } \mathtt{Oreg}) \ll 4$;

$I_1(a \cdot m, instr(w \text{ bitand } \$0F) \cdot b)$

$\geq$ [(Δ-assign), (Δ-add), (Comb-asg)]

$\Delta\, ldt(v) + 1$;

$\mathtt{Oreg} := (\text{bitnot } (((v \gg 4) \ll 4) \text{ bitor } (v \text{ bitand } \$0F))) \ll 4$;

$I_1(a \cdot m, instr(w \text{ bitand } \$0F) \cdot b)$

$=$ [Binary arithmetic]

$\Delta\, ldt(v) + 1$; $\mathtt{Oreg} := (\text{bitnot } v) \ll 4$;

$I_1(a \cdot m, instr(w \text{ bitand } \$0F) \cdot b)$

$=$ [Binary arithmetic, choice of v, definition *ldt*]

RHS . □

It is convenient to abbreviate the instruction sequence $prefix(instr, w)$ by $instr(w)$. This does not conflict with the old convention $instr(n) = [(instr, n)]$ for $n \in \mathsf{Nibble}$, because $prefix(instr, n) = instr(n) = [(instr, n)]$. We call such an instruction sequence $instr(w)$ a *prefixed instruction*. Similarly, we abbreviate for operations *op* the code sequence $prefix(\mathtt{opr}, OpCode(op))$ by *op* when confusion with the operation *op* itself is excluded by the context.

The next lemma shows that execution of the entire prefixed instruction $instr(w)$ corresponds to executing $E_1(instr)$ after loading w to the operand register (provided the operand register is cleared initially). The prefixing sequence causes an additional delay of (at most) $ldt(w)$ time units.

Lemma 10.2.3 (Prefixing and E_1).

$$\mathtt{Oreg} := 0 \;;\; I_1(a, instr(w) \cdot b) \;\geq\; \Delta\, ldt(w) \;;\; \mathtt{Oreg} := w \;;\; E_1(instr) \;;\; I_1(a \cdot instr(w), b) \;.$$

Proof. Choose m such that $instr(w) = m \cdot instr(w \text{ bitand } \$0F)$.

LHS

$\geq$ [Lemma 10.2.2]

$\Delta\, ldt(w)$; $\mathtt{Oreg} := (w \gg 4) \ll 4$; $I_1(a \cdot m, instr(w \text{ bitand } \$0F) \cdot b)$

$\geq$ [Theorem 10.1.1]

$\Delta\, ldt(w)$; $\mathtt{Oreg} := (w \gg 4) \ll 4$; $\mathtt{Oreg} := \mathtt{Oreg} \text{ bitor } (w \text{ bitand } \$0F)$;

$$
\begin{aligned}
& E_1(instr)\ ;\ I_1(a \cdot instr(w), b) \\
= \quad & [\text{(Comb-asg)}] \\
& \Delta\, ldt(w)\ ;\ \mathtt{Oreg} := ((w \gg 4) \ll 4)\ \mathsf{bitor}\,(w\ \mathsf{bitand}\ \mathtt{\$0F})\ ; \\
& E_1(instr)\ ;\ I_1(a \cdot instr(w), b) \\
= \quad & [\text{Binary arithmetic: } w = ((w \gg 4) \ll 4)\ \mathsf{bitor}\,(w\ \mathsf{bitand}\ \mathtt{\$0F})] \\
& \text{RHS}\ . \qquad \square
\end{aligned}
$$

As before we need a special lemma for jumps because $E_1(\mathtt{j})$ carries hardly any useful information. The same holds for conditional jumps that are taken.

Lemma 10.2.4 (Prefixing jumps).

(a) Suppose $c \cdot d = a \cdot \mathtt{j}(w) \cdot b$ *and* $w = |\,b\,| - |\,d\,|$. *Then*

$$
\begin{aligned}
& \mathtt{Oreg} := 0\ ;\ I_1(a, \mathtt{j}(w) \cdot b)\ \geq \\
& \quad \Delta\, ldt(w) + 3\ ;\ \mathtt{Oreg} := 0\ ;\ \mathtt{A}, \mathtt{B}, \mathtt{C} :=?\ ;\ I_1(c, d)\ .
\end{aligned}
$$

(b) Suppose $c \cdot d = a \cdot \mathtt{cj}(w) \cdot b$ *and* $w = |\,b\,| - |\,d\,|$. *Then*

$$
\begin{aligned}
& \mathtt{Oreg} := 0\ ;\ I_1(a, \mathtt{cj}(w) \cdot b)\ \geq \\
& \quad \Delta\, ldt(w) + 4\ ;\ \{\mathtt{A} = 0\}\ ;\ \mathtt{Oreg} := 0\ ;\ I_1(c, d)\ .
\end{aligned}
$$

Proof. Choose m such that $\mathtt{j}(w) = m \cdot \mathtt{j}(w\ \mathsf{bitand}\ \mathtt{\$0F})$. Proposition (a) is shown by

$$
\begin{aligned}
& \text{LHS} \\
\geq \quad & [\text{Lemma 10.2.2}] \\
& \Delta\, ldt(w)\ ;\ \mathtt{Oreg} := (w \gg 4) \ll 4\ ;\ I_1(a \cdot m, \mathtt{j}(w\ \mathsf{bitand}\ \mathtt{\$0F}) \cdot b) \\
\geq \quad & [\text{Theorem 10.1.10, (a)}] \\
& \Delta\, ldt(w)\ ;\ \Delta 3\ ;\ \mathtt{Oreg} := 0\ ;\ \mathtt{A}, \mathtt{B}, \mathtt{C} :=?\ ;\ I_1(c, d) \\
\geq \quad & [\Delta\text{-add}] \\
& \text{RHS}\ .
\end{aligned}
$$

When applying Theorem 10.1.10, we have exploited that

$$((w \gg 4) \ll 4)\ \mathsf{bitor}\,(w\ \mathsf{bitand}\ \mathtt{\$0F}) \quad = \quad w \quad = \quad |\,b\,| - |\,d\,|\ .$$

The proof of (b) is similar. □

10.2.2 Performing the Abstraction

After this preparing exploration we define the abstraction. We are interested in starting code sequences with a cleared operand register. However, we are no longer interested in the operand register itself. So the alphabet of the new abstract view is

$$\alpha_2 \stackrel{\text{def}}{=} \{\texttt{A}, \texttt{B}, \texttt{C}, \texttt{Wptr}, \texttt{Eflg}, \texttt{Mem}\} = \alpha_1 \setminus \{\texttt{Oreg}\} .$$

We perform the abstraction of I_1 as well as E_1 via the function $G_2 \in (\mathsf{Proc}_{\alpha_1} \to \mathsf{Proc}_{\alpha_2})$ which is defined by

$$G_2(P) \stackrel{\text{def}}{=} \texttt{Oreg}^+ ; [\texttt{Oreg} = 0] ; P ; \{\texttt{Oreg} = 0\} ; \texttt{Oreg}^- .$$

It hides the operand register but ensures that it is cleared before P is started. The final assertion ensures that P leaves the operand register cleared on termination. This assertion is not necessary for abstracting I_1 because I_1 does not terminate regularly. But it is required in the abstraction of E_1 to ensure that the subsequent code is again started with a cleared operand register. G_2 is induced by the simulation (R_2, S_2), where

$$R_2 \stackrel{\text{def}}{=} \{\texttt{Oreg} = 0\} ; \texttt{Oreg}^- \quad \text{and} \quad S_2 \stackrel{\text{def}}{=} \texttt{Oreg}^+ ; [\texttt{Oreg} = 0] ,$$

and is a pure data abstraction in the sense of Chap. 7. In particular it has a lower adjoint $G_2^\flat$, with which it forms a distributive Galois connection.

The new view to the Transputer's run phase is now defined by

$$I_2(a, b) \stackrel{\text{def}}{=} G_2(I_1(a, b)) .$$

Lemma 10.2.3 indicates that it is a good idea to define $E_2(\mathit{instr}, w)$, the effect of the prefixed instruction $\mathit{instr}(w)$, by

$$E_2(\mathit{instr}, w) \stackrel{\text{def}}{=} G_2(\Delta\, \mathit{ldt}(w) ; \texttt{Oreg} := w ; E_1(\mathit{instr})) ,$$

because this results in the following theorem.

Theorem 10.2.5 (General instruction theorem).

$$I_2(a, \mathit{instr}(w) \cdot b) \geq E_2(\mathit{instr}, w) ; I_2(a \cdot \mathit{instr}(w), b) .$$

Proof.

$$\begin{aligned}
& I_2(a, \mathit{instr}(w) \cdot b) \\
= \quad & [\text{Definition of } I_2, \text{ law (Assign-assume3)}] \\
& G_2(\texttt{Oreg} := 0 ; I_1(a, \mathit{instr}(w) \cdot b)) \\
\geq \quad & [\text{Lemma 10.2.3}] \\
& G_2(\Delta\, \mathit{ldt}(w) ; \texttt{Oreg} := w ; E_1(\mathit{instr}) ; I_1(a \cdot \mathit{instr}(w), b)) \\
\geq \quad & [G_2 \text{ is super-distributive w.r.t. ;}] \\
& G_2(\Delta\, \mathit{ldt}(w) ; \texttt{Oreg} := w ; E_1(\mathit{instr})) ; G_2(I_1(a \cdot \mathit{instr}(w), b)) \\
\geq \quad & [\text{Definition of } I_2 \text{ and } E_2] \\
& E_2(\mathit{instr}, w) ; I_2(a \cdot \mathit{instr}(w), b) .
\end{aligned}$$

□

The definition of $E_2(\mathit{op})$, the effect of operations viewed on the new abstraction level, is given later. Having established Theorem 10.2.5, it is interesting to investigate E_2. For example, we can prove the following approximation for the prefixed load constant instruction.

Theorem 10.2.6 (The instruction ldc).

$$E_2(\texttt{ldc}, w) \;\geq\; \Delta\, ldt(w) + 1 \;;\; \texttt{A},\texttt{B},\texttt{C} := w, \texttt{A}, \texttt{B}\ .$$

Proof.

$$\begin{array}{ll} & E_2(\texttt{ldc}, w) \\ \geq & [\text{Definition } E_2, \text{ Theorem 10.1.7}] \\ & G_2(\Delta\, ldt(w) \;;\; \texttt{Oreg} := w \;;\; \Delta 1 \;;\; \texttt{A},\texttt{B},\texttt{C},\texttt{Oreg} := \texttt{Oreg},\texttt{A},\texttt{B},0) \\ = & [(\Delta\text{-assign}), (\Delta\text{-add}), (\text{Comb-asg})] \\ & G_2(\Delta\, ldt(w) + 1 \;;\; \texttt{A},\texttt{B},\texttt{C} := w,\texttt{A},\texttt{B} \;;\; \texttt{Oreg} := 0) \\ = & [\text{Various laws}] \\ & \Delta\, ldt(w) + 1 \;;\; \texttt{A},\texttt{B},\texttt{C} := w,\texttt{A},\texttt{B} \;;\; G_2(\texttt{Oreg} := 0) \\ = & [\text{Assign-assume3}] \\ & \Delta\, ldt(w) + 1 \;;\; \texttt{A},\texttt{B},\texttt{C} := w,\texttt{A},\texttt{B} \;;\; G_2(\mathsf{Id}) \\ \geq & [G_2(\mathsf{Id}) \geq \mathsf{Id} \text{ follows from (Assert-assume-sim) and (--+-sim)}] \\ & \Delta\, ldt(w) + 1 \;;\; \texttt{A},\texttt{B},\texttt{C} := w,\texttt{A},\texttt{B}\ . \end{array}$$

□

By similar calculations the approximations for various instructions in Table 10.4 can be established.

Table 10.4. Approximations for instructions II

$E_2(\texttt{ldc}, w)$	$\geq$	$\Delta\, ldt(w) + 1 \;;\; \texttt{A},\texttt{B},\texttt{C} := w,\texttt{A},\texttt{B}$	(10.32)
$E_2(\texttt{ldl}, w)$	$\geq$	$\Delta\, ldt(w) + 2 \;;\; \{Index(\texttt{Wptr}, w) \in \mathsf{Addr}\} \;;$ $\texttt{A},\texttt{B},\texttt{C} := \texttt{Mem}(Index(\texttt{Wptr}, w)),\texttt{A},\texttt{B}$	(10.33)
$E_2(\texttt{stl}, w)$	$\geq$	$\Delta\, ldt(w) + 1 \;;\; \{AdmAdr(Index(\texttt{Wptr}, w))\} \;;$ $\texttt{Mem}[Index(\texttt{Wptr}, w)],\texttt{A},\texttt{B} := \texttt{A},\texttt{B},\texttt{C} \;;\; \texttt{C} :=?$	(10.34)
$E_2(\texttt{ldlp}, w)$	$\geq$	$\Delta\, ldt(w) + 1 \;;\; \texttt{A},\texttt{B},\texttt{C} := Index(\texttt{Wptr}, w),\texttt{A},\texttt{B}$	(10.35)
$E_2(\texttt{adc}, w)$	$\geq$	$\Delta\, ldt(w) + 1 \;;\; \texttt{A},\texttt{Eflg} := \texttt{A} + w, \texttt{Eflg} \vee AddOvFl(\texttt{A}, w)$	(10.36)
$E_2(\texttt{eqc}, w)$	$\geq$	$\Delta\, ldt(w) + 2 \;;\; \mathsf{if}\ \texttt{A} = w\ \mathsf{then}\ 1\ \mathsf{else}\ 0\ \mathsf{fi}$	(10.37)
$E_2(\texttt{cj}, w)$	$\geq$	$\Delta\, ldt(w) + 2 \;;\; \{\texttt{A} \neq 0\} \;;\; \texttt{A},\texttt{B} := \texttt{B},\texttt{C} \;;\; \texttt{C} :=?$	(10.38)

The jump theorem now reads as follows.

Theorem 10.2.7 (Jumps).

(a) *Suppose* $c \cdot d = a \cdot \texttt{j}(w) \cdot b$ *and* $w = |\,b\,| - |\,d\,|$. *Then*

$$I_2(a, \texttt{j}(w) \cdot b) \;\geq\; \Delta\, ldt(w) + 3 \;;\; \texttt{A},\texttt{B},\texttt{C} :=? \;;\; I_2(c, d)\ .$$

(b) *Suppose* $c \cdot d = a \cdot \texttt{cj}(w) \cdot b$ *and* $w = |\,b\,| - |\,d\,|$. *Then*

$$I_2(a, \texttt{cj}(w) \cdot b) \;\geq\; \Delta\, ldt(w) + 4 \;;\; \{\texttt{A} = 0\} \;;\; I_2(c, d)\ .$$

Proof. The proof of (a) is

$$I_2(a, \mathtt{j}(w) \cdot b)$$
$$= \quad \text{[Definition of } I_2\text{, law (Assign-assume3)]}$$
$$G_2(\mathtt{Oreg} := 0 \; ; \; I_1(a, \mathtt{j}(w) \cdot b))$$
$$\geq \quad \text{[Lemma 10.2.4]}$$
$$G_2(\Delta \, \mathit{ldt}(w) + 3 \; ; \; \mathtt{Oreg} := 0 \; ; \; \mathtt{A}, \mathtt{B}, \mathtt{C} :=? \; ; \; I_1(c, d))$$
$$\geq \quad [\Delta \text{ laws, (Assign-assume3)]}$$
$$\Delta \, \mathit{ldt}(w) + 3 \; ; \; G_2(\mathtt{A}, \mathtt{B}, \mathtt{C} :=? \; ; \; I_1(c, d))$$
$$\geq \quad \text{[(Ch-assume), (Initial-ch-=)]}$$
$$\Delta \, \mathit{ldt}(w) + 3 \; ; \; \mathtt{A}, \mathtt{B}, \mathtt{C} :=? \; ; \; G_2(I_1(c, d))$$
$$\geq \quad \text{[Definition of } I_2]$$
$$\Delta \, \mathit{ldt}(w) + 3 \; ; \; \mathtt{A}, \mathtt{B}, \mathtt{C} :=? \; ; \; I_2(c, d) \; .$$

The proof of (b) is similar. □

10.2.3 Operations

We are now heading for a definition for $E_2(op)$ that gives us a theorem similar to Theorem 10.2.5. An operation op is executed by applying the special function `opr` to the operand $OpCode(op)$. Let us derive an approximation for $E_2(\mathtt{opr}, OpCode(op))$ in order to motivate (and indeed to find) an appropriate definition.

Lemma 10.2.8 (Approximation for `opr`).

$$E_2(\mathtt{opr}, OpCode(op)) \;\geq\; \Delta \, \mathit{ldt}(OpCode(op)) \; ; \; \mathtt{Oreg}^+ \; ; \; E_1(op) \; ; \; \mathtt{Oreg}^- \; .$$

Proof.

$$E_2(\mathtt{opr}, OpCode(op))$$
$$\geq \quad \text{[Definition of } E_2\text{, (10.11)]}$$
$$\mathtt{Oreg}^+ \; ; \; [\mathtt{Oreg} = 0] \; ; \; \Delta \, \mathit{ldt}(OpCode(op)) \; ; \; \mathtt{Oreg} := OpCode(op) \; ;$$
$$\{CurOpr(op)\} \; ; \; E_1(op) \; ; \; \mathtt{Oreg} := 0 \; ;$$
$$\{\mathtt{Oreg} = 0\} \; ; \; \mathtt{Oreg}^-$$
$$= \quad \text{[Two times (Assign-assert2), definition } CurOpr(op)]$$
$$\mathtt{Oreg}^+ \; ; \; [\mathtt{Oreg} = 0] \; ; \; \Delta \, \mathit{ldt}(OpCode(op)) \; ; \; \mathtt{Oreg} := OpCode(op) \; ;$$
$$E_1(op) \; ; \; \mathtt{Oreg} := 0 \; ; \; \mathtt{Oreg}^-$$
$$\geq \quad \text{[(Assume), (Finalization)]}$$
$$\mathtt{Oreg}^+ \; ; \; \Delta \, \mathit{ldt}(OpCode(op)) \; ; \; \mathtt{Oreg} := OpCode(op) \; ; \; E_1(op) \; ; \; \mathtt{Oreg}^-$$
$$= \quad [\text{Initial-}\Delta]$$
$$\Delta \, \mathit{ldt}(OpCode(op)) \; ; \; \mathtt{Oreg}^+ \; ; \; \mathtt{Oreg} := OpCode(op) \; ; \; E_1(op) \; ; \; \mathtt{Oreg}^-$$

$$\geq \quad \text{[Initialization]}$$
$$\Delta\, ldt(OpCode(op))\ ;\ \texttt{Oreg}^{+}\ ;\ E_1(op)\ ;\ \texttt{Oreg}^{-}\ . \qquad \square$$

Recall that we agreed to use *op* as a short hand for the code sequence $\texttt{opr}(OpCode(op))$. Using this notation, Lemma 10.2.8 implies together with Theorem 10.2.5 that

$$I_2(a, op \cdot b)$$
$$\geq \quad [op \text{ abbreviates } \texttt{opr}(OpCode(op)), \text{ Theorem 10.2.5}]$$
$$E_2(\texttt{opr}, OpCode(op))\ ;\ I_2(a \cdot op, b)$$
$$\geq \quad \text{[Above approximation]}$$
$$\Delta\, ldt(OpCode(op))\ ;\ \texttt{Oreg}^{+}\ ;\ E_1(op)\ ;\ \texttt{Oreg}^{-}\ ;\ I_2(a \cdot op, b)\ .$$

This motivates the definition

$$E_2(op) \stackrel{\text{def}}{=} \Delta\, ldt(OpCode(op))\ ;\ \texttt{Oreg}^{+}\ ;\ E_1(op)\ ;\ \texttt{Oreg}^{-}\ ,$$

which immediately gives us the general theorem for operations we were looking for.

Theorem 10.2.9 (General operation theorem).

$$I_2(a, op \cdot b)\ \geq\ E_2(op)\ ;\ I_2(a \cdot op, b)\ .$$

Proof. The calculation above. □

Although these considerations show soundness of reasoning via $E_2(op)$, they do not at all guarantee that its definition is not too weak. To explain this point assume for a moment that we had used the weakest approximation $\bot$ for $E_2(\texttt{opr}, OpCode(op))$. Then we would have defined $E_2(op) = \bot$, which certainly would have given us Theorem 10.2.9. But $E_2(op)$ would carry no sensible information. The question is whether we were too careless when deriving the approximation for $E_2(\texttt{opr}, OpCode(op))$; for example, all the knowledge about the operand register's initial value has been thrown away in the last step of the calculation proving Lemma 10.2.8. We can justify the latter informally by pointing to the fact that none of the approximations for $E_1(op)$ in Table 10.3 or Theorem 10.1.9 depends on the operand register. But we refrain from deriving a *formal* counterpart to this informal justification because this would complicate the reasoning without contributing to its soundness. Rather we justify this empirically by the fact that we can establish useful approximations on the abstract level.

Approximation for $E_2(op)$ for various operations are collected in Table 10.5. Informally speaking they, carry the complete information about the operation's behavior, which shows that indeed our definition of $E_2(op)$ is strong enough. The approximations are obtained from those in Table 10.3 by computing $ldt(OpCode(op))$ for each of the operations *op* and applying

Table 10.5. Approximations for operations II

$$E_2(\mathtt{add}) \geq \Delta 1 \; ; \mathtt{A},\mathtt{B},\mathtt{Eflg} := \mathtt{B}+\mathtt{A},\mathtt{C},\mathtt{Eflg} \vee \mathit{AddOvFl}(\mathtt{B},\mathtt{A}) \; ; \mathtt{C} :=? \tag{10.39}$$

$$E_2(\mathtt{sub}) \geq \Delta 1 \; ; \mathtt{A},\mathtt{B},\mathtt{Eflg} := \mathtt{B}-\mathtt{A},\mathtt{C},\mathtt{Eflg} \vee \mathit{SubOvFl}(\mathtt{B},\mathtt{A}) \; ; \mathtt{C} :=? \tag{10.40}$$

$$E_2(\mathtt{mul}) \geq \Delta\, \mathit{bpw} + 7 \; ; \mathtt{A},\mathtt{B},\mathtt{Eflg} := \mathtt{B}*\mathtt{A},\mathtt{C},\mathtt{Eflg} \vee \mathit{MulOvFl}(\mathtt{B},\mathtt{A}) \; ; \mathtt{C} :=? \tag{10.41}$$

$$E_2(\mathtt{div}) \geq \Delta\, \mathit{bpw} + 11 \; ; \{\neg \mathit{DivOvFl}(\mathtt{B},\mathtt{A})\} \; ; \mathtt{A},\mathtt{B} := \mathtt{B} \div \mathtt{A},\mathtt{C} \; ; \mathtt{C} :=? \tag{10.42}$$

$$E_2(\mathtt{div}) \geq \Delta\, \mathit{bpw} + 11 \; ; \{\mathit{DivOvFl}(\mathtt{B},\mathtt{A})\} \; ; \mathtt{B},\mathtt{Eflg} := \mathtt{C},\mathsf{true} \; ; \mathtt{A},\mathtt{C} :=? \tag{10.43}$$

$$E_2(\mathtt{rem}) \geq \Delta\, \mathit{bpw} + 6 \; ; \{\neg \mathit{DivOvFl}(\mathtt{B},\mathtt{A})\} \; ; \mathtt{A},\mathtt{B} := \mathtt{B} \mathbin{\mathsf{rem}} \mathtt{A},\mathtt{C} \; ; \mathtt{C} :=? \tag{10.44}$$

$$E_2(\mathtt{rem}) \geq \Delta\, \mathit{bpw} + 6 \; ; \{\mathit{DivOvFl}(\mathtt{B},\mathtt{A})\} \; ; \mathtt{B},\mathtt{Eflg} := \mathtt{C},\mathsf{true} \; ; \mathtt{A},\mathtt{C} :=? \tag{10.45}$$

$$E_2(\mathtt{diff}) \geq \Delta 1 \; ; \mathtt{A},\mathtt{B} := \mathtt{B}-\mathtt{A},\mathtt{C} \; ; \mathtt{C} :=? \tag{10.46}$$

$$E_2(\mathtt{testerr}) \geq \Delta 4 \; ; \mathtt{A},\mathtt{B},\mathtt{C},\mathtt{Eflg} := \mathsf{if}\ \mathtt{Eflg}\ \mathsf{then}\ 0\ \mathsf{else}\ 1\ \mathsf{fi},\mathtt{A},\mathtt{B},\mathsf{false} \tag{10.47}$$

$$E_2(\mathtt{stoperr}) \geq \{\mathtt{Eflg}\} \; ; \mathsf{Stop} \tag{10.48}$$

$$E_2(\mathtt{stoperr}) \geq \Delta 3 \; ; \{\neg \mathtt{Eflg}\} \tag{10.49}$$

$$E_2(\mathtt{bcnt}) \geq \Delta 3 \; ; \mathtt{A} := \mathtt{A} * \mathit{bpw} \tag{10.50}$$

$$E_2(\mathtt{rev}) \geq \Delta 1 \; ; \mathtt{A},\mathtt{B} := \mathtt{B},\mathtt{A} \tag{10.51}$$

$$E_2(\mathtt{stopp}) \geq \mathsf{Stop} \tag{10.52}$$

$$E_2(\mathtt{not}) \geq \Delta 2 \; ; \mathtt{A} := (\mathsf{bitnot}\ \mathtt{A}) \tag{10.53}$$

$$E_2(\mathtt{mint}) \geq \Delta 2 \; ; \mathtt{A},\mathtt{B},\mathtt{C} := \mathsf{MostNeg},\mathtt{A},\mathtt{B} \tag{10.54}$$

$$E_2(\mathtt{gt}) \geq \Delta 2 \; ; \mathtt{A},\mathtt{B} := \mathsf{if}\ \mathtt{B} > \mathtt{A}\ \mathsf{then}\ 1\ \mathsf{else}\ 0\ \mathsf{fi},\mathtt{C} \; ; \mathtt{C} :=? \tag{10.55}$$

the laws about addition and deletion commands and delays. For example, the opcode of bcnt is \$34. Hence, $\mathit{ldt}(\mathit{OpCode}(\mathtt{bcnt})) = 1$ and

$$
\begin{array}{ll}
 & E_2(\mathtt{bcnt}) \\
\geq & [\text{Def. of } E_2\text{, inequality (10.26)}] \\
 & \Delta\, \mathit{ldt}(\mathit{OpCode}(\mathtt{bcnt})) \; ; \mathtt{Oreg}^{+} \; ; \Delta 2 \; ; \mathtt{A} := \mathtt{A} * \mathtt{bcnt} \; ; \mathtt{Oreg}^{-} \\
= & [(\text{Initial-}\Delta)\text{, (Initial-assign), (}-\text{-+-sim)}] \\
 & \Delta\, \mathit{ldt}(\mathit{OpCode}(\mathtt{bcnt})) \; ; \Delta 2 \; ; \mathtt{A} := \mathtt{A} * \mathtt{bcnt} \\
\geq & [\Delta\text{-add, } \mathit{ldt}(\mathit{OpCode}(\mathtt{bcnt})) = 1] \\
 & \Delta 3 \; ; \mathtt{A} := \mathtt{A} * \mathtt{bcnt} \; .
\end{array}
$$

The approximations for $E_1(\mathtt{in})$ and $E_1(\mathtt{outword})$ in Theorem 10.1.9 transfer to E_2 as well (but, of course, with reduced alphabet) as $\mathit{ldt}(\mathit{OpCode}(\mathtt{in})) = \mathit{ldt}(\mathit{OpCode}(\mathtt{outword})) = 0$.

10.3 Workspace

When reasoning about Transputer code it is often convenient to consider instead of the entire memory only a distinguished part, called the *workspace*. The workspace consists of a certain number of memory cells with addresses just above a base address, which is contained in a special register called the workspace pointer Wptr. Typically all local and auxiliary variables of a process are stored in the workspace such that it never needs to access memory cells outside. The Transputer's instruction set facilitates access to the workspace by providing instructions that allow to store and load memory cells relative to Wptr's contents. For example, the purpose of ldl (load local) applied to an operand w intuitively is to load the contents of the w'th workspace location to the accumulator A (and to shift the small stack consisting of the three accumulators A, B and C). Let us look at the semantic description provided by inequality (10.33):

$$E_2(\mathtt{ldl}, w) \ \geq \ \Delta\, \mathit{ldt}(w) + 2 \ ; \{\mathit{Index}(\mathtt{Wptr}, w) \in \mathsf{Addr}\} \ ; \\ \mathtt{A}, \mathtt{B}, \mathtt{C} := \mathtt{Mem}(\mathit{Index}(\mathtt{Wptr}, w)), \mathtt{A}, \mathtt{B} \ .$$

It embodies – inherited from the base model – the mapping of the workspace to the memory by an index calculation. Moreover, it contains an explicit assertion that the address is proper.

It is more convenient to reason about the workspace as a separate entity, if we only load from and store to the workspace and assume that its position in the memory is fixed. The workspace pointer and the memory are replaced by a single array variable Wsp of type $\mathsf{Val}_{\mathtt{Wsp}} = (\{1, \ldots, l_{\mathrm{W}}\} \to \mathsf{Word})$, where l_{W} is the number of cells that are reserved for the workspace. As a global condition we require that the workspace is disjoint from the program storage and that all its cells have proper addresses. Thus any read access to the workspace refers to a proper addresses and no write access can destroy the loaded program. This simplifies, for instance, the approximation for stl because the explicit assertion in (10.34) that the written address is admissible is no longer needed. It is replaced by the condition $1 \leq w \leq l_{\mathrm{W}}$ for stl's operand w. The behavior of ldl is now described by

$$E_3(\mathtt{ldl}, w) \ \geq \ \Delta\, \mathit{ldt}(w) + 2 \ ; \mathtt{A}, \mathtt{B}, \mathtt{C} := \mathtt{Wsp}[w], \mathtt{A}, \mathtt{B} \ ,$$

for all $1 \leq w \leq l_{\mathrm{W}}$, which is a considerably simpler inequality than (10.33).

The mapping of the workspace to the memory is reflected once and for all while performing the abstraction. Thus it need not be explicitly taken into account when reasoning on higher levels. The price to be paid for this improved simplicity is that machine code which accesses locations outside the workspace or changes the value of the workspace pointer can no longer be understood. (It is, however, sometimes possible to transfer properties that are proved about such sequences by reasoning on lower levels; but to reason about them on the higher level alone is not supported.) Similar costs accrue from the previous abstractions. From level I_1 onwards reasoning about self-modifying code has not been supported and on level I_2 prefixed instructions that are started with non-cleared operand register cannot be understood. But these limitations reflect a common discipline kept by well-structured code.

Let us now identify the memory region for the workspace. Suppose given a word address s_{W}, the *start address* of the workspace and an integer l_{W}, the *number of cells* in the workspace. We require that all workspace locations (inclusive five words below s_W that are used by some operations as additional registers)[3] have admissible addresses, i.e.

$$\forall w : \mathit{Index}(s_W, -5) \le w \le \mathit{Index}(s_W, l_W) : \mathit{AdmAdr}(\mathit{BaseAdr}(w)) \ . \tag{10.56}$$

By the definition of *AdmAdr* (10.12) this implies in particular that workspace and program memory are disjoint. As mentioned, the memory `Mem` and the workspace pointer `Wptr` are replaced by an array `Wsp` of type $\mathsf{Val}_{\mathtt{Wsp}} = (\{1, \ldots, l_W\} \to \mathsf{Word})$; thus the new alphabet is

$$\alpha_3 \stackrel{\text{def}}{=} \{\mathtt{A}, \mathtt{B}, \mathtt{C}, \mathtt{Eflg}, \mathtt{Wsp}\} = (\alpha_2 \setminus \{\mathtt{Wptr}, \mathtt{Mem}\}) \cup \{\mathtt{Wsp}\} \ .$$

The resulting view is defined via the mapping $G_3 \in (\mathsf{Proc}_{\alpha_2} \to \mathsf{Proc}_{\alpha_3})$ that is induced by the simulation (R_3, S_3):

$$\begin{aligned}
G_3(P) &\stackrel{\text{def}}{=} S_3 \ ; P \ ; R_3 \\
R_3 &\stackrel{\text{def}}{=} \mathtt{Wsp}^{\oplus} \ ; \{\mathit{WspInMem}\} \ ; \mathtt{Wptr}, \mathtt{Mem}^{-} \\
S_3 &\stackrel{\text{def}}{=} \mathtt{Wptr}, \mathtt{Mem}^{+} \ ; [\mathit{WspInMem}] \ ; \mathtt{Wsp}^{-} \\
\mathit{WspInMem} &\stackrel{\text{def}}{\equiv} \mathtt{Wptr} = s_W \wedge \\
&\qquad (\forall i : 1 \le i \le l_W : \mathtt{Wsp}(i) = \mathtt{Mem}(\mathit{Index}(s_W, i)))
\end{aligned}$$

G_3 is just the abstraction map of the Galois connection belonging to the data refinement with abstract variable `Wsp`, concrete variables `Wptr` and `Mem`, and coupling invariant *WspInMem* (see Definition 7.1.1). The predicate *WspInMem* holds iff the workspace pointer contains the correct value, viz. s_W, and the memory cells constituting the workspace contain the value of the workspace array `Wsp`. The abstract view to the behavior of partitioned code sequences, prefixed instructions, and operations is defined by

$$\begin{aligned}
I_3(a, b) &\stackrel{\text{def}}{=} G_3(I_2(a, b)) \\
E_3(\mathit{instr}, w) &\stackrel{\text{def}}{=} G_3(E_2(\mathit{instr}, w)) \\
E_3(\mathit{op}) &\stackrel{\text{def}}{=} G_3(E_2(\mathit{op})) \ .
\end{aligned}$$

G_3 is super-distributive w.r.t. ; because it is the abstraction map of a data refinement. Thus the general instruction and operation theorems transfer immediately to I_3 and E_3.

Theorem 10.3.1 (General instruction and operation theorem).

(a) $I_3(a, \mathit{instr}(w) \cdot b) \ \ge \ E_3(\mathit{instr}, w) \ ; I_3(a \cdot \mathit{instr}(w), b)$.

(b) $I_3(a, \mathit{op} \cdot b) \ \ge \ E_3(\mathit{op}) \ ; I_3(a \cdot \mathit{op}, b)$.

---

[3] This does not apply for the operations treated in this book.

Table 10.6. Approximations for instructions III

$E_3(\mathtt{ldc}, w)$	$\geq$	$\Delta\, ldt(w) + 1 \;;\; \mathtt{A,B,C} := w, \mathtt{A,B}$	(10.57)
$E_3(\mathtt{ldl}, w)$	$\geq$	$\Delta\, ldt(w) + 2 \;;\; \mathtt{A,B,C} := \mathtt{Wsp}(w), \mathtt{A,B}$, if $1 \leq w \leq l_{\mathrm{W}}$	(10.58)
$E_3(\mathtt{stl}, w)$	$\geq$	$\Delta\, ldt(w) + 1 \;;\; \mathtt{Wsp}[w], \mathtt{A,B} := \mathtt{A,B,C} \;;\; \mathtt{C} :=?$, if $1 \leq w \leq l_{\mathrm{W}}$	(10.59)
$E_3(\mathtt{stl}, 0)$	$\geq$	$\Delta 1 \;;\; \mathtt{A,B} := \mathtt{B,C} \;;\; \mathtt{C} :=?$	(10.60)
$E_3(\mathtt{ldlp}, w)$	$\geq$	$\Delta\, ldt(w) + 1 \;;\; \mathtt{A,B,C} := Index(s_{\mathrm{W}}, w), \mathtt{A,B}$	(10.61)
$E_3(\mathtt{adc}, w)$	$\geq$	$\Delta\, ldt(w) + 1 \;;\; \mathtt{A,Eflg} := \mathtt{A} + w, \mathtt{Eflg} \vee AddOvFl(\mathtt{A}, w)$	(10.62)
$E_3(\mathtt{eqc}, w)$	$\geq$	$\Delta\, ldt(w) + 2 \;;\; \mathtt{A} := \mathsf{if}\ \mathtt{A} = w\ \mathsf{then}\ 1\ \mathsf{else}\ 0\ \mathsf{fi}$	(10.63)
$E_3(\mathtt{cj}, w)$	$\geq$	$\Delta\, ldt(w) + 2 \;;\; \{\mathtt{A} \neq 0\} \;;\; \mathtt{A,B} := \mathtt{B,C} \;;\; \mathtt{C} :=?$	(10.64)

Proof. By super-distributivity of abstraction the approximations follow immediately from Theorem 10.2.5 and Theorem 10.2.9. □

Similarly, the jump theorem transfers easily.

Theorem 10.3.2 (Jumps).

(a) Suppose $c \cdot d = a \cdot \mathtt{j}(w) \cdot b$ *and* $w = |\,b\,| - |\,d\,|$. *Then*

$$I_3(a, \mathtt{j}(w) \cdot b) \;\geq\; \Delta\, ldt(w) + 3 \;;\; \mathtt{A,B,C} :=? \;;\; I_3(c, d) \;.$$

(b) Suppose $c \cdot d = a \cdot \mathtt{cj}(w) \cdot b$ *and* $w = |\,b\,| - |\,d\,|$. *Then*

$$I_3(a, \mathtt{cj}(w) \cdot b) \;\geq\; \Delta\, ldt(w) + 4 \;;\; \{\mathtt{A} = 0\} \;;\; I_3(c, d) \;.$$

Proof. By straightforward calculation one establishes that

$$S_3 \;;\; \Delta\, ldt(w) + 3 \;;\; \mathtt{A,B,C} :=? \;\geq\; \Delta\, ldt(w) + 3 \;;\; \mathtt{A,B,C} :=? \;;\; S_3$$

(or even equality of left and right hand side). By Lemma 5.3.2, which is concerned with the lifting of simulations to Galois connections between command (process) spaces, this implies

$$G_3(\Delta\, ldt(w) + 3 \;;\; \mathtt{A,B,C} :=?) \;\geq\; \Delta\, ldt(w) + 3 \;;\; \mathtt{A,B,C} :=? \;.$$

Thus (a) follows from Theorem 10.2.7 by the super-distributivity of G_3. Similarly, the proof of (b) is essentially the inequality

$$S_3 \;;\; \Delta\, ldt(w) + 4 \;;\; \{\mathtt{A} = 0\} \;\geq\; \Delta\, ldt(w) + 4 \;;\; \{\mathtt{A} = 0\} \;;\; S_3 \;,$$

which is easily established by a straightforward calculation. □

Without proof we present approximations for various instructions and operations in Table 10.6 and Table 10.7. The assertions $\{AdmAdr(w)\}$ for certain addresses w in the corresponding approximations for E_2 are implied by condition (10.56), i.e. they are equivalent to true and can therefore be removed (recall that [true] $=$ Id by the (Assert) law), which is the main motivation for the global requirement (10.56). Note that the `stl` instruction applied to 0 can be used to pop the register stack (see (10.60)).

Table 10.7. Approximations for operations III; only approximations for $E_3(\texttt{in})$ and $E_3(\texttt{outword})$ are given; the approximations in Table 10.5 for various other operations remain valid for E_3; let $i \in \{0, \dots, 3\}$

$$\begin{aligned} E_3(\texttt{in}) \geq\ & \{\mathtt{A} = bpw \wedge \mathtt{B} = \mathit{Index}(\mathsf{MostNeg}, i+4) \wedge \mathtt{C} = \mathit{Index}(\mathsf{sw}, l)\} \ ; \\ & \Delta\, \mathit{indelay}_1 \ ; \\ & \mathtt{In_i} \ ?\, \mathtt{A} \ ; \\ & \mathtt{Wsp}[l] := \mathtt{A} \ ; \\ & \mathtt{A}, \mathtt{B}, \mathtt{C} := ? \ ; \\ & \Delta\, \mathit{indelay}_2 \end{aligned} \tag{10.65}$$

$$\begin{aligned} E_3(\texttt{outword}) \geq\ & \{\mathtt{B} = \mathit{Index}(\mathsf{MostNeg}, i)\} \ ; \\ & \Delta\, \mathit{outdelay}_1 \ ; \\ & \mathtt{Out_i} \ !\, \mathtt{A} \ ; \\ & \mathtt{A}, \mathtt{B}, \mathtt{C} := ? \ ; \\ & \Delta\, \mathit{outdelay}_2 \end{aligned} \tag{10.66}$$

10.4 Symbolic Addressing

The workspace view derived in the previous section provides an abstraction of the actual memory. But workspace as an array of homogeneous components still is a low-level memory-like concept. Imperative programming languages as well as symbolic assembler languages provide another abstraction: assignable named variables of a variety of types. Such an abstraction is described in the current section.

The replacement of the workspace by a collection $x_1, \dots, x_k$ $(k \geq 0)$ of variables with value domains $T_{x_1}, \dots, T_{x_k}$ has two facets. The first so-to-speak syntactic aspect is the allocation of workspace locations for these variables. For each variable x_i we choose a distinguished workspace location that is used to hold (a representation of) its value. (For simplicity we restrict attention to a representation by single workspace cells. Representation by multiple cells or by proper parts of cells can be treated similarly but complicates the notation.)

The other more semantic aspect is the representation convention for the values of $x_1, \dots, x_k$. We capture this convention by stating a *representation relation* $R_x \subseteq T_x \times \mathsf{Word}$ for each variable $x \in \{x_1, \dots, x_k\}$. $(t, w) \in R_x$ means that the word w (stored in the workspace cell adr_x allocated for x) is a proper representation for the value t stored by x. Usually, all variables of same type are represented in the same way such that the representation relations R_{x_i} are induced by a family of representation relation $R_T \subseteq T \times \mathsf{Word}$ for the occurring data domains T (i.e. $R_x = R_{T_x}$).

For defining the abstraction and for the validity of some general theorems no characteristic knowledge about the representation relations is required. However, more specific approximations for certain instructions (`stl`, `ldl` and `in`) can be proved for concrete relations. Therefore, we define the representation relations for the data-types of our prototypic programming language

TPL, viz. for Word and Bool. Words are simply represented by themselves, so

$$R_{\mathsf{Word}} \stackrel{\text{def}}{=} \{(v,w) \mid v = w\} ,$$

i.e. $R_{\mathsf{Word}} = \mathsf{Id}_{\mathsf{Word}}$. The Boolean value tt (true) is represented by 1 and ff (false) by 0, so

$$R_{\mathsf{Bool}} \stackrel{\text{def}}{=} \{(d,w) \mid w = \mathsf{if}\ d\ \mathsf{then}\ 1\ \mathsf{else}\ 0\ \mathsf{fi}\} .$$

We choose this representation of Boolean values because it is directly supported by the Transputer's instruction set.

The above discussion shows that the abstraction to be described in this section is parameterized by the following information:

- the collection $x_1, \ldots, x_k$ of $k \geq 0$ distinct variables,
- their value domains $T_{x_1}, \ldots, T_{x_k}$,
- the representation relations $R_{x_1}, \ldots, R_{x_k}$, and
- the workspace locations $adr_{x_1}, \ldots, adr_{x_k}$.

All this information can conveniently be described by a mapping δ that assigns to each $x \in \{x_1, \ldots, x_k\}$ the triple (T_x, R_x, adr_x). We call such a mapping a *semantic dictionary* or simply *dictionary*. Let us introduce formally the set of semantic dictionaries, and – as an auxiliary notion – the set of dictionary informations, in order to state the necessary side conditions precisely.

Definition 10.4.1 (Dictionary informations, dictionaries).

(a) A dictionary information *i is a triple* (T, R, adr), *where*
- *T is a non-empty set,*
- *$R \subseteq T \times \mathsf{Word}$ is a relation, and*
- *$adr \in \{1, \ldots, l_W\}$ is a proper index of a workspace cell.*

The set of dictionary informations is called DictInfo.

(b) A (semantic) dictionary *is a mapping* $\delta \in (D \to \mathsf{DictInfo})$ *such that*

(1) $D \subseteq Y \setminus (\{\!| Tc |\!\} \cup \{\mathtt{Wsp}\})$,

(2) $\forall x \in D : \delta(x).1 = \mathsf{Val}_x$, *and*

(3) $\forall x, y \in D : x \neq y \Rightarrow \delta(x).3 \neq \delta(y).3$.

The set of semantic dictionaries is called Dict. *As convenient and intuitive shorthand notation we write T_x^δ, R_x^δ and adr_x^δ instead of $\delta(x).1$, $\delta(x).2$, and $\delta(x).3$ and even omit the superscript δ if it is clear from the context. With this convention conditions (2) and (3) read*

(2') $\forall x \in D : T_x = \mathsf{Val}_x$, *and*

(3') $\forall x, y \in D : x \neq y \Rightarrow adr_x \neq adr_y$.

(c) We call a semantic dictionary $\delta \in (D \to \mathsf{DictInfo})$ a standard dictionary *if $T_x \in \{\mathsf{Bool}, \mathsf{Word}\}$ and $R_x = R_{\mathsf{Val}_x}$ for all $x \in D$.*

The domain D of a dictionary $\delta \in (D \to \mathsf{DictInfo})$ describes the set of variables that are introduced to replace the workspace. Condition (1) avoids conflicts with the variables used in the earlier Transputer models and (2) is a technical condition that links to the global typing of variables assumed for the imperative meta-language. Condition (3) expresses that distinct variables do not share a single workspace location. Note that (3) implies that D is finite.

Semantic dictionaries correspond to symbol tables that are used commonly in compilers. However, the latter code the information syntactically while we prefer to use the value sets and representation relations directly in our mathematical consideration. Moreover, symbol tables often do not describe explicitly the representation relation but assume a fixed assignment of representation relations to types, which is separately described in the compiler's documentation. Certainly in an implemented compiler we must rely on some finite syntactic coding of semantic dictionaries. Such a syntactic coding is elaborated for translation of TPL in Chap. 13.

Let us now define the abstraction induced by a dictionary δ. The coupling invariant InWsp^δ between the new variables' and the workspace's contents is defined on the union of the old and new variables. It is thus a predicate on the alphabet

$$\alpha^\delta \stackrel{\text{def}}{=} \alpha_3 \cup \mathsf{dom}\,\delta \;=\; \{\mathtt{A}, \mathtt{B}, \mathtt{C}, \mathtt{Eflg}, \mathtt{Wsp}\} \cup \mathsf{dom}\,\delta\;.$$

(Note that the union is proper due to condition (1) in the definition of dictionaries.) InWsp^δ holds if and only if the workspace locations allocated for the new variables contain representations of the variable's contents:[4]

$$\mathit{InWsp}^\delta \stackrel{\text{def}}{\equiv} \bigwedge_{x \in \mathsf{dom}\,\delta} (x, \mathtt{Wsp}(\mathit{adr}_x)) \in R_x\;.$$

As $\mathtt{Wsp}$ is replaced by the variables in $\mathsf{dom}\,\delta$, the pre- and post-alphabet of the resulting view is

$$\alpha_4^\delta \stackrel{\text{def}}{=} \{\mathtt{A}, \mathtt{B}, \mathtt{C}, \mathtt{Eflg}\} \cup \mathsf{dom}\,\delta \;=\; \alpha_3 \setminus \mathtt{Wsp} \cup \mathsf{dom}\,\delta\;.$$

The abstraction is performed via the abstraction map $G_4^\delta : \mathsf{Proc}_{\alpha_3} \to \mathsf{Proc}_{\alpha_4^\delta}$ defined by

$$G_4^\delta(P) \stackrel{\text{def}}{=} \mathtt{Wsp}^+ \,;\, [\mathit{InWsp}^\delta] \,;\, u^- \,;\, P \,;\, u^\oplus \,;\, \{\mathit{InWsp}^\delta\} \,;\, \mathtt{Wsp}^-\;,$$

where u is a list that contains exactly one instance of each variable in $\mathsf{dom}\,\delta$. Note that the order of the variables in u is insignificant due to the reorder laws for $u^\oplus$ and u^-. G_4^δ is the abstraction map $\mathit{Ab}_{u,\mathtt{Wsp},\mathit{InWsp}^\delta}$ of the data

[4] A small technical remark: In the definition of InWsp^δ, x is lifted to a valuation function only in the first pair component, not in the indices to adr and R (this would not be well-typed). More explicitly, we could have defined

$$\mathit{InWsp}^\delta \stackrel{\text{def}}{\equiv} \bigwedge\nolimits_{x \in \mathsf{dom}\,\delta} (x^*, \mathtt{Wsp}^*(\mathit{adr}_x)) \in R_x\;.$$

Note that the lifting of the pair constructor, the element sign, etc. is still implicit.

refinement with abstract variables u, concrete variable Wsp and coupling invariant $InWsp^\delta$ and is induced by the simulation (R_4^δ, S_4^δ):

$$R_4^\delta \stackrel{\text{def}}{=} u^\oplus \,;\, \{InWsp^\delta\} \,;\, \mathtt{Wsp}^- \quad \text{and} \quad S_4^\delta \stackrel{\text{def}}{=} \mathtt{Wsp}^+ \,;\, [InWsp^\delta] \,;\, u^- \;.$$

The new view to the behavior of partitioned code sequences, prefixed instructions and operations is now consistently defined by:

$$\begin{aligned} I_4^\delta(a,b) &\stackrel{\text{def}}{=} G_4^\delta(I_3(a,b)) \\ E_4^\delta(instr,w) &\stackrel{\text{def}}{=} G_4^\delta(E_3(instr,w)) \\ E_4^\delta(op) &\stackrel{\text{def}}{=} G_4^\delta(E_3(op)) \;. \end{aligned}$$

We omit the superscript δ if it can uniquely be inferred from the context. In the remainder of this section we investigate the properties of I_4^δ and E_4^δ. In the first subsection we transfer the properties of the the third abstraction level to the new fourth abstraction level assuming a fixed dictionary δ. The second subsection investigates extensions of δ.

10.4.1 Instructions and Operations

In this subsection we assume given a fixed dictionary $\delta \in \mathsf{Dict}$ and omit all δ-superscripts.

From the results of Chap. 7 it is clear that G_4 has a lower adjoint $G_4^\flat$, with which it forms a distributive Galois connection. In particular, it is super-distributive w.r.t. ;. Thus the general instruction and operation theorem transfers immediately from I_3 to I_4.

Theorem 10.4.2 (General instruction and operation theorem).

(a) $I_4(a, instr(w) \cdot b) \;\geq\; E_4(instr,w) \,;\, I_4(a \cdot instr(w), b)$.

(b) $I_4(a, op \cdot b) \;\geq\; E_4(op) \,;\, I_4(a \cdot op, b)$.

Proof. Immediately from Theorem 10.3.1 by super-distributivity of G_4. □

Of course the jump theorem transfers as well.

Theorem 10.4.3 (Jumps).

(a) Suppose $c \cdot d = a \cdot \mathtt{j}(w) \cdot b$ *and* $w = |\,b\,| - |\,d\,|$. *Then*

$$I_4(a, \mathtt{j}(w) \cdot b) \;\geq\; \Delta\, ldt(w) + 3 \,;\, \mathtt{A},\mathtt{B},\mathtt{C} :=? \,;\, I_4(c,d) \;. \tag{10.67}$$

(b) Suppose $c \cdot d = a \cdot \mathtt{cj}(w) \cdot b$ *and* $w = |\,b\,| - |\,d\,|$. *Then*

$$I_4(a, \mathtt{cj}(w) \cdot b) \;\geq\; \Delta\, ldt(w) + 4 \,;\, \{\mathtt{A} = 0\} \,;\, I_4(c,d) \;. \tag{10.68}$$

Proof. By routine calculations one shows that

(a) $G_4(\Delta\, ldt(w) + 3 \,;\, \mathtt{A},\mathtt{B},\mathtt{C} :=?) \;\geq\; \Delta\, ldt(w) + 3 \,;\, \mathtt{A},\mathtt{B},\mathtt{C} :=?$, and
(b) $G_4(\Delta\, ldt(w) + 4 \,;\, \{\mathtt{A} = 0\}) \;\geq\; \Delta\, ldt(w) + 4 \,;\, \{\mathtt{A} = 0\}$.

The rest is clear from Theorem 10.3.2 by super-distributivity of G_4. □

Moreover, all approximations for prefixed instructions and operations in Table 10.6 and Table 10.7 that neither change nor assign to Wsp are easily seen to transfer to the new abstraction level by routine calculations. For reference purposes we collect the approximations that can be obtained in this way in Table 10.8 and Table 10.9.

Table 10.8. Approximations for instructions IV

$E_4(\mathtt{ldc}, w) \geq \Delta\, ldt(w) + 1\ ;\ \mathtt{A,B,C} := w, \mathtt{A,B}$		(10.69)
$E_4(\mathtt{stl}, 0) \geq \Delta 1\ ;\ \mathtt{A,B} := \mathtt{B,C}\ ;\ \mathtt{C} :=?$		(10.70)
$E_4(\mathtt{ldlp}, w) \geq \Delta\, ldt(w) + 1\ ;\ \mathtt{A,B,C} := Index(\mathrm{sw}, w), \mathtt{A,B}$		(10.71)
$E_4(\mathtt{adc}, w) \geq \Delta\, ldt(w) + 1\ ;\ \mathtt{A,Eflg} := \mathtt{A} + w, \mathtt{Eflg} \vee AddOvFl(\mathtt{A}, w)$		(10.72)
$E_4(\mathtt{eqc}, w) \geq \Delta\, ldt(w) + 2\ ;\ \mathtt{A} := (\mathsf{if}\ \mathtt{A} = w\ \mathsf{then}\ 1\ \mathsf{else}\ 0\ \mathsf{fi})$		(10.73)
$E_4(\mathtt{cj}, w) \geq \Delta\, ldt(w) + 2\ ;\ \{\mathtt{A} \neq 0\}\ ;\ \mathtt{A,B} := \mathtt{B,C}\ ;\ \mathtt{C} :=?$		(10.74)

By far more interesting than these immediately transfered properties is the derivation of approximations for ldl, stl and in. Let's consider ldl first. Clearly, we expect that ldl applied to adr_x somehow loads x's value to the small register stack A, B, C. But as x need not be of type Word we must take the data representation into account. The claim of the below theorem is that demonically one of x's representations is chosen and loaded to the register stack.

Theorem 10.4.4 (General ldl theorem). *Suppose $x \in \mathrm{dom}\,\delta$. Then*

$$E_4(\mathtt{ldl}, adr_x) \geq \Delta\, ldt(adr_x) + 2\ ;\ \bigwedge_{w \in \mathsf{Word}} [(x, w) \in R_x]\ ;\ \mathtt{A,B,C} := w, \mathtt{A,B}\ .$$

Proof. Let u be a list of the variables in $\mathrm{dom}\,\delta$.

$E_4(\mathtt{ldl}, adr_x)$

$\geq$ [Definition E_4, (10.58)]

$\mathtt{Wsp}^+\ ;\ [InWsp]\ ;\ u^-\ ;\ \Delta\, ldt(adr_x) + 2\ ;\ \mathtt{A,B,C} := \mathtt{Wsp}(adr_x), \mathtt{A,B}\ ;$
$u^\oplus\ ;\ \{InWsp\}\ ;\ \mathtt{Wsp}^-$

$=$ [Δ-laws,]

$\Delta\, ldt(adr_x) + 2\ ;\ \mathtt{Wsp}^+\ ;\ [InWsp]\ ;\ u^-\ ;\ \mathtt{A,B,C} := \mathtt{Wsp}(adr_x), \mathtt{A,B}\ ;$
$u^\oplus\ ;\ \{InWsp\}\ ;\ \mathtt{Wsp}^-$

$\geq$ [(Initial-assign) and ($\oplus$-−-sim)]

$\Delta\, ldt(adr_x) + 2\ ;\ \mathtt{Wsp}^+\ ;\ [InWsp]\ ;\ \mathtt{A,B,C} := \mathtt{Wsp}(adr_x), \mathtt{A,B}\ ;$
$\{InWsp\}\ ;\ \mathtt{Wsp}^-$

$$
\begin{aligned}
= \quad & [\text{(Assign-assert)}, \mathit{InWsp} \text{ idp } \mathtt{A,B,C}, [\phi] ; \{\phi\} = [\phi]] \\
& \Delta\, ldt(adr_x) + 2 ; \mathtt{Wsp}^+ ; [\mathit{InWsp}] ; \mathtt{A,B,C} := \mathtt{Wsp}(adr_x), \mathtt{A,B} ; \mathtt{Wsp}^- \\
= \quad & [\text{(Span1)}, \ . \ ; P \text{ is universally conjunctive, (Comb-assume)}] \\
& \Delta\, ldt(adr_x) + 2 ; \mathtt{Wsp}^+ ; \\
& \bigwedge_{w \in \mathsf{Word}} [w = \mathtt{Wsp}(adr_x) \wedge \mathit{InWsp}] ; \mathtt{A,B,C} := \mathtt{Wsp}(adr_x), \mathtt{A,B} ; \mathtt{Wsp}^- \\
= \quad & [\mathtt{Wsp}^+ \text{ is universally conjunctive, (Exploit-assume)}] \\
& \Delta\, ldt(adr_x) + 2 ; \\
& \bigwedge_{w \in \mathsf{Word}} \mathtt{Wsp}^+ ; [w = \mathtt{Wsp}(adr_x) \wedge \mathit{InWsp}] ; \mathtt{A,B,C} := w, \mathtt{A,B} ; \mathtt{Wsp}^- \\
\geq \quad & [\text{(Assume-antitonic) exploiting inequality derived below}] \\
& \Delta\, ldt(adr_x) + 2 ; \bigwedge_{w \in \mathsf{Word}} \mathtt{Wsp}^+ ; [(x, w) \in R_x] ; \mathtt{A,B,C} := w, \mathtt{A,B} ; \mathtt{Wsp}^- \\
= \quad & [\text{(Final-assign), (Final-assume), (−−+-sim)}] \\
& \Delta\, ldt(adr_x) + 2 ; \bigwedge_{w \in \mathsf{Word}} [(x, w) \in R_x] ; \mathtt{A,B,C} := w, \mathtt{A,B} \ .
\end{aligned}
$$

In the last but one step we exploit that

$$
\begin{aligned}
& w = \mathtt{Wsp}(adr_x) \wedge \mathit{InWsp} \\
\leq\ & w = \mathtt{Wsp}(adr_x) \wedge (x, \mathtt{Wsp}(adr_x)) \in R_x \\
\leq\ & (x, w) \in R_x \ .
\end{aligned}
$$

This completes the proof. □

For variables of type Word or Bool that are represented in the standard way we obtain simpler looking approximations.

Theorem 10.4.5 (Special `ldl` theorem). *Suppose $x \in \mathsf{dom}\,\delta$.*

(a) If $T_x = \mathsf{Word}$ and $R_x = R_{\mathsf{Word}}$ then

$$E_4(\mathtt{ldl}, adr_x) \geq \Delta\, ldt(adr_x) + 2 ; \mathtt{A,B,C} := x, \mathtt{A,B} \ .$$

(b) If $T_x = \mathsf{Bool}$ and $R_x = R_{\mathsf{Bool}}$ then

$$E_4(\mathtt{ldl}, adr_x) \geq \Delta\, ldt(adr_x) + 2 ; \mathtt{A,B,C} := \mathsf{if}\ x\ \mathsf{then}\ 1\ \mathsf{else}\ 0\ \mathsf{fi}, \mathtt{A,B} \, .$$

Proof. (a) Assume that $T_x = \mathsf{Word}$ and $R_x = R_{\mathsf{Word}}$. Then

$$
\begin{aligned}
& E_4(\mathtt{ldl}, adr_x) \\
\geq \quad & [\text{General } \mathtt{ldl} \text{ theorem}, R_x = R_{\mathsf{Word}} = \mathsf{Id}_{\mathsf{Word}}] \\
& \Delta\, ldt(adr_x) + 2 ; \bigwedge_w [x = w] ; \mathtt{A,B,C} := w, \mathtt{A,B}
\end{aligned}
$$

Table 10.9. Approximations for operations IV; let $i \in \{0, \dots, 3\}$

$$E_4(\mathtt{add}) \geq \Delta 1 \; ; \; \mathtt{A, B, Eflg} := \mathtt{B} + \mathtt{A}, \mathtt{C}, \mathtt{Eflg} \vee \mathit{AddOvFl}(\mathtt{B}, \mathtt{A}) \; ; \; \mathtt{C} :=? \qquad (10.75)$$

$$E_4(\mathtt{sub}) \geq \Delta 1 \; ; \; \mathtt{A, B, Eflg} := \mathtt{B} - \mathtt{A}, \mathtt{C}, \mathtt{Eflg} \vee \mathit{SubOvFl}(\mathtt{B}, \mathtt{A}) \; ; \; \mathtt{C} :=? \qquad (10.76)$$

$$E_4(\mathtt{mul}) \geq \Delta \, bpw + 7 \; ; \; \mathtt{A, B, Eflg} := \mathtt{B} * \mathtt{A}, \mathtt{C}, \mathtt{Eflg} \vee \mathit{MulOvFl}(\mathtt{B}, \mathtt{A}) \; ; \; \mathtt{C} :=? \qquad (10.77)$$

$$E_4(\mathtt{div}) \geq \Delta \, bpw + 11 \; ; \; \{\neg \mathit{DivOvFl}(\mathtt{B}, \mathtt{A})\} \; ; \; \mathtt{A, B} := \mathtt{B} \div \mathtt{A}, \mathtt{C} \; ; \; \mathtt{C} :=? \qquad (10.78)$$

$$E_4(\mathtt{div}) \geq \Delta \, bpw + 11 \; ; \; \{\mathit{DivOvFl}(\mathtt{B}, \mathtt{A})\} \; ; \; \mathtt{B, Eflg} := \mathtt{C}, \mathsf{true} \; ; \; \mathtt{A, C} :=? \qquad (10.79)$$

$$E_4(\mathtt{rem}) \geq \Delta \, bpw + 6 \; ; \; \{\neg \mathit{DivOvFl}(\mathtt{B}, \mathtt{A})\} \; ; \; \mathtt{A, B} := \mathtt{B} \; \mathsf{rem} \; \mathtt{A}, \mathtt{C} \; ; \; \mathtt{C} :=? \qquad (10.80)$$

$$E_4(\mathtt{rem}) \geq \Delta \, bpw + 6 \; ; \; \{\mathit{DivOvFl}(\mathtt{B}, \mathtt{A})\} \; ; \; \mathtt{B, Eflg} := \mathtt{C}, \mathsf{true} \; ; \; \mathtt{A, C} :=? \qquad (10.81)$$

$$E_4(\mathtt{diff}) \geq \Delta 1 \; ; \; \mathtt{A, B} := \mathtt{B} - \mathtt{A}, \mathtt{C} := \mathtt{C} :=? \qquad (10.82)$$

$$E_4(\mathtt{testerr}) \geq \Delta 4 \; ; \; \mathtt{A, B, C, Eflg} := \mathsf{if} \; \mathtt{Eflg} \; \mathsf{then} \; 0 \; \mathsf{else} \; 1 \; \mathsf{fi}, \mathtt{A}, \mathtt{B}, \mathsf{false} \qquad (10.83)$$

$$E_4(\mathtt{stoperr}) \geq \{\mathtt{Eflg}\} \; ; \; \mathsf{Stop} \qquad (10.84)$$

$$E_4(\mathtt{stoperr}) \geq \Delta 3 \; ; \; \{\neg \mathtt{Eflg}\} \qquad (10.85)$$

$$E_4(\mathtt{bcnt}) \geq \Delta 3 \; ; \; \mathtt{A} := \mathtt{A} * bpw \qquad (10.86)$$

$$E_4(\mathtt{rev}) \geq \Delta 1 \; ; \; \mathtt{A, B} := \mathtt{B}, \mathtt{A} \qquad (10.87)$$

$$E_4(\mathtt{stopp}) \geq \mathsf{Stop} \qquad (10.88)$$

$$E_4(\mathtt{not}) \geq \Delta 2 \; ; \; \mathtt{A} := (\mathsf{bitnot} \; \mathtt{A}) \qquad (10.89)$$

$$E_4(\mathtt{mint}) \geq \Delta 2 \; ; \; \mathtt{A, B, C} := \mathsf{MostNeg}, \mathtt{A}, \mathtt{B} \qquad (10.90)$$

$$E_4(\mathtt{gt}) \geq \Delta 2 \; ; \; \mathtt{A, B} := \mathsf{if} \; \mathtt{B} > \mathtt{A} \; \mathsf{then} \; 1 \; \mathsf{else} \; 0 \; \mathsf{fi}, \mathtt{C} \; ; \; \mathtt{C} :=? \qquad (10.91)$$

$$E_4(\mathtt{outword}) \geq \{\mathtt{B} = \mathit{Index}(\mathsf{MostNeg}, i)\} \; ; \; \Delta \, outdelay_1 \; ; \; \mathtt{Out_i} \, ! \, \mathtt{A} \; ; \; \mathtt{A, B, C} :=? \; ; \; \Delta \, outdelay_2 \qquad (10.92)$$

$=$ [Exploit-assume]

$$\Delta \, ldt(adr_x) + 2 \; ; \; \bigwedge_w [x = w] \; ; \; \mathtt{A, B, C} := x, \mathtt{A}, \mathtt{B}$$

$\geq$ [(Assume): $[\phi] \geq \mathsf{Id}$, glb of singleton equals its element]

$$\Delta \, ldt(adr_x) + 2 \; ; \; \mathtt{A, B, C} := x, \mathtt{A}, \mathtt{B} \; .$$

(b) Assume that $T_x = \mathsf{Bool}$ and $R_x = R_{\mathsf{Bool}}$. Then

$$E_4(\mathtt{ldl}, adr_x)$$

$\geq$ [General `ldl` theorem, def. of R_{Bool}]

$$\Delta \, ldt(adr_x) + 2 \; ; \; \bigwedge_w [w = \mathsf{if} \; x \; \mathsf{then} \; 1 \; \mathsf{else} \; 0 \; \mathsf{fi}] \; ; \; \mathtt{A, B, C} := w, \mathtt{A}, \mathtt{B}$$

$=$ [Exploit-assume]

$$\Delta \, ldt(adr_x) + 2 \; ;$$

$$\bigwedge_w [w = \mathsf{if} \; x \; \mathsf{then} \; 1 \; \mathsf{else} \; 0 \; \mathsf{fi}] \; ; \; \mathtt{A, B, C} := \mathsf{if} \; x \; \mathsf{then} \; 1 \; \mathsf{else} \; 0 \; \mathsf{fi}, \mathtt{A}, \mathtt{B}$$

$\geq$ [(Assume): $[\phi] \geq \mathsf{Id}$, glb of singleton equals its element]
$\Delta\, ldt(adr_x) + 2$; $\mathtt{A}, \mathtt{B}, \mathtt{C} :=$ if x then 1 else 0 fi, $\mathtt{A}, \mathtt{B}$. □

Let us now consider `stl`. The below theorem shows that `stl` applied to adr_x stores an abstraction of the value in register A to x and shifts the register stack. The theorem implies that $E_4(\mathtt{stl}, adr_x)$ chooses angelically between all the values that are represented by A's contents.

Theorem 10.4.6 (General `stl` theorem). *Suppose* $x \in \mathsf{dom}\,\delta$ *and* $e \in \mathsf{Valfct}_{T_x}$.

$$E_4(\mathtt{stl}, adr_x) \geq$$
$$\Delta\, ldt(adr_x) + 1 \;;\; \{(e, \mathtt{A}) \in R_x\} \;;\; x, \mathtt{A}, \mathtt{B} := e, \mathtt{B}, \mathtt{C} \;;\; \mathtt{C} :=? \,.$$

Proof. Let u be a list of the variables in $\mathsf{dom}\,\delta$.

$E_4(\mathtt{stl}, adr_x)$
$\geq$ [Definition E_4, (10.59)]
$\mathtt{Wsp}^+ \;;\; [\mathit{InWsp}] \;;\; u^- \;;$
$\Delta\, ldt(adr_x) + 1 \;;\; \mathtt{Wsp}[adr_x], \mathtt{A}, \mathtt{B} := \mathtt{A}, \mathtt{B}, \mathtt{C} \;;\; \mathtt{C} :=? \;;$
$u^{\oplus} \;;\; \{\mathit{InWsp}\} \;;\; \mathtt{Wsp}^-$
$=$ [Δ-laws, choice assignment laws exploiting that InWsp idp C]
$\Delta\, ldt(adr_x) + 1 \;;$
$\mathtt{Wsp}^+ \;;\; [\mathit{InWsp}] \;;\; u^- \;;\; \mathtt{Wsp}[adr_x], \mathtt{A}, \mathtt{B} := \mathtt{A}, \mathtt{B}, \mathtt{C} \;;$
$u^{\oplus} \;;\; \{\mathit{InWsp}\} \;;\; \mathtt{Wsp}^- \;;\; \mathtt{C} :=?$
$\geq$ [(Initial-assign), (Initialization)]
$\Delta\, ldt(adr_x) + 1 \;;$
$\mathtt{Wsp}^+ \;;\; [\mathit{InWsp}] \;;\; u^- \;;\; u^{\oplus} \;;\; x := e \;;\; \mathtt{Wsp}[adr_x], \mathtt{A}, \mathtt{B} := \mathtt{A}, \mathtt{B}, \mathtt{C} \;;$
$\{\mathit{InWsp}\} \;;\; \mathtt{Wsp}^- \;;\; \mathtt{C} :=?$
$\geq$ [($\oplus$-−-sim), 2× (Assign-assert)]
$\Delta\, ldt(adr_x) + 1 \;;$
$\mathtt{Wsp}^+ \;;\; [\mathit{InWsp}] \;;\; \{\mathit{InWsp}[\mathtt{Wsp}[adr_x \mapsto \mathtt{A}], \mathtt{B}, \mathtt{C}/\mathtt{Wsp}, \mathtt{A}, \mathtt{B}][e/x]\} \;;$
$x := e \;;\; \mathtt{Wsp}[adr_x], \mathtt{A}, \mathtt{B} := \mathtt{A}, \mathtt{B}, \mathtt{C} \;;\; \mathtt{Wsp}^- \;;\; \mathtt{C} :=?$
$=$ [(Finalization1), 2× (Final-assign), InWsp idp A, B]
$\Delta\, ldt(adr_x) + 1 \;;$
$\mathtt{Wsp}^+ \;;\; [\mathit{InWsp}] \;;\; \{\mathit{InWsp}[\mathtt{Wsp}[adr_x \mapsto \mathtt{A}]/\mathtt{Wsp}][e/x]\} \;;\; \mathtt{Wsp}^- \;;$
$x := e \;;\; \mathtt{A}, \mathtt{B} := \mathtt{B}, \mathtt{C} \;;\; \mathtt{C} :=?$
$=$ [(Assume-assert), (Comb-asg)]
$\Delta\, ldt(adr_x) + 1 \;;$
$\mathtt{Wsp}^+ \;;\; \{\mathit{InWsp} \Rightarrow \mathit{InWsp}[\mathtt{Wsp}[adr_x \mapsto \mathtt{A}]/\mathtt{Wsp}][e/x]\} \;;\; [\mathit{InWsp}] \;;$
$\mathtt{Wsp}^- \;;\; x, \mathtt{A}, \mathtt{B} := e, \mathtt{B}, \mathtt{C} \;;\; \mathtt{C} :=?$

$$\begin{aligned}
\geq\quad & [[\varphi] \geq \mathsf{Id}\text{, monotonicity of assertions, calculation below}] \\
& \Delta\, ldt(adr_x) + 1\ ; \\
& \mathtt{Wsp}^+\ ;\ \{(e, \mathtt{A}) \in R_x\}\ ;\ \mathtt{Wsp}^-\ ; \\
& x, \mathtt{A}, \mathtt{B} := e, \mathtt{B}, \mathtt{C}\ ;\ \mathtt{C} :=? \\
=\quad & [\text{(Final-assert), (−−+-sim)}] \\
& \Delta\, ldt(adr_x) + 1\ ;\ \{(e, \mathtt{A}) \in R_x\}\ ;\ x, \mathtt{A}, \mathtt{B} := e, \mathtt{B}, \mathtt{C}\ ;\ \mathtt{C} :=?\ .
\end{aligned}$$

In the last but one step we have exploited the inequality that is established by the calculation:

$$\begin{aligned}
& InWsp\ \Rightarrow\ InWsp[\mathtt{Wsp}[adr_x \mapsto \mathtt{A}]/\mathtt{Wsp}][e/x] \\
\equiv\quad & [\text{Distribute substitution, simplify with dictionary condition (3')}] \\
& InWsp\ \Rightarrow\ ((\bigwedge_{\substack{y \in \{x_1, \ldots, x_k\} \\ y \neq x}} (y, \mathtt{Wsp}(adr_y)) \in R_y) \wedge (e, \mathtt{A}) \in R_x) \\
\equiv\quad & [\text{The big conjunction clearly is implied by } InWsp] \\
& InWsp\ \Rightarrow\ (e, \mathtt{A}) \in R_x \\
\geq\quad & [\text{Boolean algebra}] \\
& (e, \mathtt{A}) \in R_x\ .
\end{aligned}$$

This finishes the proof of the general `stl` theorem. □

Like the general `ldl` theorem, the general `stl` theorem specializes to a simpler form for variables of type Word and Bool.

Theorem 10.4.7 (Special `stl` theorem). *Suppose* $x \in \mathsf{dom}\,\delta$.

(a) If $T_x = \mathsf{Word}$ *and* $R_x = R_{\mathsf{Word}}$ *then*

$$E_4(\mathtt{stl}, adr_x)\ \geq\ \Delta\, ldt(adr_x) + 1\ ;\ x, \mathtt{A}, \mathtt{B} := \mathtt{A}, \mathtt{B}, \mathtt{C}\ ;\ \mathtt{C} :=?\ .$$

(b) If $T_x = \mathsf{Bool}$ *and* $R_x = R_{\mathsf{Bool}}$ *then*

$$\begin{aligned}
& E_4(\mathtt{stl}, adr_x)\ \geq \\
& \quad \Delta\, ldt(adr_x) + 1\ ;\ \{\mathtt{A} \in \{0, 1\}\}\ ;\ x, \mathtt{A}, \mathtt{B} := odd(\mathtt{A}), \mathtt{B}, \mathtt{C}\ ;\ \mathtt{C} :=?\ .
\end{aligned}$$

Proof. (a) Assume that $T_x = \mathsf{Word}$ and $R_x = R_{\mathsf{Word}}$. Then

$$\begin{aligned}
& E_4(\mathtt{stl}, adr_x) \\
\geq\quad & [\text{General } \mathtt{stl} \text{ theorem applied to } e = \mathtt{A},\ R_x = R_{\mathsf{Word}} = \mathsf{Id}] \\
& \Delta\, ldt(adr_x) + 1\ ;\ \{\mathtt{A} = \mathtt{A}\}\ ;\ x, \mathtt{A}, \mathtt{B} := \mathtt{A}, \mathtt{B}, \mathtt{C}\ ;\ \mathtt{C} :=? \\
=\quad & [\{\mathtt{A} = \mathtt{A}\} = \mathsf{Id}] \\
& \Delta\, ldt(adr_x) + 1\ ;\ x, \mathtt{A}, \mathtt{B} := \mathtt{A}, \mathtt{B}, \mathtt{C}\ ;\ \mathtt{C} :=?\ .
\end{aligned}$$

(b) Assume that $T_x = \mathsf{Bool}$ and $R_x = R_{\mathsf{Bool}}$. Then

$$
\begin{aligned}
& E_4(\texttt{stl}, adr_x) \\
\geq\ & \text{[General \texttt{stl} theorem applied to } e = odd(\texttt{A}), \text{ def. } R_{\mathsf{Bool}}] \\
& \Delta\, ldt(adr_x) + 1 \,;\, \{\texttt{A} = \mathsf{if}\ odd(\texttt{A})\ \mathsf{then}\ 1\ \mathsf{else}\ 0\ \mathsf{fi}\} \,; \\
& x, \texttt{A}, \texttt{B} := odd(\texttt{A}), \texttt{B}, \texttt{C} \,;\, \texttt{C} :=? \\
=\ & [\texttt{A} \in \{0,1\} \text{ holds if and only if } \texttt{A} = \mathsf{if}\ odd(\texttt{A})\ \mathsf{then}\ 1\ \mathsf{else}\ 0\ \mathsf{fi}] \\
& \Delta\, ldt(adr_x) + 1 \,;\, \{\texttt{A} \in \{0,1\}\} \,;\, x, \texttt{A}, \texttt{B} := odd(\texttt{A}), \texttt{B}, \texttt{C} \,;\, \texttt{C} :=? \,.
\end{aligned}
$$
□

For the `in` operation we can prove the following approximation.

Theorem 10.4.8 (Approximation for `in`). *Suppose* $x \in \mathsf{dom}\,\delta$ *such that* $T_x = \mathsf{Word}$ *and* $R_x = R_{\mathsf{Word}}$. *Then for* $0 \leq i \leq 3$*:*

$$
\begin{aligned}
E_4(\texttt{in}) \geq\ & \{\texttt{A} = bpw \wedge \texttt{B} = Index(\mathsf{MostNeg}, i+4) \wedge \\
& \ \texttt{C} = Index(s_{\mathsf{W}}, adr_x))\} \,; \\
& \Delta\, indelay_1 \,; \\
& \texttt{In}_{\mathsf{i}}\, ?\, x \,; \\
& \texttt{A}, \texttt{B}, \texttt{C} :=? \,; \\
& \Delta\, indelay_2 \,.
\end{aligned}
$$

Proof. By a calculation similar to the proof of the general `stl` theorem. □

10.4.2 Extending and Restricting Dictionaries

In this subsection we investigate dictionary extensions. Interpreted the other way round the results also apply to dictionary restrictions. In the actual compiler proof the established theorems are used at two places. Firstly, they allow to cope with the allocation of auxiliary variables that are used to store intermediate results during expression evaluation; secondly, they allow an elegant treatment of local variables in blocks.

Throughout the remainder of this section we consider the following situation: δ is a dictionary, $x \in Y$ is a variable, and $i = (T, R, adr)$ is a dictionary information. u is a list of variables consisting of exactly one instance of each variable in $\mathsf{dom}\,\delta$.

We call the pair (x, i) *consistent* with δ if and only if

- $x \notin (\mathsf{dom}\,\delta \cup \{\!|\, Tc \,|\!\} \cup \{\texttt{Wsp}\})$,
- $T = \mathsf{Val}_x$, and
- $\forall y \in \mathsf{dom}\,\delta : adr_y^\delta \neq adr$.

It is easy to see that $\delta \cup \{(x, i)\}$ is again a dictionary if (x, i) is consistent with δ.

Let us first establish some refinement inequalities that relate the simulations (R_4^δ, S_4^δ) and $(R_4^{\delta \cup \{(x,i)\}}, S_4^{\delta \cup \{(x,i)\}})$.

Lemma 10.4.9 (Consistent extensions). *Suppose* (x, i) *is consistent with* δ. *Then*

(a) $R_4^\delta \geq R_4^{\delta\cup\{(x,i)\}} ; x^- \geq \{\mathtt{Wsp}(adr) \in \mathsf{rng}\, R\} ; R_4^\delta$, *and*

(b) $S_4^\delta \leq x^+ ; S_4^{\delta\cup\{(x,i)\}} \leq S_4^\delta ; [\mathtt{Wsp}(adr) \in \mathsf{rng}\, R]$.

Proof. Let us consider the proof of (a) first. It relies on the identity

$$InWsp^{\delta\cup\{(x,i)\}} = (x, \mathtt{Wsp}(adr)) \in R \wedge InWsp^\delta ,$$

which is obvious from the definition of *InWsp*. We have

$$\begin{array}{ll} & R_4^{\delta\cup\{(x,i)\}} ; x^- \\ = & [\text{Definition } R_4,\ InWsp\text{-identity above, (Comb-assert)}] \\ & u, x^\oplus ; \{(x, \mathtt{Wsp}(adr)) \in R\} ; \{InWsp^\delta\} ; \mathtt{Wsp}^- ; x^- \\ = & [\text{Add./del. laws, } ((x, \mathtt{Wsp}(adr)) \in R) \text{ } \mathsf{idp}\ u \text{ and } InWsp^\delta \text{ } \mathsf{idp}\ x] \\ & x^\oplus ; \{(x, \mathtt{Wsp}(adr)) \in R\} ; x^- ; u^\oplus ; \{InWsp^\delta\} ; \mathtt{Wsp}^- \\ = & [\text{Definition } R_4] \\ & x^\oplus ; \{(x, \mathtt{Wsp}(adr)) \in R\} ; x^- ; R_4^\delta . \end{array}$$

Together with the upper and lower estimate for $x^\oplus ; \{(x, \mathtt{Wsp}(adr)) \in R\} ; x^-$ established by the following calculation, this identity implies (a).

$$\begin{array}{ll} & \mathsf{Id} \\ = & [\oplus\text{-}-\text{-sim}] \\ & x^\oplus ; x^- \\ \geq & [\text{(Assert): } \{\phi\} \leq \mathsf{Id}] \\ & x^\oplus ; \{(x, \mathtt{Wsp}(adr)) \in R\} ; x^- \\ \geq & [\text{Restrict-angel}] \\ & \{\exists x : (x, \mathtt{Wsp}(adr)) \in R\} ; x^+ ; x^- \\ = & [(\exists x : (x, \mathtt{Wsp}(adr)) \in R) \text{ holds iff } \mathtt{Wsp}(adr) \in \mathsf{rng}\, R,\ (-\text{-}+\text{-sim})] \\ & \{\mathtt{Wsp}(adr) \in \mathsf{rng}\, R\} . \end{array}$$

From the composition properties of simulations it is clear that any of the three pairs listed below is a simulation.

- R_4^δ and S_4^δ ,
- $R_4^{\delta\cup\{(x,i)\}} ; x^-$ and $x^+ ; S_4^{\delta\cup\{(x,i)\}}$, and
- $\{\mathtt{Wsp}(adr) \in \mathsf{rng}\, R\} ; R_4^\delta$ and $S_4^\delta ; [\mathtt{Wsp}(adr) \in \mathsf{rng}\, R]$.

Thus (b) follows from (a) by Lemma 3.1.4. □

For surjective representation relations the situation is particularly simple.

Corollary 10.4.10 (Surjective consistent extensions). *Suppose (x,i) is consistent with δ. If R is surjective, i.e. if* $\mathsf{rng}\, R = \mathsf{Word}$*, then*

(a) $R_4^\delta \;=\; R_4^{\delta \cup \{(x,i)\}} \;;\, x^-$,

(b) $S_4^\delta \;=\; x^+ \;;\, S_4^{\delta \cup \{(x,i)\}}$ *, and*

(c) for all $P \in \mathsf{Proc}_{\alpha_3}$*:* $G_4^\delta(P) \;=\; x^+ \;;\, G_4^{\delta \cup \{(x,i)\}}(P) \;;\, x^-$.

Proof. If R is surjective, the predicate $\mathtt{Wsp}(adr) \in \mathsf{rng}\, R$ equals true. As $\{\mathsf{true}\}$ equals Id, Lemma 10.4.9 (a) shows that R_4^δ is both an upper and a lower estimate for $R_4^{\delta \cup \{(x,i)\}} \;;\, x^-$ in this case, which proves (a). The argument for (b) is analogous. (c) is a simple consequence of (a) and (b):

$$\begin{array}{ll} & G_4^\delta(P) \\ = & [\text{Definition } G_4^\delta] \\ & S_4^\delta \;;\, P \;;\, R_4^\delta \\ = & [\text{(a) and (b)}] \\ & x^+ \;;\, S_4^{\delta \cup \{(x,i)\}} \;;\, P \;;\, R_4^{\delta \cup \{(x,i)\}} \;;\, x^- \\ = & [\text{Definition } G_4^\delta] \\ & x^+ \;;\, G_4^{\delta \cup \{(x,i)\}} \;;\, x^- \;. \end{array}$$

□

We can now establish one of the main theorems of this subsection. It relates the Transputer views induced by δ and $\delta \cup \{(x,i)\}$ and is concerned with dictionary extensions with a surjective representation relation. It can thus be applied e.g. if x's value domain is Word and x is represented in the standard way, i.e. if $R = R_{\mathsf{Word}}$.

Theorem 10.4.11 (Consistent extension equality). *Suppose that (x,i) is consistent with δ. If R is surjective then*

$$I_4^\delta(a,b) \;=\; x^+ \;;\, I_4^{\delta \cup \{(x,i)\}}(a,b) \;;\, x^-$$

for all $a, b \in \mathsf{IS}$.

Proof. Suppose R is surjective and $a, b \in \mathsf{IS}$ are given. Then

$$\begin{array}{ll} & I_4^\delta(a,b) \\ = & [\text{Definition } I_4] \\ & G_4^\delta(I_3(a,b)) \\ = & [\text{Corollary 10.4.10}] \\ & x^+ \;;\, G_4^{\delta \cup \{(x,i)\}}(I_3(a,b)) \;;\, x^- \\ = & [\text{Definition } I_4] \\ & x^+ \;;\, I_4^{\delta \cup \{(x,i)\}}(a,b) \;;\, x^- \;. \end{array}$$

□

This theorem allows a rather simple semantic treatment of the common code generation technique for a block construct $\texttt{begin}\ x : \pi\ \texttt{end}$ that introduces x as a new[5] variable if the chosen representation relation is surjective. The meaning of such a block construct is given by

$$M(\texttt{begin}\ x : \pi\ \texttt{end}) \ = \ x^+ \ ; M(\pi) \ ; x^- \ ,$$

where $M(\pi)$ is the meaning of the block's body π. Suppose the representation of the variables that are used outside the block is described by a certain dictionary δ. Then we choose for x a new location adr that is not yet used and a representation relation $R \subseteq T \times \mathsf{Word}$ (T is the value domain of x) and translate the body π w.r.t. the extended dictionary $\delta' = \delta \cup \{(x, i)\}$, where $i = (T, R, adr)$. This results in code m that satisfies – ignoring the timing for a moment –

$$I_4^{\delta'}(a, m \cdot b) \ \geq \ M(\pi) \ ; I_4^{\delta'}(a \cdot m, b)$$

for all surrounding code pieces a, b. (See Chap. 11 for a discussion why this is a reasonable condition.) Theorem 10.4.11 now implies that m is correct code for the entire block if R is surjective, for we have for all $a, b \in \mathsf{IS}$:

$$\begin{array}{ll} & I_4^{\delta}(a, m \cdot b) \\ = & [\text{Theorem 10.4.11}] \\ & x^+ \ ; I_4^{\delta'}(a, m \cdot b) \ ; x^- \\ \geq & [m \text{ is correct code for } \pi \text{ w.r.t. dictionary } \delta'] \\ & x^+ \ ; M(\pi) \ ; I_4^{\delta'}(a \cdot m, b) \ ; x^- \\ \geq & [x^- \ ; x^+ \leq \mathsf{Id}] \\ & x^+ \ ; M(\pi) \ ; x^- \ ; x^+ \ ; I_4^{\delta'}(a \cdot m, b) \ ; x^- \\ = & [\text{Def. of meaning of blocks, Theorem 10.4.11}] \\ & M(\texttt{begin}\ x : \pi\ \texttt{end}) \ ; I_4^{\delta}(a \cdot m, b) \ . \end{array}$$

But this works out so simple only if R is surjective. What is the problem when this condition is violated? R being surjective means that every possible contents of the workspace cell $\texttt{Wsp}[adr]$ can be interpreted as representing a value of x. The problem with a non-surjective representation relation R is caused by the additional conjunct $(x, \texttt{Wsp}[adr]) \in R$ that is present in $InWsp^{\delta'}$ but not in $InWsp^{\delta}$. Intuitively the additional initial assumption $[(x, \texttt{Wsp}[adr]) \in R]$ in $I_4^{\delta'}$ implies that in $x^+ \ ; I_4^{\delta'}(a, b) \ ; x^-$ only computations from states in which $\texttt{Wsp}[adr]$ contains a value $w \in \mathsf{rng}\, R$ are considered, while $I_4^{\delta}(a, b)$ does not embody such a condition. In contrast, the additional assertion $\{(x, \texttt{Wsp}[adr]) \in R\}$ has no consequence because $I_3(a, b)$ – inherited from *Run* – does not terminate. As a computation might depend on $\texttt{Wsp}[adr]$'s

[5] For simplicity we assume here that a block construct must not redeclare a variable that is already used outside the block.

contents, $I_4^\delta(a,b)$ can thus be less deterministic. Therefore, in the general case only an inequality is valid.

Theorem 10.4.12 (General consistent extension inequality). *Suppose (x,i) is consistent with δ and let $\delta' = \delta \cup \{(x,i)\}$. Then*

$$x^+ \;;\; I_4^{\delta'}(a,b) \;;\; x^- \;\geq\; I_4^\delta(a,b) \;.$$

Proof.

$$\begin{array}{ll} & x^+ \;;\; I_4^{\delta'}(a,b) \;;\; x^- \\ = & \text{[Def. } I_4\text{]} \\ & x^+ \;;\; S_4^{\delta'} \;;\; I_3(a,b) \;;\; R_4^{\delta'} \;;\; x^- \\ \geq & \text{[Consistent Extension Lemma 10.4.9]} \\ & S_4^{\delta} \;;\; I_3(a,b) \;;\; R_4^{\delta'} \;;\; x^- \\ = & \text{[Analog of Lemma 10.1.6 for } I_3 \text{ where } X = R_4^{\delta'} \;;\; x^- \text{ and } Y = R_4^{\delta}\text{]} \\ & S_4^{\delta} \;;\; I_3(a,b) \;;\; R_4^{\delta} \\ = & \text{[Def. } I_4\text{]} \\ & I_4^{\delta}(a,b) \;. \end{array}$$

□

Unfortunately, Theorem 10.4.12 does not suffice for the reasoning about implementation of block constructs because the reverse inequality is also needed as the reader might check by looking again at the above calculation.

These considerations seem to indicate that reasonable representation relations must be surjective, which would severely restrict the choice of representation relations. R_{Bool}, for instance, is *not* surjective! Fortunately we can work with non-surjective representation relations but only with special care. If a local variable x in a block is represented according to a non-surjective relation R, we must add an initial piece of code to code for the block body in order to obtain correct code for the block. This piece of code must initialize the workspace location allocated for x by some value in the range of R. We cannot reason about the effect of such initialization code on the level I_4, because the workspace is not visible there. Instead we have to refer to the level I_3.

Definition 10.4.13 (Initialization code). *Let $m \in \mathsf{IS}$, $i = (T, R, adr) \in$ $\mathsf{DictInfo}$ and $d \in \mathsf{Time}$. Then we call m* initialization code for i that needs at most d time units for execution, *$\mathsf{IC}(m,i,d)$ for short, iff there is $e \in \mathsf{Valfct}_{\mathsf{Word}}$ such that*

(a) $\mathsf{rng}\, e \subseteq \mathsf{rng}\, R$, *and*

(b) $I_3(a, m \cdot b) \;\geq\; \Delta d \;;\; \mathtt{Wsp}[adr] := e \;;\; \mathtt{A,B,C,Eflg} :=? \;;\; I_3(a \cdot m, b)$ *for all* $a, b \in \mathsf{IS}$.

The intuition is that e describes the value with which $\mathtt{Wsp}(adr)$ is initialized. This value might depend on the initial state but a corresponding abstract value must always exist, which is ensured by (a). Condition (b) expresses that the initialization code m indeed performs the initialization. We allow m to use the registers $\mathtt{A}, \mathtt{B}, \mathtt{C}, \mathtt{Eflg}$.

Theorem 10.4.14 (Initialized consistent extension). *Suppose (x, i) is consistent with δ. Let $m \in \mathsf{IS}$, $w \in \mathsf{Word}$, and $d \in \mathsf{Time}$. If $\mathsf{IC}(m, i, d)$ then*

$$I_4^\delta(a, m \cdot b) \;\geq\; \varDelta\, d\ ;\ \mathtt{A}, \mathtt{B}, \mathtt{C}, \mathtt{Eflg} :=?\ ;\ x^+\ ;\ I_4^{\delta \cup \{(x,i)\}}(a \cdot m, b)\ ;\ x^-$$

for all $a, b \in \mathsf{IS}$.

Proof. Let $a, b \in \mathsf{IS}$ and assume that $\mathsf{IC}(m, i, d)$ holds. First of all,

$$\begin{array}{cl}
 & \mathtt{Wsp}[adr] := e\ ;\ [\mathtt{Wsp}(adr) \in \mathsf{rng}\, R] \\
= & \quad [\text{Assign-assert}] \\
 & [e \in \mathsf{rng}\, R]\ ;\ \mathtt{Wsp}[adr] := e \\
= & \quad [e \in \mathsf{rng}\, R \text{ equals } \mathbf{true} \text{ due to condition (a) in def. of } \mathsf{IC}(m, i, d)] \\
 & \mathtt{Wsp}[adr] := e\ .
\end{array}$$

Now,

$$\begin{array}{cl}
 & I_4^\delta(a, m \cdot b) \\
= & \quad [\text{Definition } I_4^\delta] \\
 & S_4^\delta\ ;\ I_3(a, m \cdot b)\ ;\ R_4^\delta \\
\geq & \quad [\text{Condition (b) in def. of } \mathsf{IC}(m, i, d)] \\
 & S_4^\delta\ ;\ \varDelta\, d\ ;\ \mathtt{Wsp}[adr] := e\ ;\ \mathtt{A}, \mathtt{B}, \mathtt{C}, \mathtt{Eflg} :=?\ ;\ I_3(a \cdot m, b)\ ;\ R_4^\delta \\
= & \quad [\varDelta\text{-laws, above identity}] \\
 & \varDelta\, d\ ;\ S_4^\delta\ ;\ \mathtt{Wsp}[adr] := e\ ;\ [\mathtt{Wsp}(adr) \in \mathsf{rng}\, R]\ ; \\
 & \mathtt{A}, \mathtt{B}, \mathtt{C}, \mathtt{Eflg} :=?\ ;\ I_3(a \cdot m, b)\ ;\ R_4^\delta \\
= & \quad [\text{Def. } S_4^\delta, \text{ asg. laws, } \mathit{InWsp}^\delta \text{ idp } \mathtt{Wsp}[adr] \text{ as } (x, i) \text{ is consist. with } \delta] \\
 & \varDelta\, d\ ;\ \mathtt{Wsp}^+\ ;\ \mathtt{Wsp}[adr] := e\ ;\ [\mathit{InWsp}^\delta]\ ;\ u^-\ ;\ [\mathtt{Wsp}(adr) \in \mathsf{rng}\, R]\ ; \\
 & \mathtt{A}, \mathtt{B}, \mathtt{C}, \mathtt{Eflg} :=?\ ;\ I_3(a \cdot m, b)\ ;\ R_4^\delta \\
\geq & \quad [\text{(Initialization), definition } S_4^\delta] \\
 & \varDelta\, d\ ;\ S_4^\delta\ ;\ [\mathtt{Wsp}(adr) \in \mathsf{rng}\, R]\ ;\ \mathtt{A}, \mathtt{B}, \mathtt{C}, \mathtt{Eflg} :=?\ ;\ I_3(a \cdot m, b)\ ;\ R_4^\delta \\
\geq & \quad [\text{Lemma 10.4.9 properties (a) and (b)}] \\
 & \varDelta\, d\ ;\ x^+\ ;\ S_4^{\delta \cup \{(x,i)\}}\ ;\ \mathtt{A}, \mathtt{B}, \mathtt{C}, \mathtt{Eflg} :=?\ ;\ I_3(a \cdot m, b)\ ;\ R_4^{\delta \cup \{(x,i)\}}\ ;\ x^- \\
= & \quad [\text{Choice asg. laws using } \mathit{InWsp}^\delta\text{ 's idp. from } \mathtt{A}, \mathtt{B}, \mathtt{C}, \mathtt{Eflg}, \text{ def. } I_4^\delta] \\
 & \varDelta\, d\ ;\ \mathtt{A}, \mathtt{B}, \mathtt{C}, \mathtt{Eflg} :=?\ ;\ x^+\ ;\ I_4^{\delta \cup \{(x,i)\}}(a \cdot m, b)\ ;\ x^-\ .
\end{array}$$

□

Together with the general extension inequality in Theorem 10.4.12 this theorem is sufficient for reasoning about the implementation of blocks. The above notion of correct initialization code is just an example out of a family of similar notions. The choice assignment $\mathtt{A,B,C,Eflg} :=?$, for instance, could be removed from the right hand side in condition (b). Theorem 10.4.14 would then also look simpler. However, the resulting theorem would be almost useless because initialization code that uses none of the registers hardly ever exists if R is not surjective. On the other hand, we could define more general notions. For example, we could allow the initialization code to write to other unused workspace locations.

10.5 Forgetting About Registers

The previous section provides a view to the behavior of Transputer machine programs in which the registers $\mathtt{A,B,C,Eflg}$ and the variables in $\mathsf{dom}\,\delta$ are visible as well as the communications on the link channels. Such a view is appropriate for tackling expression translation where δ introduces the variables occurring in the source expression together with some *auxiliary variables* that are used to store intermediate results. Complete TPL programs, however, have no visible variables or registers; only communications on the link channels are visible. In order to have a comparable view to the Transputer we must hide all registers and variables. Variables can be hidden by restricting the dictionary δ exploiting the consistent extension theorems established in the previous section. In this section we define a new view that hides the registers. The new level – like the previous one – is parameterized by a dictionary δ. It thus provides appropriate views for treatment of TPL statement translation (with a dictionary introducing the variables occurring in the statement) as well as TPL program translation (with an empty dictionary).

Let Reg stand for the list of variables $\mathtt{A,B,C,Eflg}$ and suppose $\delta \in \mathsf{Dict}$. The alphabet of the new view is

$$\alpha_5 \stackrel{\text{def}}{=} \mathsf{dom}\,\delta = \alpha_4^\delta \setminus \{\mathtt{A,B,C,Eflg}\} .$$

The abstraction is performed via the abstraction map $G_5^\delta : \mathsf{Proc}_{\alpha_4^\delta} \to \mathsf{Proc}_{\alpha_5^\delta}$,

$$G_5^\delta(P) \stackrel{\text{def}}{=} Reg^+ \,;\, P \,;\, Reg^- ,$$

induced by the simulation (R_5^δ, S_5^δ),

$$R_5^\delta \stackrel{\text{def}}{=} Reg^- \quad \text{and} \quad S_5^\delta \stackrel{\text{def}}{=} Reg^+ .$$

Once again G_5^δ can be considered the abstraction map of a data abstraction, viz. one with the trivial invariant ‘true’. The hierarchy of views is extended by the definition

$$I_5^\delta(a,b) \stackrel{\text{def}}{=} G_5^\delta(I_4^\delta(a,b)) .$$

As before we omit the superscript δ if it is clear from context. Of course we could straightforwardly define corresponding abstractions for prefixed instructions and operations. The general instruction and operation theorem would transfer immediately. However, unlike on the previous levels, the abstractions for prefixed instructions and operations would carry very little information because the effect of instructions and operations is generally linked to the registers, which are no longer visible.[6] Generally, only the effect of longer instruction sequences (like the entire code for an assignment statement or an entire program) has a sensible interpretation on the new level. Usually we derive knowledge about behavior of code sequences first on the lower levels from the behavior of single instructions and transfer it to the fifth level directly by its definition.

There are two notable exceptions: the jump instruction `j` and the `stopp` operation have sensible interpretations as shown by the following two theorems. They can advantageously be used when reasoning about the implementation of the control structures, which is done 'on level I_5'.

Theorem 10.5.1 (Unconditional jump). *Let* $\delta \in \mathsf{Dict}$. *If* $a \cdot \mathtt{j}(w) \cdot b = c \cdot d$ *and* $w = |b| - |d|$ *then*

$$I_5^\delta(a, \mathtt{j}(w) \cdot b) \;\geq\; \Delta\, ldt(w) + 3 \;;\; I_5^\delta(c, d) \;.$$

Proof. The theorem is seen from the calculation:

$$\begin{aligned}
& I_5(a, \mathtt{j}(w) \cdot b) \\
\geq \quad & [\text{Definition } I_5,\ (10.67)] \\
& Reg^+ \;;\; \Delta\, ldt(w) + 3 \;;\; \mathtt{A}, \mathtt{B}, \mathtt{C} := ? \;;\; I_4(c, d) \;;\; Reg^- \\
= \quad & [(\text{Initial-}\Delta),\ (\text{Ch-initialization-}=)] \\
& \Delta\, ldt(w) + 3 \;;\; Reg^+ \;;\; I_4(c, d) \;;\; Reg^- \\
= \quad & [\text{Definition } I_5] \\
& \Delta\, ldt(w) + 3 \;;\; I_5(c, d) \;.
\end{aligned}$$

□

A similar theorem for conditional jumps is connected to the correctness predicate for (Boolean) expression translation and is thus given only in Sect. 12.

Theorem 10.5.2 (`stopp`). *Let* $\delta \in \mathsf{Dict}$. *Then* $I_5^\delta(a, \mathtt{stopp} \cdot b) \;\geq\; \mathsf{Stop}$.

Proof. The property is shown by the little calculation

$$I_5(a, \mathtt{stopp} \cdot b)$$

---

[6] Just as a curio we note that an approximation for `stl` would look

$$E_5(\mathtt{stl}, adr_x) \quad\geq\quad \Delta\, ldt(adr_x) + 1 \;;\; x := ?$$

for a word variable $x \in \mathsf{dom}\,\delta$ represented in the standard way.

$=$ [Definition I_5]

$Reg^+ \ ; I_4(a, \mathtt{stopp} \cdot b) \ ; Reg^-$

$\geq$ [10.88]

$Reg^+ \ ; \mathsf{Stop} \ ; I_4(a \cdot \mathtt{stopp}, b) \ ; Reg^-$

$=$ [(Stop-zero), (Initial-stop)]

Stop . □

The consistent extension theorems for I_4 transfer easily to I_5, which results in the following theorem.

Theorem 10.5.3 (Consistent extensions). *Let* $a, b, m \in \mathsf{IS}$, $w \in \mathsf{Word}$, *and* $d \in \mathsf{Time}$. *Suppose* (x, i) *is consistent with* δ, *where* $i = (T, R, adr)$.

(a) The inequality $I_5^\delta(a, b) \leq x^+ \ ; I_5^{\delta \cup \{(x,i)\}}(a, b) \ ; x^-$ *is generally valid.*
(b) If $\mathsf{IC}(m, i, d)$ *then* $I_5^\delta(a, m \cdot b) \geq \Delta d \ ; x^+ \ ; I_5^{\delta \cup \{(x,i)\}}(a \cdot m, b) \ ; x^-$.
(c) If R *is surjective then* $I_5^\delta(a, b) = x^+ \ ; I_5^{\delta \cup \{(x,i)\}}(a, b) \ ; x^-$.

Proof. We present only the proof of (b). The proofs of (a) and (c) from the corresponding theorems about I_4 are even simpler.

Suppose $\mathsf{IC}(m, i, d)$ holds. Then

$I_5^\delta(a, m \cdot b)$

$=$ [Definition I_5]

$Reg^+ \ ; I_4^\delta(a, m \cdot b) \ ; Reg^-$

$\geq$ [Theorem 10.4.14]

$Reg^+ \ ; \Delta d \ ; \mathtt{A,B,C,Eflg} := ? \ ; x^+ \ ; I_4^{\delta \cup \{(x,i)\}}(a \cdot m, b) \ ; x^- \ ; Reg^-$

$=$ [Various laws about addition and deletion commands]

$\Delta d \ ; x^+ \ ; Reg^+ \ ; I_4^{\delta \cup \{(x,i)\}}(a \cdot m, b) \ ; Reg^- \ ; x^-$

$=$ [Definition I_5]

$\Delta d \ ; x^+ \ ; I_5^{\delta \cup \{(x,i)\}}(a \cdot m, b) \ ; x^-$. □

10.6 Discussion

We have now arrived at the top of the hierarchy of views to the Transputer. Although some of the considerations have been motivated by matters of translation – particularly the introduction of symbolic variables and the study of dictionary extensions – we have not really talked about translation up to now but have just seen increasingly abstract interpretations of the same syntactic objects, viz. machine programs. This will change in the next chapter where we define the compiling-correctness relations for the different syntactic categories of TPL. They fix the required semantic relationship between source and target code. The consistency of the hierarchy enables to choose different views when defining the conditions for different syntactic categories of TPL, which largely simplifies the definitions and, later, the reasoning. In fact it is one of the main motivations for studying the hierarchy of views for the purpose of translation.

11. Compiling-Correctness Relations

The specification of a code generator is the interface between the user and the compiler designer. Two extreme styles of specification, implicit and explicit ones, serve their respective needs differently well. By an *explicit* (or *syntactic*) specification we mean a mapping that assigns concrete target code to syntactic source programs. A typical form in which an explicit specification can be presented is a mapping that is defined inductively over the structure of source programs with possibly some additional parameters like the symbol table. It is a convenient starting point for the implementation. However, it is unsatisfactory for the user who is not so much interested in the concrete code generated for his source program but wants to transfer (correctness) properties to the target code which have been established for the source program. He is thus served better by an *implicit* (or *semantic*) specification that fixes the required and achieved relationship between the behavior of a source program and corresponding target code. Such a specification, however, is too implicit as starting point for the implementation. Consequently, we need both an implicit and an explicit specification for compiling. The proof of their mutual consistency is sometimes called *compiling verification.*

In the traditional setup of compiler verification the implicit specification is formulated as a correctness condition to be fulfilled by the explicit specification. Usually one assumes that both specifications are completely known before the compiling verification starts. In practice, however, it is difficult to construct the two specifications independently in a consistent way, which would lead to iterations of proof attempts for slightly changed specifications.

C.A.R. Hoare proposes in [41] to start from a semantic specification and to present the explicit specification as a collection of theorems instead of an inductively defined function. In order to explain the idea assume for a moment that $C(s,t)$ is the relation 't is correct target code for s' defined in terms of the semantics of source and target programs s and t.[1] The idea is now to establish for each source language constructor op, which builds the composed statement $op(s_1,\ldots,s_n)$ from $n \geq 0$ component statements $s_1,\ldots,s_n$, a theorem of the form

$$C(s_1,t_1) \wedge \cdots \wedge C(s_n,t_n) \quad \Rightarrow \quad C(op(s_1,\ldots,s_n), ctx(t_1,\ldots,t_n)) \ ,$$

[1] In practice C has additional parameters.

where *ctx* is a target language context. Such a theorem shows one possible way to construct correct code for $op(s_1, \ldots, s_n)$ from correct code pieces $t_1, \ldots, t_n$ for the component statements $s_1, \ldots, s_n$, viz. putting $t_1, \ldots, t_n$ into the context *ctx*. For an atomic statements, i.e. for $n = 0$, the theorem degenerates to the form

$$C(op, ctx) ,$$

and provides thus a piece of code *ctx* that correctly implements the atomic statement *op*. It is quite easy to define an inductive function that is correct w.r.t. C, i.e. an explicit specification consistent with C, from a collection of such theorems. In practice we have a family of correctness relations $(C_{cat})_{cat}$, one for each syntactic category *cat* of the source language, and most of the relations have additional parameters like the dictionary that describes the representation conventions for the variables.

Often the first definition of these relations that captures our intuitive expectation about the behavior of correct code must be strengthened in order to make theorems of the above form valid. The reason is the well-know phenomenon that inductive arguments often require to strengthen the proved property: as described above, the theorems provide essentially an inductive specification of correct code. This strengthening might make the relations less intelligible, which conflicts with their other purpose, viz. to provide a convenient interface for the user. Fortunately, for TPL this problem does not matter. The user is interested mainly in the correctness relation for complete programs, called CP below. As programs cannot be components of larger syntactic objects in TPL, the definition of CP is not influenced by inductive considerations, in contrast to the correctness predicates for statement and expression translation, called CS and CE. Indeed this has been one of the reasons for introducing a separate category of programs in TPL. Another approach to defuse the conflict between compositional specification and ease of interfacing is to provide two different correctness predicates for one single category, one for the compositional specification of code and another one, which is proved to be implied by the first one, to comfort the user.

To present explicit code generator specifications as collections of theorems on implicit ones facilitates an incremental, modular construction of the explicit specification and focuses on its correctness. Another advantage is that certain aspects can be left implicit in early stages of the development, which enhances modularity further. For example, we do not fix the concrete allocation scheme for the memory in the first phase of the code generator development for TPL. This relieves the (first phase of the) code generator correctness proof from the details of a specific scheme and facilitates the reuse of the verification for various schemes. On the other hand it implies that we have to invest a second phase to arrive at a really explicit specification (see Chap. 13).

Another advantage is according to Hoare that extensions of the source language are easily tackled. The only necessary effort should be to prove theorems for the new constructs because the theorems for the old constructs remain valid. While this is true for small extensions it is questionable whether this applies to essential ones as well. In our opinion it is very likely that essential additions to the source language require further strengthening of the correctness relations in order to allow a compositional specification of code for the new constructs, which might invalidate the theorems for the old constructs.

In the remainder of this chapter we motivate and define the compiling-correctness relations for the three syntactic categories of TPL and for monadic and binary operators, which amounts to an implicit code generator specification. In the next chapter we prove a collection of translation theorems. This provides an explicit specification, from which a code generator can be implemented without further semantic consideration. As an example we develop in Chap. 13 an implementation by a functional program. As mentioned, we do not decide for a specific storage allocation scheme in the translation theorems. In order to resolve this we study in Chap. 13, before developing the functional implementation, refined versions of the compiling-correctness relations.

11.1 Programs

We assume that the user of a TPL program is only interested in the communications on the external channels and that changes to variables are not directly observable. Therefore, we required TPL programs to have no free variables (see Table 9.2). A comparable view to the behavior of a Transputer that executes an instruction sequence m starting with m's first instruction is provided by $I_5^{\emptyset}(\varepsilon, m)$. This motivates the following definition.

Definition 11.1.1 (Correct program translation).
Suppose given prog $\in$ Prog *and* $m \in$ IS. *We call* m correct code *for prog iff*

$$I_5^{\emptyset}(\varepsilon, m) \;\geq\; \mathsf{MP}(prog) \ .$$

We abbreviate this property by $\mathsf{CP}(prog, m)$.

The astounding simplicity of Definition 11.1.1 stems from the fact that the details of and the preconditions for the execution of m are hidden in the definition of $I_5^{\emptyset}$. Most likely, however, the user is not willing to learn the entire hierarchy of views in order to understand what is guaranteed about the target code. It is thus interesting to derive a direct relationship between $\mathsf{MP}(prog)$ and *Run* that is implied by $\mathsf{CP}(prog, m)$.

First of all we can prove an upper estimate for $I_5^{\emptyset}$. Recall that Tc stands for the list `A`, `B`, `C`, `Eflg`, `Oreg`, `Wptr`, `Ip`, `Mem` of the internal components in the Transputer base model.

Lemma 11.1.2 (Upper estimate for $I_5^\emptyset$). *Let $m \in \mathsf{IS}$ be a machine program. Then*

$$I_5^\emptyset(\varepsilon, m) \;\leq\; Tc^+ \;;\; [\mathit{Loaded}(m) \wedge \mathtt{Ip} = s_\mathrm{P} \wedge \mathtt{Oreg} = 0 \wedge \mathtt{Wptr} = s_\mathrm{W}] \;;\; \mathit{Run} \;;\; Tc^- \;.$$

Proof. By definition $I_5^\emptyset(\varepsilon, m) \;=\; S_5^\emptyset \;;\; S_4^\emptyset \;;\; S_3 \;;\; S_2 \;;\; S_1^{\varepsilon,m} \;;\; \mathit{Run} \;;\; R_1^{\varepsilon,m} \;;\; R_2 \;;\; R_3 \;;\; R_4^\emptyset \;;\; R_5^\emptyset$. Let us consider the composition of the S_i's and R_i's separately. We have

$$\begin{array}{ll}
& S_5^\emptyset \;;\; S_4^\emptyset \;;\; S_3 \;;\; S_2 \;;\; S_1^{\varepsilon,m} \\
= & [\text{Definition } S_4^\emptyset] \\
& S_5^\emptyset \;;\; \mathtt{Wsp}^+ \;;\; [\mathit{InWsp}^\emptyset] \;;\; \varepsilon^- \;;\; S_3 \;;\; S_2 \;;\; S_1^{\varepsilon,m} \\
= & [\mathit{InWsp}^\emptyset \equiv \mathsf{true}, \text{(Assume)}, \text{(--empty)}, \text{definition } S_3] \\
& S_5^\emptyset \;;\; \mathtt{Wsp}^+ \;;\; \mathtt{Wptr},\mathtt{Mem}^+ \;;\; [\mathit{WspInMem}] \;;\; \mathtt{Wsp}^- \;;\; S_2 \;;\; S_1^{\varepsilon,m} \\
\leq & [\text{(+--–union)}, \text{(Restrict-demon)}] \\
& S_5^\emptyset \;;\; \mathtt{Wptr},\mathtt{Mem}^+ \;;\; [\mathbf{E}_{\mathtt{Wsp}}(\mathit{WspInMem})] \;;\; \mathtt{Wsp}^\oplus \;;\; \mathtt{Wsp}^- \;;\; S_2 \;;\; S_1^{\varepsilon,m} \\
= & [\mathbf{E}_{\mathtt{Wsp}}(\mathit{WspInMem}) \equiv (\mathtt{Wptr} = s_\mathrm{W}), (\oplus\text{-–-sim}), \text{defs } S_5^\emptyset, S_2, S_1^{\varepsilon,m}] \\
& \mathit{Reg}^+ \;;\; \mathtt{Wptr},\mathtt{Mem}^+ \;;\; [\mathtt{Wptr} = s_\mathrm{W}] \;;\; \mathtt{Oreg}^+ \;;\; [\mathtt{Oreg} = 0] \;;\; \mathtt{Ip}^+ \;;\; [\Lambda(\varepsilon, m)] \\
= & [\text{(Initial-assume)}, \text{(+-union)}, \text{(Comb-assume)}] \\
& \mathit{Reg},\mathtt{Wptr},\mathtt{Mem},\mathtt{Oreg},\mathtt{Ip}^+ \;;\; [\mathtt{Wptr} = s_\mathrm{W} \wedge \mathtt{Oreg} = 0 \wedge \Lambda(\varepsilon, m)] \\
= & [\text{(+-reorder)}, \text{def. } Tc, \text{def. } \Lambda(\varepsilon, m), \text{commutativity of } \wedge] \\
& Tc^+ \;;\; [\mathit{Loaded}(m) \wedge \mathtt{Ip} = s_\mathrm{P} \wedge \mathtt{Oreg} = 0 \wedge \mathtt{Wptr} = s_\mathrm{W}]
\end{array}$$

and

$$\begin{array}{ll}
& R_1^{\varepsilon,m} \;;\; R_2 \;;\; R_3 \;;\; R_4^\emptyset \;;\; R_5^\emptyset \\
= & [\text{Definitions}] \\
& \{\Lambda(\varepsilon, m)\} \;;\; \mathtt{Ip}^- \;;\; \{\mathtt{Oreg} = 0\} \;;\; \mathtt{Oreg}^- \;; \\
& \mathtt{Wsp}^\oplus \;;\; \{\mathit{WspInMem}\} \;;\; \mathtt{Wptr},\mathtt{Mem}^- \;;\; \varepsilon^+ \;;\; \{\mathit{InWsp}^\emptyset\} \;;\; \mathtt{Wsp}^- \;;\; \mathit{Reg}^- \\
\leq & [\text{(Assert) gives that } \{\phi\} \leq \mathsf{Id} \text{ for all } \phi] \\
& \mathtt{Ip}^- \;;\; \mathtt{Oreg}^- \;;\; \mathtt{Wsp}^\oplus \;;\; \mathtt{Wptr},\mathtt{Mem}^- \;;\; \varepsilon^+ \;;\; \mathtt{Wsp}^- \;;\; \mathit{Reg}^- \\
= & [\text{(+-empty)}, (\oplus\text{-–-comm})] \\
& \mathtt{Ip}^- \;;\; \mathtt{Oreg}^- \;;\; \mathtt{Wptr},\mathtt{Mem}^- \;;\; \mathtt{Wsp}^\oplus \;;\; \mathtt{Wsp}^- \;;\; \mathit{Reg}^- \\
= & [(\oplus\text{-–-sim}), \text{(--union)}, \text{(--reorder)}, \text{definition } Tc] \\
& Tc^- \;.
\end{array}$$

Together with the identity for $I_5^\emptyset(\varepsilon, m)$ presented at the beginning of this proof, the inequalities established by these calculations imply the claim of the lemma. □

From this upper estimate we can establish the following theorem that directly relates the source program's semantics to certain executions of the *Run* phase induced by correct code m.

Theorem 11.1.3 (Direct relationship to run phase). *Suppose prog* $\in$ Prog *and* $m \in$ IS. *If* CP(*prog*, m) *then*

$$\mathsf{MP}(prog) \;\leq\; Tc^{+} \;;\; [\mathit{Loaded}(m) \wedge \mathtt{Ip} = s_{\mathrm{P}} \wedge \mathtt{Oreg} = 0 \wedge \mathtt{Wptr} = s_{\mathrm{W}}] \;;\; \mathit{Run} \;;\; Tc^{-} \;.$$

Proof. Immediate from Lemma 11.1.2, the definition of CP, and transitivity of $\leq$. □

The initial assumption $[\mathit{Loaded}(m) \wedge \mathtt{Ip} = s_{\mathrm{P}} \wedge \mathtt{Oreg} = 0 \wedge \mathtt{Wptr} = s_{\mathrm{W}}]$ clearly states the obligation for the loader or boot program that starts an instruction sequence m generated by a compiler developed according to CP: it must put the Transputer into a state where m is loaded and the instruction pointer, the operand register, and the workspace pointer are initialized appropriately.

Our considerations apply to all values of the global constants $s_{\mathrm{P}}, l_{\mathrm{P}}, s_{\mathrm{W}}, l_{\mathrm{W}}$ that satisfy the global assumption (10.56). Recall that $s_{\mathrm{P}}, l_{\mathrm{P}}, s_{\mathrm{W}}, l_{\mathrm{W}}$ parameterize the program storage and the workspace and that (10.56) expresses their disjointness.

11.2 Statements

Suppose *stat* $\in \mathsf{Stat}_V$ is a well-formed TPL statement the free variables of which are contained in $V \subseteq Z$. Its meaning is given by $\mathsf{MS}_V(stat)$. Formalizing standard practice we use a semantic dictionary to describe how the variables in V are represented on the target processor. So assume that $\delta \in$ Dict is given such that $\mathsf{dom}\,\delta = V$.

As explained in the introduction to this chapter, the correctness predicate for statement translation is complex because it must allow a compositional treatment of translation. We motivate it stepwise.

A suitable view for comparing the behavior of a machine program m with $\mathsf{MS}_V(stat)$ is induced by I_5^{δ} because the alphabet of the resulting process equals the alphabet of $\mathsf{MS}_V(stat)$. A first idea is to use

$$I_5^{\delta}(\varepsilon, m) \;\geq\; \mathsf{MS}(stat)$$

as the notion of correct implementation. But – inherited from the initial description by the *Run* process – $I_5^{\delta}(\varepsilon, m)$ does not terminate in contrast to $\mathsf{MS}(stat)$. (For programs this does not matter as we agreed in the definition of MP that programs stop finally; stopping can be achieved by a final `stopp` instruction in m.) The main purpose of termination of *stat* is to transfer control to its sequential successor. Therefore, it is sufficient to require that control is transferred to the code just following m if $\mathsf{MS}(stat)$ terminates. This leads to the condition

$$I_5^{\delta}(\varepsilon, m \cdot b) \;\geq\; \mathsf{MS}(stat) \;;\; I_5^{\delta}(m, b) \tag{11.1}$$

for all code sequences b.

Another difficulty is that the code for a component statement typically is not positioned at the beginning of the program memory but just after the code of its sequential predecessor. This results in the idea to provide not just a 'post-context' b as in (11.1) but also a 'pre-context' a. So we arrive at the requirement

$$I_5^{\delta}(a, m \cdot b) \;\geq\; \mathsf{MS}(stat) \;;\; I_5^{\delta}(a \cdot m, b) \tag{11.2}$$

for all code sequences a, b. The intuitive interpretation is as follows. If $a \cdot m \cdot b$ is started with the first instruction of m then the effect is as least as good as the source program's behavior $\mathsf{MS}(stat)$ followed by the behavior arising from starting $a \cdot m \cdot b$ just after m. This predicate leads to a particularly simple treatment of sequential composition and would be sufficient for an untimed language.

Since timing is reflected in both the source and target language semantics, condition (11.2) also speaks about correct timing. Unfortunately, it does not allow a compositional treatment of the upper bounds in statements. We therefore add another parameter E to the correctness predicate,which specifies a bound that can be guaranteed for the source statement. This results in the requirement

$$I_5^{\delta}(a, m \cdot b) \;\geq\; |\,\mathsf{MS}(stat)\,| \preceq E \;;\; I_5^{\delta}(a \cdot m, b) \;,$$

for all code sequences a, b.

A further complication is that we want to justify the assumption of immediate execution for internal constructs of the timed source language TPL. Intuitively this is possible because only communications are directly observable. However, the code implementing e.g. an assignment in the source language certainly needs time to execute. The idea is to shift excess time of code implementing internal activity to a sequentially successive process that is compiled to a machine program needing less time than allowed by the source [23]. This can be accomplished by adding two further parameters L and R to the correctness predicate, where L states the excess time which can be absorbed from the sequential predecessor and R states the excess time that is handed over to the sequential successor for absorption. This leads to the following definition.

Definition 11.2.1 (Correct statement translation). *Suppose given* $\delta \in \mathsf{Dict}$, $stat \in \mathsf{Stat}_{\mathsf{dom}\,\delta}$, $m \in \mathsf{IS}$, *and* $E, L, R \in \mathsf{Time}$. *We say that* m *implements stat w.r.t.* δ*, absorbing excess time* L *from its sequential predecessor, exporting excess time* R *to its sequential successor, under time bound* E*, iff for all* $a, b \in \mathsf{IS}$

$$\Delta L \; ; I_5^\delta(a, m \cdot b) \;\geq\; |\,\mathsf{MS}_{\mathsf{dom}\,\delta}(stat)\,| \preceq E \; ; \Delta R \; ; I_5^\delta(a \cdot m, b) \; .$$

For brevity, we denote this implementation property by $\mathsf{CS}(stat, m, \delta, L, R, E)$.

The condition $stat \in \mathsf{Stat}_{\mathsf{dom}\,\delta}$ expresses that all free variables in *stat* are bound by δ. It ensures well-definedness of $\mathsf{MS}_{\mathsf{dom}\,\delta}(stat)$.

11.3 Expressions

The representation of the value domains Bool and Word occurring for TPL expressions has already been described in Sect. 10.4 by the two relations R_{Bool} and R_{Word}. It is easy to see that both R_{Bool} and R_{Word} are functions, i.e. that each value has a unique representation. We can thus use the functional notation $R_{\mathsf{Bool}}(v)$ and $R_{\mathsf{Word}}(w)$ for the words that represent the Boolean value v and word value w. As a reminder we note that

$$R_{\mathsf{Bool}}(v) \;=\; \mathsf{if}\ v\ \mathsf{then}\ 1\ \mathsf{else}\ 0\ \mathsf{fi} \quad \text{and} \quad R_{\mathsf{Word}}(w) \;=\; w \; .$$

What do we expect from a Transputer instruction sequence m that is to implement a TPL expression $expr \in \mathsf{Expr}_V$? Intuitively its execution should evaluate *expr* in the current state; the result should be left in register `A`. A formal statement of this property has to take into account the chosen representation of values. Recalling that $\mathsf{SE}(expr)(V)$ is the value domain of *expr*,

$$Rep_V(expr) \;\stackrel{\text{def}}{=}\; R_{\mathsf{SE}(expr)(V)}(\mathsf{ME}_V(expr))$$

is the word valuation function that delivers for each state the represented result of *expr*. We omit the index V if it is clear from the context.

We need not speak explicitly about the representation of the variables in the correctness predicate because we can use the appropriate view to m's behavior. Obviously the symbolic variables in the source expression as well as the registers must be visible. Such a view is provided by I_4^δ, where δ is a dictionary with $\mathsf{dom}\,\delta = V$. Like for statements it is sensible to put m into a pre- and post-context. So the first idea is to use the following predicate as notion of correct implementation of an expression *expr* by a code sequence m:

$$I_4(a, m \cdot b) \;\geq\; \mathtt{A} := Rep(expr) \; ; I_4(a \cdot m, b) \;\; \text{for all } a, b \in \mathsf{IS}. \tag{11.3}$$

Although clearly sufficient it is too restrictive in the following respects.

- It does not allow m to spend time for execution. We resolve this by adding a delay to the right hand side and a parameter E to the correctness predicate, which provides an upper bound on the execution time.
- It requires that the other accumulators `B`, `C` and the error flag `Eflg` are left unchanged. This is resolved by adding a choice assignment to the right hand side.

Our actual definition is as follows.

Definition 11.3.1 (Correct expression translation). *Suppose given* $\delta \in$ Dict, *expr* $\in \mathsf{Expr}_{\mathsf{dom}\,\delta}$, $m \in$ IS, *and* $E \in$ Time. *We say that* m *implements expr w.r.t.* δ *needing at most* E *time units for execution, iff for all* $a, b \in$ IS

$$I_4(a, m \cdot b) \;\geq\; \Delta E \;;\; \mathtt{A} := Rep(expr) \;;\; \mathtt{B}, \mathtt{C}, \mathtt{Eflg} :=? \;;\; I_4(a \cdot m, b) \;.$$

We denote this property by $\mathsf{CE}(expr, m, \delta, E)$.

11.4 Monadic and Binary Operators

Code for monadic and binary expressions consists of code that loads the value of the subexpression(s) to the register stack A, B, C together with some final piece of code that is specific for the respective operator. The correctness predicate for monadic and binary operators to be defined in this section are concerned with the behavior of this final piece m of code. The task of m is to calculate the result from the arguments expected on the register stack. It has to take into account the representation of values by words. By convention the result is left in register A. Note that this convention is consistent with the convention for expressions. Like for expressions the code is considered in an arbitrary pre- and post-context. It is allowed to change the registers B, C, Eflg arbitrarily and to spend a certain amount of time for execution which is controlled by a parameter E of the correctness predicate.

Definition 11.4.1 (Compiling relation for monadic operators). *Let mop* $\in$ Mop, $m \in$ IS, $E \in$ Time *and* $A, B \in \{\mathsf{Bool}, \mathsf{Word}\}$ *such that* $\mathsf{MM}(mop) \in (A \to B)$. *We say that* m implements *mop* needing at most E time units for execution *iff there is* $f \in (\mathsf{Word} \to \mathsf{Word})$ *such that*

(a) $f(R_A(a)) = R_B(\mathsf{MM}(mop)(a))$ *for all* $a \in A$ *and*

(b) $I_4^\delta(a, m \cdot b) \;\geq\; \Delta E \;;\; \mathtt{A} := f(\mathtt{A}) \;;\; \mathtt{B}, \mathtt{C}, \mathtt{Eflg} :=? \;;\; I_4^\delta(a \cdot m, b)$ *for all* $a, b \in$ IS, $\delta \in$ Dict.

For brevity, we denote this property by $\mathsf{CM}(mop, m, E)$.

The purpose of f is to mirror $\mathsf{MM}(mop)$ on the representations, which is ensured by condition (a).

The correctness predicate for binary operators is similar. The code expects the first argument in register B and the second one in register A. This order of arguments is supported directly by the Transputer's instruction sets as can be seen e.g. from the behavior of the operation sub.

Definition 11.4.2 (Compiling relation for binary operators). *Suppose given bop* $\in$ Bop, $m \in$ IS, $E \in$ Time *and* $A, B, C \in \{\mathsf{Bool}, \mathsf{Word}\}$ *such that* $\mathsf{MM}(mop) \in (A \times B \to C)$. *We say that* m implements *bop* needing at most E time units for execution *iff there is* $f \in (\mathsf{Word} \times \mathsf{Word} \to \mathsf{Word})$ *such that* *(a)* $f(R_A(a), R_B(b)) = R_C(\mathsf{MM}(bop)(a,b))$ *for all* $a \in A, b \in B$ *and*

(b) $I_4^\delta(a, m \cdot b) \;\geq\; \Delta E \; ; \; \mathtt{A} := f(\mathtt{B}, \mathtt{A}) \; ; \; \mathtt{B}, \mathtt{C}, \mathtt{Eflg} :=? \; ; \; I_4^\delta(a \cdot m, b)$ *for all* $a, b \in \mathsf{IS}$, $\delta \in \mathsf{Dict}$.

For brevity, we denote this property by $\mathsf{CB}(bop, m, E)$.

The compiling-correctness relations for expressions, monadic and binary operators take advantage of the fact that all operators are interpreted by total functions. Otherwise we would have to choose and specify the error behavior resulting from operator applications outside their domain.

12. Translation Theorems

The purpose of this chapter is to establish for each syntactic constructor of TPL a theorem that shows how correct code for a composed construct can be obtained from correct code for the components. As mentioned earlier, a complete set of such theorems is a stepping-stone on the path to a code generator program. In the first section we establish some lemmata that are useful for shortening the proofs of the translation theorems.

Throughout this chapter we suppose given $\delta \in \mathsf{Dict}$, $V = \mathsf{dom}\,\delta$, $stat, stat_1, stat_2 \in \mathsf{Stat}_V$, $expr$, $expr_1$, $expr_2 \in \mathsf{Expr}_V$, m, m_0, m_1, $m_2 \in \mathsf{IS}$, L, L_1, L_2, R, R_1, R_2, E, E_0, E_1, $E_2 \in \mathsf{Time}$, w, w_1, $w_2 \in \mathsf{Word}$.

12.1 Preliminaries

The first lemma is concerned with CS's timing parameters and is an immediate consequence of the refinement laws for time bounds and delays. A similar lemma can be proved for CE.

Lemma 12.1.1 (Weakening timing parameters). *Suppose*

(a) $L_1 \leq L$,

(b) $R_1 \geq R$, *and*

(c) $E_1 \geq E$.

Then $\mathsf{CS}(stat, m, \delta, L, R, E)$ *implies* $\mathsf{CS}(stat, m, \delta, L_1, R_1, E_1)$.

Proof. If $\mathsf{CS}(stat, m, \delta, L, R, E)$ holds, we have for all $a, b \in \mathsf{IS}$

$$\begin{aligned}
& \Delta\, L_1 \;;\; I_5^\delta(a, m \cdot b) \\
\geq \quad & [(\Delta\text{-refine}):\ L_1 \leq L] \\
& \Delta\, L \;;\; I_5^\delta(a, m \cdot b) \\
\geq \quad & [\mathsf{CS}(stat, m, \delta, L, R, E)] \\
& |\,\mathsf{MS}(stat)\,| \preceq E \;;\; \Delta\, R \;;\; I_5^\delta(a \cdot m, b) \\
\geq \quad & [(\Delta\text{-refine}):\ R_1 \geq R,\ (\text{Bound-refine}):\ E_1 \geq E] \\
& |\,\mathsf{MS}(stat)\,| \preceq E_1 \;;\; \Delta\, R_1 \;;\; I_5^\delta(a \cdot m, b)\ .
\end{aligned}$$

□

CE is defined w.r.t. I_4 and CS w.r.t. I_5. The following lemma gives a lower estimate for expression code viewed at level I_5. It is useful when considering translation of statements that have expressions as components.

Lemma 12.1.2 (CE at level I_5). *Suppose* $\mathsf{CE}(expr, m, \delta, E)$. *Then*

$$I_5^\delta(a, m \cdot b) \;\geq\; \Delta E \;;\; Reg^+ \;;\; \mathtt{A} := Rep(expr) \;;\; I_4^\delta(a \cdot m, b) \;;\; Reg^-$$

for all $a, b \in \mathsf{IS}$.

Proof. For all $a, b \in \mathsf{IS}$ we have

$$\begin{array}{ll} & I_5^\delta(a, m \cdot b) \\ \geq & [\text{Definition of } I_5] \\ & Reg^+ \;;\; I_4^\delta(a, m \cdot b) \;;\; Reg^- \\ \geq & [\mathsf{CE}(expr, m, \delta, E)] \\ & Reg^+ \;;\; \Delta E \;;\; \mathtt{A} := Rep(expr) \;;\; \mathtt{B,C,Eflg} :=? \;;\; I_4^\delta(a \cdot m, b) \;;\; Reg^- \\ = & [\text{(Ch-asg): } Rep(expr) \text{ is independent of } \mathtt{B,C,Eflg}] \\ & Reg^+ \;;\; \Delta E \;;\; \mathtt{B,C,Eflg} :=? \;;\; \mathtt{A} := Rep(expr) \;;\; I_4^\delta(a \cdot m, b) \;;\; Reg^- \\ = & [\text{(Initial-}\Delta\text{), (Ch-initialization-=)}] \\ & \Delta E \;;\; Reg^+ \;;\; \mathtt{A} := Rep(expr) \;;\; I_4^\delta(a \cdot m, b) \;;\; Reg^- \;. \end{array}$$

□

In Sect. 10.5 we saw that single instructions cannot sensibly be interpreted on level I_5 in isolation (except of `stopp` and `j`). The next two lemmata show that conditional jump instructions have a sensible interpretation if they follow on correct code for a Boolean expression.

We consider the following situation: $expr \in \mathsf{Expr}_V$ is a well-formed Boolean TPL expression (i.e. $\mathsf{SE}(expr)(V) = \mathsf{Bool}$), $m \in \mathsf{IS}$, $w \in \mathsf{Word}$ and $E \in \mathsf{Time}$. If *expr* evaluates to true in the initial state the jump is not taken.

Lemma 12.1.3 (Conditional jumps that are not taken).
If $\mathsf{CE}(expr, m, \delta, E)$ *then*

$$\begin{array}{l} I_5^\delta(a, m \cdot \mathtt{cj}(w) \cdot b) \;\geq \\ \qquad \{\mathsf{ME}_V(expr)\} \;;\; \Delta E + ldt(w) + 2 \;;\; I_5^\delta(a \cdot m \cdot \mathtt{cj}(l), b) \end{array}$$

for all $a, b \in \mathsf{IS}$.

Proof. For all $a, b \in \mathsf{IS}$

$$\begin{array}{ll} & I_5^\delta(a, m \cdot \mathtt{cj}(w) \cdot b) \\ \geq & [\mathsf{CE}(expr, m, \delta, E), \text{ Lemma 12.1.2}] \\ & \Delta E \;;\; Reg^+ \;;\; \mathtt{A} := Rep(expr) \;;\; I_4^\delta(a \cdot m, \mathtt{cj}(w) \cdot b) \;;\; Reg^- \\ \geq & [\text{Theorem 10.4.2, (10.74)}] \\ & \Delta E \;;\; Reg^+ \;;\; \mathtt{A} := Rep(expr) \;;\; \Delta\, ldt(w) + 2 \;;\; \{\mathtt{A} \neq 0\} \;;\; \mathtt{A,B} := \mathtt{B,C} \;;\; \mathtt{C} :=? \;; \\ & I_4^\delta(a \cdot m \cdot \mathtt{cj}(w), b) \;;\; Reg^- \end{array}$$

$$
\begin{aligned}
= \quad & [\Delta\text{-laws}] \\
& \Delta\, E + \mathit{ldt}(w) + 2 \; ; \; \mathit{Reg}^+ \; ; \; \mathtt{A} := \mathit{Rep}(\mathit{expr}) \; ; \; \{\mathtt{A} \neq 0\} \; ; \; \mathtt{A}, \mathtt{B} := \mathtt{B}, \mathtt{C} \; ; \; \mathtt{C} :=? \; ; \\
& I_4^\delta(a \cdot m \cdot \mathtt{cj}(w), b) \; ; \; \mathit{Reg}^- \\
= \quad & [\text{(Assign-assert), (Initial-assert): } \mathit{Rep}(\mathit{expr}) \text{ is independent from } \mathit{Reg}] \\
& \Delta\, E + \mathit{ldt}(w) + 2 \; ; \; \{\mathit{Rep}(\mathit{expr}) \neq 0\} \; ; \; \mathit{Reg}^+ \; ; \; \mathtt{A} := \mathit{Rep}(\mathit{expr}) \; ; \; \mathtt{A}, \mathtt{B} := \mathtt{B}, \mathtt{C} \; ; \\
& \mathtt{C} :=? \; ; \; I_4^\delta(a \cdot m \cdot \mathtt{cj}(w), b) \; ; \; \mathit{Reg}^- \\
\geq \quad & [\mathit{Rep}(\mathit{expr}) \neq 0 \text{ iff } \mathsf{ME}_V(\mathit{expr}), \text{(Initialization), (Ch-initialization-=)}] \\
& \Delta\, E + \mathit{ldt}(w) + 2 \; ; \; \{\mathsf{ME}_V(\mathit{expr})\} \; ; \; \mathit{Reg}^+ \; ; \; I_4^\delta(a \cdot m \cdot \mathtt{cj}(w), b) \; ; \; \mathit{Reg}^- \\
= \quad & [(\Delta\text{-assert}), \text{Definition } I_5] \\
& \{\mathsf{ME}_V(\mathit{expr})\} \; ; \; \Delta\, E + \mathit{ldt}(w) + 2 \; ; \; I_5^\delta(a \cdot m \cdot \mathtt{cj}(w), b) \; .
\end{aligned}
$$

□

If, on the other hand, *expr* evaluates to false in the initial state, the jump is taken.

Lemma 12.1.4 (Conditional jumps that are taken). *Let $a, b, c, d \in \mathsf{IS}$. If*

(a) $\mathsf{CE}(\mathit{expr}, m, \delta, E)$,

(b) $c \cdot d \; = \; a \cdot m \cdot \mathtt{cj}(w) \cdot b$, *and*

(c) $w \; = \; |\, b \,| - |\, d \,|$

then $I_5^\delta(a, m \cdot \mathtt{cj}(w) \cdot b) \;\geq\; \{\neg \mathsf{ME}_V(\mathit{expr})\} \; ; \; \Delta\, E + \mathit{ldt}(w) + 4 \; ; \; I_5^\delta(c, d)$.

Proof. We have

$$
\begin{aligned}
& I_5^\delta(a, m \cdot \mathtt{cj}(w) \cdot b) \\
\geq \quad & [\mathsf{CE}(\mathit{expr}, m, \delta, E), \text{Lemma 12.1.2, (10.68)}] \\
& \Delta\, E \; ; \; \mathit{Reg}^+ \; ; \; \mathtt{A} := \mathit{Rep}(\mathit{expr}) \; ; \; \Delta\, \mathit{ldt}(w) + 4 \; ; \; \{\mathtt{A} = 0\} \; ; \; I_4^\delta(c, d) \; ; \; \mathit{Reg}^- \\
\geq \quad & [\text{Calculation as in the previous proof}] \\
& \{\neg \mathsf{ME}_V(\mathit{expr})\} \; ; \; \Delta\, E + \mathit{ldt}(w) + 4 \; ; \; I_5^\delta(c, d) \; .
\end{aligned}
$$

□

The two cases of a conditional jump can also be described together by a conditional.

Corollary 12.1.5 (Conditional jumps). *Suppose $a, b, c, d \in \mathsf{IS}$. If*

(a) $\mathsf{CE}(\mathit{expr}, m, \delta, E)$,

(b) $c \cdot d \; = \; a \cdot m \cdot \mathtt{cj}(w) \cdot b$, *and*

(c) $w \; = \; |\, b \,| - |\, d \,|$

then

$$
\begin{aligned}
I_5^\delta(a, m \cdot \mathtt{cj}(w) \cdot b) \;\geq\; & (\Delta\, E + \mathit{ldt}(w) + 2 \; ; \; I_5^\delta(a \cdot m \cdot \mathtt{cj}(w), b)) \\
& \lhd \; \mathsf{ME}_V(\mathit{expr}) \; \rhd \\
& (\Delta\, E + \mathit{ldt}(w) + 4 \; ; \; I_5^\delta(c, d)) \; .
\end{aligned}
$$

Proof. The claimed inequality follows from Lemma 12.1.3 and Lemma 12.1.4 by the modularization lemma (Lemma 5.7.10). □

The evaluation of the second argument of a binary expression must not destroy the value that has already been determined for the first argument. The standard technique is to save the result of the first subexpression's evaluation to an auxiliary variable, from where it is restored after the evaluation of the second subexpression. Storing to and loading from variables is done by `stl` and `ldl` instructions. The code for the second argument expression thus typically is surrounded by a `stl` and a `ldl` instruction (to the same new location). The next lemma investigates this code pattern in isolation and provides an inequality similar to the definition of CE. Execution of this code pattern leaves the result of the expression evaluation in register B instead of register A and does not change A. The allocation of a new auxiliary variable is described by a consistent dictionary extension. For the semantic reasoning we use the consistent extension theorem concerning surjective representation relations from Sect. 10.4.

Lemma 12.1.6 (Preserving register A). *Suppose given $x \in Y$ and $i = (\mathsf{Word}, R_{\mathsf{Word}}, adr) \in \mathsf{DictInfo}$ such that (x, i) is consistent with δ. Let $\delta' = \delta \cup \{(x, i)\}$. If $\mathsf{CE}(expr, m_1, \delta', E_1)$ and $m = \mathtt{stl}(adr) \cdot m_1 \cdot \mathtt{ldl}(adr)$ then*

$$I_4^\delta(a, m \cdot b) \geq$$
$$\Delta\, E_1 + 2 * ldt(adr) + 3 \; ; \mathtt{B} := Rep(expr) \; ; \mathtt{C}, \mathtt{Eflg} :=? \; ; I_4^\delta(a \cdot m, b) \;,$$

for all $a, b \in \mathsf{IS}$.

Proof. For arbitrary $a, b \in \mathsf{IS}$ it is

$$
\begin{aligned}
& I_4^\delta(a, \mathtt{stl}(adr) \cdot m_1 \cdot \mathtt{ldl}(adr) \cdot b) \\
= \quad & [\text{Surjective consistent extension theorem (Theorem 10.4.11)}] \\
& x^+ \; ; I_4^{\delta'}(a, \mathtt{stl}(adr) \cdot m_1 \cdot \mathtt{ldl}(adr) \cdot b) \; ; x^- \\
\geq \quad & [\text{Theorem 10.4.7 (a)}, \mathsf{CE}(expr, m_1, \delta', E_1), \text{Theorem 10.4.5 (a)}] \\
& x^+ \; ; \Delta\, ldt(adr) + 1 \; ; x, \mathtt{A}, \mathtt{B} := \mathtt{A}, \mathtt{B}, \mathtt{C} \; ; \mathtt{C} :=? \; ; \\
& \Delta\, E_1 \; ; \mathtt{A} := Rep(expr) \; ; \mathtt{B}, \mathtt{C}, \mathtt{Eflg} :=? \; ; \\
& \Delta\, ldt(adr) + 2 \; ; \mathtt{A}, \mathtt{B}, \mathtt{C} := x, \mathtt{A}, \mathtt{B} \; ; \\
& I_4^{\delta'}(a \cdot \mathtt{stl}(adr) \cdot m_1 \cdot \mathtt{ldl}(adr), b) \; ; x^- \\
= \quad & [\Delta\text{-laws}] \\
& \Delta\, E_1 + 2 * ldt(adr) + 3 \; ; x^+ \; ; x, \mathtt{A}, \mathtt{B} := \mathtt{A}, \mathtt{B}, \mathtt{C} \; ; \mathtt{C} :=? \; ; \\
& \mathtt{A} := Rep(expr) \; ; \mathtt{B}, \mathtt{C}, \mathtt{Eflg} :=? \; ; \\
& \mathtt{A}, \mathtt{B}, \mathtt{C} := x, \mathtt{A}, \mathtt{B} \; ; \\
& I_4^{\delta'}(a \cdot \mathtt{stl}(adr) \cdot m_1 \cdot \mathtt{ldl}(adr), b) \; ; x^- \\
\geq \quad & [(\text{Ch-comm}): Rep(expr) \text{ idp. } \mathtt{C} \text{ and } x, \mathtt{A} \text{ idp. } \mathtt{B}, \mathtt{C}, \mathtt{Eflg}, (\text{Ch-union})] \\
& \Delta\, E_1 + 2 * ldt(adr) + 3 \; ; x^+ \; ; \\
& x, \mathtt{A}, \mathtt{B} := \mathtt{A}, \mathtt{B}, \mathtt{C} \; ; \mathtt{A} := Rep(expr) \; ; \mathtt{A}, \mathtt{B} := x, \mathtt{A} \; ; \\
& \mathtt{C}, \mathtt{Eflg} :=? \; ; I_4^{\delta'}(a \cdot \mathtt{stl}(adr) \cdot m_1 \cdot \mathtt{ldl}(adr), b) \; ; x^-
\end{aligned}
$$

$$\begin{aligned}
= \quad & [(\text{Comb-asg}): \mathit{Rep}(\mathit{expr}) \text{ idp. } x, \mathtt{A}, \mathtt{B}] \\
& \Delta\, E_1 + 2 * \mathit{ldt}(\mathit{adr}) + 3 \;;\; x^+ \;;\; x, \mathtt{A}, \mathtt{B} := \mathtt{A}, \mathtt{A}, \mathit{Rep}(\mathit{expr}) \;; \\
& \mathtt{C}, \mathtt{Eflg} :=? \;;\; I_4^{\delta'}(a \cdot \mathtt{stl}(\mathit{adr}) \cdot m_1 \cdot \mathtt{ldl}(\mathit{adr}), b) \;;\; x^- \\
= \quad & [(\text{Identity-asg}), (\text{Comb-asg})] \\
& \Delta\, E_1 + 2 * \mathit{ldt}(\mathit{adr}) + 3 \;;\; x^+ \;;\; x := \mathtt{A} \;;\; \mathtt{B} := \mathit{Rep}(\mathit{expr}) \;; \\
& \mathtt{C}, \mathtt{Eflg} :=? \;;\; I_4^{\delta'}(a \cdot \mathtt{stl}(\mathit{adr}) \cdot m_1 \cdot \mathtt{ldl}(\mathit{adr}), b) \;;\; x^- \\
\geq \quad & [(\text{Initialization}), (\text{Initial-assign}), (\text{Initial-ch-=})] \\
& \Delta\, E_1 + 2 * \mathit{ldt}(\mathit{adr}) + 3 \;;\; \mathtt{B} := \mathit{Rep}(\mathit{expr}) \;;\; \mathtt{C}, \mathtt{Eflg} :=? \;; \\
& x^+ \;;\; I_4^{\delta'}(a \cdot \mathtt{stl}(\mathit{adr}) \cdot m_1 \cdot \mathtt{ldl}(\mathit{adr}), b) \;;\; x^- \\
= \quad & [\text{Surjective consistent extension theorem (Theorem 10.4.11)}] \\
& \Delta\, E_1 + 2 * \mathit{ldt}(\mathit{adr}) + 3 \;;\; \mathtt{B} := \mathit{Rep}(\mathit{expr}) \;;\; \mathtt{C}, \mathtt{Eflg} :=? \;; \\
& I_4^{\delta}(a \cdot \mathtt{stl}(\mathit{adr}) \cdot m_1 \cdot \mathtt{ldl}(\mathit{adr}), b) \;,
\end{aligned}$$

which shows the claimed property. □

12.2 Programs

Let us now consider translation of TPL programs. Formalizing standard praxis the main part of the code for a program **prog** $(stat)$ is provided by code for the program body *stat* w.r.t. an empty dictionary. We must add a final `stopp` operation because we agreed that TPL programs stop if their body terminates. As the `stopp` operation can absorb arbitrary final delays of the code for the program body and as there is no global timing requirement for complete programs, the timing parameters for the translation of *stat* can be arbitrarily chosen.

Theorem 12.2.1 (Programs). *Suppose* **prog** $(stat) \in \mathsf{Prog}$.
If $\mathsf{CS}(stat, m, \emptyset, L, R, E)$ *then* $\mathsf{CP}(\underline{\mathbf{prog}}\,(stat), m \cdot \mathtt{stopp})$.

Proof. The proof is the calculation

$$\begin{aligned}
& I_5^{\emptyset}(\varepsilon, m \cdot \mathtt{stopp}) \\
\geq \quad & [\Delta\, L \leq \mathsf{Id}] \\
& \Delta\, L \;;\; I_5^{\emptyset}(\varepsilon, m \cdot \mathtt{stopp}) \\
\geq \quad & [\mathsf{CS}(stat, m, \emptyset, L, R, E)] \\
& |\, \mathsf{MS}_{\emptyset}(stat)\, | \preceq E \;;\; \Delta\, R \;;\; I_5^{\emptyset}(m, \mathtt{stopp}) \\
\geq \quad & [(\text{Bound-intro}), \text{Theorem 10.5.2}] \\
& \mathsf{MS}_{\emptyset}(stat) \;;\; \Delta\, R \;;\; \mathsf{Stop} \\
= \quad & [\Delta\text{-stop}] \\
& \mathsf{MS}_{\emptyset}(stat) \;;\; \mathsf{Stop} \\
= \quad & [\text{Definition } \mathsf{MP}] \\
& \mathsf{MP}(\underline{\mathbf{prog}}\,(stat)) \;.
\end{aligned}$$

□

12.3 Statements

We now consider translation of TPL statements. Without much further ado we prove a theorem for each statement constructor. In most cases we do not verbalize the timing conditions. Their exact form usually has been detected during calculation of the proofs and is given in the theorems.

The skip-statement can be implemented by the empty code sequence.

Theorem 12.3.1 (Skip). *If* $R \geq L$ *then* $\mathsf{CS}(\underline{\mathbf{skip}}, \varepsilon, \delta, L, R, E)$.

Proof. For any $a, b \in \mathsf{IS}$ we have

$$\begin{array}{ll} & \Delta L \; ; \; I_5^\delta(a, \varepsilon \cdot b) \\ = & [\mathsf{Id} \text{ is unit of } ;,\ \varepsilon \text{ is unit of concatenation}] \\ & \mathsf{Id} \; ; \; \Delta L \; ; \; I_5^\delta(a \cdot \varepsilon, b) \\ \geq & [(\text{Bound-}\mathsf{Id}),\ (\Delta\text{-refine}){:}\ R \geq L] \\ & |\,\mathsf{Id}\,| \preceq E \; ; \; \Delta R \; ; \; I_5^\delta(a \cdot \varepsilon, b) \\ = & [\text{Definition } \mathsf{MS}] \\ & |\,\mathsf{MS}_V(\underline{\mathbf{skip}})\,| \preceq E \; ; \; \Delta R \; ; \; I_5^\delta(a \cdot \varepsilon, b) \ . \end{array}$$

□

The stop-statement is correctly implemented by the `stopp` operation.

Theorem 12.3.2 (Stop). $\mathsf{CS}(\underline{\mathbf{stop}}, \mathtt{stopp}, \delta, L, R, \infty)$.

Proof. Suppose $a, b \in \mathsf{IS}$ are given.

$$\begin{array}{ll} & \Delta L \; ; \; I_5^\delta(a, \mathtt{stopp} \cdot b) \\ \geq & [10.5.2] \\ & \Delta L \; ; \; \mathsf{Stop} \\ = & [(\Delta\text{-stop}),\ (\text{Stop-zero})] \\ & \mathsf{Stop} \; ; \; \Delta R \; ; \; I_5^\delta(a \cdot \mathtt{stopp}, b) \\ = & [\text{Void-bound}] \\ & |\,\mathsf{Stop}\,| \preceq \infty \; ; \; \Delta R \; ; \; I_5^\delta(a \cdot \mathtt{stopp}, b) \\ = & [\text{Definition } \mathsf{MS}] \\ & |\,\mathsf{MS}_V(\underline{\mathbf{stop}})\,| \preceq \infty \; ; \; \Delta R \; ; \; I_5^\delta(a \cdot \mathtt{stopp}, b) \ . \end{array}$$

□

The proposed code for an assignment statement $\underline{\mathbf{assign}}(x, expr) \in \mathsf{Stat}_V$ is composed from code that evaluates *expr* and a `stl`-instruction that stores the result value to the location allocated for x.

Theorem 12.3.3 (Assignments). *Suppose given an assignment statement* $\underline{\mathbf{assign}}(x, expr) \in \mathsf{Stat}_V$. *If*

(a) $\mathsf{CE}(expr, m_1, \delta, E_1)$,

(b) $m = m_1 \cdot \mathtt{stl}(adr_x)$,

(c) $R \geq L + E_1 + ldt(adr_x) + 1$, *and*

(d) $R_x = R_{\mathsf{Val}_x}$

then $\mathsf{CS}(\underline{\textbf{assign}}\,(x, expr), m, \delta, L, R, E)$.

Condition (d) requires that x is represented in the standard way. If x is represented differently we have to add code that adapts the standard representation used by the expression code.

Proof. For arbitrary $a, b \in \mathsf{IS}$ we have

$$
\begin{array}{ll}
 & \Delta L \; ; \; I_5^\delta(a, m_1 \cdot \mathtt{stl}(adr_x) \cdot b) \\
\geq & [\mathsf{CE}(expr, m_1, \delta, E_1), \text{ Lemma 12.1.2}] \\
 & \Delta L \; ; \; \Delta E_1 \; ; \; Reg^+ \; ; \; \mathtt{A} := Rep(expr) \; ; \; I_4^\delta(a \cdot m_1, \mathtt{stl}(adr_x) \cdot b) \; ; \; Reg^- \\
\geq & [(\Delta\text{-add}), \text{ Theorems 10.4.2 and 10.4.6 applied to } e = \mathsf{ME}_V(expr)] \\
 & \Delta L + E_1 \; ; \; Reg^+ \; ; \; \mathtt{A} := Rep(expr) \; ; \\
 & \Delta\, ldt(adr_x) + 1 \; ; \; \{(\mathsf{ME}_V(expr), \mathtt{A}) \in R_x\} \; ; \; x, \mathtt{A}, \mathtt{B} := \mathsf{ME}_V(expr), \mathtt{B}, \mathtt{C} \; ; \; \mathtt{C} :=? \; ; \\
 & I_4^\delta(a \cdot m_1 \cdot \mathtt{stl}(adr_x), b) \; ; \; Reg^- \\
\geq & [\Delta\text{-laws}, \; m = m_1 \cdot \mathtt{stl}(adr_x), \text{ (Conv1)}] \\
 & \Delta L + E_1 + ldt(adr_x) + 1 \; ; \; Reg^+ \; ; \; \mathtt{A} := Rep(expr) \; ; \\
 & \{(\mathsf{ME}_V(expr), \mathtt{A}) \in R_x\} \; ; \; x := \mathsf{ME}_V(expr) \; ; \; \mathtt{A}, \mathtt{B}, \mathtt{C} :=? \; ; \\
 & I_4^\delta(a \cdot m, b) \; ; \; Reg^- \\
\geq & [(\Delta\text{-refine}): R \geq L + E_1 + ldt(adr_x) + 1, \text{ (Assign-assert)}] \\
 & \Delta R \; ; \; Reg^+ \; ; \; \{(\mathsf{ME}_V(expr), Rep(expr)) \in R_x\} \; ; \\
 & \mathtt{A} := Rep(expr) \; ; \; x := \mathsf{ME}_V(expr) \; ; \; \mathtt{A}, \mathtt{B}, \mathtt{C} :=? \; ; \\
 & I_4^\delta(a \cdot m, b) \; ; \; Reg^- \\
= & [(\mathsf{ME}_V(expr), Rep(expr)) \in R_x \text{ equals } \mathsf{true} \text{ (see below)}] \\
 & \Delta R \; ; \; Reg^+ \; ; \; \mathtt{A} := Rep(expr) \; ; \; x := \mathsf{ME}_V(expr) \; ; \; \mathtt{A}, \mathtt{B}, \mathtt{C} :=? \; ; \\
 & I_4^\delta(a \cdot m, b) \; ; \; Reg^- \\
\geq & [\text{(Initialization), (Initial-assign), (Ch-initialization-=)}] \\
 & \Delta R \; ; \; x := \mathsf{ME}_V(expr) \; ; \; Reg^+ \; ; \; I_4^\delta(a \cdot m, b) \; ; \; Reg^- \\
= & [(\Delta\text{-assign}), \text{ (Bound-asg)}] \\
 & |\, x := \mathsf{ME}_V(expr) \,| \preceq E \; ; \; \Delta R \; ; \; Reg^+ \; ; \; I_4^\delta(a \cdot m, b) \; ; \; Reg^- \\
= & [\text{Definitions } \mathsf{MS} \text{ and } I_5^\delta] \\
 & |\, \mathsf{MS}_V(\underline{\textbf{assign}}\,(x, expr)) \,| \preceq E \; ; \; \Delta R \; ; \; I_5^\delta(a \cdot m, b) \; .
\end{array}
$$

It remains to be shown that $(\mathsf{ME}_V(expr), Rep(expr)) \in R_x$ equals true. First of all, $\mathsf{Val}_x = \mathsf{SE}(expr)(V)$ and $x \in V$ because $\underline{\textbf{assign}}\,(x, expr) \in \mathsf{Stat}_V$ is well-formed. Thus

$$
\begin{array}{ll}
 & (\mathsf{ME}_V(expr), Rep(expr)) \\
= & [\text{Definition of } Rep, \; \mathsf{Val}_x = \mathsf{SE}(expr)(V)] \\
 & (\mathsf{ME}_V(expr), R_{\mathsf{Val}_x}(\mathsf{ME}_V(expr))) \\
\in & [\text{Trivial}] \\
 & R_{\mathsf{Val}_x}
\end{array}
$$

$$
\begin{aligned}
= &\quad \text{[Assumption]}\\
&R_x \ .
\end{aligned}
$$

This completes the proof. □

The next theorem is concerned with translation of output statements.

Theorem 12.3.4 (Output statements). *Suppose given an output statement* **output** $(\mathtt{Out_i}, expr) \in \mathsf{Stat}_V$ *$(0 \le i \le 3)$. If*

(a) $\mathsf{CE}(expr, m_1, \delta, E_1)$,

(b) $m \ = \ m_1 \cdot \mathtt{mint} \cdot \mathtt{ldc}(i) \cdot \mathtt{bcnt} \cdot \mathtt{add} \cdot \mathtt{rev} \cdot \mathtt{outword}$,

(c) $R \ \ge \ outdelay_2$, *and*

(d) $E \ \ge \ L + E_1 + outdelay_1 + 8$

then $\mathsf{CS}($**output** $(\mathtt{Out_i}, expr), m, \delta, L, R, E)$.

Proof. Let $m' = \mathtt{mint} \cdot \mathtt{ldc}(i) \cdot \mathtt{bcnt} \cdot \mathtt{add} \cdot \mathtt{rev}$, i.e. $m = m_1 \cdot m' \cdot \mathtt{outword}$. Note first that $expr$ is a word expression because **output** $(\mathtt{Out_i}, expr)$ is well-formed. Moreover, for arbitrary code sequences c, d

$$
\begin{aligned}
&I_4^\delta(c, m' \cdot \mathtt{outword} \cdot d)\\
\ge &\quad \text{[Theorems 10.4.2, Tables 10.8 \& 10.9]}\\
&\Delta 2 \ ; \mathtt{A}, \mathtt{B}, \mathtt{C} := \mathsf{MostNeg}, \mathtt{A}, \mathtt{B} \ ;\\
&\Delta \, ldt(i) + 1 \ ; \mathtt{A}, \mathtt{B}, \mathtt{C} := i, \mathtt{A}, \mathtt{B} \ ;\\
&\Delta 3 \ ; \mathtt{A} := \mathtt{A} * bpw \ ;\\
&\Delta 1 \ ; \mathtt{A}, \mathtt{B}, \mathtt{Eflg} := \mathtt{B} + \mathtt{A}, \mathtt{C}, \mathtt{Eflg} \vee AddOvFl(\mathtt{B}, \mathtt{A}) \ ; \mathtt{C} :=? \ ;\\
&\Delta 1 \ ; \mathtt{A}, \mathtt{B} := \mathtt{B}, \mathtt{A} \ ;\\
&I_4^\delta(c \cdot m', \mathtt{outword} \cdot d)\\
\ge &\quad [(\Delta\text{-assign}), (\Delta\text{-choice}), (\Delta\text{-add}), \ ldt(i) = 0 \text{ since } 0 \le i \le 3]\\
&\Delta 8 \ ; \mathtt{A}, \mathtt{B}, \mathtt{C} := \mathsf{MostNeg}, \mathtt{A}, \mathtt{B} \ ;\\
&\mathtt{A}, \mathtt{B}, \mathtt{C} := i, \mathtt{A}, \mathtt{B} \ ;\\
&\mathtt{A} := \mathtt{A} * bpw \ ;\\
&\mathtt{A}, \mathtt{B}, \mathtt{Eflg} := \mathtt{B} + \mathtt{A}, \mathtt{C}, \mathtt{Eflg} \vee AddOvFl(\mathtt{B}, \mathtt{A}) \ ; \mathtt{C} :=? \ ;\\
&\mathtt{A}, \mathtt{B} := \mathtt{B}, \mathtt{A} \ ;\\
&I_4^\delta(c \cdot m', \mathtt{outword} \cdot d)\\
\ge &\quad \text{[(Conv1), (Ch-asg)]}\\
&\Delta 8 \ ; \mathtt{A}, \mathtt{B}, \mathtt{C} := \mathsf{MostNeg}, \mathtt{A}, \mathtt{B} \ ;\\
&\mathtt{A}, \mathtt{B}, \mathtt{C} := i, \mathtt{A}, \mathtt{B} \ ;\\
&\mathtt{A} := \mathtt{A} * bpw \ ;\\
&\mathtt{A}, \mathtt{B} := \mathtt{B} + \mathtt{A}, \mathtt{C} \ ;\\
&\mathtt{A}, \mathtt{B} := \mathtt{B}, \mathtt{A} \ ; \mathtt{C}, \mathtt{Eflg} :=? \ ;\\
&I_4^\delta(c \cdot m', \mathtt{outword} \cdot d)\\
\ge &\quad \text{[Comb-asg]}\\
&\Delta 8 \ ; \mathtt{A}, \mathtt{B}, C := \mathtt{A}, \mathsf{MostNeg} + i * bpw, \mathtt{A} \ ; \mathtt{C}, \mathtt{Eflg} :=? \ ; I_4^\delta(c \cdot m', \mathtt{outword} \cdot d)\\
\ge &\quad \text{[(Identity-asg), (Conv1), Theorem 10.4.2, (10.92)]}\\
&\Delta 8 \ ; \mathtt{B} := \mathsf{MostNeg} + i * bpw \ ; \mathtt{C}, \mathtt{Eflg} :=? \ ;
\end{aligned}
$$

$\{\mathtt{B} = \mathit{Index}(\mathsf{MostNeg}, i)\}$; $\Delta\, outdelay_1$; $\mathtt{Out_i}\,!\,\mathtt{A}$; $\mathtt{A,B,C} :=?$; $\Delta\, outdelay_2$;
$I_4^\delta(c \cdot m' \cdot \mathtt{outword}, d)$

$=$ [(Ch-assert1), (Assign-assert)]
$\Delta\, 8$; $\{\mathsf{MostNeg} + i * bpw = \mathit{Index}(\mathsf{MostNeg}, i)\}$; $\mathtt{B} := \mathsf{MostNeg} + i * bpw$;
$\mathtt{C,Eflg} :=?$; $\Delta\, outdelay_1$; $\mathtt{Out_i}\,!\,\mathtt{A}$; $\mathtt{A,B,C} :=?$; $\Delta\, outdelay_2$;
$I_4^\delta(c \cdot m' \cdot \mathtt{outword}, d)$

$=$ [Def. Index: $\{\mathsf{MostNeg} + i * bpw = \mathit{Index}(\mathsf{MostNeg}, i)\} = \{\mathsf{true}\} = \mathsf{Id}$]
$\Delta\, 8$; $\mathtt{B} := \mathsf{MostNeg} + i * bpw$;
$\mathtt{C,Eflg} :=?$; $\Delta\, outdelay_1$; $\mathtt{Out_i}\,!\,\mathtt{A}$; $\mathtt{A,B,C} :=?$; $\Delta\, outdelay_2$;
$I_4^\delta(c \cdot m' \cdot \mathtt{outword}, d)$

$\geq$ [(Conv1), Δ-laws]
$\Delta\, outdelay_1 + 8$; $\mathtt{B,C,Eflg} :=?$; $\mathtt{Out_i}\,!\,\mathtt{A}$; $\mathtt{A,B,C} :=?$; $\Delta\, outdelay_2$;
$I_4^\delta(c \cdot m' \cdot \mathtt{outword}, d)$

$\geq$ [(Ch-ass-output), (Ch-union)]
$\Delta\, outdelay_1 + 8$; $\mathtt{Out_i}\,!\,\mathtt{A}$; $\mathtt{A,B,C,Eflg} :=?$; $\Delta\, outdelay_2$;
$I_4^\delta(c \cdot m' \cdot \mathtt{outword}, d)$.

Using this inequation we prove $\mathsf{CS}(\underline{\mathbf{output}}\,(\mathtt{Out_i}, expr), m, \delta, L, R, E)$ by the following calculation that applies to arbitrary $a, b \in \mathsf{IS}$:

$\Delta\, L$; $I_5^\delta(a, m \cdot b)$

$\geq$ [$\mathsf{CE}(expr, m_1, \delta, E_1)$, Lemma 12.1.2, above calculation]
$\Delta\, L$; $\Delta\, E_1$; Reg^+ ; $\mathtt{A} := Rep(expr)$;
$\Delta\, outdelay_1 + 8$; $\mathtt{Out_i}\,!\,\mathtt{A}$; $\mathtt{A,B,C,Eflg} :=?$;
$\Delta\, outdelay_2$; $I_4^\delta(a \cdot m, b)$; Reg^-

$=$ [Δ-laws]
$\Delta\, L + E_1 + outdelay_1 + 8$; Reg^+ ; $\mathtt{A} := Rep(expr)$;
$\mathtt{Out_i}\,!\,\mathtt{A}$; $\mathtt{A,B,C,Eflg} :=?$;
$\Delta\, outdelay_2$; $I_4^\delta(a \cdot m, b)$; Reg^-

$=$ [(Δ-refine): $E \geq L + E_1 + outdelay_1 + 8$, (Assign-output), (Cancel1)]
$\Delta\, E$; Reg^+ ; $\mathtt{Out_i}\,!\,Rep(expr)$; $\mathtt{A,B,C,Eflg} :=?$;
$\Delta\, outdelay_2$; $I_4^\delta(a \cdot m, b)$; Reg^-

$=$ [$expr$ is word expr; so $Rep(expr) = \mathsf{ME}(expr)$]
$\Delta\, E$; Reg^+ ; $\mathtt{Out_i}\,!\,\mathsf{ME}(expr)$; $\mathtt{A,B,C,Eflg} :=?$;
$\Delta\, outdelay_2$; $I_4^\delta(a \cdot m, b)$; Reg^-

$=$ [(Initial-output): $\mathsf{ME}(expr)$ idp Reg, (Ch-initialization-=), (Initial-Δ)]
$\Delta\, E$; $\mathtt{Out_i}\,!\,\mathsf{ME}(expr)$; $\Delta\, outdelay_2$; Reg^+ ; $I_4^\delta(a \cdot m, b)$; Reg^-

$=$ [(Δ-bound), (Bound-final), Definition I_5^δ]
$|\, \Delta\, \infty$; $\mathtt{Out_i}\,!\,\mathsf{ME}(expr)\,| \preceq E$; $\Delta\, outdelay_2$; $I_5^\delta(a \cdot m, b)$

$\geq$ [(Δ-refine): $R \geq outdelay_2$, def. MS]
$|\, \mathsf{MS}(\underline{\mathbf{output}}\,(\mathtt{Out_i}, expr))\,| \preceq E$; $\Delta\, R$; $I_5^\delta(a \cdot m, b)$. □

Input statements can be translated as follows.

Theorem 12.3.5 (Input statements). *Suppose given an input statement* $\underline{\textbf{input}}\,(\texttt{In}_\texttt{i}, x) \in \mathsf{Stat}_V$ $(0 \le i \le 3)$. *If*

(a) $m \;=\; \texttt{ldlp}(adr_x) \cdot \texttt{mint} \cdot \texttt{ldc}(i+4) \cdot \texttt{bcnt} \cdot \texttt{add} \cdot \texttt{ldc}(1) \cdot \texttt{bcnt} \cdot \texttt{in},$

(b) $R \;\ge\; indelay_2$, *and*

(c) $E \;\ge\; L + ldt(adr_x) + indelay_1 + 12$

then $\mathsf{CS}(\underline{\textbf{input}}\,(\texttt{In}_\texttt{i}, x), m, \delta, L, R, E)$.

Proof. The proof is similar to the one for output statement translation. □

As expected a sequential composition can be implemented by the concatenation of code for the component statements. The code for the second statement must be prepared to absorb (at least) the excess time exported by the code for the first statement.

Theorem 12.3.6 (Sequential composition). *If*

(a) $\mathsf{CS}(stat_1, m_1, \delta, L_1, R_1, E_1)$,

(b) $\mathsf{CS}(stat_2, m_2, \delta, L_2, R_2, E_2)$, *and*

(c) $R_1 \le L_2$

then $\mathsf{CS}(\underline{\textbf{seq}}\,(stat_1, stat_2), m_1 \cdot m_2, \delta, L_1, R_2, E_1 + E_2)$.

Proof. By definition of CS we have $stat_1, stat_2 \in \mathsf{Stat}_V$, which implies that $\underline{\textbf{seq}}\,(stat_1, stat_2) \in \mathsf{Stat}_V$. Moreover, we have for arbitrary $a, b \in \mathsf{IS}$

$$\begin{array}{ll}
& \Delta\, L_1 \;;\; I_5^\delta(a, m_1 \cdot m_2 \cdot b) \\
\ge & [\mathsf{CS}(stat_1, m_1, \delta, L_1, R_1, E_1)] \\
& |\,\mathsf{MS}_V(stat_1)\,| \preceq E_1 \;;\; \Delta\, R_1 \;;\; I_5^\delta(a \cdot m_1, m_2 \cdot b) \\
\ge & [(\Delta\text{-refine}): R_1 \le L_2] \\
& |\,\mathsf{MS}_V(stat_1)\,| \preceq E_1 \;;\; \Delta\, L_2 \;;\; I_5^\delta(a \cdot m_1, m_2 \cdot b) \\
\ge & [\mathsf{CS}(stat_2, m_2, \delta, L_2, R_2, E_2)] \\
& |\,\mathsf{MS}_V(stat_1)\,| \preceq E_1 \;;\; |\,\mathsf{MS}_V(stat_2)\,| \preceq E_2 \;;\; \Delta\, R_2 \;;\; I_5^\delta(a \cdot m_1 \cdot m_2, b) \\
\ge & [\text{Bound-add}] \\
& |\,\mathsf{MS}_V(stat_1) \;;\; \mathsf{MS}_V(stat_2)\,| \preceq E_1 + E_2 \;;\; \Delta\, R_2 \;;\; I_5^\delta(a \cdot m_1 \cdot m_2, b) \\
= & [\text{Definition } \mathsf{MS}] \\
& |\,\mathsf{MS}_V(\underline{\textbf{seq}}\,(stat_1, stat_2))\,| \preceq E_1 + E_2 \;;\; \Delta\, R_2 \;;\; I_5^\delta(a \cdot m_1 \cdot m_2, b)\;.
\end{array}$$

□

Checking time bounds is quite simple because the parameter E of the correctness predicate has been introduced for this very purpose. A compiler encountering an upper bound operator in the source statement only needs to check whether the required time bound is more liberal than the one asserted for the code generated for the enclosed statement. If it is, no further action is necessary, as the real-time requirement expressed by the bound is met. If it is less liberal, on the other hand, the source statement cannot be adequately compiled with the given code generation strategy, and should be rejected.

Theorem 12.3.7 (Time bounds). *If* $\mathsf{CS}(stat, m, \delta, L, R, E)$ *and* $E \leq t$ *then* $\mathsf{CS}(\underline{\textbf{upperbound}}(stat, t), m, \delta, L, R, E)$.

Proof. According to the definition of CS, we have $stat \in \mathsf{Stat}_V$. This implies $\underline{\textbf{upperbound}}(stat, t) \in \mathsf{Stat}_V$. Moreover, for all $a, b \in \mathsf{IS}$:

$$\begin{aligned}
& \Delta L \ ; \ I_5^\delta(a, m \cdot b) \\
\geq \quad & [\mathsf{CS}(stat, m, \delta, L, R, E)] \\
& |\, \mathsf{MS}_V(stat) \,| \preceq E \ ; \ \Delta R \ ; \ I_5^\delta(a \cdot m, b) \\
= \quad & [\text{(Bound-comb)}, \ Min(E, t) = E \text{ as } E \leq t] \\
& |\,|\, \mathsf{MS}_V(stat) \,| \preceq t \,| \preceq E \ ; \ \Delta R \ ; \ I_5^\delta(a \cdot m, b) \\
= \quad & [\text{Definition MS}] \\
& |\, \mathsf{MS}_V(\underline{\textbf{upperbound}}(stat, t)) \,| \preceq E \ ; \ \Delta R \ ; \ I_5^\delta(a \cdot m, b) \ .
\end{aligned}$$

□

Formalizing standard practice the code for a block $\underline{\textbf{block}}(x, stat)$ w.r.t. a dictionary δ is provided essentially by code for *stat* w.r.t. a dictionary with an additional binding for x to a new location. As discussed in Sect. 10.4 the location for x must be initialized with a (word) value that has an abstract counterpart. Block code is thus composed of an initialization code piece for x and the code for the body *stat*. The code for *stat* must – in addition to the delay that is to be absorbed by the block – absorb the delay caused by the initialization code.

Theorem 12.3.8 (Blocks). *Suppose* $\underline{\textbf{block}}(x, stat) \in \mathsf{Stat}_V$, $i \in \mathsf{DictInfo}$. *If*

(a) (x, i) *is consistent with* δ,

(b) $\mathsf{IC}(m_0, i, E_0)$, *and*

(c) $\mathsf{CS}(stat, m_1, \delta \cup \{(x, i)\}, L + E_0, R, E)$

then $\mathsf{CS}(\underline{\textbf{block}}(x, stat), m_0 \cdot m_1, \delta, L, R, E)$.

Condition (a) ensures that actually a new location has been chosen and condition (b) says that execution of m_0 initializes the workspace location allocated for variable x.

Proof. The proof is essentially an application of the consistent extension theorem (Theorem 10.5.3). For arbitrary $a, b \in \mathsf{IS}$

$$\begin{aligned}
& \Delta L \ ; \ I_5^\delta(a, m_0 \cdot m_1 \cdot b) \\
\geq \quad & [\text{Consistent extension theorem (Theorem 10.5.3), (b) using } \mathsf{IC}(m_0, i, E_0)] \\
& \Delta L \ ; \ \Delta E_0 \ ; \ x^+ \ ; \ I_5^{\delta \cup \{(x,i)\}}(a \cdot m_0, m_1 \cdot b) \ ; \ x^- \\
= \quad & [(\Delta\text{-add}), (\text{Initial-}\Delta)] \\
& x^+ \ ; \ \Delta L + E_0 \ ; \ I_5^{\delta \cup \{(x,i)\}}(a \cdot m_0, m_1 \cdot b) \ ; \ x^- \\
\geq \quad & [\mathsf{CS}(stat, m_1, \delta \cup \{(x, i)\}, L + E_0, R, E)] \\
& x^+ \ ; \ \big|\, \mathsf{MS}_{V \cup \{x\}}(stat) \,\big| \preceq E \ ; \ \Delta R \ ; \ I_5^{\delta \cup \{(x,i)\}}(a \cdot m_0 \cdot m_1, b) \ ; \ x^-
\end{aligned}$$

$$\begin{aligned}
\geq\ & [\text{--+-sim, (Initial-}\Delta)] \\
& x^+ \ ;\ \big|\,\mathsf{MS}_{V\cup\{x\}}(\mathit{stat})\,\big| \preceq E \ ;\ x^- \ ;\ \Delta R \ ;\ x^+ \ ;\ I_5^{\delta\cup\{(x,i)\}}(a\cdot m_0\cdot m_1, b) \ ;\ x^- \\
\geq\ & [\text{Consistent extension theorem (Theorem 10.5.3), (a)}] \\
& x^+ \ ;\ \big|\,\mathsf{MS}_{V\cup\{x\}}(\mathit{stat})\,\big| \preceq E \ ;\ x^- \ ;\ \Delta R \ ;\ I_5^{\delta}(a\cdot m_0\cdot m_1, b) \\
=\ & [\text{(Bound-initial), (Bound-final)}] \\
& \big|\,x^+ \ ;\ \mathsf{MS}_{V\cup\{x\}}(\mathit{stat}) \ ;\ x^-\,\big| \preceq E \ ;\ \Delta R \ ;\ I_5^{\delta}(a\cdot m_0\cdot m_1, b) \\
=\ & [\text{Definition } \mathsf{MS}] \\
& |\,\mathsf{MS}_V(\,\underline{\mathbf{block}}\,(x,\mathit{stat}))\,| \preceq E \ ;\ \Delta R \ ;\ I_5^{\delta}(a\cdot m_0\cdot m_1, b)\ .
\end{aligned}$$

□

Having established the block translation theorem, it is interesting to study concrete initialization code patterns. In well-formed TPL programs all declared variables have domain Bool or Word. The representation conventions for these variables are fixed by the dictionary δ. In practice the standard conventions described by the relations R_{Bool} and R_{Word} are used. Concrete initialization code pattern for variables that are represented according to these relations are provided by the next theorem.

As words are represented by themselves, locations for word variables need not be initialized, which means that the empty code sequence is correct initialization code. For Boolean variables it is sufficient to write the value 0 to the allocated location *adr*, which can be achieved by the code sequence $\texttt{ldc}(0)\cdot\texttt{stl}(\mathit{adr})$. (Another possibility is, of course, to write the value 1.)

Theorem 12.3.9 (Initialization code). *Let* $i = (T, R, \mathit{adr}) \in \mathsf{DictInfo}$.

(a) If $T = \mathsf{Word}$ *and* $R = R_{\mathsf{Word}}$ *then* $\mathsf{IC}(\varepsilon, i, 0)$.

(b) If $T = \mathsf{Bool}$ *and* $R = R_{\mathsf{Bool}}$ *then* $\mathsf{IC}(\texttt{ldc}(0)\cdot\texttt{stl}(\mathit{adr}), i, \mathit{ldt}(\mathit{adr})+2)$.

Proof. (a): Suppose $T = \mathsf{Word}$ and $R = R_{\mathsf{Word}}$. Choose $e \equiv \texttt{Wsp}(\mathit{adr})$. Clearly, $\mathsf{rng}\, e \subseteq \mathsf{rng}\, R$ because $\mathsf{rng}\, R = \mathsf{Word}$. Moreover,

$$\begin{aligned}
& I_3(a, \varepsilon\cdot b) \\
\geq\ & [\varepsilon \text{ is unit of concatenation, } (\Delta\text{-void}), \text{(Identity-asg), (Ch-Id)}] \\
& \Delta\, 0 \ ;\ \texttt{Wsp}[\mathit{adr}] := e \ ;\ \texttt{A},\texttt{B},\texttt{C},\texttt{Eflg} :=?\ ;\ I_3(a\cdot\varepsilon, b)\ .
\end{aligned}$$

(b): Suppose $T = \mathsf{Bool}$ and $R = R_{\mathsf{Word}}$. Choose $e \equiv 0$. Then $\mathsf{rng}\, e = \{0\} \subseteq \mathsf{rng}\, R_{\mathsf{Bool}} = R$. Furthermore,

$$\begin{aligned}
& I_3(a, \texttt{ldc}(0)\cdot\texttt{stl}(\mathit{adr})\cdot b) \\
\geq\ & [\text{Gen. instr. theorem, (10.57), (10.59): } 0 \leq \mathit{adr} \leq l_{\mathrm{W}} \text{ since } i \in \mathsf{DictInfo}] \\
& \Delta\, \mathit{ldt}(0)+1 \ ;\ \texttt{A},\texttt{B},\texttt{C} := 0,\texttt{A},\texttt{B}\ ; \\
& \Delta\, \mathit{ldt}(\mathit{adr})+1 \ ;\ \texttt{Wsp}[\mathit{adr}],\texttt{A},\texttt{B} := \texttt{A},\texttt{B},\texttt{C}\ ;\ \texttt{C} :=?\ ; \\
& I_3(a\cdot\texttt{ldc}(0)\cdot\texttt{stl}(\mathit{adr}), b) \\
=\ & [(\Delta\text{-assign}), (\Delta\text{-add}), \mathit{ldt}(0) = 0, \text{(Comb-asg)}] \\
& \Delta\, \mathit{ldt}(\mathit{adr})+2 \ ;\ \texttt{Wsp}[\mathit{adr}],\texttt{A},\texttt{B},\texttt{C} := 0,\texttt{A},\texttt{B},\texttt{B}\ ;\ \texttt{C} :=?\ ; \\
& I_3(a\cdot\texttt{ldc}(0)\cdot\texttt{stl}(\mathit{adr}), b)
\end{aligned}$$

$\geq$ [$e \equiv 0$, (Conv1), (Ch-Id)]
$\Delta\, ldt(adr) + 2$; $\mathtt{Wsp}[adr] := e$; $\mathtt{A},\mathtt{B},\mathtt{C},\mathtt{Eflg} :=?$;
$I_3(a \cdot \mathtt{ldc}(0) \cdot \mathtt{stl}(adr), b)$. □

We now consider translation of conditionals. The proposed code is straightforward

Theorem 12.3.10 (Conditionals). *Suppose* $\underline{\mathbf{if}}(expr, stat_1, stat_2) \in \mathsf{Stat}_V$. *If*

(a) $\mathsf{CE}(expr, m_0, \delta, E_0)$,
(b) $\mathsf{CS}(stat_1, m_1, \delta, L_1, R_1, E_1)$,
(c) $\mathsf{CS}(stat_2, m_2, \delta, L_2, R_2, E_2)$,
(d) $m \;=\; m_0 \cdot \mathtt{cj}(w_1) \cdot m_1 \cdot \mathtt{j}(w_2) \cdot m_2$,
(e) $w_1 \;=\; |\, m_1 \cdot \mathtt{j}(w_2)\,|$ *and* $w_2 \;=\; |\, m_2\,|$,
(f) $L_1 \;\geq\; L + E_0 + ldt(w_1) + 2$ *and* $L_2 \;\geq\; L + E_0 + ldt(w_1) + 4$,
(g) $R \;\geq\; \mathsf{Max}\{R_1 + ldt(w_2) + 3, R_2\}$, *and*
(h) $E \;\geq\; \mathsf{Max}\{E_1, E_2\}$

then $\mathsf{CS}(\underline{\mathbf{if}}(expr, stat_1, stat_2), m, \delta, L, R, E)$.

Proof. Let $a, b \in \mathsf{IS}$.

ΔL ; $I_5^\delta(a, m_0 \cdot \mathtt{cj}(w_1) \cdot m_1 \cdot \mathtt{j}(w_2) \cdot m_2 \cdot b)$
$\geq$ [Lemma 12.1.5: cond. (e) implies $w_1 = |\, m_1 \cdot \mathtt{j}(w_2) \cdot m_2 \cdot b\,| - |\, m_2 \cdot b\,|$]
ΔL ;
$(\Delta E_0 + ldt(w_1) + 2$; $I_5^\delta(a \cdot m_0 \cdot \mathtt{cj}(w_1), m_1 \cdot \mathtt{j}(w_2) \cdot m_2 \cdot b))$
$\lhd\, \mathsf{ME}(expr) \rhd$
$(\Delta E_0 + ldt(w_1) + 4$; $I_5^\delta(a \cdot m_0 \cdot \mathtt{cj}(w_1) \cdot m_1 \cdot \mathtt{j}(w_2), m_2 \cdot b))$
$\geq$ [(Δ-cond), (Δ-add)]
$(\Delta L + E_0 + ldt(w_1) + 2$; $I_5^\delta(a \cdot m_0 \cdot \mathtt{cj}(w_1), m_1 \cdot \mathtt{j}(w_2) \cdot m_2 \cdot b))$
$\lhd\, \mathsf{ME}(expr) \rhd$
$(\Delta L + E_0 + ldt(w_1) + 4$; $I_5^\delta(a \cdot m_0 \cdot \mathtt{cj}(w_1) \cdot m_1 \cdot \mathtt{j}(w_2), m_2 \cdot b))$
$\geq$ [(Δ-refine): condition (f)]
$(\Delta L_1$; $I_5^\delta(a \cdot m_0 \cdot \mathtt{cj}(w_1), m_1 \cdot \mathtt{j}(w_2) \cdot m_2 \cdot b))$
$\lhd\, \mathsf{ME}(expr) \rhd$
$(\Delta L_2$; $I_5^\delta(a \cdot m_0 \cdot \mathtt{cj}(w_1) \cdot m_1 \cdot \mathtt{j}(w_2), m_2 \cdot b))$
$\geq$ [$\mathsf{CS}(P_1, m_1, \delta, L_1, R_1, E_1)$ and $\mathsf{CS}(stat_2, m_2, \delta, L_2, R_2, E_2)$]
$(|\, \mathsf{MS}(stat_1)\,| \preceq E_1$; ΔR_1 ; $I_5^\delta(a \cdot m_0 \cdot \mathtt{cj}(w_1) \cdot m_1, \mathtt{j}(w_2) \cdot m_2 \cdot b))$
$\lhd\, \mathsf{ME}(expr) \rhd$
$(|\, \mathsf{MS}(stat_2)\,| \preceq E_2$; ΔR_2 ; $I_5^\delta(a \cdot m, b))$
$\geq$ [Theorem 10.5.1: condition (e) implies $w_2 = |\, m_2 \cdot b\,| - |\, b\,|$]
$(|\, \mathsf{MS}(stat_1)\,| \preceq E_1$; ΔR_1 ; $\Delta\, ldt(w_2) + 3$; $I_5^\delta(a \cdot m, b))$
$\lhd\, \mathsf{ME}(expr) \rhd$

$$(|\mathsf{MS}(stat_2)| \preceq E_2 \,;\, \Delta R_2 \,;\, I_5^\delta(a\cdot m, b))$$

$\geq$ [(Δ-add), (Δ-refine): condition (g), (Bound-refine): condition (h)]

$$(|\mathsf{MS}(stat_1)| \preceq E \,;\, \Delta R \,;\, I_5^\delta(a\cdot m, b))$$
$$\lhd\ \mathsf{ME}(expr)\ \rhd$$
$$(|\mathsf{MS}(stat_2)| \preceq E \,;\, \Delta R \,;\, I_5^\delta(a\cdot m, b))$$

$=$ [;-cond-leftwards]

$$((|\mathsf{MS}(stat_1)| \preceq E) \lhd \mathsf{ME}(expr) \rhd (|\mathsf{MS}(stat_2)| \preceq E)) \,;\, \Delta R \,;\, I_5^\delta(a\cdot m, b)$$

$=$ [Bound-cond]

$$|\mathsf{MS}(stat_1) \lhd \mathsf{ME}(expr) \rhd \mathsf{MS}(stat_2)| \preceq E \,;\, \Delta R \,;\, I_5^\delta(a\cdot m, b)$$

$=$ [Definition MS]

$$|\mathsf{MS}(\underline{\mathbf{if}}(expr, stat_1, stat_2))| \preceq E \,;\, \Delta R \,;\, I_5^\delta(a\cdot m, b)\ . \qquad \square$$

Loop code is composed of code for evaluation of the guard and code for the body glued together by some jumps. While the code is straightforward it is difficult to guess correct timing conditions. They are, however, easily detected during the proof, which is an advantage of a formal approach.

Theorem 12.3.11 (While-loops). *Let* $\underline{\mathbf{while}}(expr, stat) \in \mathsf{Stat}_V$ *be a loop statement. If*

(a) $\mathsf{CE}(expr, m_0, \delta, E_0)$,
(b) $\mathsf{CS}(stat, m_1, \delta, L_1, R_1, E_1)$,
(c) $m = m_0 \cdot \mathsf{cj}(w_1) \cdot m_1 \cdot \mathsf{j}(w_2)$,
(d) $w_1 = |m_1 \cdot \mathsf{j}(w_2)|$ *and* $w_2 = -|m|$,
(e) $L_1 \geq L + E_0 + ldt(w_1) + 2$,
(f) $L \geq R_1 + ldt(w_2) + 3$, *and*
(g) $R \geq L + E_0 + ldt(w_1) + 4$

then $\mathsf{CS}(\underline{\mathbf{while}}(expr, stat), m, \delta, L, R, \infty)$.

Proof. Let $W \in (\mathsf{Proc}_V \to \mathsf{Proc}_V)$, $W(X) = (\mathsf{MS}(stat) \,;\, X) \lhd \mathsf{ME}(expr) \rhd \mathsf{Id}$. According to the definition of MS for loops we have to show that for all code sequences a, b

$$\Delta L \,;\, I_5^\delta(a, m\cdot b) \;\geq\; |\mu W| \preceq \infty \,;\, \Delta R \,;\, I_5^\delta(a\cdot m, b)\ ,$$

which by the law (Void-bound) is equivalent to

$$\Delta L \,;\, I_5^\delta(a, m\cdot b) \;\geq\; \mu W \,;\, \Delta R \,;\, I_5^\delta(a\cdot m, b)\ . \tag{12.1}$$

Suppose given arbitrary $a, b \in \mathsf{IS}$. Let $P = \Delta R \,;\, I_5^\delta(a\cdot m, b)$ and define $H \in (\mathsf{Proc}_V \to \mathsf{Proc}_V)$ by $H(X) = X \,;\, P$. Then we must show:

$$\Delta L \,;\, I_5^\delta(a, m\cdot b) \;\geq\; H(\mu W)\ . \tag{12.2}$$

Define $V \in (\mathsf{Proc}_V \to \mathsf{Proc}_V)$ by $V(X) = (\mathsf{MS}(stat) \,;\, X) \lhd \mathsf{ME}(expr) \rhd P$. For all $X \in \mathsf{Proc}_V$ we have

$$H(W(X)) \underset{\substack{\uparrow\\ \text{[Definitions]}}}{=} ((\mathsf{MS}(stat)\ ;\ X) \lhd \mathsf{ME}(expr) \rhd \mathsf{Id})\ ;\ P$$

$$\underset{\substack{\uparrow\\ \text{[;-cond-leftwards]}}}{=} (\mathsf{MS}(stat)\ ;\ X\ ;\ P) \lhd \mathsf{ME}(expr) \rhd P \underset{\substack{\uparrow\\ \text{[Definitions]}}}{=} V(H(X))\ .$$

Moreover, H is universally disjunctive (see Sect. 5.6) and hence in particular $\perp$-strict and $\vee$-continuous. Therefore, the transfer lemma (Theorem 2.3.3) yields $H(\mu W) = \mu V$. So inequality (12.2) is equivalent to

$$\Delta L\ ;\ I_5^\delta(a, m \cdot b)\ \geq\ \mu V\ .$$

According to Lemma 2.3.2 it is sufficient to show

$$\Delta L\ ;\ I_5^\delta(a, m \cdot b)\ \geq\ V(\Delta L\ ;\ I_5^\delta(a, m \cdot b))\ ,$$

which unfolds to

$$\begin{aligned}&\Delta L\ ;\ I_5^\delta(a, m \cdot b)\ \geq\\ &\qquad(\mathsf{MS}(stat)\ ;\ \Delta L\ ;\ I_5^\delta(a, m \cdot b)) \lhd \mathsf{ME}(expr) \rhd (\Delta R\ ;\ I_5^\delta(a \cdot m, b))\ .\end{aligned}$$

By the modularization lemma (Lemma 5.7.10) this inequality is valid if and only if
(a) $\Delta L\ ;\ I_5^\delta(a, m \cdot b)\ \geq\ \{\mathsf{ME}(expr)\}\ ;\ \mathsf{MS}(stat)\ ;\ \Delta L\ ;\ I_5^\delta(a, m \cdot b)$ and
(b) $\Delta L\ ;\ I_5^\delta(a, m \cdot b)\ \geq\ \{\neg\mathsf{ME}(expr)\}\ ;\ \Delta R\ ;\ I_5^\delta(a \cdot m, b)$.
These two inequalities are established by the following calculations.

$$\begin{aligned}
&\Delta L\ ;\ I_5^\delta(a, m \cdot b)\\
\geq\ &\quad[\mathsf{CE}(expr, m_0, \delta, E_0),\ \text{Lemma 12.1.3}]\\
&\Delta L\ ;\ \{\mathsf{ME}(expr)\}\ ;\ \Delta\, E_0 + ldt(w_1) + 2\ ;\ I_5^\delta(a \cdot m_0 \cdot \mathsf{cj}(w_1), m_1 \cdot \mathsf{j}(w_2) \cdot b)\\
\geq\ &\quad[(\Delta\text{-assert}),\ (\Delta\text{-add}),\ (\Delta\text{-refine}):\ \text{condition (e)}]\\
&\{\mathsf{ME}(expr)\}\ ;\ \Delta L_1\ ;\ I_5^\delta(a \cdot m_0 \cdot \mathsf{cj}(w_1), m_1 \cdot \mathsf{j}(w_2) \cdot b)\\
\geq\ &\quad[\mathsf{CS}(stat, m_1, \delta, L_1, R_1, E_1)]\\
&\{\mathsf{ME}(expr)\}\ ;\ |\,\mathsf{MS}(stat)\,| \preceq E_1\ ;\ \Delta R_1\ ;\ I_5^\delta(a \cdot m_0 \cdot \mathsf{cj}(w_1) \cdot m_1, \mathsf{j}(w_2) \cdot b)\\
\geq\ &\quad[(\text{Bound-intro}),\ \text{Theorem 10.5.1: condition (d) implies } w_2 = |\,b\,| - |\,m \cdot b\,|]\\
&\{\mathsf{ME}(expr)\}\ ;\ \mathsf{MS}(stat)\ ;\ \Delta R_1\ ;\ \Delta\, ldt(w_2) + 3\ ;\ I_5^\delta(a, m \cdot b)\\
\geq\ &\quad[(\Delta\text{-add}),\ (\Delta\text{-refine}):\ \text{condition (f)}]\\
&\{\mathsf{ME}(expr)\}\ ;\ \mathsf{MS}(stat)\ ;\ \Delta L\ ;\ I_5^\delta(a, m \cdot b)\ .
\end{aligned}$$

This proves (a). The proof of (b) is even simpler.

$$\begin{aligned}
&\Delta L\ ;\ I_5^\delta(a, m \cdot b)\\
\geq\ &\quad[\mathsf{CE}(expr, m_0, \delta, E_0),\ \text{Lemma 12.1.4: (d) gives } w_1 = |\,m_1 \cdot \mathsf{j}(w_2) \cdot b\,| - |\,b\,|]\\
&\Delta L\ ;\ \{\neg\mathsf{ME}(expr)\}\ ;\ \Delta\, E_0 + ldt(w_1) + 4\ ;\ I_5^\delta(a \cdot m, b)\\
=\ &\quad[(\Delta\text{-assert}),\ (\Delta\text{-add})]\\
&\{\neg\mathsf{ME}(expr)\}\ ;\ \Delta\, L + E_0 + ldt(w_1) + 4\ ;\ I_5^\delta(a \cdot m, b)\\
\geq\ &\quad[(\Delta\text{-refine}):\ \text{condition (g)}]\\
&\{\neg\mathsf{ME}(expr)\}\ ;\ \Delta R\ ;\ I_5^\delta(a \cdot m, b)\ .
\end{aligned}$$

This finishes the proof of the loop translation theorem. □

If the loop body *stat* has an internal path, the code m_1 for *stat* possibly shifts at least as much excess time to the successor than absorbed from the predecessor.[1] So in this case we have $R_1 \geq L_1$. It is easy to see that then no finite L exists that satisfies condition (e) as well as condition (f). (L must be strictly smaller than L_1 and strictly greater than R_1.) Nevertheless the loop translation theorem can be applicable with $L = \infty$. Note that by condition (g) then R must be ∞ as well so that only a trivial timing property can be guaranteed for the loop.

12.4 Expressions

We now investigate translation of expressions. We start with atomic expressions.

For a constant expressions it suffices to load just the appropriate value with an `ldc` instruction.

Theorem 12.4.1 (Constants). *Suppose* $\underline{\textbf{const}}\,(k) \in \mathsf{Expr}_V$ *is a constant TPL expression of type* $T = \mathsf{SE}(\underline{\textbf{const}}\,(k))(V)$. *If*

(a) $w \;=\; R_T(k)$, *i.e.* w *is the word that represents* k, *and*

(b) $E \;\geq\; \mathit{ldt}(w) + 1$

then $\mathsf{CE}(\mathit{expr}, \mathtt{ldc}(w), \delta, E)$.

Proof. For all $a, b \in \mathsf{IS}$ we have

$$
\begin{aligned}
& I_4^\delta(a, \mathtt{ldc}(w) \cdot b) \\
\geq\; & \quad [\text{Theorem 10.4.2, (10.69)}] \\
& \Delta\, \mathit{ldt}(w) + 1 \;;\; \mathtt{A}, \mathtt{B}, \mathtt{C} := w, \mathtt{A}, \mathtt{B} \;;\; I_4^\delta(a \cdot \mathtt{ldc}(w), b) \\
\geq\; & \quad [(\Delta\text{-refine}){:}\ E \geq \mathit{ldt}(w) + 1,\ (\text{Conv1}),\ (\text{Ch-Id})] \\
& \Delta\, E \;;\; \mathtt{A} := w \;;\; \mathtt{B}, \mathtt{C}, \mathtt{Eflg} :=? \;;\; I_4^\delta(a \cdot \mathtt{ldc}(w), b) \\
=\; & \quad [w = R_T(k) = R_T(\mathsf{ME}_V(\underline{\textbf{const}}\,(k))) = \mathit{Rep}(\underline{\textbf{const}}\,(k))] \\
& \Delta\, E \;;\; \mathtt{A} := \mathit{Rep}(\underline{\textbf{const}}\,(k)) \;;\; \mathtt{B}, \mathtt{C}, \mathtt{Eflg} :=? \;;\; I_4^\delta(a \cdot \mathtt{ldc}(w), b) \;.
\end{aligned}
$$

□

The value of a variable x can be loaded using a `ldl` instruction provided the variable is represented in the standard way.

Theorem 12.4.2 (Variables). *Suppose* $\underline{\textbf{var}}\,(x) \in \mathsf{Expr}_V$. *If*

(a) $R_x \;=\; R_{\mathsf{Val}_x}$ *and*

(b) $E \;\geq\; \mathit{ldt}(\mathit{adr}_x) + 2$

---

[1] Strictly speaking, this applies to *dynamic* program paths. However, a compiler might work with timing information valid for all *static* paths because it cannot gain complete knowledge whether a static program path is dynamically possible or not.

then $\mathsf{CE}(\underline{\mathbf{var}}\,(x), \mathtt{ldl}(adr_x), \delta, E)$.

Proof. According to the definition of TPL, x can be either of type Bool or Word. We give the proof only for the case T_x = Bool. For arbitrary $a, b \in$ IS it is

$$
\begin{array}{ll}
 & I_4^\delta(a, \mathtt{ldl}(adr_x) \cdot b) \\
\geq & [10.4.5\ \text{part(b)}] \\
 & \Delta\, ldt(adr_x) + 2 \ ;\ \mathtt{A,B,C} := \mathsf{if}\ x\ \mathsf{then}\ 1\ \mathsf{else}\ 0\ \mathsf{fi}, \mathtt{A,B}\ ;\ I_4^\delta(a \cdot \mathtt{ldl}(adr_x), b) \\
\geq & [(\text{Conv1}),\ (\text{Ch-Id})] \\
 & \Delta\, ldt(adr_x) + 2 \ ;\ \mathtt{A} := \mathsf{if}\ x\ \mathsf{then}\ 1\ \mathsf{else}\ 0\ \mathsf{fi}\ ;\ \mathtt{B,C,Eflg} :=?\ ; \\
 & I_4^\delta(a \cdot \mathtt{ldl}(adr_x), b) \\
\geq & [(\Delta\text{-refine}):\ E \geq ldt(adr_x) + 2] \\
 & \Delta E\ ;\ \mathtt{A} := \mathsf{if}\ x\ \mathsf{then}\ 1\ \mathsf{else}\ 0\ \mathsf{fi}\ ;\ \mathtt{B,C,Eflg} :=?\ ;\ I_4^\delta(a \cdot \mathtt{ldl}(adr_x), b) \\
\geq & [\mathsf{if}\ x\ \mathsf{then}\ 1\ \mathsf{else}\ 0\ \mathsf{fi} = R_{\mathsf{Bool}}(x) = Rep(\underline{\mathbf{var}}\,(x))] \\
 & \Delta E\ ;\ \mathtt{A} := Rep(\underline{\mathbf{var}}\,(x))\ ;\ \mathtt{B,C,Eflg} :=?\ ;\ I_4^\delta(a \cdot \mathtt{ldl}(adr_x), b)\ .
\end{array}
$$

The proof for the case T_x = Word is similar. □

We now consider translation of expressions that apply a monadic operator to a subexpression.

Theorem 12.4.3 (Monadic expressions). *Suppose* $\underline{\mathbf{mon}}\,(mop, expr) \in \mathsf{Expr}_V$. *If*

(a) $\mathsf{CM}(mop, m_0, E_0)$,

(b) $\mathsf{CE}(expr, m_1, \delta, E_1)$,

(c) $m = m_1 \cdot m_0$, *and*

(d) $E \geq E_0 + E_1$

then $\mathsf{CE}(\underline{\mathbf{mon}}\,(mop, expr), m, \delta, E)$.

Proof. Let $A, B \in \{\mathsf{Bool}, \mathsf{Word}\}$ such that $\mathsf{MM}(mop) \in (A \to B)$ and choose f as in the definition of CM. $\mathsf{SE}(expr)(V)$ equals A because $\underline{\mathbf{mon}}\,(mop, expr)$ is well-formed . Hence,

$$
\begin{array}{ll}
 & f(Rep(expr)) \\
= & [\text{Def. } Rep] \\
 & f(R_A(\mathsf{ME}_V(expr))) \\
= & [\text{Choice of } f] \\
 & R_B(\mathsf{MM}(mop)(\mathsf{ME}_V(expr))) \\
= & [\text{Def. ME}] \\
 & R_B(\mathsf{ME}_V(\underline{\mathbf{mon}}\,(mop, expr))) \\
= & [\text{Def. } Rep] \\
 & Rep(\underline{\mathbf{mon}}\,(mop, expr))\ .
\end{array}
$$

Now, for all $a, b \in$ IS

$$
I_4^\delta(a, m_1 \cdot m_0 \cdot b)
$$

$\geq$ [$\mathsf{CE}(expr, m_1, \delta, E_1)$, $\mathsf{CM}(mop, m_0, E_0)$]

$\Delta\, E_1$; $\mathtt{A} := Rep(expr)$; $\mathtt{B}, \mathtt{C}, \mathtt{Eflg} :=?$;

$\Delta\, E_0$; $\mathtt{A} := f(\mathtt{A})$; $\mathtt{B}, \mathtt{C}, \mathtt{Eflg} :=?$

$I_4^\delta(a \cdot m_1 \cdot m_0, b)$

$\geq$ [Δ-laws, (Ch-comm): $f(\mathtt{A})$ idp. of $\mathtt{B}, \mathtt{C}, \mathtt{Eflg}$, (Ch-union)]

$\Delta\, E_0 + E_1$; $\mathtt{A} := Rep(expr)$; $\mathtt{A} := f(\mathtt{A})$; $\mathtt{B}, \mathtt{C}, \mathtt{Eflg} :=?$; $I_4^\delta(a \cdot m_1 \cdot m_0, b)$

$=$ [(Comb-asg), above calculation]

$\Delta\, E_0 + E_1$; $\mathtt{A} := Rep(\underline{\mathbf{mon}}\,(mop, expr))$; $\mathtt{B}, \mathtt{C}, \mathtt{Eflg} :=?$; $I_4^\delta(a \cdot m_1 \cdot m_0, b)$

$\geq$ [(Δ-refine): $E \geq E_0 + E_1$]

$\Delta\, E$; $\mathtt{A} := Rep(\underline{\mathbf{mon}}\,(mop, expr))$; $\mathtt{B}, \mathtt{C}, \mathtt{Eflg} :=?$; $I_4^\delta(a \cdot m_1 \cdot m_0, b)$.

This completes the proof. □

Now we consider the translation of binary expressions. The idea of the code is as follows. First the second subexpression is evaluated and the result is stored to an auxiliary variable. Afterwards the first subexpression is evaluated and the value of the second subexpression is loaded from the auxiliary variable. In the resulting state, register B contains the first argument and register A the second one, which is just the appropriate situation for applying code that implements the operator according to CB. We describe the allocation of the auxiliary variable by means of a consistent extension to the dictionary.

Theorem 12.4.4 (Binary expressions). *Let* $\underline{\mathbf{bin}}\,(bop, expr_1, expr_2) \in \mathsf{Expr}_V$ *and assume that* $x \in Y$ *and* $i = (\mathsf{Word}, R_{\mathsf{Word}}, adr) \in \mathsf{DictInfo}$. *Let* $\delta' = \delta \cup \{(x, i)\}$. *If*

(a) (x, i) *is consistent with* δ,

(b) $\mathsf{CB}(bop, m_0, E_0)$,

(c) $\mathsf{CE}(expr_1, m_1, \delta', E_1)$ *and* $\mathsf{CE}(expr_2, m_2, \delta, E_2)$,

(d) $m = m_2 \cdot \mathtt{stl}(adr) \cdot m_1 \cdot \mathtt{ldl}(adr) \cdot m_0$, *and*

(e) $E \geq E_0 + E_1 + E_2 + 2 * ldt(adr) + 3$

then $\mathsf{CE}(\underline{\mathbf{bin}}\,(bop, expr_1, expr_2), m, \delta, E)$.

This implementation uses only the first two registers from the register stack A, B, C. It is possible to generate faster and shorter code, e.g. by the scheme described in [46, Sect. 5.3], exploiting that intermediate results need not always be saved to an auxiliary variable. Although there is no fundamental difficulty in justifying such an optimized translation technique it complicates the proof slightly, which is the reason why we consider here only the very homogeneous scheme described above.

Proof. Let $A, B, C \in \{\mathsf{Bool}, \mathsf{Word}\}$ such that $\mathsf{MB}(bop) \in (A \times B \to C)$ and choose f as in the definition of CB. Since $\underline{\mathbf{bin}}\,(bop, expr_1, expr_2)$ is well-formed, $\mathsf{SE}(expr_1)(V)$ equals A and $\mathsf{SE}(expr_2)(V)$ equals B. Thus

$$
\begin{aligned}
& f(Rep(expr_1), Rep(expr_2)) \\
= \quad & [\text{Def. } Rep] \\
& f(R_A(\mathsf{ME}_V(expr_1)), R_B(\mathsf{ME}_V(expr_2))) \\
= \quad & [\text{Choice of } f] \\
& R_C(\mathsf{MB}(bop)(\mathsf{ME}_V(expr_1), \mathsf{ME}_V(expr_2))) \\
= \quad & [\text{Def. } \mathsf{ME}] \\
& R_B(\mathsf{ME}_V(\underline{\mathbf{bin}}(bop, expr_1, expr_2))) \\
= \quad & [\text{Def. } Rep] \\
& Rep(\underline{\mathbf{bin}}(bop, expr_1, expr_2)) \ .
\end{aligned}
$$

Using this identity we can calculate for arbitrary $a, b \in \mathsf{IS}$ as follows:

$$
\begin{aligned}
& I_4^\delta(a, m_2 \cdot \mathtt{stl}(adr) \cdot m_1 \cdot \mathtt{ldl}(adr) \cdot m_0 \cdot b) \\
\geq \quad & [\mathsf{CE}(expr_2, m_2, \delta, E_2), \mathsf{CE}(expr_1, m_1, \delta', E_1), \text{Lemma 12.1.6}] \\
& \Delta E_2 \ ; \mathtt{A} := Rep(expr_2) \ ; \mathtt{B}, \mathtt{C}, \mathtt{Eflg} :=? \ ; \\
& \Delta E_1 + 2 * ldt(adr) + 3 \ ; \mathtt{B} := Rep(expr_1) \ ; \mathtt{C}, \mathtt{Eflg} :=? \ ; \\
& I_4^\delta(a \cdot m_2 \cdot \mathtt{stl}(adr) \cdot m_1 \cdot \mathtt{ldl}(adr), m_0 \cdot b) \\
\geq \quad & [\mathsf{CB}(bop, m_0, E_0)] \\
& \Delta E_2 \ ; \mathtt{A} := Rep(expr_2) \ ; \mathtt{B}, \mathtt{C}, \mathtt{Eflg} :=? \ ; \\
& \Delta E_1 + 2 * ldt(adr) + 3 \ ; \mathtt{B} := Rep(expr_1) \ ; \mathtt{C}, \mathtt{Eflg} :=? \ ; \\
& \Delta E_0 \ ; \mathtt{A} := f(\mathtt{B}, \mathtt{A}) \ ; \mathtt{B}, \mathtt{C}, \mathtt{Eflg} :=? \ ; \\
& I_4^\delta(a \cdot m_2 \cdot \mathtt{stl}(adr) \cdot m_1 \cdot \mathtt{ldl}(adr) \cdot m_0, b) \\
\geq \quad & [\Delta\text{-laws, (Ch-comm): } Rep(expr_1) \text{ idp. of } \mathtt{B}, \mathtt{C}, \mathtt{Eflg}, \text{(Ch-union)}] \\
& \Delta E_0 + E_1 + E_2 + 2 * ldt(adr) + 3 \ ; \mathtt{A} := Rep(expr_2) \ ; \\
& \mathtt{B} := Rep(expr_1) \ ; \mathtt{C}, \mathtt{Eflg} :=? \ ; \\
& \mathtt{A} := f(\mathtt{B}, \mathtt{A}) \ ; \mathtt{B}, \mathtt{C}, \mathtt{Eflg} :=? \ ; \\
& I_4^\delta(a \cdot m_2 \cdot \mathtt{stl}(adr) \cdot m_1 \cdot \mathtt{ldl}(adr) \cdot m_0, b) \\
\geq \quad & [(\Delta\text{-refine}): \text{(e), (Ch-comm): } f(\mathtt{B}, \mathtt{A}) \text{ idp. of } \mathtt{C}, \mathtt{Eflg}, \text{(Ch-union)}] \\
& \Delta E \ ; \mathtt{A} := Rep(expr_2) \ ; \mathtt{B} := Rep(expr_1) \ ; \mathtt{A} := f(\mathtt{B}, \mathtt{A}) \ ; \\
& \mathtt{B}, \mathtt{C}, \mathtt{Eflg} :=? \ ; I_4^\delta(a \cdot m_2 \cdot \mathtt{stl}(adr) \cdot m_1 \cdot \mathtt{ldl}(adr) \cdot m_0, b) \\
= \quad & [\text{Comb-asg}] \\
& \Delta E \ ; \mathtt{A}, \mathtt{B} := f(Rep(expr_1), Rep(expr_2)), Rep(expr_1) \ ; \\
& \mathtt{B}, \mathtt{C}, \mathtt{Eflg} :=? \ ; I_4^\delta(a \cdot m_2 \cdot \mathtt{stl}(adr) \cdot m_1 \cdot \mathtt{ldl}(adr) \cdot m_0, b) \\
\geq \quad & [\text{Above calculation, (Cancel1)}] \\
& \Delta E \ ; \mathtt{A} := Rep(\underline{\mathbf{bin}}(bop, expr_1, expr_2)) \ ; \\
& \mathtt{B}, \mathtt{C}, \mathtt{Eflg} :=? \ ; I_4^\delta(a \cdot m_2 \cdot \mathtt{stl}(adr) \cdot m_1 \cdot \mathtt{ldl}(adr) \cdot m_0, b) \ .
\end{aligned}
$$

□

12.5 Monadic Operators

We now consider translation of the monadic operators **not**, **plus** and **minus**. First of all, we consider the Boolean operator **not**. It can be implemented by a comparison to 0.

Theorem 12.5.1 (Boolean negation). $\mathsf{CM}(\underline{\mathbf{not}}, \mathsf{eqc}(0), 2)$.

Proof. Let $f \in (\mathsf{Word} \to \mathsf{Word})$ be the function defined by $f(x) = \mathsf{if}\ x = 0\ \mathsf{then}\ 1\ \mathsf{else}\ 0\ \mathsf{fi}$. As shown by the following table, f satisfies condition (a) in the definition of CM (Definition 11.4.1):

a	$R_{\mathsf{Bool}}(a)$	$f(R_{\mathsf{Bool}}(a))$	$\mathsf{MM}(\underline{\mathbf{not}})(a)$	$R_{\mathsf{Bool}}(\mathsf{MM}(\underline{\mathbf{not}})(a))$
tt	1	0	ff	0
ff	0	1	tt	1

Furthermore, (b) holds because

$$\begin{aligned} & I_4^\delta(a, \mathsf{eqc}(0) \cdot b) \\ \geq \quad & [10.4.2, 10.73] \\ & \Delta\, ldt(0) + 2 \,;\, \mathtt{A} := \mathsf{if}\ \mathtt{A} = 0\ \mathsf{then}\ 1\ \mathsf{else}\ 0\ \mathsf{fi} \,;\, I_4^\delta(a \cdot \mathsf{eqc}(0), b) \\ \geq \quad & [ldt(0) = 0, \text{definition of } f, \text{(Ch-Id)}] \\ & \Delta\, 2 \,;\, \mathtt{A} := f(\mathtt{A}) \,;\, \mathtt{B}, \mathtt{C}, \mathtt{Eflg} :=? \,;\, I_4^\delta(a \cdot \mathsf{eqc}(0), b) \end{aligned}$$

for arbitrary $a, b \in \mathsf{IS}$, $\delta \in \mathsf{Dict}$. □

The monadic operator + can simply be ignored, which means that the empty code sequence is a correct implementation.

Theorem 12.5.2 (Monadic +). $\mathsf{CM}(\underline{\mathbf{plus}}, \varepsilon, 0)$.

Proof. $\mathsf{MM}(\underline{\mathbf{plus}})$ is the identity on Word. Choosing $f = \mathsf{Id}_{\mathsf{Word}}$, condition (a) in the definition of CM is trivially satisfied. The proof of (b) just exploits some laws about Id in order to introduce the operators on the right hand side:

$$\begin{aligned} & I_4^\delta(a, \varepsilon \cdot b) \\ = \quad & [(\Delta\text{-void}), \text{(Identity-asg)}, \varepsilon \text{ is unit of concatenation}] \\ & \Delta\, 0 \,;\, \mathtt{A} := \mathtt{A} \,;\, I_4^\delta(a \cdot \varepsilon, b) \\ \geq \quad & [\text{Definition } f, \text{(Ch-Id)}] \\ & \Delta\, 0 \,;\, \mathtt{A} := f(\mathtt{A}) \,;\, \mathtt{B}, \mathtt{C}, \mathtt{Eflg} :=? \,;\, I_4^\delta(a \cdot \varepsilon, b)\ . \end{aligned}$$

□

Translation of integer negation is described by the next theorem.

Theorem 12.5.3 (Word negation). $\mathsf{CM}(\underline{\mathbf{minus}}, \mathtt{not} \cdot \mathtt{adc}(1), 3)$.

Proof. Choose $f \in (\mathsf{Word} \to \mathsf{Word})$ such that $f(x) = -x$. Two's complement arithmetic together with the convention that $\mathsf{MostNeg} = -\mathsf{MostNeg}$ shows that $f(x) = (\mathsf{bitnot}\ x) + 1$ for all $x \in \mathsf{Word}$. As $R_{\mathsf{Word}} = \mathsf{Id}_{\mathsf{Word}}$ and $\mathsf{MM}(\underline{\mathbf{minus}}) = f$, condition (a) in the definition of CM is trivial. Condition (b) is proved by the little calculation

$$\begin{aligned} & I_4^\delta(a, \mathtt{not} \cdot \mathtt{adc}(1) \cdot b) \\ \geq \quad & [(10.89), (10.72)] \\ & \Delta\, 2 \,;\, \mathtt{A} := (\mathsf{bitnot}\ \mathtt{A}) \,; \\ & \Delta\, ldt(1) + 1 \,;\, \mathtt{A}, \mathtt{Eflg} := \mathtt{A} + 1, \mathtt{Eflg} \vee AddOvFl(\mathtt{A}, 1) \,; \\ & I_4^\delta(a \cdot \mathtt{not} \cdot \mathtt{adc}(1), b) \end{aligned}$$

$\geq$ [Δ-laws, $ldt(1) = 0$, (Comb-asg)]

$\Delta 3$; $\mathtt{A}, \mathtt{Eflg} := (\mathsf{bitnot}\ \mathtt{A}) + 1, \mathtt{Eflg} \vee AddOvFl(\mathtt{A}, 1)$; $I_4^\delta(a \cdot \mathtt{not} \cdot \mathsf{adc}(1), b)$

$\geq$ [$f(x) = (\mathsf{bitnot}\ x) + 1$, (Ch-Id), (Conv1)]

$\Delta 3$; $\mathtt{A} := f(\mathtt{A})$; $\mathtt{B}, \mathtt{C}, \mathtt{Eflg} :=?$; $I_4^\delta(a \cdot \mathtt{not} \cdot \mathsf{adc}(1), b)$

for arbitrarily chosen $a, b \in \mathsf{IS}$, $\delta \in \mathsf{Dict}$. □

12.6 Binary Operators

12.6.1 Arithmetic Operators

When proving translation theorems for the binary arithmetic operators it proves sensible to choose $f = \mathsf{MB}(bop)$. This renders condition (a) in the definition of CB trivial as R_{Word} is the identity on Word. In the proofs we, therefore, present only the calculations establishing condition (b).

Theorem 12.6.1 (Addition). $\mathsf{CB}(\underline{\mathbf{plus}}, \mathsf{add}, 1)$.

Proof. For arbitrary $a, b \in \mathsf{IS}$, $\delta \in \mathsf{Dict}$ we have

$I_4^\delta(a, \mathsf{add} \cdot b)$

$\geq$ [Theorem 10.4.2, (10.75)]

$\Delta 1$; $\mathtt{A}, \mathtt{B}, \mathtt{Eflg} := \mathtt{B} + \mathtt{A}, \mathtt{C}, \mathtt{Eflg} \vee AddOvFl(\mathtt{B}, \mathtt{A})$; $\mathtt{C} :=?$; $I_4^\delta(a \cdot \mathsf{add}, b)$

$\geq$ [(Conv1), $f(x, y) = \mathsf{MB}(\underline{\mathbf{plus}})(x, y) = x + y$]

$\Delta 1$; $\mathtt{A} := f(\mathtt{B}, \mathtt{A})$; $\mathtt{B}, \mathtt{C}, \mathtt{Eflg} :=?$; $I_4^\delta(a \cdot \mathsf{add}, b)$. □

The following two theorems that consider translation of the subtraction and multiplication operator are just as easily proved from the approximations given for the corresponding operations in Table 10.9. We omit their proofs.

Theorem 12.6.2 (Subtraction). $\mathsf{CB}(\underline{\mathbf{minus}}, \mathsf{sub}, 1)$.

Theorem 12.6.3 (Multiplication). $\mathsf{CB}(\underline{\mathbf{times}}, \mathtt{mul}, bpw + 7)$.

For the division operators <u>**div**</u> and <u>**rem**</u> more complex code must be generated. The reason is that we interpret the division operators, like all other operators, by total functions. By convention the division operations on Word yield 0 in all cases that traditionally are considered 'undefined'. However, the Transputer does not guarantee anything about the value left in register `A` by the corresponding operations `div` and `rem` in case of an overflow as we see from the axioms and approximations for `div` and `rem`. It is therefore wrong to use just those two operations as implementing code for <u>**div**</u> and <u>**rem**</u>. One possible solution is to check explicitly whether the arguments are in the domain of the 'traditional' partial division operations. However, this leads to rather long code. Another idea is to exploit that `div` and `rem` set the error flag in the 'undefined' cases. We adopt this solution.

The code sequences start with $\texttt{testerr}\cdot\texttt{ldc}(0)$. The purpose of the initial `testerr` operation is to reset the error flag. However, it also loads 0 to the register stack if the error flag was set and 1 otherwise. As we are not interested in the old value of the error flag we remove it from the stack by $\texttt{stl}(0)$. Then we execute `div` or `rem`. The purpose of the final piece of code is to load 0 to `A` if the error flag has been set by `div` resp. `rem` and to leave `A` unchanged otherwise. This is achieved by the code sequence $\texttt{testerr}\cdot\texttt{cj}(0)$. Of course $\texttt{cj}(0)$ always transfers control to the subsequent instruction. We exploit here that `cj` shifts the stack if the jump is not taken (i.e. if `A` does not contain 0) but leaves it unchanged otherwise. This fortunately is just what is needed after the `testerr` operation has loaded the value 0 to the stack if the error flag was set and 1 otherwise.

Theorem 12.6.4 (Division & Remainder).

(a) $\mathsf{CB}(\underline{\mathbf{div}}, \texttt{testerr}\cdot\texttt{stl}(0)\cdot\texttt{div}\cdot\texttt{testerr}\cdot\texttt{cj}(0), \mathit{bpw}+24)$.
(b) $\mathsf{CB}(\underline{\mathbf{rem}}, \texttt{testerr}\cdot\texttt{stl}(0)\cdot\texttt{rem}\cdot\texttt{testerr}\cdot\texttt{cj}(0), \mathit{bpw}+19)$.

Proof. Let $\delta \in \mathsf{Dict}$. First of all, we see that for all code sequences c, d

$$
\begin{array}{ll}
 & I_4^\delta(c, \texttt{testerr}\cdot\texttt{stl}(0)\cdot d) \\
\geq & [I_4\text{-instruction and operation theorem, (10.83), (10.70)}] \\
 & \Delta 4\ ;\ \texttt{A},\texttt{B},\texttt{C},\texttt{Eflg} := \mathsf{if}\ \texttt{Eflg}\ \mathsf{then}\ 0\ \mathsf{else}\ 1\ \mathsf{fi}, \texttt{A},\texttt{B},\mathsf{false}\ ; \\
 & \Delta 1\ ;\ \texttt{A},\texttt{B} := \texttt{B},\texttt{C}\ ;\ \texttt{C} :=?\ ;\ I_4^\delta(c\cdot\texttt{testerr}\cdot\texttt{stl}(0), d) \\
\geq & [\Delta\text{-laws, (Comb-asg)}] \\
 & \Delta 5\ ;\ \texttt{A},\texttt{B},\texttt{Eflg} := \texttt{A},\texttt{B},\mathsf{false}\ ;\ \texttt{C} :=?\ ;\ I_4^\delta(c\cdot\texttt{testerr}\cdot\texttt{stl}(0), d) \\
= & [\text{Identity-asg}] \\
 & \Delta 5\ ;\ \texttt{Eflg} := \mathsf{false}\ ;\ \texttt{C} :=?\ ;\ I_4^\delta(c\cdot\texttt{testerr}\cdot\texttt{stl}(0), d)\ .
\end{array}
$$

Secondly, for all code sequences c, d

$$
\begin{array}{ll}
 & I_4^\delta(c, \texttt{cj}(0)\cdot d) \\
\geq & [(10.74),\ (10.68)] \\
 & \{\texttt{A}=0\}\ ;\ \Delta\, \mathit{ldt}(0)+4\ ;\ I_4^\delta(c\cdot\texttt{cj}(0), d) \\
 & \vee \\
 & \{\texttt{A}\neq 0\}\ ;\ \Delta\, \mathit{ldt}(0)+2\ ;\ \texttt{A},\texttt{B} := \texttt{B},\texttt{C}\ ;\ \texttt{C} :=?\ ;\ I_4^\delta(c\cdot\texttt{cj}(0), d) \\
\geq & [\mathit{ldt}(0)=0,\ \text{(Identity-asg), (Ch-Id), } \Delta\text{-laws, (Conv1)}] \\
 & \{\texttt{A}=0\}\ ;\ \texttt{A} := \texttt{A}\ ;\ \texttt{B},\texttt{C} :=?\ ;\ \Delta 4\ ;\ I_4^\delta(c\cdot\texttt{cj}(0), d) \\
 & \vee \\
 & \{\texttt{A}\neq 0\}\ ;\ \texttt{A} := \texttt{B}\ ;\ \texttt{B},\texttt{C} :=?\ ;\ \Delta 2\ ;\ I_4^\delta(c\cdot\texttt{cj}(0), d) \\
= & \left[\text{(Exploit-assert) using that } \begin{array}{l} \texttt{A}=0 \Rightarrow \texttt{A} = \mathsf{if}\ \texttt{A}=0\ \mathsf{then}\ 0\ \mathsf{else}\ \texttt{B}\ \mathsf{fi}\ \text{and} \\ \texttt{A}\neq 0 \Rightarrow \texttt{B} = \mathsf{if}\ \texttt{A}=0\ \mathsf{then}\ 0\ \mathsf{else}\ \texttt{B}\ \mathsf{fi} \end{array}\right] \\
 & \{\texttt{A}=0\}\ ;\ \texttt{A} := \mathsf{if}\ \texttt{A}=0\ \mathsf{then}\ 0\ \mathsf{else}\ \texttt{B}\ \mathsf{fi}\ ;\ \texttt{B},\texttt{C} :=?\ ;\ \Delta 4\ ;\ I_4^\delta(c\cdot\texttt{cj}(0), d) \\
 & \vee \\
 & \{\texttt{A}\neq 0\}\ ;\ \texttt{A} := \mathsf{if}\ \texttt{A}=0\ \mathsf{then}\ 0\ \mathsf{else}\ \texttt{B}\ \mathsf{fi}\ ;\ \texttt{B},\texttt{C} :=?\ ;\ \Delta 2\ ;\ I_4^\delta(c\cdot\texttt{cj}(0), d)
\end{array}
$$

$\geq$ [(Δ-refine), . ; P is universally-disjunctive for all P]
$(\{\mathtt{A}=0\} \vee \{\mathtt{A}\neq 0\})$;
$\mathtt{A} := \text{if } \mathtt{A}=0 \text{ then } 0 \text{ else } \mathtt{B} \text{ fi} \; ; \; \mathtt{B},\mathtt{C} :=? \; ; \; \Delta 4 \; ; \; I_4^\delta(c \cdot \mathtt{cj}(0), d)$
$=$ [$\{\mathtt{A}=0\} \vee \{\mathtt{A}\neq 0\} = \{\mathtt{A}=0 \vee \mathtt{A}\neq 0\} = \{\text{true}\} = \text{Id}$]
$\mathtt{A} := \text{if } \mathtt{A}=0 \text{ then } 0 \text{ else } \mathtt{B} \text{ fi} \; ; \; \mathtt{B},\mathtt{C} :=? \; ; \; \Delta 4 \; ; \; I_4^\delta(c \cdot \mathtt{cj}(0), d)$.

Using this inequality, which formalizes our above remark about $\mathtt{cj}(0)$, we see that for all $c, d \in \mathsf{IS}$

$I_4^\delta(c, \mathtt{testerr} \cdot \mathtt{cj}(0) \cdot d)$
$\geq$ [Theorem 10.4.2, (10.83), inequality above]
$\Delta 4 \; ; \; \mathtt{A},\mathtt{B},\mathtt{C},\mathtt{Eflg} := \text{if } \mathtt{Eflg} \text{ then } 0 \text{ else } 1 \text{ fi}, \mathtt{A}, \mathtt{B}, \text{false}$;
$\mathtt{A} := \text{if } \mathtt{A}=0 \text{ then } 0 \text{ else } \mathtt{B} \text{ fi} \; ; \; \mathtt{B},\mathtt{C} :=? \; ; \; \Delta 4$;
$I_4^\delta(c \cdot \mathtt{testerr} \cdot \mathtt{cj}(0), d)$
$\geq$ [Δ-laws, (Comb-asg), (Conv1)]
$\Delta 8 \; ; \; \mathtt{A} := \text{if if } \mathtt{Eflg} \text{ then } 0 \text{ else } 1 \text{ fi} = 0 \text{ then } 0 \text{ else } \mathtt{A} \text{ fi} \; ; \; \mathtt{B},\mathtt{C},\mathtt{Eflg} :=?$;
$I_4^\delta(c \cdot \mathtt{testerr} \cdot \mathtt{cj}(0), d)$
$=$ [Simplification]
$\Delta 8 \; ; \; \mathtt{A} := \text{if } \mathtt{Eflg} \text{ then } 0 \text{ else } \mathtt{A} \text{ fi} \; ; \; \mathtt{B},\mathtt{C},\mathtt{Eflg} :=?$;
$I_4^\delta(c \cdot \mathtt{testerr} \cdot \mathtt{cj}(0), d)$.

In order to prove (a) we check condition (a) of CB's definition for $m = \mathtt{testerr} \cdot \mathtt{stl}(0) \cdot \mathtt{div} \cdot \mathtt{testerr} \cdot \mathtt{cj}(0)$ and $E = bpw + 24$. Since $\div$ is a word operator we choose $f \in (\text{Word} \times \text{Word} \to \text{Word})$, $f(x,y) = x \div y$.

$I_4^\delta(a, m \cdot b)$
$\geq$ [Calculations above, (10.78), (10.79)]
$\Delta 5 \; ; \; \mathtt{Eflg} := \text{false} \; ; \; \mathtt{C} :=? \; ; \; \Delta\, bpw + 11$;
$((\mathtt{A},\mathtt{B} := \mathtt{B} \div \mathtt{A}, \mathtt{C} \; ; \; \mathtt{C} :=?) \lhd \neg \mathit{DivOvFl}(\mathtt{B},\mathtt{A}) \rhd (\mathtt{B},\mathtt{Eflg} := \mathtt{C}, \text{true} \; ; \; \mathtt{A},\mathtt{C} :=?))$;
$\Delta 8 \; ; \; \mathtt{A} := \text{if } \mathtt{Eflg} \text{ then } 0 \text{ else } \mathtt{A} \text{ fi} \; ; \; \mathtt{B},\mathtt{C},\mathtt{Eflg} :=?$;
$I_4^\delta(a \cdot m, b)$
$\geq$ [Δ-laws, (Conv1)]
$\Delta\, bpw + 24 \; ; \; \mathtt{Eflg} := \text{false} \; ; \; \mathtt{C} :=?$;
$((\mathtt{A} := \mathtt{B} \div \mathtt{A} \; ; \; \mathtt{B},\mathtt{C} :=?) \lhd \neg \mathit{DivOvFl}(\mathtt{B},\mathtt{A}) \rhd (\mathtt{Eflg} := \text{true} \; ; \; \mathtt{A},\mathtt{B},\mathtt{C} :=?))$;
$\mathtt{A} := \text{if } \mathtt{Eflg} \text{ then } 0 \text{ else } \mathtt{A} \text{ fi} \; ; \; \mathtt{B},\mathtt{C},\mathtt{Eflg} :=?$;
$I_4^\delta(a \cdot m, b)$
$=$ [(Ch-asg), (Assign-cond), (;-cond-leftwards), (Ch-comm)]
$\Delta\, bpw + 24 \; ; \; \mathtt{C} :=?$;
$((\mathtt{Eflg} := \text{false} \; ; \; \mathtt{A} := \mathtt{B} \div \mathtt{A} \; ; \; \mathtt{A} := \text{if } \mathtt{Eflg} \text{ then } 0 \text{ else } \mathtt{A} \text{ fi} \; ; \; \mathtt{B},\mathtt{C} :=?)$
$\lhd \neg \mathit{DivOvFl}(\mathtt{B},\mathtt{A}) \rhd$
$(\mathtt{Eflg} := \text{false} \; ; \; \mathtt{Eflg} := \text{true} \; ; \; \mathtt{A} := \text{if } \mathtt{Eflg} \text{ then } 0 \text{ else } \mathtt{A} \text{ fi} \; ; \; \mathtt{B},\mathtt{C} :=?))$;
$\mathtt{B},\mathtt{C},\mathtt{Eflg} :=?$;
$I_4^\delta(a \cdot m, b)$
$\geq$ [Comb-asg]
$\Delta\, bpw + 24 \; ; \; \mathtt{C} :=?$;

$((\mathtt{A}, \mathtt{Eflg} := \mathsf{if\ false\ then\ } 0 \mathsf{\ else\ } \mathtt{B} \div \mathtt{A} \mathsf{\ fi}, \mathsf{false}\ ;\ \mathtt{B}, \mathtt{C} :=?)$
$\triangleleft \neg \mathit{DivOvFl}(\mathtt{B}, \mathtt{A}) \triangleright$
$(\mathtt{A}, \mathtt{Eflg} := \mathsf{if\ true\ then\ } 0 \mathsf{\ else\ } \mathtt{A} \mathsf{\ fi}, \mathsf{true}\ ;\ \mathtt{B}, \mathtt{C} :=?))\ ;$
$\mathtt{B}, \mathtt{C}, \mathtt{Eflg} :=?\ ;$
$I_4^\delta(a \cdot m, b)$
$\geq$ [Simplification, (Exploit-cond): $\mathit{DivOvFl}(\mathtt{B}, \mathtt{A}) \Rightarrow 0 = \mathtt{B} \div \mathtt{A}$, (Conv1)]
$\varDelta\, bpw + 24\ ;\ \mathtt{C} :=?\ ;$
$((\mathtt{A} := \mathtt{B} \div \mathtt{A}\ ;\ \mathtt{B}, \mathtt{C}, \mathtt{Eflg} :=?)$
$\triangleleft \neg \mathit{DivOvFl}(\mathtt{B}, \mathtt{A}) \triangleright$
$(\mathtt{A} := \mathtt{B} \div \mathtt{A}\ ;\ \mathtt{B}, \mathtt{C}, \mathtt{Eflg} :=?))\ ;$
$\mathtt{B}, \mathtt{C}, \mathtt{Eflg} :=?\ ;$
$I_4^\delta(a \cdot m, b)$
$=$ [Void-cond]
$\varDelta\, bpw + 24\ ;\ \mathtt{C} :=?\ ;\ \mathtt{A} := \mathtt{B} \div \mathtt{A}\ ;\ \mathtt{B}, \mathtt{C}, \mathtt{Eflg} :=?\ ;\ \mathtt{B}, \mathtt{C}, \mathtt{Eflg} :=?\ ;\ I_4^\delta(a \cdot m, b)$
$=$ [(Ch-asg), (Ch-union), def. f]
$\varDelta\, bpw + 24\ ;\ \mathtt{A} := f(\mathtt{B}, \mathtt{A})\ ;\ \mathtt{B}, \mathtt{C}, \mathtt{Eflg} :=?\ ;\ I_4^\delta(a \cdot m, b)\ .$

The proof of (b) is by an analogous calculation. □

12.6.2 Relational Operators

Equality can be checked by taking the difference of the arguments and comparing the result with 0.

Theorem 12.6.5 (Equal). $\mathsf{CB}(\underline{\mathbf{eq}}, \mathtt{diff} \cdot \mathsf{eqc}(0), 3)\ .$

Proof. Choose $f \in (\mathsf{Word} \times \mathsf{Word} \to \mathsf{Word})$ such that $f(x, y) = \mathsf{if\ } x - y = 0 \mathsf{\ then\ } 1 \mathsf{\ else\ } 0 \mathsf{\ fi}$. Then condition (a) of CB's definition is seen from

$R_{\mathsf{Bool}}(\mathsf{MM}(\underline{\mathbf{eq}})(x, y))$
$=$ [Defs]
$\mathsf{if\ } x = y \mathsf{\ then\ } 1 \mathsf{\ else\ } 0 \mathsf{\ fi}$
$=$ [$x = y$ iff $x - y = 0$]
$\mathsf{if\ } x - y = 0 \mathsf{\ then\ } 1 \mathsf{\ else\ } 0 \mathsf{\ fi}$
$=$ [Defs]
$f(R_{\mathsf{Word}}(x), R_{\mathsf{Word}}(y))$

and (b) from the calculation

$I_4^\delta(a, \mathtt{diff} \cdot \mathsf{eqc}(0) \cdot b)$
$\geq$ [(10.82), (10.73)]
$\varDelta 1\ ;\ \mathtt{A}, \mathtt{B} := \mathtt{B} - \mathtt{A}, \mathtt{C}\ ;\ \mathtt{C} :=?\ ;$
$\varDelta\, \mathit{ldt}(0) + 2\ ;\ \mathtt{A} := \mathsf{if\ } \mathtt{A} = 0 \mathsf{\ then\ } 1 \mathsf{\ else\ } 0 \mathsf{\ fi}\ ;$
$I_4^\delta(a \cdot \mathtt{diff} \cdot \mathsf{eqc}(0), b)$
$\geq$ [$\varDelta$-laws, $\mathit{ldt}(0) = 0$, (Ch-comm): $\mathsf{if\ } \mathtt{A} = 0 \mathsf{\ then\ } 1 \mathsf{\ else\ } 0 \mathsf{\ fi}$ is idp. of $\mathtt{C}$]
$\varDelta 3\ ;\ \mathtt{A}, \mathtt{B} := \mathtt{B} - \mathtt{A}, \mathtt{C}\ ;\ \mathtt{A} := \mathsf{if\ } \mathtt{A} = 0 \mathsf{\ then\ } 1 \mathsf{\ else\ } 0 \mathsf{\ fi}\ ;\ \mathtt{C} :=?\ ;$

$$I_4^\delta(a \cdot \texttt{diff} \cdot \mathsf{eqc}(0), b)$$
$$= \quad \text{[Comb-asg]}$$
$$\varDelta 3 \; ; \; \texttt{A}, \texttt{B} := \mathsf{if}\ \texttt{B} - \texttt{A} = 0\ \mathsf{then}\ 1\ \mathsf{else}\ 0\ \mathsf{fi}, \texttt{C} \; ; \; \texttt{C} :=? \; ; \; I_4^\delta(a \cdot \texttt{diff} \cdot \mathsf{eqc}(0), b)$$
$$\geq \quad \text{[(Conv1), (Ch-Id), Definition } f\text{]}$$
$$\varDelta 3 \; ; \; \texttt{A} := f(\texttt{B}, \texttt{A}) \; ; \; \texttt{C} :=? \; ; \; I_4^\delta(a \cdot \texttt{diff} \cdot \mathsf{eqc}(0), b)$$

for $a, b \in \mathsf{IS}$ and $\delta \in \mathsf{Dict}$. □

The proofs for all the remaining operators proceed in the same fashion. Condition (a) follows easily by simple word or Boolean arithmetic and (b) by simplifying the sequences of approximations obtained by repeated application of the instruction and operation theorems of Sect. 10.4. We present the remaining theorems for the relational operators without further ado and omit the full proofs but give the definitions of f as a hint.

Theorem 12.6.6 (Greater). $\mathsf{CB}(\underline{\mathbf{ge}}, \mathtt{gt}, 2)$.

Proof. Choose $f(x,y) = \mathsf{if}\ x > y\ \mathsf{then}\ 1\ \mathsf{else}\ 0\ \mathsf{fi}$. □

Theorem 12.6.7 (Not equal). $\mathsf{CB}(\underline{\mathbf{ne}}, \texttt{diff} \cdot \mathsf{eqc}(0) \cdot \mathsf{eqc}(0), 5)$.

Proof. Choose $f(x,y) = \mathsf{if}\ (\mathsf{if}\ x - y = 0\ \mathsf{then}\ 1\ \mathsf{else}\ 0\ \mathsf{fi}) = 0\ \mathsf{then}\ 1\ \mathsf{else}\ 0\ \mathsf{fi}$. □

Theorem 12.6.8 (Less). $\mathsf{CB}(\underline{\mathbf{le}}, \texttt{rev} \cdot \mathtt{gt}, 3)$.

Proof. Choose $f(x,y) = \mathsf{if}\ y > x\ \mathsf{then}\ 1\ \mathsf{else}\ 0\ \mathsf{fi}$. □

Theorem 12.6.9 (Greater-or-equal). $\mathsf{CB}(\underline{\mathbf{geq}}, \texttt{rev} \cdot \mathtt{gt} \cdot \mathsf{eqc}(0), 5)$.

Proof. Choose $f(x,y) = \mathsf{if}\ (\mathsf{if}\ y > x\ \mathsf{then}\ 1\ \mathsf{else}\ 0\ \mathsf{fi}) = 0\ \mathsf{then}\ 1\ \mathsf{else}\ 0\ \mathsf{fi}$. □

Theorem 12.6.10 (Less-or-equal). $\mathsf{CB}(\underline{\mathbf{leq}}, \mathtt{gt} \cdot \mathsf{eqc}(0), 4)$.

Proof. Choose $f(x,y) = \mathsf{if}\ (\mathsf{if}\ x > y\ \mathsf{then}\ 1\ \mathsf{else}\ 0\ \mathsf{fi}) = 0\ \mathsf{then}\ 1\ \mathsf{else}\ 0\ \mathsf{fi}$. □

12.6.3 Boolean Operators

As all operators are interpreted by total functions, expression evaluation can never be 'undefined'. Thus 'short circuit' evaluation of Boolean operators which does not evaluate the second argument if the result is already determined by the first one is a safe evaluation strategy. Short circuit evaluation increases performance in the mean case. But our objective is the guarantee of upper bounds that are valid even in the worst case. These upper bounds are not improved by short-circuit evaluation. Therefore, we evaluate Boolean expressions by the standard scheme, which results in a homogeneous approach for all binary expressions.

Theorem 12.6.11 (And). $\mathsf{CB}(\underline{\mathbf{and}}, \mathtt{add} \cdot \mathsf{eqc}(2), 3)$.

Proof. Choose $f(x,y) = \text{if } x+y = 2 \text{ then } 1 \text{ else } 0 \text{ fi}$. Then – as required by condition (a) of CB's definition – $f(R_{\text{Bool}}(r), R_{\text{Bool}}(s)) = R_{\text{Bool}}(\text{MB}(\underline{\textbf{and}})(r,s))$ holds for all $(r,s) \in \text{Bool} \times \text{Bool}$ as demonstrated by the following table:

r	s	$R_{\text{Bool}}(r)$	$R_{\text{Bool}}(s)$	$R_{\text{Bool}}(r) + R_{\text{Bool}}(s)$	$f(R_{\text{Bool}}(r), R_{\text{Bool}}(s))$	$\text{MB}(\underline{\textbf{and}})(r,s)$
tt	tt	1	1	2	1	tt
tt	ff	1	0	1	0	ff
ff	tt	0	1	1	0	ff
ff	ff	0	0	0	0	ff

Furthermore, for arbitrary a, b:

$$\begin{aligned}
& I_4^\delta(a, \mathbf{add} \cdot \mathtt{eqc}(2) \cdot d) \\
\geq\ & \quad [\text{Theorem 10.4.2, (10.75), (10.73)}] \\
& \Delta 1 \ ; \mathtt{A}, \mathtt{B}, \mathtt{Eflg} := \mathtt{B} + \mathtt{A}, \mathtt{C}, \mathtt{Eflg} \vee \mathit{AddOvFl}(\mathtt{B}, \mathtt{A}) \ ; \mathtt{C} :=? \ ; \\
& \Delta\, \mathit{ldt}(2) + 2 \ ; \mathtt{A} := \text{if } \mathtt{A} = 2 \text{ then } 1 \text{ else } 0 \text{ fi} \ ; \\
& I_4^\delta(a \cdot \mathbf{add} \cdot \mathtt{eqc}(2), b) \\
=\ & \quad [(\Delta\text{-assign}), (\Delta\text{-add}), \mathit{ldt}(2) = 0] \\
& \Delta 3 \ ; \mathtt{A}, \mathtt{B}, \mathtt{Eflg} := \mathtt{B} + \mathtt{A}, \mathtt{C}, \mathtt{Eflg} \vee \mathit{AddOvFl}(\mathtt{B}, \mathtt{A}) \ ; \mathtt{C} :=? \ ; \\
& \mathtt{A} := (1 \lhd \mathtt{A} = 2 \rhd 0) \ ; \\
& I_4^\delta(a \cdot \mathbf{add} \cdot \mathtt{eqc}(2), b) \\
\geq\ & \quad [(\text{Ch-comm}), (\text{Comb-asg}), (\text{Conv1}), \text{Definition } f] \\
& \Delta 3 \ ; \mathtt{A} := f(\mathtt{B}, \mathtt{A}) \ ; \mathtt{B}, \mathtt{C}, \mathtt{Eflg} :=? \ ; I_4^\delta(a \cdot \mathbf{add} \cdot \mathtt{eqc}(2), b) \ ,
\end{aligned}$$

which establishes condition (b). □

Finally, we consider the Boolean operator $\underline{\textbf{or}}$.

Theorem 12.6.12 (Or). $\text{CB}(\underline{\textbf{or}}, \mathbf{add} \cdot \mathtt{ldc}(0) \cdot \mathtt{gt}, 4)$.

Proof. Choose $f(x,y) = \text{if } x + y > 0 \text{ then } 1 \text{ else } 0 \text{ fi}$. The following table shows condition (a):

r	s	$R_{\text{Bool}}(r)$	$R_{\text{Bool}}(s)$	$f(R_{\text{Bool}}(r), R_{\text{Bool}}(s))$	$\text{MB}(\underline{\textbf{or}})(r,s)$
tt	tt	1	1	1	tt
tt	ff	1	0	1	tt
ff	tt	0	1	1	tt
ff	ff	0	0	0	ff

Condition (b) follows by a straightforward calculation. □

13. A Functional Implementation

The translation theorems of the previous chapter provide a basis for the implementation of a code generator but they do not yet determine the style of the implementation. For instance, attribute grammars can be used or a recursive-descent parser extended by code generation actions. To justify the correctness of a specific implementation requires additional considerations. But the necessary arguments are of a different nature than the deliberations up to now: they are no longer concerned directly with semantic issues. Semantic reasoning is separated from the further considerations by the translation theorems.

In this chapter we head for an implementation by an (abstract) functional program. For this behalf we develop a collection of code generation or *compiling functions*. The basic strategy for their construction is to separate the parameters of the compiling-correctness relations appropriately into argument and result components. Suitable instantiation of the translation theorems shows how the result for a composed construct can be obtained from results for the component constructs (with appropriately chosen additional parameters).

Before we actually construct the compiling functions we address the following topics that advantageously are treated separately from the transition to functions by refining the compiling-correctness relations.

(a) Up to now it has been convenient to assume that the constants s_P, l_P, s_W and l_W, which parameterize the position of the program storage and the workspace in the actual memory, are globally fixed. But in practice these constants are not known at compile time but are chosen only at loading time. Actually we expect that a compiler does not rely on concrete values for these constants but delivers information about the storage requirements in addition to the target code, which enables the loader to choose suitable values. There are only a few distinguished places where knowledge about the aforementioned constants is assumed or exploited:
   - The predicate *Loaded* requires that the loaded program is not longer than l_P.
   - The global assumption (10.56) formally expresses that program storage and workspace must be mapped to disjoint areas of the memory.

- The locations assigned to variables by a dictionary δ must be in the range $1 \le adr \le l_W$.

It is the task of the loader, which chooses the concrete values for the constants, to ensure the first two conditions. Its choice of l_W is restricted by an additional parameter *lu* (*'last used'*) of the refined correctness predicates that states a minimum requirement. (Of course, *lu* is to become a result component of the compiling functions.) Formally, the refined correctness predicates ensure semantic correctness only if $l_W \ge lu$. This condition is exploited to guarantee well-definedness of the dictionaries used.

(b) The allocation of auxiliary workspace locations for the intermediate results of expression evaluation has been described by a dictionary extension (see Theorem 12.4.4). While it is convenient to refer to auxiliary variables in the semantic reasoning, their names are of no significance for the actual translation. Only the workspace address of the new locations is needed when code is generated. How can we avoid that the code generator must choose arbitrary names for them? The idea is to use a stack-like allocation schema. Formally, we furnish the refined correctness predicates with an additional parameter *ff* (*'first free'*) that ensures that all workspace locations above *ff* (inclusive the location with address *ff*) are unused. The locations that are not contained in the dictionary but are below *ff* play the role of auxiliary variables.
A related point is that the code generator should be enabled to determine a new, unused location easily without inspecting the entire dictionary. This is also with the new parameter *ff*.

(c) In an implemented code generator we cannot use semantic dictionaries but must use some syntactic coding. For that purpose we introduce *syntactic dictionaries* below.

Item (a) actually extends the specification of the code generator, which now has to deliver *lu* in addition to the target code. In contrast, (b) and (c) are concerned with the implementation; the aim of (b) is to increase its efficiency and (c) is required by the means that are available in the assumed implementation formalism. These matters could be treated one after another by successive refinements of the correctness predicates. We prefer here to treat them together in order to avoid too many development phases.

13.1 Syntactic Dictionaries

Let us now define syntactic dictionaries.

Definition 13.1.1 (Syntactic dictionaries).

(a) A syntactic dictionary information *is a pair* (s, adr) *consisting of a a* sort symbol $s \in \{\underline{\textbf{bool}}, \underline{\textbf{word}}\}$ *and a positive number* $adr \in \mathbb{N}_{>0}$. *The set of syntactic dictionary entries is denoted by* SyntDictInfo.

(*b*) *A syntactic dictionary* ρ *is a function from a set of variables* $D \subseteq Z$ *to* SyntDictInfo. *(Recall that* Z *is the set of variables that may appear in TPL programs.) The set of syntactic dictionaries is called* SyntDict*:*

$$\mathsf{SyntDict} \stackrel{\text{def}}{=} \{\rho \mid \textit{there is } D \subseteq Z \textit{ such that } \rho \in (D \to \mathsf{SyntDictInfo})\}.$$

We range over SyntDict *by* ρ *and write for* $x \in \mathsf{dom}\,\rho$ *– like for semantic dictionaries –* s^ρ_x *and* adr^ρ_x *for* $\rho(x).1$ *and* $\rho(x).2$.

Syntactic dictionaries as defined here are still rather abstract entities but they are concrete enough to allow a straightforward implementation in a modern functional language, like Standard ML [58, 85]. Of course in a 'real' compiler one would invest some effort to provide an implementation that allows an efficient access to the entries, e.g. by using some hashing scheme. But this is outside the scope of this book.

The next definition describes the abstract (semantic) dictionary represented by a syntactic dictionary.

Definition 13.1.2 (Represented semantic objects).

(*a*) *The data domain represented by a sort symbol* s *is denoted by* $\widehat{s}$. *More specifically,* $\widehat{\mathbf{bool}} = \mathsf{Bool}$ *and* $\widehat{\mathbf{word}} = \mathsf{Word}$.
(*b*) *The semantic dictionary information represented by a syntactic dictionary* (s, adr) *is* $\widehat{(s, adr)} = (\widehat{s}, R_{\widehat{s}}, adr)$, *where* R_{Bool} *and* R_{Word} *are the standard representation relations for Boolean and word values defined in Chap. 10.*
(*c*) *The* standard dictionary $\widehat{\rho}$ represented by a syntactic dictionary ρ *is defined by* $\mathsf{dom}\,\widehat{\rho} = \mathsf{dom}\,\rho$ *and* $\widehat{\rho}(x) = \widehat{\rho(x)}$ *for all* $x \in \mathsf{dom}\,\rho$.

Due to the side conditions for semantic dictionaries, $\widehat{\rho}$ actually is a (standard) dictionary only if

- all variables are mapped to proper workspace locations, i.e. $adr^\rho_x \in \{1, \ldots, l_{\mathsf{W}}\}$ for all $x \in \mathsf{dom}\,\rho$,
- ρ is *injective in the locations*, i.e. $adr^\rho_x \neq adr^\rho_y$ for any two distinct $x, y \in \mathsf{dom}\,\rho$, and
- ρ is *type-correct*, i.e. $\widehat{S^\rho_x} = \mathsf{Val}_x$.

13.2 Refined Correctness Relations

We are now prepared to define the refined correctness relations. The additional parameters have been motivated and explained at the beginning of this chapter. We also refine the predicate for initialization code.

Definition 13.2.1 (Refined correctness predicates). *Let* $prog \in \mathsf{Prog}$, $stat \in \mathsf{Stat}$, $expr \in \mathsf{Expr}$, $m \in \mathsf{IS}$, $\rho \in \mathsf{SyntDict}$, $adr \in \mathsf{IN}_{>0}$, $\delta \in \mathsf{Dict}$, $f\!f, lu \in \mathsf{IN}$, $s \in \{\,\underline{\mathbf{bool}}, \underline{\mathbf{word}}\,\}$, *and* $L, R, E \in \mathsf{Time}$.

(a) *We say* δ comprises ρ and does not exceed address ff, *if* $\widehat{\rho} \subseteq \delta$, $\mathsf{dom}\,\delta \setminus \mathsf{dom}\,\rho \subseteq \mathsf{Aux}$, *and* $adr_x^\delta < \mathit{ff}$ *for all* $x \in \mathsf{dom}\,\delta$. *Such a dictionary* δ *is also called a* (ρ, ff)-dictionary *for short.*
(b) *We say that* m implements $prog$ provided at least lu workspace cells are available *and write* $\mathsf{CP}'(prog, m, lu)$ *for short, if* $lu > l_{\mathrm{W}}$ *or* $\mathsf{CP}(prog, m)$ *holds.*
(c) $\mathsf{CS}'(stat, m, \rho, \mathit{ff}, lu, L, R, E)$ *holds if* $lu > l_{\mathrm{W}}$ *or* $\mathsf{CS}(stat, m, \delta, L, R, E)$ *holds for all* (ρ, ff)*-dictionaries* δ.
(d) $\mathsf{CE}'(expr, m, \rho, \mathit{ff}, lu, E)$ *holds if* $lu > l_{\mathrm{W}}$ *or* $\mathsf{CE}(expr, m, \delta, E)$ *holds for all* (ρ, ff)*-dictionaries* δ.
(e) $\mathsf{IC}'(m, s, adr, E)$ *holds if* $\mathsf{IC}(m, \widehat{(s, adr)}, E)$.

CS', CE' and IC' can be verbalized in a similar way as CP'. Due to the large number of parameters, however, such a verbalization is not really helpful. The transition from δ to the pair (ρ, ff) can be interpreted as a data refinement. The representation relation is just the relationship verbalized as 'δ is a (ρ, ff)-dictionary'. Note that in general there is no functional relationship from the concrete entity (ρ, ff) to the abstract entity δ. The reason is that we had to choose arbitrary names for auxiliary variables, when arguing with the original compiling-correctness relations, while an implementation need not choose names at all.

13.3 Refined Translation Theorems

The translation theorems of Chap. 12 transfer to the refined correctness predicates. It is important to understand that the proofs for these refined translation theorems do not require semantic argumentation but twiddle only with the parameters of the correctness predicates. The proofs are particularly simple if the described translation does not affect the dictionary. As typical examples we show the refined version of the program translation theorem and of the theorem for sequential composition.

Theorem 13.3.1 (Program translation refined). *Let* $\underline{\mathbf{prog}}\,(stat) \in \mathsf{Prog}$ *and suppose* $\mathsf{CS}'(stat, m, \emptyset, 1, lu, L, R, E)$. *Then* $\mathsf{CP}'(prog, m \cdot \mathtt{stopp}, lu)$.

Proof. If $lu > l_{\mathrm{W}}$ there is nothing to be shown, so assume $lu \leq l_{\mathrm{W}}$. Clearly, $\emptyset$ is an $(\emptyset, 1)$-dictionary. Hence $\mathsf{CS}'(stat, m, \emptyset, 1, lu, L, R, E)$ implies $\mathsf{CS}(stat, m, \emptyset, L, R, E)$. Thus $\mathsf{CP}(\underline{\mathbf{prog}}\,(stat), m \cdot \mathtt{stopp})$ by Theorem 12.2.1. □

Theorem 13.3.2 (Sequential composition translation refined). *Suppose*

(a) $\mathsf{CS}'(stat_1, m_1, \rho, \mathit{ff}, lu_1, L, M, E_1)$ *and*
(b) $\mathsf{CS}'(stat_2, m_2, \rho, \mathit{ff}, lu_2, M, R, E_2)$.

Then $\mathsf{CS}'(\underline{\mathbf{seq}}(stat_1, stat_2), m_1 \cdot m_2, \rho, f\!f, \mathsf{Max}\{lu_1, lu_2\}, L, R, E_1 + E_2)$.

Proof. Assume $\mathsf{Max}\{lu_1, lu_2\} \le l_W$ and suppose given a $(\rho, f\!f)$-dictionary δ. Clearly, $lu_1 \le l_W$ and $lu_2 \le l_W$. By definition of CS' thus

- $\mathsf{CS}(stat_1, m_1, \delta, L, M, E_1)$ because of (a) and
- $\mathsf{CS}(stat_2, m_2, \delta, M, R, E_2)$ because of (b).

Theorem 12.3.6 yields $\mathsf{CS}(\underline{\mathbf{seq}}(stat_1, stat_2), m_1 \cdot m_2, \delta, L, R, E_1 + E_2)$. □

The translation patterns in the theorems for blocks and binary expressions, however, affect the dictionary. Therefore, we elaborate the refined theorems for them here. The strategy is to allocate the location $f\!f$ for the local or auxiliary variable.

Let $V = \mathsf{dom}\,\rho$. The refined translation theorem for blocks looks as follows.

Theorem 13.3.3 (Block translation refined). *Suppose* $\underline{\mathbf{block}}(x, stat) \in \mathsf{Stat}_V$,

(a) $\widehat{s} = \mathsf{Val}_x$,

(b) $\mathsf{IC}'(m_0, s, f\!f, E_0)$, *and*

(c) $\mathsf{CS}'(stat, m_1, \rho \cup \{(x, (s, f\!f))\}, f\!f + 1, lu, L + E_0, R, E)$.

Then $\mathsf{CS}'(\underline{\mathbf{block}}(x, stat), m_0 \cdot m_1, \rho, f\!f, \mathsf{Max}\{f\!f, lu\}, L, R, E)$.

Proof. If $\mathsf{Max}\{f\!f, lu\} > l_W$, the proposition holds trivially. Thus assume $\mathsf{Max}\{f\!f, lu\} \le l_W$, which implies $f\!f \le l_W$ and $lu \le l_W$. Assume given a $(\rho, f\!f)$-dictionary δ. We have to show $\mathsf{CS}(\underline{\mathbf{block}}(x, stat), m_0 \cdot m_1, \delta, L, R, E)$. Of course, the idea is to apply Theorem 12.3.8.

Choose $i = \widehat{(s, f\!f)}$ and let $\rho' = \rho \cup \{(x, (s, f\!f))\}$. i is indeed a dictionary information because $f\!f \le l_W$. We check the preconditions of the block translation Theorem 12.3.8.

(a) That (x, i) is consistent with δ follows from the assumption that δ is a $(\rho, f\!f)$-dictionary and $\underline{\mathbf{block}}(x, stat) \in \mathsf{Stat}_V$.
(b) $\mathsf{IC}(m_0, i, E_0)$ follows immediately from $\mathsf{IC}'(m_0, s, f\!f, E_0)$.
(c) $\mathsf{CS}(stat, m_1, \delta \cup \{(x, i)\}, L + E_0, R, E)$ follows from $\mathsf{CS}'(stat, m_1, \rho', f\!f + 1, lu, L + E_0, R, E)$ because $\delta \cup \{(x, i)\}$ is a $(\rho', f\!f + 1)$- dictionary. The latter is quite easy to show.

Thus Theorem 12.3.8 tells us that $\mathsf{CS}(\underline{\mathbf{block}}(x, stat), m_0 \cdot m_1, \delta, L, R, E)$ holds. □

This is the refined version of the translation theorem for binary expressions. The idea is to use location $f\!f$ for storing the intermediate result and to translate the first sub-expression w.r.t. an incremented $f\!f$-parameter.

Theorem 13.3.4 (Binary expression translation refined). *Suppose* $\underline{\mathbf{bin}}(bop, expr_1, expr_2) \in \mathsf{Expr}_V$, *(a)* $\mathsf{CB}(bop, m_0, E_0)$,

(b) $\mathsf{CE}'(expr_1, m_1, \rho, \mathit{ff}+1, lu_1, E_1)$,

(c) $\mathsf{CE}'(expr_2, m_2, \rho, \mathit{ff}, lu_2, E_2)$,

(d) $m = m_2 \cdot \mathtt{stl}(\mathit{ff}) \cdot m_1 \cdot \mathtt{ldl}(\mathit{ff}) \cdot m_0$, *and*

(e) $E \geq E_0 + E_1 + E_2 + 2 * ldt(\mathit{ff}) + 3$.

Then $\mathsf{CE}'(\underline{\mathbf{bin}}(bop, expr_1, expr_2), m, \rho, \mathit{ff}, \mathsf{Max}\{\mathit{ff}, lu_1, lu_2\}, E)$.

Proof. Suppose given a (ρ, ff)-dictionary δ. If $\mathsf{Max}\{\mathit{ff}, lu_1, lu_2\} > l_W$ the result holds trivially, so let us assume $\mathsf{Max}\{\mathit{ff}, lu_1, lu_2\} \leq l_W$. Clearly, this implies $\mathit{ff} \leq l_W$, $lu_1 \leq l_W$ and $lu_2 \leq l_W$. We have to show that $\mathsf{CE}(\underline{\mathbf{bin}}(bop, expr_1, expr_2), m, \delta, E)$ holds, and of course we want to conclude this with the binary expression translation Theorem 12.4.4. So, choose a new variable $x \in \mathsf{Aux} \setminus (\mathsf{dom}\,\delta \cup \{\!\!\{ Tc \}\!\!\} \cup \{\mathtt{Wsp}\})$ with value domain Word. (Without loss of generality we can assume that such a variable exists because $\mathsf{dom}\,\delta \cup \{\!\!\{ Tc \}\!\!\} \cup \{\mathtt{Wsp}\}$ is finite.) Let $i = (\mathsf{Word}, R_{\mathsf{Word}}, \mathit{ff})$. i is indeed a dictionary information as $\mathit{ff} \leq l_W$. It is easy to see that (x, i) is consistent with δ; essentially this holds because $adr_x^\delta < \mathit{ff}$ for all $x \in \mathsf{dom}\,\delta$. Let $\delta' = \delta \cup \{(x, i)\}$. In order to apply Theorem 12.4.4 we must only show $\mathsf{CE}(expr_1, m_1, \delta', E_1)$ and $\mathsf{CE}(expr_2, m_2, \delta, E_2)$ as the other conditions are explicitly required here as well.

- Clearly, $\widehat{\rho} \subseteq \delta'$ ($\widehat{\rho}$ is even contained in δ). Moreover, $adr_x^{\delta'} < \mathit{ff}+1$ for all $x \in \mathsf{dom}\,\delta'$. Hence δ' is a $(\rho, \mathit{ff}+1)$ dictionary. Therefore, $\mathsf{CE}'(expr_1, m_1, \rho, \mathit{ff}+1, lu_1, E_1)$ implies $\mathsf{CE}(expr_1, m_1, \delta', E_1)$ because $lu_1 \leq l_W$.
- As mentioned above $lu_2 \leq l_W$, and by its very choice δ is a (ρ, ff)-dictionary. Thus (c) implies $\mathsf{CE}(expr_2, m_2, \delta, E_2)$.

Now, Theorem 12.4.4 yields $\mathsf{CE}(\underline{\mathbf{bin}}(bop, expr_1, expr_2), m, \delta, E)$. □

We do not present the complete collection of refined translation theorems here; we think the reader can imagine how they look like. In an actual development, however, they should be documented as an intermediate stage.

13.4 Compiling Functions

From the refined translation theorems we now construct the compiling functions. As mentioned, the basic strategy for the construction is to separate the parameters of the refined correctness predicates into argument and result components. More specifically, we define three functions EP, ES, EE for the translation of programs, statements and expression respectively, a function EI corresponding to IC′ that provides initialization code, and functions EB and EM corresponding to CB and CM that provide code for binary and monadic operators. We use the following separation between argument and result components that has already been prepared in the form of the translation theorems:

- EP has *prog* as argument and m, lu as result,
- ES has $stat, \rho, ff, L$ as arguments and m, lu, R, E as result,
- EE has $expr, \rho, ff$ as arguments and m, lu, E as result,
- EB has *bop* as argument and m, E as result,
- EM has *mop* as argument and m, E as result, and
- EI has s, *adr* as arguments and m, E as result.

The signature of the compiling functions is summarized in Table 13.1.

Table 13.1. Signature of compiling functions

$\mathsf{EP} \in (\mathsf{Prog} \xrightarrow{\text{part.}} \mathsf{IS} \times \mathbb{N})$	Programs
$\mathsf{ES} \in (\mathsf{Stat} \times \mathsf{SyntDict} \times \mathbb{N} \times \mathsf{Time} \xrightarrow{\text{part.}} \mathsf{IS} \times \mathbb{N} \times \mathsf{Time} \times \mathsf{Time})$	Statements
$\mathsf{EE} \in (\mathsf{Expr} \times \mathsf{SyntDict} \times \mathbb{N} \xrightarrow{\text{part.}} \mathsf{IS} \times \mathbb{N} \times \mathsf{Time})$	Expressions
$\mathsf{EB} \in (\mathsf{Bop} \xrightarrow{\text{part.}} \mathsf{IS} \times \mathsf{Time})$	Binary operators
$\mathsf{EM} \in (\mathsf{Mop} \xrightarrow{\text{part.}} \mathsf{IS} \times \mathsf{Time})$	Monadic operators
$\mathsf{EI} \in (\{\underline{\mathbf{bool}}, \underline{\mathbf{word}}\} \times \mathbb{N}_{>0} \xrightarrow{\text{part.}} \mathsf{IS} \times \mathsf{Time})$	Initialization code

It can turn out during translation that a time bound cannot be guaranteed with the given translation strategy. By convention the compiling functions are undefined in this case; thus they are partial functions. In practice an error message would be generated pointing to the time bound in the source program that caused the problem. The compiling functions are defined in such a way that the following theorem becomes valid. By convention validity of an equality implies definedness of its left and right hand side. So, for instance, the antecedent $\mathsf{EP}(prog) = (m, lu)$ in (a) requires in particular that $\mathsf{EP}(prog)$ is defined.

Theorem 13.4.1 (Correctness of explicit specification). *Let prog* $\in$ Prog, *stat* $\in \mathsf{Stat}_V$, *and expr* $\in \mathsf{Expr}_V$, *where* $V = \mathrm{dom}\,\rho$.

(a) $\mathsf{EP}(prog) = (m, lu)$ *implies* $\mathsf{CP}'(prog, m, lu)$.
(b) $\mathsf{ES}(stat, \rho, ff, L) = (m, lu, R, E)$ *implies* $\mathsf{CS}'(stat, m, \rho, ff, lu, L, R, E)$.
(c) $\mathsf{EE}(expr, \rho, ff) = (m, lu, E)$ *implies* $\mathsf{CE}'(expr, m, \rho, ff, lu, E)$.
(d) $\mathsf{EB}(bop) = (m, E)$ *implies* $\mathsf{CB}(bop, m, E)$.
(e) $\mathsf{EM}(mop) = (m, E)$ *implies* $\mathsf{CM}(mop, m, E)$.
(f) $\mathsf{EI}(s, ff) = (m, E)$ *implies* $CI(m, s, ff, E)$.

Based on the refined translation theorems the concrete definition of the compiling functions is straightforward in most cases and is presented in Table 13.2, Table 13.3, Table 13.5, and Table 13.4. Exceptions are the clauses for

Table 13.2. Compiling clauses for programs and statements except loops

$\mathsf{EP}(\underline{\mathbf{prog}}\,(stat))$ $= (m, lu) \quad \text{where } (m, lu, R, E) = \mathsf{ES}(stat, \emptyset, 1, 0)$
$\mathsf{ES}(\underline{\mathbf{skip}}, \rho, \mathit{ff}, L)$ $= (\varepsilon, 0, L, 0)$
$\mathsf{ES}(\underline{\mathbf{stop}}, \rho, \mathit{ff}, L)$ $= (\mathtt{stopp}, 0, 0, \infty)$
$\mathsf{ES}(\underline{\mathbf{assign}}\,(x, expr), \rho, \mathit{ff}, L)$ $= (m_1 \cdot \mathtt{stl}(adr_x^\rho), lu_1, L + E_1 + ldt(adr_x^\rho) + 1, 0)$ $\text{where } (m_1, lu_1, E_1) = \mathsf{EE}(expr, \rho, \mathit{ff})$
$\mathsf{ES}(\underline{\mathbf{output}}\,(\mathtt{Out_i}, expr), \rho, \mathit{ff}, L)$ $= (m, lu_1, outdelay_2, L + E_1 + outdelay_1 + 8)$ $\text{where } (m_1, lu_1, E_1) = \mathsf{EE}(expr, \rho, \mathit{ff})$ $\text{and } m = m_1 \cdot \mathtt{mint} \cdot \mathtt{ldc}(i) \cdot \mathtt{bcnt} \cdot \mathtt{add} \cdot \mathtt{rev} \cdot \mathtt{outword}$
$\mathsf{ES}(\underline{\mathbf{input}}\,(\mathtt{In_i}, x), \rho, \mathit{ff}, L)$ $= (m, 0, indelay_2, L + ldt(adr_x^\rho) + indelay_1 + 12)$ $\text{where } m = \mathtt{ldlp}(adr_x^\rho) \cdot \mathtt{mint} \cdot \mathtt{ldc}(i+4) \cdot \mathtt{bcnt} \cdot \mathtt{add} \cdot \mathtt{ldc}(1) \cdot \mathtt{bcnt} \cdot \mathtt{in}$
$\mathsf{ES}(\underline{\mathbf{seq}}\,(stat_1, stat_2), \rho, \mathit{ff}, L)$ $= (m_1 \cdot m_2, \mathsf{Max}\{lu_1, lu_2\}, R, E_1 + E_2)$ $\text{where } (m_1, lu_1, M, E_1) = \mathsf{ES}(stat_1, \rho, \mathit{ff}, L)$ $\text{and } (m_2, lu_2, R, E_2) = \mathsf{ES}(stat_2, \rho, \mathit{ff}, M)$
$\mathsf{ES}(\underline{\mathbf{upperbound}}\,(stat, t), \rho, \mathit{ff}, L)$ $= \begin{cases} (m, lu, R, E) & \text{if } E \le t \\ \text{undefined} & \text{otherwise} \end{cases}$ $\text{where } (m, lu, R, E) = \mathsf{ES}(stat, \rho, \mathit{ff}, L)$
$\mathsf{ES}(\underline{\mathbf{block}}\,(x, stat), \rho, \mathit{ff}, L)$ $= (m_0 \cdot m_1, \rho, \mathit{ff}, \mathsf{Max}\{\mathit{ff}, lu\}, L, R, E)$ $\text{where } s \text{ is chosen such that } \widehat{s} = \mathsf{Val}_x$ $\text{and } (m_0, E_0) = \mathsf{EI}(s, \mathit{ff})$ $\text{and } (m_1, lu, R, E) = \mathsf{ES}(stat, \rho \cup \{(x, (s, \mathit{ff}))\}, \mathit{ff} + 1, L + E_0)$
$\mathsf{ES}(\underline{\mathbf{if}}\,(expr, stat_1, stat_2), \rho, \mathit{ff}, L)$ $= (m, \mathsf{Max}\{lu_0, lu_1, lu_2\}, \mathsf{Max}\{R_1 + ldt(w_2) + 2, R_2\}, \mathsf{Max}\{E_1, E_2\})$ $\text{where } (m_0, lu_0, E_0) = \mathsf{EE}(expr, \rho, \mathit{ff})$ $\text{and } (m_1, lu_1, R_1, E_1) = \mathsf{ES}(stat_1, \rho, \mathit{ff}, L + E_0 + 2 * bpw + 1)$ $\text{and } (m_2, lu_2, R_2, E_2) = \mathsf{ES}(stat_2, \rho, \mathit{ff}, L + E_0 + 2 * bpw + 3)$ $\text{and } w_2 = \lvert m_2 \rvert$ $\text{and } w_1 = \lvert m_1 \cdot \mathtt{j}(w_2) \rvert$ $\text{and } m = m_0 \cdot \mathtt{cj}(w_1) \cdot m_1 \cdot \mathtt{j}(w_2) \cdot m_2$

Table 13.3. Compiling clause for loops

$$
\begin{aligned}
&\mathsf{ES}(\underline{\textbf{while}}\,(expr, stat), \rho, \mathit{ff}, L)\\
&\quad = (m, \mathsf{Max}\{lu_0, lu_1\}, L + E_0 + ldt(w_1) + 4, \infty)\\
&\qquad \text{if } L \;\geq\; R_1 + 2 * bpw + 2\\
&\qquad \text{where } (m_0, lu_0, E_0) \;=\; \mathsf{EE}(expr, \rho, \mathit{ff})\\
&\qquad\quad \text{and } (m_1, lu_1, R_1, E_1) \;=\; \mathsf{ES}(stat, \rho, \mathit{ff}, L + E_0 + 2 * bpw + 1)\\
&\qquad\quad \text{and } (w_1, w_2) = \mathsf{WJ}(|\, m_1 \,|, |\, m_2 \,|)\\
&\qquad\quad \text{and } m = m_0 \cdot \mathtt{cj}(w_1) \cdot m_2 \cdot \mathtt{j}(w_2)\\
&\quad = (m', \mathsf{Max}\{lu_0, lu_1'\}, L' + E_0 + ldt(w_1) + 4, \infty)\\
&\qquad \text{if } L' \;\geq\; R_1' + 2 * bpw + 2\\
&\qquad \text{where } L' \;=\; R_1 + 2 * bpw + 2\\
&\qquad\quad \text{and } (m_1', lu_1', R_1', E_1') \;=\; \mathsf{ES}(stat, \rho, \mathit{ff}, L' + E_0 + 2 * bpw + 1)\\
&\qquad\quad \text{and } (w_1', w_2') = \mathsf{WJ}(|\, m_1' \,|, |\, m_2' \,|)\\
&\qquad\quad \text{and } m' = m_0 \cdot \mathtt{cj}(w_1') \cdot m_2' \cdot \mathtt{j}(w_2')\\
&\quad = (m'', \mathsf{Max}\{lu_0, lu_1''\}, \infty, \infty)\\
&\qquad \text{otherwise}\\
&\qquad \text{where } (m_1'', lu_1'', R_1'', E_1'') \;=\; \mathsf{ES}(stat, \rho, \mathit{ff}, \infty)\\
&\qquad\quad \text{and } (w_1'', w_2'') = \mathsf{WJ}(|\, m_1'' \,|, |\, m_2'' \,|)\\
&\qquad\quad \text{and } m'' = m_0 \cdot \mathtt{cj}(w_1'') \cdot m_2'' \cdot \mathtt{j}(w_2'')
\end{aligned}
$$

Table 13.4. Compiling clauses for expressions

$$
\mathsf{EE}(\underline{\textbf{const}}\,(k), \rho, \mathit{ff}) = (\mathtt{ldc}(w), 0, ldt(w) + 1) \quad \text{where } w = \begin{cases} k & \text{if } k \in \mathsf{Word} \\ 0 & \text{if } k = \mathsf{ff} \\ 1 & \text{if } k = \mathsf{tt} \end{cases}
$$

$$
\mathsf{EE}(\underline{\textbf{var}}\,(x), \rho, \mathit{ff}) = (\mathtt{ldl}(adr_x^\rho), 0, ldt(adr_x^\rho + 2))
$$

$$
\begin{aligned}
\mathsf{EE}(\underline{\textbf{mon}}\,(mop, expr), \rho, \mathit{ff}) &= (m_1 \cdot m_0, lu, E_0 + E_1)\\
&\quad \text{where } (m_0, E_0) = \mathsf{EM}(mop)\\
&\quad\text{and } (m_1, lu, E_1) = \mathsf{EE}(expr, \rho, \mathit{ff})
\end{aligned}
$$

$$
\begin{aligned}
\mathsf{EE}(\underline{\textbf{bin}}\,(bop, expr_1, expr_2), \rho, \mathit{ff}) &= (m, \mathsf{Max}\{\mathit{ff}, lu_1, lu_2\}, E)\\
&\quad \text{where } (m_0, E_0) = \mathsf{EB}(bop)\\
&\quad\text{and } (m_1, lu_1, E_1) = \mathsf{EE}(expr_1, \rho, \mathit{ff} + 1)\\
&\quad\text{and } (m_2, lu_2, E_2) = \mathsf{EE}(expr_2, \rho, \mathit{ff})\\
&\quad\text{and } m = m_2 \cdot \mathtt{stl}(\mathit{ff}) \cdot m_1 \cdot \mathtt{ldl}(\mathit{ff}) \cdot m_0\\
&\quad\text{and } E = E_0 + E_1 + E_2 + 2 * ldt(\mathit{ff}) + 3
\end{aligned}
$$

Table 13.5. Clauses for initialization code and operators

$\mathsf{EI}(\underline{\textbf{word}}, \mathit{ff})$	$=$	$(\varepsilon, 0)$
$\mathsf{EI}(\underline{\textbf{bool}}, \mathit{ff})$	$=$	$(\texttt{ldc}(0) \cdot \texttt{stl}(\mathit{ff}), \mathit{ldt}(\mathit{ff}) + 2)$
$\mathsf{EB}(\underline{\textbf{plus}})$	$=$	$(\texttt{add}, 1)$
$\mathsf{EB}(\underline{\textbf{minus}})$	$=$	$(\texttt{sub}, 1)$
$\mathsf{EB}(\underline{\textbf{times}})$	$=$	$(\texttt{mul}, \mathit{bpw} + 7)$
$\mathsf{EB}(\underline{\textbf{div}})$	$=$	$(\texttt{testerr} \cdot \texttt{stl}(0) \cdot \texttt{div} \cdot \texttt{testerr} \cdot \texttt{cj}(0), \mathit{bpw} + 24)$
$\mathsf{EB}(\underline{\textbf{rem}})$	$=$	$(\texttt{testerr} \cdot \texttt{stl}(0) \cdot \texttt{rem} \cdot \texttt{testerr} \cdot \texttt{cj}(0), \mathit{bpw} + 19)$
$\mathsf{EB}(\underline{\textbf{eq}})$	$=$	$(\texttt{diff} \cdot \texttt{eqc}(0), 3)$
$\mathsf{EB}(\underline{\textbf{ge}})$	$=$	$(\texttt{gt}, 2)$
$\mathsf{EB}(\underline{\textbf{ne}})$	$=$	$(\texttt{diff} \cdot \texttt{eqc}(0) \cdot \texttt{eqc}(0), 5)$
$\mathsf{EB}(\underline{\textbf{le}})$	$=$	$(\texttt{rev} \cdot \texttt{gt}, 3)$
$\mathsf{EB}(\underline{\textbf{geq}})$	$=$	$(\texttt{rev} \cdot \texttt{gt} \cdot \texttt{eqc}(0), 5)$
$\mathsf{EB}(\underline{\textbf{leq}})$	$=$	$(\texttt{gt} \cdot \texttt{eqc}(0), 4)$
$\mathsf{EB}(\underline{\textbf{and}})$	$=$	$(\texttt{add} \cdot \texttt{eqc}(2), 3)$
$\mathsf{EB}(\underline{\textbf{or}})$	$=$	$(\texttt{add} \cdot \texttt{ldc}(0) \cdot \texttt{gt}, 4)$
$\mathsf{EM}(\underline{\textbf{not}})$	$=$	$(\texttt{eqc}(0), 2)$
$\mathsf{EM}(\underline{\textbf{plus}})$	$=$	$(\varepsilon, 0)$
$\mathsf{EM}(\underline{\textbf{minus}})$	$=$	$(\texttt{not} \cdot \texttt{adc}(1), 3)$

conditionals and loops that are discussed below. We choose for L in recursive calls and for lu, R and E in the result the smallest values that can be justified with the refined translation theorems because they provide the strongest available information. In a number of clauses in Table 13.2, Table 13.3 and Table 13.4 intermediate results are introduced after the keywords 'where' and 'and'. We assume that 'where' as well as 'and' is 'strict' such that a clause's value is undefined if this holds for some intermediate result. We have taken care that there are no cross-dependencies between intermediate result such that the specification is indeed fully constructive. More specifically, the intermediate results can always be determined from top to bottom. It is this requirement of full constructiveness that causes the problems with conditionals and loops. The three clauses for **while** are to be inspected from top to bottom and the first applicable clause is to be used. The function WJ (*'while jumps'*) in the `while` clauses calculates the arguments for the jump instructions and is defined later in this chapter when discussing how loop translation was made fully constructive.

The proof that Theorem 13.4.1 is actually valid is by structural induction. For each source construct the property to be shown is essentially given by the corresponding (refined) translation theorem. Although we do not want to explicate the structural induction, there is a subtle point that should be mentioned. By the assumptions $stat \in \mathsf{Stat}_V$ and $expr \in \mathsf{Expr}_V$ in Theorem 13.4.1, the relationship between compiling functions and refined correctness predicates is valid only if the source statements or expressions are well-formed w.r.t. the set of variables in the domain of the dictionary. This condition is necessary because most translation theorems rely on a similar assumption (see e.g. the condition $\underline{\mathbf{block}}\,(x, stat) \in \mathsf{Stat}_V$ in Theorem 13.3.3). It must be ensured when the compiling functions are applied to sub-statements or expressions because otherwise the delivered results cannot sensibly be interpreted. Fortunately this proof obligation is always immediate by well-formedness of the composed source construct w.r.t. the given dictionary.

13.4.1 Constructive Translation of Conditionals

Let us now discuss the problems with conditionals and loops and the solution that was chosen in Table 13.2 and Table 13.3. We consider conditionals first, for which the refined translation theorem looks as follows.

Theorem 13.4.2 (Conditional translation refined).
Suppose $\underline{\mathbf{if}}\,(expr, stat_1, stat_2) \in \mathsf{Stat}_V$,

(a) $\mathsf{CE}'(expr, m_0, \rho, \mathit{ff}, lu_0, E_0)$,
(b) $\mathsf{CS}'(stat_1, m_1, \rho, \mathit{ff}, lu_1, L_1, R_1, E_1)$,
(c) $\mathsf{CS}'(stat_2, m_2, \rho, \mathit{ff}, lu_2, L_2, R_2, E_2)$,
(d) $m = m_0 \cdot \mathtt{cj}(w_1) \cdot m_1 \cdot \mathtt{j}(w_2) \cdot m_2$,
(e) $w_1 = |\, m_1 \cdot \mathtt{j}(w_2)\,|$ *and* $w_2 = |\, m_2\,|$,
(f) $L_1 \geq L + E_0 + ldt(w_1) + 2$ *and* $L_2 \geq L + E_0 + ldt(w_1) + 4$,
(g) $R \geq \mathsf{Max}\{R_1 + ldt(w_2) + 3, R_2\}$, *and*
(h) $E \geq \mathsf{Max}\{E_1, E_2\}$.

Then $\mathsf{CS}'(\underline{\mathbf{if}}\,(expr, stat_1, stat_2), m, \rho, \mathit{ff}, \mathsf{Max}\{lu_0, lu_1, lu_2\}, L, R, E)$.

When translating the 'then' and 'else' part, we would ideally like to choose the smallest values justified by this theorem for the arguments L_1 and L_2. By condition (f) these are $L_1 = L+E_0+ldt(w_1)+2$ and $L_2 = L+E_0+ldt(w_1)+4$. But w_1 depends on m_1 and w_2 on m_2, i.e. on the results for the 'then' and 'else' part. Therefore, we cannot choose these values before we have available the results. The solution adopted in Table 13.2 is to use weaker (that is larger) values for L_1 and L_2, which is possible because Theorem 13.4.2 requires only inequalities. We exploit the following upper estimate for *ldt*.

Lemma 13.4.3 (Upper bound for *ldt*). *For all* $w \in \mathsf{Word}$,

$$ldt(w) \leq 2 * bpw - 1 \ .$$

Proof. The representation of a word w consists of at most $2 * bpw$ nibbles. $ldt(w)$ is the number of leading `pfix`/`nfix` instructions that are needed to provide the operand w. As the least significant nibble is provided by the instruction to be executed itself, this can be done with at most $(2 * bpw - 1)$ `pfix` instructions. The use of `nfix` instructions in the actual prefixing scheme only improves this figure.

If you do not want to rely on this intuitive explanation you might prove the estimate directly from the definition of *ldt*.

- For $w = 0$ the claimed inequality clearly holds because $ldt(0) = 0$.
- By induction on i one can prove that $16^i \leq w < 16^{i+1}$ implies $ldt(w) = i$.
- This immediately yields the claimed inequality for positive w because $w < 16^{2*bpw}$ for all words.
- For negative words w, $ldt(w) = ldt((\mathsf{bitnot}\ w) \gg 4) + 1$ by definition. It is easy to see that $(\mathsf{bitnot}\ w) \gg 4$ is positive and less than $16^{2*bpw-1}$. By the property proved by induction, $ldt((\mathsf{bitnot}\ w) \gg 4) + 1 \leq 2 * bpw - 1$. □

By this upper estimate, Theorem 13.4.2 remains valid if condition (f) is replaced by

(f') $L_1 \geq L + E_0 + 2 * bpw + 1$ and $L_2 \geq L + E_0 + 2 * bpw + 3$.

We have applied this weaker condition when constructing the clause for translation of conditionals.

13.4.2 Constructive Translation of Loops

Even more considerations were necessary to make loop translation constructive. Let us have a look at the refined translation theorem in order to explain the problems.

Theorem 13.4.4 (Loop translation refined).
Suppose `while`$(expr, stat) \in \mathsf{Stat}_V$,

(a) $\mathsf{CE}'(expr, m_0, \rho, f\!f, lu_0, E_0)$,
(b) $\mathsf{CS}'(stat, m_1, \rho, f\!f, lu_1, L_1, R_1, E_1)$,
(c) $m = m_0 \cdot \mathtt{cj}(w_1) \cdot m_1 \cdot \mathtt{j}(w_2)$,
(d) $w_1 = |\, m_1 \cdot \mathtt{j}(w_2) \,|$ *and* $w_2 = -|\, m \,|$,
(e) $L_1 \geq L + E_0 + ldt(w_1) + 2$,
(f) $L \geq R_1 + ldt(w_2) + 3$, *and*
(g) $R \geq L + E_0 + ldt(w_1) + 4$.

Then $\mathsf{CS}'(\underline{\mathbf{while}}\,(expr, stat), m, \rho, f\!f, \mathsf{Max}\{lu_0, lu_1\}, L, R, \infty)$.

The following problems must be solved when deriving a constructive specification from this theorem.

1) w_1 and w_2 are mutually dependent; w_2 even depends on itself (via m).
2) The conditions (e) and (f) on L_1 and L depend on m_1 and m_2 via w_1 and w_2.
3) The condition (f) must be guaranteed, which is somewhat unfortunate as by the chosen translation strategy L is an input while R_1 is an output of the translation of the body.

Let us consider problem 1) first. Letting $s_1 = |w_1|$ and $s_2 = |w_2|$ we have to find a solution for the following system of equations.

$$\begin{aligned} w_1 &= |\,\mathsf{j}(w_2)\,| + s_1 \\ w_2 &= -(|\,\mathsf{cj}(w_1)\,| + |\,\mathsf{j}(w_2)\,| + s_1 + s_2) \end{aligned}$$

This is equivalent to finding a fixpoint of $f_{s_1,s_2} \in (\mathsf{Int} \times \mathsf{Int} \to \mathsf{Int} \times \mathsf{Int})$,

$$f_{s_1,s_2}(x,y) \;=\; (|\,\mathsf{j}(y)\,| + s,\; -(|\,\mathsf{cj}(x)\,| + |\,\mathsf{j}(y)\,| + s_1 + s_2))\;.$$

One can show that f_{s_1,s_2} is monotonic and bounded w.r.t. the order $\leq \times \geq$ on $\mathsf{Int} \times \mathsf{Int}$ and that this implies that it has a least fixpoint (w.r.t. $\leq \times \geq$). Moreover, this fixpoint can be finitely approximated from $(0,0)$, i.e. it can be obtained by applying $h_{s_1,s_2} \in (\mathsf{Int} \times \mathsf{Int} \overset{\text{part.}}{\longrightarrow} \mathsf{Int} \times \mathsf{Int})$ to the argument $(0,0)$, where h_{s_1,s_2} is the least defined partial function satisfying

$$\begin{aligned} &h_{s_1,s_2}(x,y) \;= \\ &\qquad \mathsf{if}\ f_{s_1,s_2}(x,y) = (x,y)\ \mathsf{then}\ (x,y)\ \mathsf{else}\ h_{s_1,s_2}(f_{s_1,s_2}(x,y))\ \mathsf{fi}\;. \end{aligned}$$

Hence, we define $\mathsf{WJ} \in (\mathsf{Int} \times \mathsf{Int} \overset{\text{part.}}{\longrightarrow} \mathsf{Int} \times \mathsf{Int})$, the function that is used in the loop translation clauses in Table 13.3 to determine a pair (w_1, w_2) that satisfies the above equation system, by

$$\mathsf{WJ}(s_1, s_2) \;=\; h_{s_1,s_2}(0,0)\;.$$

We refrain from formalizing the above remarks about the least fixpoint of f_{s_1,s_2} and from giving a proof that $h_{s_1,s_2}(0,0)$ is indeed the smallest fixpoint of f_{s_1,s_2}. While this is interesting for the 'completeness' and 'optimality' of the code generator specified by the compiling functions it is not necessary for its 'soundness', for which partial correctness of WJ suffices. Partial correctness, however, is quite easily shown by a fixpoint induction for h_{s_1,s_2}. For that purpose recall the fixpoint induction principle on complete partial orders (cpos), i.e. partial orders that have a least element and are chain-complete (see, e.g., [51] for an introduction to cpo theory).

Theorem 13.4.5 (Fixpoint induction (de Bakker, Scott)). *Suppose $(M, \sqsubseteq)$ is a complete partial order, φ is a continuous function on M and $P \subseteq M$. If*

(a) for every chain $C \subseteq P$ (w.r.t. $\sqsubseteq$) the least upper bound $\sqcup C$ is in P (P is admissible*),*
(b) $\bot \in P$ (induction basis), and

(c) $\forall x \in M : x \in P \Rightarrow f(x) \in P$ *(induction step)*

then $\mu f \in P$.

The partial correctness result for WJ, on which we rely in the translation clauses for loops, is stated in the following lemma.

Lemma 13.4.6 (Partial correctness of WJ). *Let* $s_1, s_2, w_1, w_2 \in \mathsf{Int}$. *If* $\mathsf{WJ}(s_1, s_2) = (w_1, w_2)$ *then* (w_1, w_2) *is a fixpoint of* f_{s_1,s_2}.

Proof. Let us write h for h_{s_1,s_2} and f for f_{s_1,s_2}, and let $M = (\mathsf{Int} \times \mathsf{Int} \xrightarrow{\text{part.}} \mathsf{Int} \times \mathsf{Int})$ be the set of partial functions on $\mathsf{Int} \times \mathsf{Int}$. It is clear that h is the least fixpoint of the functional $\varphi \in (M \to M)$,

$$\varphi(g)(x,y) \;=\; \mathsf{if}\ f(x,y) = (x,y)\ \mathsf{then}\ (x,y)\ \mathsf{else}\ g(f(x,y))\ \mathsf{fi}\ ,$$

w.r.t. the 'definedness order' $\sqsubseteq$ on M, which is defined by

$$g \sqsubseteq g' \quad \text{iff} \quad (x,y) \in \mathsf{dom}\, g \text{ implies } (x,y) \in \mathsf{dom}\, g' \text{ and } g(x,y) = g'(x,y)$$

(or simply by $g \subseteq g'$ if functions are, as usual, identified with their graph). We show by a fixpoint induction that $\mu\varphi$ is a member of the following set:

$$\mathsf{Prop} \;=\; \{g \mid \forall x, y : (x,y) \in \mathsf{dom}\, g \Rightarrow g(x,y) \text{ is a fixpoint of } f\}\ .$$

This implies the claim of the lemma, as $\mathsf{WJ}(s_1, s_2)$ equals $(\mu\varphi)(0,0)$ by definition. Let us now perform the fixpoint induction.

Admissibility: If $(g_i)_{i\in I}$ is a chain in Prop and $(x,y) \in \mathsf{dom}\,(\bigsqcup_{i\in I} g_i)$, then there is an $i \in I$ such that $(x,y) \in \mathsf{dom}\, g_i$ and $(\bigsqcup_{i\in I} g_i)(x,y) = g_i(x,y)$. But $g_i(x,y)$ is a fixpoint of f because $g_i \in \mathsf{Prop}$.

Induction basis: The totally undefined function $\perp_M$ trivially is in Prop because there is no pair $(x,y) \in \mathsf{dom} \perp_M$.

Induction step: Assume $g \in \mathsf{Prop}$ and suppose given $(x,y) \in \mathsf{dom}\, \varphi(g)$. If $f(x,y) = (x,y)$ then $\varphi(g)(x,y) = (x,y)$, which clearly is a fixpoint of f by assumption. If, on the other hand, $f(x,y) \neq (x,y)$ then $\varphi(g)(x,y) = g(f(x,y))$. In particular $f(x,y)$ is in $\mathsf{dom}\, g$ and $\varphi(g)(x,y) = g(f(x,y))$ is a fixpoint of f since $g \in \mathsf{Prop}$. □

Let us now turn attention to problem 2). It can be resolved by the technique that was applied for conditionals: (e) and (f) are replaced by the weaker conditions

(e') $L_1 \geq L + E_0 + 2 * bpw + 1$ and

(f') $L \geq R_1 + 2 * bpw + 2$.

A simple approach for solving problem 3) is to check after the generation of the code for the body whether condition (f) – or rather (f') – holds or not. If it holds we are done. If, on the other hand, it does not hold then the source program is rejected. Unfortunately, this simple approach rejects too many programs. In the compiling clause for loops, L is the amount of excess time that must be absorbed from the sequential predecessor of the loop. Condition (f) expresses that – because of possibly occurring iteration – the loop must also be able to absorb the excess time caused by the body (plus the time needed for the backwards jump). There is no reason why the latter typically should be smaller than L; but if it is not, the simple approach rejects the loop!

We can do better by exploiting that, by the analog of Lemma 12.1.1 for CS', it suffices to find an $L' \geq L$ satisfying the conditions. Let us formulate the resulting corollary to Theorem 13.4.4 explicitly in order not to obscure the discussion. On this occasion we also replace (e) and (f) by (e') and (f') and describe the calculation of w_1 and w_2 explicitly.

Corollary 13.4.7 (Loop translation refined further).
Suppose $\texttt{while}(expr, stat) \in \mathsf{Stat}_V$,

(a) $\mathsf{CE}'(expr, m_0, \rho, \mathit{ff}, lu_0, E_0)$,
(b) $\mathsf{CS}'(stat, m_1, \rho, \mathit{ff}, lu_1, L_1, R_1, E_1)$,
(c) $m = m_0 \cdot \mathtt{cj}(w_1) \cdot m_1 \cdot \mathtt{j}(w_2)$,
(d) $(w_1, w_2) = \mathsf{WJ}(|\, m_1\,|, |\, m_2\,|)$,
(e) $L_1 \geq L' + E_0 + 2 * bpw + 1$,
(f) $L' \geq R_1 + 2 * bpw + 2$,
(g) $R \geq L' + E_0 + ldt(w_1) + 4$, *and*
(h) $L' \geq L$.

Then $\mathsf{CS}'(\underline{\textbf{while}}\,(expr, stat), m, \rho, \mathit{ff}, \mathsf{Max}\{lu_0, lu_1\}, L, R, \infty)$.

Proof. By Lemma 13.4.6, condition (d) implies that w_1 and w_2 satisfy condition (d) of Theorem 13.4.4. Hence, by that theorem, conditions (a) – (g) imply $\mathsf{CS}'(\underline{\textbf{while}}\,(expr, stat), m, \rho, \mathit{ff}, \mathsf{Max}\{lu_0, lu_1\}, L', R, \infty)$. Exploiting (h), $\mathsf{CS}'(\underline{\textbf{while}}\,(expr, stat), m, \rho, \mathit{ff}, \mathsf{Max}\{lu_0, lu_1\}, L, R, \infty)$ follows by the analog of Lemma 12.1.1 for CS'. □

We must now decide how to choose L'. In the clause in Table 13.2 we have applied an iterative approach. First the body is translated assuming $L' = L$. If with the resulting value for R_1 condition (g) is valid, we can use the result immediately as in the 'simple approach' sketched above. Otherwise, the body is translated again choosing $L' = R_1 + 2 * bpw + 2$ because this promises to make condition (g) valid. This second translation of the body can result in another value of the time to be exported by the body called R_1' for differentiation. We must check whether condition (g) is valid for L' and the new value R_1'. If this is the case we are done. Otherwise, we could try further iteration. But an informal consideration indicates that $R_1 < R_1'$ means that there is a linear relationship between the L parameter for the body and the resulting R component of the result caused by a static internal path through the loop body.[1] Therefore, further iteration is useless as it cannot result in a solution. But there is one distinguished value for L', viz. $L' = \infty$, for which the translation nevertheless might succeed. This value is tried finally. Note that condition (g) implies that R must then be ∞ as well.

In an actual implementation of the iterative solution we would possibly exploit that the code component of the compiling functions does not depend on the timing parameters and, therefore, w_1, w_2 and m need not be calculated for every iteration.

13.5 Discussion

It is straightforward to write from the compiling functions a functional program, say in Standard ML [58, 85]. We have done this [69] for translation of a similar language, viz. TimedPL, a prototypic hard-real time programming language that has been considered in the ProCoS project. Only little additional effort was necessary concerning the representation of the data types due to the rich type system available in Standard ML.

The difficulties in deriving the constructive specification for conditional and loop compilation indicate that the chosen translation strategy is too naive. This seems particularly true for the determination of timing information, which called for the iteration in the loop translation. In essence the compiling functions provide a one-pass translation, which might be a too demanding goal. Possibly it is a better strategy to annotate an abstract source program tree in a first phase with the target code and to determine the timing information in a second phase. This could nicely be described by an attribute grammar. Another solution is to look for a better parameterization of the timing information. Anyhow, the purpose of this chapter has not been to develop an efficient implementation but to show at an example the construction of an implementation from the translation theorems of Chap. 12.

Compiling functions can be interpreted in two ways. On the one hand, they can be seen as a functional implementation. On the other hand, they can be considered to provide a truly explicit code generator specification. Thus one might use them as a starting point for the construction of implementations in other styles, which could be more convenient than basing the construction on translation theorems because compiling functions are fully constructive. However, rather arbitrary design decision have been made during the transition to the compiling functions, and other decisions might be more adequate for other non-functional styles. Altogether a collection of theorems seems to be a better interface between semantic verification and implementation, because it leaves more freedom to the implementation while already relieving it from semantic considerations.

[1] Note that correctness of ES is not affected by this informal consideration, which is the reason why we do not discuss it formally.

A user of the code generator provided by EP will probably not be satisfied with the information that the compiler is correct w.r.t. the refined correctness relations because he will not be willing to learn all the details of the semantic hierarchy and of the correctness relations. Therefore, we provide the following theorem, which has been prepared with Theorem 11.1.3, that gives a relationship between semantics of a source program and executions of the Transputer induced by the generated target code. The Transputer is viewed according to the base model as this is the ultimate reference point; all the other views should be internal to the code generator verification.

Theorem 13.5.1 (User interface). *Suppose $prog \in \mathsf{Prog}$, $m \in \mathsf{IS}$ and $lu \in \mathsf{IN}$ such that* $\mathsf{EP}(prog) = (m, lu)$. *If $lu \leq l_W$ then*

$$\mathsf{MP}(prog) \;\leq\; Tc^+ \;;\; [Loaded(m) \wedge \mathtt{Ip} = s_P \wedge \mathtt{Oreg} = 0 \wedge \mathtt{Wptr} = s_W] \;;\; Run \;;\; Tc^- \;.$$

Proof. Suppose $lu \leq l_W$. By Theorem 13.4.1, (a), we have $\mathsf{CP}'(prog, m, lu)$. Because of $lu \leq l_W$, the definition of CP' tells us that $\mathsf{CP}(prog, m)$. The claimed inequality now follows as an application of Theorem 11.1.3. □

The initial assumption $[Loaded(m) \wedge \mathtt{Ip} = s_P \wedge \mathtt{Oreg} = 0 \wedge \mathtt{Wptr} = s_W]$ states the obligation of the loader or boot program that starts an instruction sequence m generated by EP. Its task is to put the Transputer into a state where m is loaded and the instruction pointer, the operand register, and the workspace pointer are initialized appropriately.

As all considerations in this book apply to all values of the global constants s_P, l_P, s_W, l_W parameterizing the program storage and the workspace, a user of the code generator (or a loader program) can choose these constants after the code has been generated. The above theorem shows that it is a good idea to choose l_W such that $l_W \geq lu$. (Of course $l_P \geq |m|$ must hold as well because otherwise $Loaded(m)$ cannot hold.) The chosen constants must also satisfy the global assumption (10.56) (see p. 158), which expresses that program storage and workspace are disjoint.

14. Conclusion

After a long journey we have reached a prototypic implementation of a code generator for TPL by means of the compiling functions. Now the time has come to draw some conclusions from the experiences gained along the way.

In the introduction we said that the ultimate goal of this line of research is a methodology for the provably correct construction of code generators. Such a construction bases on intuitive ideas, and a proposed methodology must foster their stepwise capture and formalization. This book contributes a case study for a provably correct construction. First we developed from a base model of the target processor a hierarchy of increasingly abstract views. Afterwards we defined semantic correctness conditions that relate source and target code using appropriate views from the aforementioned hierarchy. Then we established a collection of translation theorems. They provide concrete code patterns that are correct if various side conditions are fulfilled. We designed the theorems by guessing the code patterns; the side conditions were detected during the proof. The translation theorems provide a basis from which an implementation can be developed without further semantic reasoning. We demonstrated this with a functional implementation.

Whether the applied approach is viable as a general methodology can, of course, not definitively be judged on the basis of a single case study. A first answer, however, is indicated by the number of detours and iterations that were necessary when preparing this book. The parts that actually concerned the translation, i.e. the hierarchy of views, the translation theorems, and the construction of the functional implementation, were rather stable, which suggests that the approach is indeed adequate.[1] Revisions of the formal contents of these parts were caused mainly by modifications to the underlying imperative meta-notation and by the intention to treat certain phenomena in greater generality. We considered, for instance, in a first version only symbolic variables of type Word. There were only two related points that had to be revised. In the first exposition dictionaries were global parameters of the development, which prohibited a proper treatment of dictionary extensions and block translation; and we dealt with translation of binary expressions not by dictionary extensions but by an explicit parameter naming free locations.

[1] This is not to deny that we had to fight against technical details often. But most of them could be solved locally without affecting topics far away.

The matter that caused most revisions was the decision for the formal basis of the imperative meta-notation. For instance, we had to decide whether to use a syntactic or a semantic approach. Another question that caused a lot of trouble was how to deal with the alphabet of processes. In an intermediate stage we opted for a homogeneous space and used various block operators instead of addition and deletion commands. But this tended to obscure the presentation because the embedding into the homogeneous space gleamed through at various places. We have now used an inhomogeneous algebra of commands together with overloading of the command constructors.

Practical compiler verification is largely a documentation problem. Many details must be considered, and there is a real danger that essential considerations are hidden under a mountain of technicalities. A modular structure as chosen in this book is intended to facilitate conceptual insights as well as rigorous control by many local, independent checks. A possible problem is that the complexity might go into the structure of the exposition. Whether the style of presentation in this book actually increases confidence into the finally developed code generator must be left to the judgment of the reader. Possibly real belief can only be achieved by a mechanical replay of the proofs, which promises to detect writing errors that are easily overlooked by a human reader. There has already been some work on re-doing proofs from a draft of (the second part of) this book with the PVS prover [75, 76] by K.-H. Buth and T. Meyer [16, 56] at Kiel. H. Pfeifer et. al. at Ulm have also done work on supporting refinement proofs with the PVS prover [77]. Moreover, in a recent effort with PVS they have applied the idea of mutually consistent views to the target processor, albeit in a different semantic framework.

Besides easing preparation and comprehensibility of proofs and providing insight, modularity has another advantage: it facilitates reuse. At many places in this book the interface between different kinds of considerations is given by a certain collection of theorems. The models on which these theorems rely can be exchanged if only the theorems remain valid. Moreover, the theorems can be applied for different purposes. Let us discuss some examples.

- The model of the imperative meta-notation can be exchanged. If the command laws remain valid, all the theorems in the semantic hierarchy and all translation theorems remain valid.[2] In this way the laws seal the consideration against the concrete underlying model. (This, of course, is an old observation that has been reported by many other researchers and underlies any axiomatic method.) To change the underlying model seems promising e.g. for providing a semantics that can properly explain external choice and parallelism.
- The views to the Transputer's behavior can be reused for translation of other source languages or other purposes that require reasoning about ma-

[2] Of course the axioms in the Transputer base model and the semantics of TPL must be reasonable with the new interpretation as well.

chine code. This seems reasonable in particular for the lower levels that are not at all specific for translation of TPL.
- The collection of translation theorems provides a basis for different implementations.

In our opinion it is reasonable to adopt a pragmatic position with respect to the facts that are proved. It can largely reduce the burden of proof obligations to prove propositions rigorously only if they contribute to the correctness of the ultimate code generator, but to rely for facts that only concern its 'completeness' on informal arguments. Let us name some examples of this strategy.

- When deriving the hierarchy of views to the Transputer we did not establish a formal criterion that the chosen abstractions are strong enough. This follows only empirically from the fact that reasoning based on the abstractions was successful.
- When providing a constructive specification of loop translation we justified only informally that the function WJ that calculates the length of jumps actually is defined for any arising input. Furthermore, we did not prove formally that two attempts to translate the body are sufficient and that further iteration is useless. In both cases correctness of the compilation is not affected. The informal arguments addresses only the question if results are obtained as often as possible, which is 'completeness' somehow.

A question bothering us during the course of this work is why informal argumentation sometimes is more efficient than its rigorous counterpart. Often an informal argument can be given in just a few words, but its formalization requires a much larger effort. A partial answer is that the informal argument relies on implicit side conditions and assumptions and is thus, strictly speaking, only partially sound. But in our opinion there is also another, deeper reason. In informal argumentation we are free to choose a view to the phenomenon that fits to the problem at hand. But when arguing rigorously we fix a certain model as a reference point and tackle all questions with respect to that model. For some questions the informal argument might break the structure of this single reference model. This indicates that rigorous reasoning can be made more efficient by providing instead of one single reference model a number of mutual consistent models such that an appropriate one can be selected for the purpose at hand. We exploited this observation at various places.

- At least two different intuitions are connected to the command notation: their formal interpretation as predicate transformers and an operational intuition. Although the latter has no formal status, it can guide the reasoning.
- Various consistent models for the behavior of the Transputer are provided by the hierarchy of views.

The advantage of rigorous reasoning over informal argumentation is that it uncovers hidden assumptions and side conditions. Moreover, there are some questions that can only be solved with a formal reference point. An example in the context of this book is the correct statement of the timing conditions in the translation theorems, in particular for loops. Although the conditions are easily interpreted intuitively a posteriori, it is very difficult to guess them correctly before performing the calculations in the proofs.

14.1 Topics for Future Research

At the end of a research enterprise there are often more questions than in the beginning. Let us discuss some possible directions of future research.

14.1.1 Extensions

More Sophisticated Timing Guarantees. A real challenge is to allow state-dependent time bounds in source programs and to guarantee non-trivial time bounds for statements containing loops. Of course this will result in undecidable problems in general. A first idea might be to find useful decidable subsets but this seems to be rather unrealistic. More promising is to let the compiler rely on some support by the program designer.

One approach is that the program designer provides invariants as annotations to the program, which can be exploited by the compiler. Another approach is that the compiler generates, in addition to the target code, a bunch of verification conditions, validity of which guarantees the timing correctness of the code. It is then the task of the program designer to prove these verification conditions, possibly with the aid of a mechanical proof assistant. In both cases a satisfactory solution that is not too demanding for the program designer requires to combine timing reasoning with information obtained from data-flow analysis and compiler technology with mechanical prover technology.

Semantic Model. The predicate transformer semantics of communicating commands could be extended to explain properly external choice and parallel composition. A first idea is to use a further special variable that record refusal or readiness sets.

Alternatives. This extension of the semantic model should enable to treat Occam-like alternatives, which requires in particular to model the special operations for their implementation provided by the Transputer. A further challenge is to combine alternatives with upper bound timing in a way that is useful for program design and implementable on actual hardware.

14.1.2 Improvements

Separate the Reasoning About Timing. It is interesting to consider how the reasoning about the timing correctness of code can be separated from the reasoning about its logical correctness. Possibly one can work with different views for timing and logical behavior that afterwards are combined. More generally, a collection of abstract views derived from a common concrete model need not necessarily be organized as a linear hierarchy as advocated in this monograph.

Independence Notion. When deriving the hierarchy of views we often had to transfer approximations that intuitively were independent of the variables parameterizing the abstraction. We then relied on routine calculations. The question is whether there is a useful formal notion of independence that is easily checked by a syntactic criterion and implies 'trivial' abstraction.

More Efficient Data Abstraction Reasoning. A related point is to establish and exploit compositionality properties of data abstraction similar to the compositionality properties of data refinement studied in [63, 66] in order to reduce the amount of explicit calculation.

Parameterization of Timing. We applied an iterative approach for determining timing information for loops. It is conceivable that the need for iteration can be avoided by using another parameterization in the implementation that allows a more complete description of possible timing parameters.

14.1.3 Modifications

Partial Correctness. We used preservation of total correctness as underlying notion of refinement. It is interesting to consider preservation of partial correctness instead. We expect that most arguments remain valid because weakest preconditions and weakest liberal preconditions coincide for the basic constructors. But the definition of loops must be changed and the interesting question is to prove a translation theorem for loops. In [68] we studied this question in a simple setting.

Implementation Style. We should consider the transition from a collection of translation theorems to more practical compiler implementation means like attribute grammars particularly from a correctness point of view.

Other Translation Tasks. The idea of stepwise deriving abstract views could be applied to other processors and to other translation situations. In particular it is interesting to consider more drastic abstractions like stacks and unrestricted number domains that are possible if an acceptable failure behavior is available.

References

1. M. Abadi and L. Lamport. The existence of refinement mappings. *Theoretical Computer Science*, 82:253–284, 1991.
2. K. R. Apt and G. D. Plotkin. Countable nondeterminism and random assignment. *Journal of the ACM*, 33(4):724–767, 1986.
3. R. J. R. Back. *Correctness Preserving Program Refinements: Proof Theory and Applications*, volume 131 of *Mathematical Center Tracts*. Mathematical Centre, Amsterdam, 1980.
4. R. J. R. Back. Refinement calculus, lattices and higher order logic. In M. Broy, editor, *Program Design Calculi (Proceedings of 1992 Marktoberdorf Summer School)*. Springer-Verlag, 1993.
5. R. J. R. Back and J. von Wright. Refinement calculus, Part I: Sequential nondeterministic programs. In J. W. de Bakker, W.-P. de Roever, and G. Rozenberg, editors, *Stepwise Refinement of Distributed Systems — Models, Formalisms, Correctness. REX Workshop*, volume 430 of *LNCS*, pages 42–66. Springer-Verlag, 1989.
6. R. J. R. Back and J. von Wright. Duality in specification languages: A lattice theoretic approach. *Acta Informatica*, 27(7):583–625, 1990.
7. W. R. Bevier, W. A. Hunt, Jr., and W. D. Young. Towards verified execution environments. Technical Report 5, Computational Logic, Inc., Austin, Texas, USA, February 1987.
8. G. Birkhoff. *Lattice Theory*, volume 25 of *Amer. Math. Soc. Collog. Publ.* Amer. Math. Soc., 1940.
9. G. Birkhoff. *Lattice Theory*. Amer. Math. Soc., third edition, 1967.
10. D. Bjørner and C. B. Jones, editors. *The Vienna Development Method*, volume 61 of *LNCS*. Springer-Verlag, 1978.
11. E. Börger and I. Durdanović. Correctness of compiling occam to transputer code. *The Computer Journal*, 39(1), 1996.
12. E. Börger, I. Durdanović, and D. Rosenzweig. Occam: Specification and compiler correctness. Part I: The primary model. In E.-R. Olderog, editor, *Proceedings IFIP TC2 Working Conference on Programming: Concepts, Methods and Calculi (PROCOMET '94)*, pages 489–508. North-Holland, 1994.
13. J. P. Bowen et al. A ProCoS II project description: ESPRIT Basic Research project 7071. *Bulletin of the European Association for Theoretical Computer Science (EATCS)*, 50:128–137, June 1993.
14. S. D. Brookes, C. A. R. Hoare, and A. W. Roscoe. A theory of communicating sequential processes. *Journal of the ACM*, 31(7):560–599, 1984.
15. G. M. Brown. Towards truly delay-insensitive circuit realizations of process algebras. In G. Jones and M. Sheeran, editors, *Designing Correct Circuits*, Workshops in Computing, pages 120–131. Springer-Verlag, 1991.

16. K.-H. Buth. Automated code generator verification based on algebraic laws. ProCoS Technical Report [Kiel KHB 5/1], Christian-Albrechts-Universität Kiel, Germany, September 1995.
17. W. Chen and J. T. Udding. Towards a calculus of data refinement. In *Mathematics of Program Construction*, volume 375 of *LNCS*, New York, 1989. Springer-Verlag.
18. P. Cousot and R. Cousot. Abstract interpretation frameworks. *J. Logic Computat.*, 4(2):511–547, 1992.
19. J. W. de Bakker. *Mathematical Theory of Program Correctness.* Prentice-Hall International, 1980.
20. E. W. Dijkstra. Guarded commands, nondeterminacy and formal derivation of programs. *Communications of the ACM*, 18(8):453–457, August 1975.
21. E. W. Dijkstra. *A Discipline of Programming.* Prentice Hall, 1976.
22. E. W. Dijkstra and C. S. Scholten. *Predicate Calculus and Program Semantics.* Texts and Monographs in Computer Science. Springer-Verlay, 1990.
23. M. Fränzle and M. Müller-Olm. Towards provably correct code generation for a hard real-time programming language. In P. A. Fritzson, editor, *Compiler Construction '94, 5th International Conference Edinburgh U.K.*, volume 786 of *LNCS*, pages 294–308. Springer-Verlag, April 1994.
24. M. Fränzle and B. von Karger. Proposal for a programming language core for ProCoS II. ProCoS Technical Report [Kiel MF 11/3], Christian-Albrechts-Universität Kiel, Germany, August 1993.
25. P. H. B. Gardiner and C. C. Morgan. Data refinement of predicate transformers. *Theoretical Computer Science*, 87, 1991. Also in [62].
26. P. H. B. Gardiner and P. K. Pandya. Reasoning algebraically about recursion. *Science of Computer Programming*, 18:271–280, 1992.
27. R. Gerber and S. Hong. Timing constraint refinement and structural code motion. *IEEE Transaction on Software Engineering*, 21:389–404, May 1995.
28. W. Goerigk, A. Dold, T. Gaul, G. Goos, A. Heberle, F. W. von Henke, U. Hoffmann, H. Langmaack, H. Pfeifer, H. Ruess, and W. Zimmermann. Compiler correctness and implementation. Verification: The Verifix approach. Poster session of CC'96 (Compiler Construction '96), 1996.
29. G. Grätzer. *General Lattice Theory.* Birkhäuser Verlag, 1978.
30. D. Gries. *The Science of Programming.* Springer-Verlag, 1981.
31. D. Gries. Lectures on data refinement. In M. Broy, editor, *Programming and Mathematical Method (Proceedings of 1990 Marktoberdorf Summer School)*, pages 213–244. Springer-Verlag, 1992.
32. D. Gries and J. Prins. A new notion of encapsulation. In *Proc. SIGPLAN '85 Symposium on Language Issues in Programming Environments*, pages 131–139, Seattle, Washington, June 1985.
33. J. D. Guttman, J. D. Ramsdell, and V. Swarup. The VLISP verified scheme system. *Lisp and Symbolic Computation*, 8:33–110, 1995.
34. J. D. Guttman, J. D. Ramsdell, and M. Wand. VLISP: A verified implementation of scheme. *Lisp and Symbolic Computation*, 8:5–32, 1995.
35. J. He, C. A. R. Hoare, M. Fränzle, M. Müller-Olm, E.-R. Olderog, M. Schenke, M. R. Hansen, A. P. Ravn, and H. Rischel. Provably correct systems. In H. Langmaack, W.-P. de Roever, and J. Vytopil, editors, *Proceedings of the 3rd International Symposium on "Formal Techniques in Real-Time and Fault-Tolerant Systems", Lübeck, Germany*, volume 863 of *LNCS*, pages 288–335. Springer-Verlag, September 1994.

36. He Jifeng, I. Page, and J. P. Bowen. Towards a provably correct hardware implementation of Occam. In G. J. Milne and L. Pierre, editors, *Correct Hardware Design and Verification Methods*, volume 683 of *LNCS*, pages 214–225. Springer-Verlag, 1993.
37. H. Herrlich and M. Hušek. Galois connections. In A. Melton, editor, *Mathematical Foundations of Programming Semantics*, volume 239 of *LNCS*, pages 122–134. Springer-Verlag, 1985.
38. W. H. Hesselink. Predicate-transformer semantics of general recursion. *Acta Informatica*, 26(4):309–332, 1989.
39. C. A. R. Hoare. Proof of correctness of data representation. *Acta Informatica*, 1:271–281, 1972.
40. C. A. R. Hoare. *Communicating Sequential Processes*. Prentice Hall, 1985.
41. C. A. R. Hoare. Refinement algebra proves correctness of compiling specifications. In C. C. Morgan and J. C. P. Woodcock, editors, *3rd Refinement Workshop*, Workshops in Computer Science, pages 33–48. Springer-Verlag, 1991.
42. C. A. R. Hoare, I. J. Hayes, H. Jifeng, C. C. Morgan, A. W. Roscoe, J. W. Sanders, I. H. Sorenson, J. M. Spivey, and B. A. Sufrin. Laws of programming. *Communications of the ACM*, 30(8):672–687, August 1987.
43. C. A. R. Hoare, H. Jifeng, and A. Sampaio. Normal form approach to compiler design. *Acta Informatica*, 30:701–739, 1993.
44. C. A. R. Hoare, H. Jifeng, and J. W. Sanders. Prespecification in data refinement. *Information Processing Letters*, 25:71–76, 1887.
45. inmos limited. *Occam2 Reference Manual*. Prentice Hall International, first edition, 1988.
46. inmos limited. *Transputer Instruction Set – A Compiler Writer's Guide*. Prentice Hall International, first edition, 1988.
47. C. B. Jones. *Systematic Software Development Using VDM*. Prentice Hall, 1986.
48. J. J. Joyce. Totally verified systems: Linking verified software to verified hardware. In Leeser and Brown [50], pages 177–201.
49. J.-L. Lassez, V. L. Nguyen, and E. A. Sonenberg. Fixed point theorems and semantics: A folk tale. *Information Processing Letters*, 14(3):112–116, 1982.
50. M. Leeser and G. Brown, editors. *Hardware Specification, Verification and Synthesis: Mathematical Aspects*, volume 408 of *LNCS*, 1990.
51. J. Loeckx and K. Sieber. *The Foundations of Program Verification*. John Wiley & Sons and B. G. Teubner, second edition, 1987.
52. A. J. Martin. The design of a delay-insensitive microprocessor: An example of circuit synthesis by program transformation. In Leeser and Brown [50], pages 244–259.
53. Mathematics of Program Construction Group. Fixed-point calculus. *Information Processing Letters*, 53(3):131–136, 1995.
54. J. McCarthy and J. Painter. Correctness of a compiler for arithmetic expressions. In J. Schwarz, editor, *Proc. Symp. Applied Mathematics*, pages 33–41. American Mathematical Society, 1967.
55. A. Melton, D. A. Schmidt, and G. E. Strecker. Galois connections and computer science applications. In D. Pitt, S. Abramsky, A. Poigné, and D. Rydeheard, editors, *Category Theory and Computer Programming*, volume 240 of *LNCS*, pages 299–312. Springer-Verlag, 1985.
56. T. Meyer. Anwendung von PVS zur Codegenerator-Verifikation. Diplomarbeit, Christian-Albrechts-Universität Kiel, November 1995.
57. R. Milne and C. Strachey. *A Theory of Programming Language Semantics*. Chapman and Hall, 1976.

58. R. Milner, M. Tofte, and R. Harper. *The Definition of Standard ML*. The MIT Press, 1990.
59. J. S. Moore. A mechanically verified language implementation. *Journal of Automated Reasoning*, 5(4):461–492, 1989.
60. C. Morgan. Data refinement by miracles. *Information Processing Letters*, 26:243–246, 1988. Also in [62].
61. C. Morgan. The specification statement. *TOPLAS*, 10(3), 1988. Also in [62].
62. C. Morgan and T. V. (Eds.). *On the Refinement Calculus*. Springer-Verlag, 1994.
63. C. Morgan and P. H. B. Gardiner. Data refinement by calculation. *Acta Informatica*, 27, 1991. Also in [62].
64. F. L. Morris. Advice on structuring compilers and proving them correct. In *Proceedings ACM Symposium on Principles of Programming Languages*, pages 144–152, 1973.
65. J. M. Morris. A theoretical basis for stepwise refinement and the programming calculus. *Science of Computer Programming*, 9:287–306, 1987.
66. J. M. Morris. Laws of data refinement. *Acta Informatica*, 26:287–308, 1989.
67. M. Müller-Olm. The concrete syntax of TimedPL. ProCoS Technical Report [Kiel MMO 13/3], Christian-Albrechts-Universität Kiel, Germany, August 1995.
68. M. Müller-Olm. An exercise in compiler verification. Available from the author, 1995.
69. M. Müller-Olm. A short description of the prototype compiler. ProCoS Technical Report [Kiel MMO 14/1], Christian-Albrechts-Universität Kiel, Germany, August 1995.
70. G. Nelson. A generalization of Dijkstra's calculus. *ACM Transactions on Programming Languages and Systems*, 11(4):517–561, October 1989.
71. T. S. Norvell. Machine code programs are predicates too. In D. Till, editor, *6th Refinement Workshop*, Workshops in Computing. Springer-Verlag and British Computer Society, 1994.
72. E.-R. Olderog and C. A. R. Hoare. Specification-oriented semantics for communicating processes. *Acta Informatica*, 23:9–66, 1986.
73. D. P. Oliva, J. D. Ramsdell, and M. Wand. The VLISP verified PreScheme compiler. *Lisp and Symbolic Computation*, 8:111–182, 1995.
74. O. Ore. Galois connexions. *Trans. Amer. Math. Soc.*, 55:493–513, 1944.
75. S. Owre, N. Shankar, and J. M. Rushby. *The PVS Specification Language (Beta Release)*. Computer Science Laboratory, SRI International, Menlo Park, CA, June 1993.
76. S. Owre, N. Shankar, and J. M. Rushby. *User Guide for the PVS Specification and Verification System (Beta Release)*. Computer Science Laboratory, SRI International, Menlo Park, CA, March 1993.
77. H. Pfeifer et. al. Supporting refinement calculus proofs in PVS. Verifix Working Paper [Verifix/Ulm 3.0], University of Ulm, Germany, 1996.
78. W. Polak. *Compiler Specification and Verification*, volume 124 of *Lecture Notes in Computer Science*. Springer-Verlag, 1981.
79. A. Sampaio. *An Algebraic Approach To Compiler Design*. PhD thesis, Oxford University Computing Laboratory, October 1993.
80. D. A. Schmidt. *Denotational Semantics: A Methodology for Language Development*. Wm. G. Brown Publishers, 1986.
81. J. Schmidt. Beiträge zur Filtertheorie II. *Math. Nachr.*, 10:197–232, 1953.
82. J. E. Stoy. *Denotational Semantics: The Scott-Strachey Approach to Programming Language Theory*. The MIT Press, 1977.
83. A. Tarski. A lattice-theoretical fixpoint theorem and its application. *Pacific Journal of Mathematics*, 5:285–309, 1955.

84. J. W. Thatcher, E. G. Wagner, and J. B. Wright. More on advice on structuring compilers and proving them correct. *Theoretical Computer Science*, 15:223–249, 1981.
85. Å. Wikström. *Functional Programming Using Standard ML*. Prentice Hall, first edition, 1987.
86. M. W. Wilkes and J. B. Stringer. Micro-programming and the design of the control circuits in an electronic digital computer. *Proc. Cambridge Phil. Soc.*, 49:230–238, 1953. also *Annals of Hist. Comp.* **8**, 2 (1986) 121–126.

Index

Springer and the environment

Vol. 1249: W. McCune (Ed.), Automated Deduction – CADE-14. Proceedings, 1997. XIV, 462 pages. 1997. (Subseries LNAI).

Vol. 1250: A. Olivé, J.A. Pastor (Eds.), Advanced Information Systems Engineering. Proceedings, 1997. XI, 451 pages. 1997.

Vol. 1251: K. Hardy, J. Briggs (Eds.), Reliable Software Technologies – Ada-Europe '97. Proceedings, 1997. VIII, 293 pages. 1997.

Vol. 1252: B. ter Haar Romeny, L. Florack, J. Koenderink, M. Viergever (Eds.), Scale-Space Theory in Computer Vision. Proceedings, 1997. IX, 365 pages. 1997.

Vol. 1253: G. Bilardi, A. Ferreira, R. Lüling, J. Rolim (Eds.), Solving Irregularly Structured Problems in Parallel. Proceedings, 1997. X, 287 pages. 1997.

Vol. 1254: O. Grumberg (Ed.), Computer Aided Verification. Proceedings, 1997. XI, 486 pages. 1997.

Vol. 1255: T. Mora, H. Mattson (Eds.), Applied Algebra, Algebraic Algorithms and Error-Correcting Codes. Proceedings, 1997. X, 353 pages. 1997.

Vol. 1256: P. Degano, R. Gorrieri, A. Marchetti-Spaccamela (Eds.), Automata, Languages and Programming. Proceedings, 1997. XVI, 862 pages. 1997.

Vol. 1258: D. van Dalen, M. Bezem (Eds.), Computer Science Logic. Proceedings, 1996. VIII, 473 pages. 1997.

Vol. 1259: T. Higuchi, M. Iwata, W. Liu (Eds.), Evolvable Systems: From Biology to Hardware. Proceedings, 1996. XI, 484 pages. 1997.

Vol. 1260: D. Raymond, D. Wood, S. Yu (Eds.), Automata Implementation. Proceedings, 1996. VIII, 189 pages. 1997.

Vol. 1261: J. Mycielski, G. Rozenberg, A. Salomaa (Eds.), Structures in Logic and Computer Science. X, 371 pages. 1997.

Vol. 1262: M. Scholl, A. Voisard (Eds.), Advances in Spatial Databases. Proceedings, 1997. XI, 379 pages. 1997.

Vol. 1263: J. Komorowski, J. Zytkow (Eds.), Principles of Data Mining and Knowledge Discovery. Proceedings, 1997. IX, 397 pages. 1997. (Subseries LNAI).

Vol. 1264: A. Apostolico, J. Hein (Eds.), Combinatorial Pattern Matching. Proceedings, 1997. VIII, 277 pages. 1997.

Vol. 1265: J. Dix, U. Furbach, A. Nerode (Eds.), Logic Programming and Nonmonotonic Reasoning. Proceedings, 1997. X, 453 pages. 1997. (Subseries LNAI).

Vol. 1266: D.B. Leake, E. Plaza (Eds.), Case-Based Reasoning Research and Development. Proceedings, 1997. XIII, 648 pages. 1997 (Subseries LNAI).

Vol. 1267: E. Biham (Ed.), Fast Software Encryption. Proceedings, 1997. VIII, 289 pages. 1997.

Vol. 1268: W. Kluge (Ed.), Implementation of Functional Languages. Proceedings, 1996. XI, 284 pages. 1997.

Vol. 1269: J. Rolim (Ed.), Randomization and Approximation Techniques in Computer Science. Proceedings, 1997. VIII, 227 pages. 1997.

Vol. 1270: V. Varadharajan, J. Pieprzyk, Y. Mu (Eds.), Information Security and Privacy. Proceedings, 1997. XI, 337 pages. 1997.

Vol. 1271: C. Small, P. Douglas, R. Johnson, P. King, N. Martin (Eds.), Advances in Databases. Proceedings, 1997. XI, 233 pages. 1997.

Vol. 1272: F. Dehne, A. Rau-Chaplin, J.-R. Sack, R. Tamassia (Eds.), Algorithms and Data Structures. Proceedings, 1997. X, 476 pages. 1997.

Vol. 1273: P. Antsaklis, W. Kohn, A. Nerode, S. Sastry (Eds.), Hybrid Systems IV. X, 405 pages. 1997.

Vol. 1274: T. Masuda, Y. Masunaga, M. Tsukamoto (Eds.), Worldwide Computing and Its Applications. Proceedings, 1997. XVI, 443 pages. 1997.

Vol. 1275: E.L. Gunter, A. Felty (Eds.), Theorem Proving in Higher Order Logics. Proceedings, 1997. VIII, 339 pages. 1997.

Vol. 1276: T. Jiang, D.T. Lee (Eds.), Computing and Combinatorics. Proceedings, 1997. XI, 522 pages. 1997.

Vol. 1277: V. Malyshkin (Ed.), Parallel Computing Technologies. Proceedings, 1997. XII, 455 pages. 1997.

Vol. 1278: R. Hofestädt, T. Lengauer, M. Löffler, D. Schomburg (Eds.), Bioinformatics. Proceedings, 1996. XI, 222 pages. 1997.

Vol. 1279: B. S. Chlebus, L. Czaja (Eds.), Fundamentals of Computation Theory. Proceedings, 1997. XI, 475 pages. 1997.

Vol. 1280: X. Liu, P. Cohen, M. Berthold (Eds.), Advances in Intelligent Data Analysis. Proceedings, 1997. XII, 621 pages. 1997.

Vol. 1281: M. Abadi, T. Ito (Eds.), Theoretical Aspects of Computer Software. Proceedings, 1997. XI, 639 pages. 1997.

Vol. 1282: D. Garlan, D. Le Métayer (Eds.), Coordination Languages and Models. Proceedings, 1997. X, 435 pages. 1997.

Vol. 1283: M. Müller-Olm, Modular Compiler Verification. XV, 250 pages. 1997.

Vol. 1284: R. Burkard, G. Woeginger (Eds.), Algorithms — ESA '97. Proceedings, 1997. XI, 515 pages. 1997.

Vol. 1285: X. Jao, J.-H. Kim, T. Furuhashi (Eds.), Simulated Evolution and Learning. Proceedings, 1996. VIII, 231 pages. 1997. (Subseries LNAI).

Vol. 1286: C. Zhang, D. Lukose (Eds.), Multi-Agent Systems. Proceedings, 1996. VII, 195 pages. 1997. (Subseries LNAI).

Vol. 1289: G. Gottlob, A. Leitsch, D. Mundici (Eds.), Computational Logic and Proof Theory. Proceedings, 1997. VIII, 348 pages. 1997.

Vol. 1292: H. Glaser, P. Hartel, H. Kuchen (Eds.), Programming Languages: Implementations, Logigs, and Programs. Proceedings, 1997. XI, 425 pages. 1997.

Vol. 1294: B.S. Kaliski Jr. (Ed.), Advances in Cryptology — CRYPTO '97. Proceedings, 1997. XII, 539 pages. 1997.

Vol. 1299: M.T. Pazienza (Ed.), Information Extraction. Proceedings, 1997. IX, 213 pages. 1997. (Subseries LNAI).

Vol. 1300: C. Lengauer, M. Griebl, S. Gorlatch (Eds.), Euro-Par'97 Parallel Processing. Proceedings, 1997. XXX, 1379 pages. 1997.